Building a Sustainable Political Economy: SPERI Research & Policy

Series Editors
Colin Hay
SPERI
University of Sheffield
Sheffield, UK

Anthony Payne
SPERI
University of Sheffield
Sheffield, UK

"The Northern Powerhouse has been surrounded by hype and rhetoric. Here is the absolutely vital corrective: a collection of chapters exploring the historical, territorial and structural reality of the political economy of the North. Packed with evidence, assembled with exemplary scholarship."
—Michael Moran, *Emeritus Professor of Government at University of Manchester, UK*

"At last, a serious academic contribution to the Northern Powerhouse debate that takes on the agglomeraniacs and Treasury tinkerers both empirically and philosophically. Despite offering a withering critique of progress to date, this book is far from pessimistic and instead represents a clarion call for a progressive, pan-Northern politics putting the North of England once again at the vanguard of economic and democratic reinvention."
—Ed Cox, *Director at IPPR North, UK*

"This book offers new insights into the political economy of the North of England. The topics covered are wide-ranging – from science policy to economic development – but the common theme is the policy agendas needed to address the North-South divide (and why existing approaches have failed). Berry and Giovannini's important book is required reading for academics and policy-makers interested in this agenda."
—Neil Lee, *Assistant Professor of Economic Geography at London School of Economics and Political Science, UK*

The Sheffield Political Economy Research Institute (SPERI) is an innovation in higher education research and outreach. It brings together leading international researchers in the social sciences, policy makers, journalists and opinion formers to reassess and develop proposals in response to the political and economic issues posed by the current combination of financial crisis, shifting economic power and environmental threat. Building a Sustainable Political Economy: SPERI Research & Policy will serve as a key outlet for SPERI's published work. Each title will summarise and disseminate to an academic and postgraduate student audience, as well as directly to policy-makers and journalists, key policy-oriented research findings designed to further the development of a more sustainable future for the national, regional and world economy following the global financial crisis. It takes a holistic and interdisciplinary view of political economy in which the local, national, regional and global interact at all times and in complex ways. The SPERI research agenda, and hence the focus of the series, seeks to explore the core economic and political questions that require us to develop a new sustainable model of political economy at all times and in complex ways.

More information about this series at
http://www.springer.com/series/14879

Craig Berry · Arianna Giovannini
Editors

Developing England's North

The Political Economy of the Northern Powerhouse

Editors
Craig Berry
University of Sheffield
Sheffield, UK

Arianna Giovannini
De Montfort University
Leicester, UK

Building a Sustainable Political Economy: SPERI Research & Policy
ISBN 978-3-319-62559-1   ISBN 978-3-319-62560-7   (eBook)
https://doi.org/10.1007/978-3-319-62560-7

Library of Congress Control Number: 2017948250

Cover illustration: Pattern adapted from an Indian cotton print produced in the 19th century

Printed on acid-free paper

This Palgrave Macmillan imprint is published by Springer Nature
The registered company is Springer International Publishing AG
The registered company address is: Gewerbestrasse 11, 6330 Cham, Switzerland

Dedicated to the memory of Jo Cox MP (1974–2016)
Proud daughter of the North, citizen of the world, inspiration to us all

CONTENTS

LIST OF FIGURES

LIST OF TABLES

CHAPTER 1

Introduction: Powerhouse Politics and Economic Development in the North

Craig Berry and Arianna Giovannini

Abstract Why the North, why now and what is new? This chapter establishes the scholarly and real-world contexts within which the pursuit of economic development in the North should be studied. It discusses the Northern Powerhouse agenda, recent changes related to Brexit, the persistence of geographical inequalities between England's regions, the historical context of devolution, the experience of deindustrialisation and the broader patterns of global capitalist restructuring within which Northern economic development is situated. The chapter also summarises the book's contents and discusses how the North can be defined—and indeed what attempts to define the North tell us about the politics of economic development.

Keywords Brexit · Capitalist restructuring · Development · Devolution · North–South divide · Northern Powerhouse

C. Berry (✉)
Sheffield Political Economy Research Institute, University of Sheffield, Sheffield, UK
e-mail: craig.berry@sheffield.ac.uk

A. Giovannini
Department of Politics and Public Policy, De Montfort University, Leicester, UK
e-mail: arianna.giovannini@dmu.ac.uk

© The Author(s) 2018
C. Berry and A. Giovannini (eds.), *Developing England's North*,
Building a Sustainable Political Economy: SPERI Research & Policy,
https://doi.org/10.1007/978-3-319-62560-7_1

1

The North of England has rarely featured in national debates in the UK as much as it has done since the 2008 financial crisis, and particularly the 2010–2016 period when George Osborne—a son of London but a parliamentary representative for Tatton in the Northern county of Cheshire—served as Chancellor of the Exchequer. In exploring the pursuit of economic development in the North, this volume seeks to account for both the genealogy of the North's renewed (and possibly short-lived) significance to national politics, and how related political processes can be characterised. Essentially, this work is motivated by the need to understand how the Northern economy has become politicised, the implications of this, and the specific forms that politicisation has taken, after a long period of discursive neglect. In a nutshell: why the North, why now and what is new? By necessity, the political economy of the North must be studied in relation to the political economy of the UK as a whole, and indeed relationships between the UK economy, its constituent geographies and the rest of the world. The fact that the North is north *of* somewhere else is of course a key feature of its political economy. Yet this relationship with the South of England is merely one of an infinite number of ways in which the North is materialised as a political–economic space. The economy of the North of England is produced, and reproduced, by processes of formal and informal governance at the myriad of geographical scales, including overlapping (and often contradictory) internal structures and processes within the North. Encouraging greater cross-fertilisation among political economy and economic geography (and related disciplines) is therefore one of the main aims of this volume.

'Brexit'—the UK's decision, in the referendum of 23 June 2016, to withdraw from the European Union (EU)—looms large over the book's content. Like the UK in general, most parts of the North are highly integrated with, and as such dependent upon, at least in the short term, the wider European economy. More generally, the EU's political and economic structures and processes are in an integral dimension of the (evolving) political economy of the North. Interestingly, the areas of the UK (including large parts of the North) where jobs and production are most dependent on European economic integration (and indeed EU investment) are those that voted most strongly to leave; it is a myth that the big cities, principally London (but also the Northern 'core cities'), have higher levels of economic interaction with the continent (Los et al. 2017; Hunt et al. 2016). This is a fact that should not be forgotten, uncomfortable as it is for some commentators: the population of the North chose Brexit, albeit against the advice of the region's leaders—just as Northern elites are often complicit in the maintenance of national political–economic practices, even though (as many chapters of this book will argue) such practices help to keep the residents of the North poorer. Brexit will undoubtedly, over time, reorder the means by which economic life in the North is governed. Yet this is not a book about Brexit and the North. Above all, we do not know, at the time of writing, whether the UK will experience (or choose) a 'soft' or 'hard' Brexit; in practice, there will be degrees of stiffness across the different spheres through which Brexit will be operationalised, and we may yet see the form and extent of Brexit differentiated by geography within the UK. More generally, there are, quite apart from Brexit, innumerable local, national and international processes which, as they progress, threaten to reorder economic governance within the North. Historically, the North's development and prosperity have been shaped far more by its status within the British political economy than it by the UK's relationship with the EU.

The book's empirical focus is therefore the multitude of post-crisis policy agendas which have newly exposed the (global) political economy of the North, chiefly Osborne's Northern Powerhouse framing, but also the broader devolution agenda. Exploring the Northern Powerhouse and devolution may (or may not) help us begin to understand the many implications of Brexit for the North, but is also an urgent task in its own right—not least because initiatives related to the Northern Powerhouse and devolution have been largely driven by Whitehall, and Brexit will in all likelihood *increase* the formal authority of Whitehall over Northern cities and regions (as well as perhaps also offering new opportunities, in the longer term, for more substantial forms of devolution). The fact that the Northern Powerhouse as a specific discursive ploy appears to have been marginalised within the Theresa May government is worth pondering—as it is by several of the book's chapters—but should probably not be exaggerated. Moreover, we should not overstate the extent to which the Northern Powerhouse encompassed a distinctive and original set of tangible policy initiatives. Many of the policies that fell under this framework have links with very long-standing agendas, many of which are still being pursued, albeit with a little less fanfare. And crucially, there are as yet no reasons to conclude that the assumptions about the North (and its economic imperatives) which underpinned discourse and practice related to the Northern Powerhouse have been expunged from the architecture of central government—not least because the Northern Powerhouse agenda appears to have merely reflected these pre-existing assumptions.

WHAT IS THE NORTH?

We recognise that we mean by 'the North' is not entirely obvious from the term itself. At the same time, notwithstanding some debate over 'borderline' areas, we would contend that most people in the UK have a general understanding of what is, and what is not, considered the North of England, and that this understanding is usually upheld in scholarship on the North. The book has not been compiled on the basis of an editorial line on how to define the North, although it is worth noting that all chapters implicitly share the view that the definition of the North that has at times been explicit in officialdom—being composed of the regions of the North West, North East and Yorkshire and Humberside—is largely accurate.

It is of course not possible to tell the story of the North without referring to places unambiguously outside of these three regions. This is in part, first, because other parts of the UK resemble North in terms of socio-economic outcomes. Danny Dorling (2010, 2011), one of the leading scholars of the so-called 'North–South divide', actually includes Scotland, Wales, Northern Ireland and a large chunk of the Midlands in his definition of the North, given similarities in outcomes such as household income and life expectancy. The Northern regions are disadvantaged, but not uniquely so within the UK. It is also because, second, the North is not a distinct economic space. Generally speaking, it obviously interacts with the domestic and international economies; moreover, we should not assume that the North's constituent parts interact with each other economically more than they do with 'exogenous' areas. We cannot understand how the Northern economy (or economies) functions without also understanding these wider relationships and processes. Yet none of this means that the North cannot be distinguished analytically. The North may not be uniquely disadvantaged but there may be (relatively) distinct explanations for its disadvantage. Similarly, while it may be necessary to locate the North in its wider political–economic contexts, the way in which these contexts shape specifically Northern economic life is a legitimate object of inquiry.

We would also offer a note of caution about a predominantly spatial understanding of the North. The book's central disciplinary perspective is that of political economy, and its analysis generally focuses therefore on how the exercise of power across multiple spheres shapes Northern economic life, or the way in which the North interacts with the rest. The relevant spheres may be local, national or international. The lack of any formal institutional framework through which the North as a whole is governed may make this exercise challenging empirically—but arguably underlines the urgency of understanding the wider political processes which shape the North (Hayton et al. 2016). A political economy perspective also encourages us to focus on the social construction of the North, and the framing of its spatial identity by elite forces. Any simple understanding of the North's characteristics or boundaries is belied by an inherently complex social reality, but the delineation of the North is itself an act of power in need of interrogation (Paasi 2000; Jessop 2012, 2015). Indeed, it is not difficult to detect the power relations implicit in the notion that the North is different, unique or even 'foreign' from English or British norms—a notion that is reinforced even in narratives and policy initiatives that are designed ostensibly to benefit the North (such as the Northern Powerhouse, or the coalition government's earlier 'Northern Futures', or New Labour's 'The Northern Way'—all of which enjoyed local as well as national support among policy elites). The North has acquired meaning in subservience.

THE POLITICAL–ECONOMIC ENVIRONMENT

As with any volume of this nature, the book's empirical scope is broad, and its analysis multi-tonal. However, four key dimensions of the North's political–economic environment underpin the book's intellectual agenda and its contribution to the existing literature:

- The persistence of geographical inequalities within the UK, and in particular between the North and South of England.
- Long-standing (yet partial) attempts to devolve powers from the UK central government to the North and its localities.
- The experience of deindustrialisation in the North (and the imperative to 'rebalance' the economy towards industry in the wake of the financial crisis).
- A wider, transnational process of capitalist restructuring within which the North is implicated quite acutely.

Undoubtedly, as suggested above, the notion of North–South divide has become a trope for the persistence of economic—but also political, social and cultural—inequalities between the North and South of England (Martin 1993; Jewell 1994). The concept rests on the presence of structural differences (in terms of economic development, employment, education, life expectancy, etc.) between a prospering South and a 'lagging behind' North (Dorling 2010). Crucially, as Baker and Billinge (2004) argue, the North–South divide has a history both as a *reality* (especially in economic terms) and as a *representation of reality* (portrayed and reproduced in a number of political, social and cultural narratives as well as in the popular imagination), which has persisted in shaping the spatial imaginary of the North as subordinated to the South. There are serious and long-standing geographical inequalities within the UK, for which (within England at least) the North–South divide is a *simplifying* but not *simplistic* description. From a political economy perspective, however, it is important to note additionally that the dichotomy underpinning the North–South divide has been 'institutionalised' by successive governments since at least the 1970s. Indeed, the need to address disparities between the North and the South has provided the rationale both for economic and social reforms and, most recently, for justifying state restructuring.

Yet, an agenda of helping the North rather than empowering the North (and indeed disempowering the South), invariably pursued without a clear analysis of why the North–South divide exists, has led to uneven, partial and 'messy' attempts at bridging the North–South divide. These attempts often crystallise inequalities, as Northern economic development is reduced to a fairly technocratic area of social or regional policy, while the economic development of the country as a whole remains the focus of the sovereign institutions at the centre. The Northern Powerhouse, insofar as it can be associated with concrete policy initiatives, ostensibly represents another attempt to help the North through the lens of national institutions and a national growth model, based on the notion that the North needs to 'catch up' with the South. Furthermore, the agenda implicitly inscribes the notion of Northern dependency on the already-existing economic powerhouse in the South, and as such blurs seamlessly into an austerity agenda which prescribes *less* central government support for Northern regions, so that the North might be better equipped to help itself (Berry 2016a).

Of course, many in the policymaking community would argue that the centre has sought to empower the North (as well as other regions and nations in the UK) through devolution. Yet moves towards devolution are tied up in the institutional churn that characterises the centre's orientation towards the North more generally, and in recent years have also been strongly associated with austerity (Pike et al. 2016). Devolution to the North does, however, have a longer genealogy. Over the past decades (and in particular since 1997), devolution has been presented by successive governments as a means to address the governance of uneven development in England. Decentralisation, though, has itself developed in an uneven manner, taking different forms and meanings, and focusing on different scales under different administrations. From the late 1990s onwards, devolution to the North of England revolved around a diverse set of 'spatial imaginaries', spanning from administrative regions (as the basis for Regional Development Agencies and directly elected regional assemblies) to cities and/or city-regions and, most recently, combined authorities of local councils (usually linked after 2010, loosely, with a Local Enterprise Partnership) (Giovannini 2016). The common thread to these approaches is that they frame the North within a centripetal narrative according to which Whitehall 'knows best' how to address the North's problems—leading to devolution policies negotiated mainly between national and local elites, and involving feeble powers, modest budgets, vast liabilities and the maintenance of substantial control from the centre (Giovannini 2016: 592; Deas 2014). Thus, devolution in the North of England has followed a characteristically bewildering and underwhelming path—leading to complexity, experimentation, fragmentation and incoherence with largely negative implications for territorial equity and justice (Pike and Tomaney 2009), as well as for local politics and democracy (Tomaney 2016; Prosser et al. 2017).

Indeed, the problematic nature of devolution in the North has been thrown into sharp relief in the context of the Northern Powerhouse, showing continuity with past experiences. On the one hand, the devolution deals currently endorsed by the government continue to be tightly connected with the pursuit of local economic growth, which is one of the *leitmotifs* of the Northern Powerhouse agenda. On the other hand, however, the economic dividend of devolution deals grounded in the idea of agglomerative urban growth is far from clear (Haughton et al. 2016). In essence, the Northern Powerhouse is being advanced within a patchwork of 'territorial fixes' rather than coherent and cohesive decentralisation policies across the North. Some argue that devolution in the North, as a result, is promoting a 'deep(ening) neoliberalisation of territorial politics' (Brenner et al. 2010), in which interregional inequality is not only tolerated, but becomes the norm (Deas 2014: 2309)—and local elites, rather than central government, will be the principal culprits of failures to 'catch up'. While this understanding is arguable, we can certainly say, more generally, that moves towards devolution have always had a rather ambiguous identity with the politics of economic development in the North, embodying a dynamic of emasculation through democratisation. Despite the apparent wake-up call of the 2008 crisis, there are few reasons to believe that the present moment is different substantively from previous devolutionary moments in this regard.

The main economic context in which concerns about the North–South divide, and efforts towards enabling the North to develop, have emerged (and re-emerged) is deindustrialisation. In recent years, especially since the 2008 crisis, national policy elites have begun to problematise the decline of manufacturing industries and advocate a 'rebalancing' of the UK economy from London-based (financial) services back towards manufacturing industries based predominantly in the North and Midlands. As such, both the experience of deindustrialisation, and more recent attempts to mitigate its seemingly negative consequences, form a crucial background to the book's analyses of the political economy of development in the North. Deindustrialisation in terms of declining employment in manufacturing industries has of course been experienced throughout the advanced capitalist economies, rather than the UK alone. However, it has been steeper in the UK elsewhere, and ultimately led to significant reductions in manufacturing output as well as employment, associated as it is with the UK's long-standing productivity problem (Berry 2016c; Rowthorn and Coutts 2013). Deindustrialisation also has particular geographical implications for the UK, given that it is predominantly London and the South East where high-value 'post-industrial' economic activities are concentrated. While some Northern cities have now developed strengths in some knowledge-based service industries, many places remain scarred by the loss of large-scale manufacturing employment, and the UK has a much more significant degree of inequality *within* regions than comparable countries, as towns and smaller cities in the North are 'left behind' by regional centres (Hudson 2013; McCann 2016).

Ostensibly, rebalancing signifies an attempt to revive UK manufacturing, particularly in the North. There have been several incarnations of an industrial strategy for the UK in recent years, most obviously under Vince Cable (as Secretary of State for Business, Innovation and Skills) under the coalition government in 2012, and after the ascendance of Theresa May to the premiership in 2016. Both initiatives have earmarked the growth of high-value manufacturing as important to the UK's economic future, although both, despite the obvious geographical connotations of the wider rebalancing agenda, are also relatively 'place-blind' (Berry 2016b). Furthermore, we can question the extent to which rebalancing is a genuinely transformative agenda. Clearly, the notion of *re*balancing suggests that there once was balance, and the implication therefore is that all is required is a set of technocratic adjustments to the economy's current path, rather than wholesale reform. There are no problems inherent in the UK economy's sectoral or geographical composition; rather, its constituent industries and localities have simply become a little disorderly. That the Northern Powerhouse agenda is understood as helping to deliver rebalancing helps us to understand both its limited ambitions, and the concentration of the agenda on helping the North to catch up rather than on the relationship between the North and other parts of the British political economy (Berry and Hay 2016; Froud et al. 2011; Lee 2015).

The UK's experience of, and quintessential acquiescence to, deindustrialisation cannot be divorced from much broader processes of restructuring in the global capitalist system. This restructuring, known simplistically as 'globalisation' but associated in more sophisticated terms with the development of new global production networks as the West deindustrialises, is inherently spatial in nature. It both emerges from and reinforces the existence of 'core' and 'periphery' zones within the global economy, as large cities within the West become more integrated with each other and cities in the rapidly industrialising semi-periphery. Geographical inequalities within highly developed economies are at the same time enhanced, as core cities become increasingly detached from their neighbouring regions domestically (Peck and Theodore 2007). One of the ironies of globalisation is that it has actually taken the form of localisation, whereby economies trade in intermediate or semi-finished goods with nearby countries rather than specialising in particular finished goods for which a wider, more global market exists. More trade over smaller distances and new, complex patterns of specialisation and convergence are the results of this transformation (McCann 2008). The exception that proves the rule is financial services, as services that are developed and produced entirely within a single city, that is, financial centres such as London, are sold as finished products—although the customers generally, and by necessity, come to London to consume these products rather than importing them across borders.

These macro-level processes cannot possibly account for recent developments in the Northern economy in any satisfactory way. While global capitalist restructuring appears to have exacerbated inequalities between England's North and South (McCann 2016), in many ways the UK's extant economic geography provides an exemplary case of the core/periphery dynamics that have emerged in other developed economies. Nevertheless, these broader, global processes are an important part of the picture of what economic development looks like, and could look like, in the North. It is interesting that many of the largest cities in the North have adopted the mantle of 'core cities', although they are not in any meaningful sense part of the 'core' zone of the global economy in the way that London is. It is hard to imagine, given the deeply embedded nature of North–South relations in the UK, that entering the ranks of global core cities alongside London could become a realistic goal for Northern cities in the foreseeable future, especially in the wake of Brexit. The more pertinent point for our purposes, perhaps, is that both national and local political leaders in the UK have internalised this process of restructuring to the extent that it is seen as the only possible route to sustainable economic development, even if the route is a highly uncertain one for most localities. This might help us to understand why there has been so little sustained opposition within public debates to the coalition and Conservative governments' agendas around devolution, local growth and the Northern Powerhouse, and indeed why national and local elites have often sought to insulate these agendas from democratic scrutiny.

The Book

The idea of this book stems from a workshop held at the University of Sheffield in November 2015, titled 'The Political Economy of the Northern Powerhouse', which was part of a series of events organised by the White Rose Consortium for the North of England project (WRCN) in 2015–2016. The workshop brought together a unique range of scholars from several disciplines, united most of all by wonderment that the issues around the political and economic life of the North of England most of us had been studying—and indeed living, in most cases—for many years had suddenly been thrust into the national spotlight. More specifically, contributors were asked to consider the following:

- The uneven and evolving nature of economic life in the North of England, including industrial composition, and the impact of social structures and processes on the Northern economy.
- The economic relationships between Northern regions, the rest of the UK, and the European and global economies.
- Approaches to economic development (and its governance) in policymaking processes and/or academic research.
- The relationship between culture, identity and political processes within or affecting the North, especially in relation to the rise of Englishness as a political identity.
- The operation of political parties (and their subnational structures) within political processes within or affecting the North.
- The relationship between urban development, economic geography and political processes within or affecting the North.
- The emerging character of UK central government (which will of course retain significant powers over macroeconomic policy) as political authority becomes more localised.
- Epistemological and methodological issues related to the analysis of the political economy of the North of England.

Admittedly, this was a very ambitious agenda, which we inevitably did not manage to meet in full. But we considered it an urgent agenda nevertheless—and we still do. This book has been compiled in hope of advancing it further, concretising the fruitful exchanges generated on the day, and hoping to inspire further research and debates in the testing years ahead for the North. We are grateful to the White Rose University Consortium for funding the workshop and the wider WRCN project. Most of the chapters in this volume are updated versions of the papers presented at the workshop, and those that have been added are authored by some of the workshop's non-presenting participants, inspired by the discussion it encompassed.

The book is organised into three parts. The first part focuses on economic policymaking structures and practices in the context of the evolving economic relationships between the North and the rest of the

UK. In Chap. 2, Martin and Gardiner report on a major new research programme into structural transformation within urban economies to assess the scale of the challenge facing those concerned with local economic development in Northern England. They show that a North–South pattern of spatial economic imbalance was already well established in the nineteenth century, despite popular misconceptions of the North's industrial past. Using novel data, the authors then show how major Northern cities have lagged even further behind in recent decades in terms of the growth of employment, output and productivity. Crucially, this problem is not readily attributed to Northern cities being 'too small', as the advocates of vogue-ish thinking around urban agglomeration might claim; what is arguably more important is the fact that London has long enjoyed the position of hosting all of the key economic, financial and political institutions that govern the economy and determine national economic policy. As such, spatial imbalance in the UK is not solely an economic issue: it is also one of the major spatial imbalances in the location and operation of the key levers of economic, financial, political and administrative power. The authors conclude that spatial economic imbalance in the UK is an entrenched, persistent and indeed institutionalised feature of the national political economy, and that the partial devolution of fiscal powers and policies to city-regions in the North will have only a limited impact on what has long been a systemic and deep-seated London-centric bias in Britain's national political economy.

Lee takes up similar themes in Chap. 3. He argues that the political economy of England's Northern Powerhouse cannot be understood in isolation from that of its 'Southern Powerhouse' neighbour. The chapter challenges the notion that the UK's relative economic decline can be attributed to the absence of a state-led technocratic industrial modernisation programme, and contends instead that public policy and governance arrangements in contemporary England are the outcome of the long-term strategic priorities of the English (latterly British) developmental state, fashioned by its pilot agency, the Treasury. As such, the Northern Powerhouse agenda should be understood as simply the latest political narrative in a long-standing tradition of British statecraft which has subordinated the interests of development in the North of England to those of the global financial and commercial interests of the City of London.

In Chap. 4, Berry focuses more forensically on issues raised in Chaps. 2 and 3, that is, the decline of manufacturing industries in Northern England. The chapter is structured around 'the three Ds' of the Northern Powerhouse: deindustrialisation, devolution and, most arrestingly, 'de-development'. Contesting the view that the Northern Powerhouse can be understood primarily as a process of institutional or constitutional reform, it instead locates the agenda within the long (but limited) history of UK industrial policy. It argues that regional policy has always substituted for industrial policy in the UK state's 'horizontal' support for manufacturing, and that devolution to Northern city-regions is therefore the ultimate expression of *laissez-faire* industrial policy. However, the agenda touches upon post-crisis concerns around place and empowerment, even while it serves to *reduce* the control of Northern citizens over their own local economies by offering only a narrow understanding of how economies develop. Indeed, insofar as Northern regions have very little control over the structures and practices that govern its economic make-up, and as such have no way of bucking its subservient role within processes of global capitalist restructuring, the North may be stuck in a de-development trap. In Chap. 5, Flanagan and Wilsdon ask whether the long-standing concentration of science-related investments—one of the few functioning features of UK industrial policy—is likely to be reversed. They document the bias towards 'golden triangle' investments within UK science and innovation policy on the basis of a place-blind policy framework, and consider the extent to which more recent developments show that the North's scientific assets, such as its world-class universities, are finally beginning to be recognised by policymakers as integral to the UK's economic prospects.

The second part of the book focuses on city-regional governance and local politics, with each chapter considering the myriad ways in which issues around place are becoming an important feature of British political life. In Chap. 6, Gray, Dickinson and Pugalis consider whether the approach to subnational development that underpins the Northern Powerhouse narrative represents a serious and coherent attempt at bridging the economic North–South divide. The analysis focuses on the evolution of the government's cities and local growth agenda (CLOG) in the North of England and its relationship with the Northern Powerhouse, with particular emphasis on agglomeration theories, and draws on empirical data in the form of interviews with stakeholders in the North. The authors find several flaws in this relationship, arguing that the Northern Powerhouse is a 'piggyback initiative' that has spawned a wide range of policies, interventions and funding announcements with little attempt at strategic coordination. They conclude that subnational policy in the North, as manifest in CLOG and the Northern Powerhouse, is distinctively disorderly. This approach limits the development of place-specific governance and policy and, most importantly, is unlikely to lead to a rebalancing of the economy.

In Chap. 7, Giovannini develops a critical analysis of the uneven governance of devolution deals in Yorkshire. Drawing on the findings of interviews with local stakeholders, she assesses the opportunities and challenges offered by devolution deals in the region. She concludes that although economic development is *perceived* as a key asset of devolution, in practice the current top-down approach to 'devo deals' is promoting local divisions and is fostering intra-regional inequalities. As a result, devolution in Yorkshire is leading to a system of governance that is highly fragmented and problematic in political, economic and democratic terms. Crucially, the new fractures created within Yorkshire could end up hampering from within not only the devolution process, but also the wider Northern Powerhouse agenda. In Chap. 8, Evans and Blakeley focus on the other side of the Pennines, in assessing the interconnection between devolution to combined authorities (CAs) in the North and the Northern Powerhouse, based on the benchmark case study of 'Devo Manc'. The authors find that the institutional maturity of Greater Manchester Combined Authority (GMCA) and its central role in the promotion of the Independent Economic Review to develop an economic strategy for the Northern Powerhouse have been key to defining its leadership role in the context of the CAs initiative. They argue therefore that in the existing governance vacuum of the Northern Powerhouse, the leadership of the GMCA will provide a fulcrum. However, they also emphasise that there remains uncertainty about the long-term sustainability of both the CAs project and the Northern Powerhouse, and suggest that decisions concerning the Northern transport interconnectivity and the impact of the 'metro-mayors' elections will be decisive tests of their viability.

In Chap. 9, Martin, Schafran and Taylor consider devolution in the North of England through the lens of history. Arguing that current debates about Northern English cities and their role in national economic strategies cannot be read simply through contemporary politics, they trace the long history of policy and planning discourses about the North, of which the Northern Powerhouse, they argue, is the latest incarnation. Drawing on Dave Russell's (2004) chronology of key historical moments in which Northern English cities have been particularly significant in

cultural narratives of the nation, the authors develop an analysis of concurrent tensions in debates about planning and governance which have
shaped specific (and often 'negative') constructions and perceptions of
the North. Focussing on representations about the North of England
over the last two centuries, their study sheds light on the presence of four
interlocking themes: the dominating role of London in directing debates
about the North; a tension between political and spatial approaches to
planning; the characterisation of cities in the North as intrinsically problematic; and the continued issue of poverty in these cities.

The third part of the book deals more specifically with issues of inequality in the North, and the possibility that these may be exacerbated
by initiatives related to the Northern Powerhouse, particularly in the
context of austerity. In Chap. 10, Jones, Beel and Rees Jones focus on
the way in which city-regions (as the central spatial political units within
the Northern Powerhouse) are constructed, and shed light on how civil
society is being (re)positioned within a fast-changing governance landscape. To achieve this, they draw on the case of two key city-regions
within the Northern Powerhouse: Greater Manchester and Sheffield. By
analysing the findings of interviews with civil society actors in these two
areas, the authors argue that the current approach to city-regional economic development and devolution is falling short of its promises and,
by perpetuating uneven dynamics of 'inclusion' and 'exclusion', continues to exacerbate uneven development and undermine the project of
spatial rebalancing in the North. Crucially, they note the presence of a
clear divide between the actors who have been enabled to have a voice
and 'lead' within the devolution city-region agenda and those who have
been marginalised in this process. They emphasise how new 'citizenship
regimes' implemented within city-regions place civil society outside of
decision-making processes that underpin devolution deals, whilst simultaneously (and paradoxically) expecting civil society to deal with the
fallout from continuing uneven development, socio-spatial inequalities
and austerity. They conclude that there is a need to integrate the 'social'
alongside the 'economic' within both devolution and the Northern
Powerhouse if a more inclusive growth strategy, embedded in a sustainable system of governance, is to be achieved.

In Chap. 11, Muldoon-Smith and Greenhalgh examine how the
Northern Powerhouse agenda will be financed, focusing principally on
the government's Business Rate Retention Scheme (BRRS). The chapter
explains local government finance in England, focusing on its evolution

from a centralised model to one based on the parallel rubrics of localism and local economic growth. The chapter's analysis focuses on three interrelated themes: liability and growth potential, demand divergence and the nature of local commercial property markets. The authors conclude that, by bringing the civic realm into closer proximity to already financialised property markets, the BRRS has begun to roll out the conditions that will allow parts of the Northern Powerhouse to enter an era of 'civic financialisation' and entrepreneurial activity. However, asymmetries between commercial property markets, economic conditions and welfare needs across the North of England could also create a defined set of 'winners' and 'losers' (that is, those that can take part in autonomous civic financialisation and those that remain reliant on a system of redistribution and equalisation)—thus casting doubts on the coherence and long-term sustainability of the Northern Powerhouse agenda and the way in which it's financed.

Chapter 12, by Bailey, covers similar territory, albeit focusing on the recomposition of the tax system within the UK more generally, and in particular the implications of this process for local economic development in the North. The chapter argues that tax reform will concentrate capital available for reinvestment in those local economies which are already affluent and growing, and in all likelihood further disadvantage Northern regions. The recomposition of the tax system therefore inaugurates a 'race to the bottom' between polities who will be encouraged to offer increasingly 'business friendly' tax environments. This is being discursively rationalised as part of a strategy to address the UK's uneven development, but instead is likely to exacerbate regional inequalities. Finally, the concluding chapter draws together the main themes of the book, summarises the lessons for future scholarship on the North, and sketches an alternative policy agenda designed to deliver economic development and political empowerment for the North.

REFERENCES

Baker, A., and M. Billinge. 2004. *Geographies of England: The North–South divide, material and imagined.* Oxford: Oxford University Press.

Berry, C. 2016a. *Austerity politics and UK economic policy.* Basingstoke: Palgrave.

Berry, C. 2016b. Industrial policy change in the post-crisis British economy: Policy innovation in an incomplete and institutional environment. *British Journal of Politics and International Relations* 18 (4): 829–847.

Berry, C. 2016c. UK manufacturing decline since the crisis in historical perspective. *SPERI British Political Economy Brief No. 25*. Available at: http://speri.dept.shef.ac.uk/2016/10/20/british-manufacturing-has-entered-a-new-phase-of-decline-new-speri-brief/. Accessed 14 March 2017.

Berry, C., and C. Hay. 2016. The Great British 'rebalancing' act: The construction and implementation of an economic imperative for exceptional times. *British Journal of Politics and International Relations* 18 (1): 3–25.

Brenner, N., J. Peck, and N. Theodore. 2010. After neoliberalization? *Globalizations* 7 (3): 327–345.

Deas, I. 2014. The search for territorial fixes in subnational governance: City-regions and the disputed emergence of post-political consensus in Manchester, England. *Urban Studies* 51 (11): 2285–2314.

Dorling, D. 2010. Persistent North–South divides. In *The economic geography of the UK*, ed. N.M. Coe and A. Jones, 12–28. London: Sage.

Dorling, D. 2011. *So you think you know about Britain*. London: Constable.

Froud, J., S. Johal, J. Law, A. Leaver, and K. Williams. 2011. Rebalancing the economy (or buyer's remorse). CRESC Working paper No. 87. Available from: http://www.cresc.ac.uk/publications/rebalancing-the-economy-or-buyers-remorse. Accessed 28 February 2014.

Giovannini, A. 2016. Towards a "New English Regionalism" in the North? The case of Yorkshire First. *The Political Quarterly* 87 (4): 590–600.

Haughton, G., I. Deas, S. Hincks, and K. Ward. 2016. Mythic Manchester: Devo Manc, the Northern Powerhouse and rebalancing the English economy. *Cambridge Journal of Regions, Economy and Society* 9: 355–370.

Hayton, R., A. Giovannini, and C. Berry. 2016. Introduction. In *The politics of the north: Governance, territory and identity in northern England*, ed. R. Hayton, A. Giovannini, and C. Berry. Leeds: University of Leeds, 6–11. Available from: http://speri.dept.shef.ac.uk/wp-content/uploads/2016/01/Politics-of-the-North-Hayton-Giovannini-Berry.pdf. Accessed 14 March 2017.

Hudson, R. 2013. Thatcherism and its geographical legacies: The new map of socio-spatial inequality in the divided kingdom. *The Geographical Journal* 179 (4): 377–381.

Hunt, T., S. Lavery, W. Vittery, and C. Berry. 2016. UK regions and European structural and investment funds. *SPERI British Political Economy Brief No.25*. Available at: http://speri.dept.shef.ac.uk/wp-content/uploads/2016/05/Brief24-UK-regions-and-European-structural-and-investment-funds.pdf. Accessed 14 March 2017.

Jessop, B. 2012. Cultural political economy, spatial imaginaries, regional economic dynamics. *CPERC Working paper 2012–2*. Available from: http://www.lancaster.ac.uk/cperc/docs/Jessop%20CPERC%20Working%20Paper%202012-02.pdf. Accessed 14 March 2017.

Jessop, B. 2015. *The state: Past, present, future*. Cambridge: Polity Press.

Jewell, H. 1994. *The North–South divide: The origins of northern consciousness in England*. Manchester: Manchester University Press.

Lee, S. 2015. Indebted and unbalanced: The political economy of the coalition. In *The conservative-liberal coalition: Examining the Cameron-Clegg Government*, ed. M. Beech and S. Lee, 16–35. Basingstoke: Palgrave Macmillan.

Los, B., P. McCann, J. Springford, and M. Thissen. 2017, forthcoming. The mismatch between local voting and the local economic consequences of Brexit. *Regional Studies*.

Martin, R. 1993. Remapping British regional policy: The end of the North–South divide? *Regional Studies* 27 (8): 797–805.

McCann, P. 2008. Globalization and economic geography: The world is curved, not flat. *Cambridge Journal of Regions, Economy and Society* 1 (3): 351–370.

McCann, P. 2016. *The UK regional-national economic problem: Geography, globalisation and governance*. London: Routledge.

Paasi, A. 2000. Territorial identities as social constructs. *Hagar—International Social Science Review* 1 (2): 91–113.

Peck, J., and N. Theodore. 2007. Variegated capitalism. *Human Geography* 31 (6): 731–772.

Pike, A., and J. Tomaney. 2009. The state and uneven development: The governance of economic development in England in the post-devolution UK. *Cambridge Journal of Regions, Economy and Society* 2 (1): 13–34.

Pike, A., M. Coombes, P. O'Brien, and J. Tomaney. 2016. Austerity states, institutional dismantling and the governance of sub-national economic development: The demise of the regional development agencies in England. *Spatial Economics Research Centre Discussion Paper 206*. Available from: http://www.spatialeconomics.ac.uk/textonly/SERC/publications/download/sercdp0206.pdf. Accessed 14 March 2017.

Prosser, B., A. Renwick, A. Giovannini, M. Sandford, M. Flinders, W. Jennings, G. Smith, P. Spada, G. Stoker, and K. Ghose. 2017. Citizen Participation and changing governance: Cases of devolution in England. *Policy & Politics* 45 (2): 251–269.

Rowthorn, R., and K. Coutts. 2013. Deindustrialisation and the balance of payments in advanced economies, Foresight/Government Office for Science Future of Manufacturing Project Evidence Paper 31. Available from: https://www.gov.uk/government/uploads/system/uploads/attachment_data/file/283905/ep31-de-industrialisation-and-balance-of-payments.pdf. Accessed 11 August 2016.

Tomaney, J. 2016. Limits of devolution: Localism, economics and post-democracy. *The Political Quarterly* 87 (4): 546–552.

Authors' Biography

Craig Berry is Deputy Director of the Sheffield Political Economy Research Institute at the University of Sheffield. His previous roles include Policy Advisor at HM Treasury, Pensions Policy Officer at the Trades Union Congress, and Head of Policy and Senior Researcher at the International Longevity Centre-UK, and he has taught at the University of Warwick and University of Manchester. He published *Globalisation and Ideology in Britain* in 2011 and *Austerity Politics and UK Economic Policy* in 2015.

Arianna Giovannini is Senior Lecturer in Local Politics at the Department of Politics and Public Policy, De Montfort University (DMU), where she is also a member of the Local Governance Research Unit (LGRU) and the Centre for Urban Research on Austerity (CURA). Before joining DMU she was a researcher at the Sheffield Political Economy Research Institute (SPERI), University of Sheffield, where she is now an Honorary Research Fellow, and a research assistant for the White Rose Consortium for the North of England project at POLIS, University of Leeds. Her research focuses on devolution, territorial and political identity, regionalism and democracy—with a particular emphasis on the 'English Question' and the North of England. She has published widely on these themes in leading academic journals such as *Political Studies, Policy & Politics* and *The Political Quarterly*.

PART I

Economic Policy and the Political Economy of Northern Development

Reviving the 'Northern Powerhouse' and Spatially Rebalancing the British Economy: The Scale of the Challenge

Ron Martin and Ben Gardiner

Abstract George Osborne's Northern Powerhouse agenda was based on the idea that Northern cities are 'individually strong but collectively not strong enough. The whole is less than the sum of its parts'. Few would probably disagree with the basic intent and aspiration behind this declaration, or that the UK economy has become too dominated by London, but this chapter argues that both the dominant diagnosis of the problem, and the main policies being advanced to solve it, are more debatable. It is in fact questionable whether Northern cities are as economically strong 'individually' as Osborne's claim suggests. There is more to a city's economic success than just size and density, and the argument that greater connectivity to London promised by the High

R. Martin (✉)
Department of Geography, and a Research Associate of the Centre for
Business Research in the Judge Business School, University of Cambridge,
Cambridge, UK
e-mail: rlm1@cam.ac.uk

B. Gardiner
University of Cambridge, Cambridge, UK
e-mail: bcg29@cam.ac.uk

© The Author(s) 2018
C. Berry and A. Giovannini (eds.), *Developing England's North*,
Building a Sustainable Political Economy: SPERI Research & Policy,
https://doi.org/10.1007/978-3-319-62560-7_2

23

Speed 2 rail project will benefit Northern cities is highly contestable. Moreover, devolution could even intensify economic and social disparities both among Northern cities themselves and in relation to the more advantageous position of London with regard to fiscal devolution. The lagging performance of Northern cities (and regions) and the challenge confronting their catch up with London need to be understood in terms of the historical development of the national political economy, and how that development has favoured a certain disposition towards and role in the evolving process of globalisation.

Keywords Agglomeration · Economic development · Exports Northern cities · Northern Powerhouse · Regional inequality

From the late 1970s and early 1980s onwards a very particular model of economic growth was championed across many of the advanced nations, and indeed beyond.[1] Based on deregulation, privatisation, financialisation and enthusiastic belief in ever-deeper free market globalisation, this model was hailed as finally bringing an end to recessions and inflation, driving a new age of stable growth; what in the USA became labelled as the 'Great Moderation' (Bernanke 2004), and in the UK as a new 'NICE' era (of *n*on-*i*nflationary *c*ontinued *e*xpansion).[2] Above all, it was a model driven by a dramatic and seemingly unstoppable expansion of finance and banking. Banks made record profits, the world's financial centres prospered, and many regions and cities, indeed whole nations, experienced rapid growth on the back of the booming housing and real estate markets that the banks were eager to fund and profit from. In the UK, the financial success of London was openly celebrated by the Labour government at the time, and even held up as a model for the rest of the country to follow. As then Chancellor of the Exchequer, Gordon Brown, argued in his Mansion House speech in June 2007:

> I believe it will be said of this age, the first decades of the 21st century, that out of the greatest restructuring of the global economy, perhaps even greater than the industrial revolution, a new world order was created.... [M]ost importantly of all in the new world order... [t]he financial services sector in Britain, and the City of London at the centre of it ... shows how we can excel in a world of global competition. Britain needs more of the vigour, ingenuity and aspiration that you [London's financial class] already demonstrate is the hallmark of your success. (Brown 2010)

No sooner had this praise been lavished, however, than the economic boom on which it was based was brought to an abrupt halt. The financial crisis revealed the boom for what it was, a form of development that was highly *unbalanced*: on a global level, between creditor and debtor nations (especially China and the USA respectively); within the Eurozone, between the strong core members such as Germany and France, and the weaker peripheral members such as Spain, Italy and Portugal; and within countries, between consumption and investment, between services and production, between state revenues and spending, between rich and poor, and, spatially, between different cities and regions. For while the 'long boom' between the early 1990s and 2007 may have lifted most regions and cities, it lifted some much more than others. Indeed, in some instances (the UK is a particularly prominent case) it reinforced regional inequalities.

In recognition of these inequalities, since 2010, when the Conservative–Liberal Coalition Government came to power, a new spatial imaginary has risen to the fore in UK government policy thinking on the need to 'spatially rebalance' the national economy. The argument is that the financial crisis of 2007–2008 had exposed the fact that the economy had become too dependent for growth on a narrow range of activities—especially finance—and on one corner of the country, namely London and the Greater South East. As David Cameron, shortly after he had been elected Prime Minister, opined:

> Our economy has become more and more unbalanced... Today our economy is heavily reliant on just a few industries and a few regions – particularly London and the South East. This really matters. An economy with such a narrow foundation for growth is fundamentally unstable and wasteful – because we are not making use of the talent out there in all parts of our United Kingdom. (Cameron 2010)

The Deputy Prime Minister, Nick Clegg, held to a similar view:

> For years, our prosperity has been pinned on financial wizardry in London's Square Mile, with other sectors and other regions left behind. That imbalance left us hugely exposed when the banking crisis hit. And now Britain has a budget deficit higher than at any time since the Second World War. It is time to correct that imbalance. We need to spread growth across the whole country and across all sectors. (Clegg 2010)

And yet more recently, Theresa May, David Cameron's successor as Prime Minister, once again stressed the need to secure an economy that's fair and where everyone plays by the same rules. That means acting to tackle some of the economy's structural problems that hold people back. Things like the shortage of affordable homes. The need to make big decisions on – and invest in - our infrastructure. The need to rebalance the economy across sectors and areas in order to spread wealth and prosperity around the country. (May 2016)

The coalition government's initial response was to prosecute a new localism, a new 'local growth agenda' (H.M Government 2010). Local Enterprise Partnerships (to replace the previous Regional Development Agencies) were established, together with a regional growth fund, local enterprise zones, city deals and various other measures, all intended to promote local growth and greater 'spatial balance' across the economy. And then, from mid-2014 onwards, then Chancellor George Osborne began to talk of his offensive to promote what he called a 'Northern Powerhouse' to rival London in scale and dynamism:

> Something remarkable has happened to London over these recent decades. It has become a global capital, the home of international finance, attracting the young, the ambitious, the wealthy and the entrepreneurial from around the world in their tens of thousands. And it's a great strength for our country that it contains such a global city... But something remarkable has happened here in Manchester, and in Liverpool and Leeds and Newcastle and other Northern cities over these last thirty years too. The once hollowed-out city centres are thriving again, with growing universities, iconic museums and cultural events, and huge improvements to the quality of life... The cities of the North are individually strong, but collectively not strong enough. The whole is less than the sum of its parts. So the powerhouse of London dominates more and more. And that's not healthy for our economy... We need a Northern Powerhouse too. Not one city, but a collection of Northern cities—sufficiently close to each other that combined can take on the world. (Osborne 2014)

However, at the same time the government has also been anxious that the growth of London is not hindered or compromised in any way. Herein lies a key conundrum: how to achieve a greater degree of 'spatial balance' in the economy whilst also wanting to protect and enhance the gains from spatial agglomeration of economic activity and growth in the already prosperous London–South East mega-region. Much of the debate surrounding this issue has revolved around a stark question: is London good or bad for the rest of the UK? On the one side are those who point to the benefits of the Greater London economic machine in generating demand for goods and services in the rest of the UK, as a vital source of export earnings, and as a major contributor to the taxes needed to help fund welfare payments and public spending across the nation as a whole (see for example City of London Corporation 2011, 2014). But on the other side are those who see London as akin to a 'country apart', even a quasi-independent 'city-state', as a region which has become increasingly detached from the rest of the UK in terms of its level of prosperity, its economic growth, its global orientation and its cyclical behaviour (Deutsche Bank 2013). Some go further, and regard it as having become a sort of 'economic black hole', sucking in key human and financial resources from, and to the detriment of, the rest of the country. For example, Vince Cable, when he was Secretary of State for Business in the Coalition Government, was quite emphatic that

One of the big problems that we have at the moment... is that London is becoming a kind of giant suction machine, draining the life out of the rest of the country. (Cable 2013)

A similar view was subsequently voiced by Scotland's First Minister:

London has a centrifugal pull on talent, investment and business from the rest of Europe and the world. That brings benefits to the broader UK economy. But as we know, that same centrifugal pull is felt by the rest of us across the UK, often to our detriment. The challenge for us all is how to balance this in our best interests – not by engaging in a race to the bottom, but by using our powers to create long-term comparative advantage and genuine economic value. (Sturgeon 2014)

This 'spatial imbalance' in the UK economy, of an economy tipped too far in favour of London and the South East, is not in fact some new or recent feature, but a long-standing problem, one that goes back to the Victorian period if not earlier. We have been here before, repeatedly. As early as 1919, Sir Halford Mackinder, successively a prominent Oxford political geographer, Director of the London School of Economics, and Liberal Unionist (Conservative) MP, had argued for a more 'balanced' national socio-economy:

As long as you allow a great metropolis to drain most of the best young brains from the local communities, to cite only one aspect of what goes on, so long must organizations centre unduly in the metropolis and become inevitably an organization of nation-wide classes and interests. (Mackinder 1919)

Barely two decades later, in equally direct terms, the milestone report of the Barlow Commission in 1940 on the distribution of the nation's industrial population expressed a similar view, again in language highly prescient of that used by Vince Cable nearly 75 years later:

The contribution in one area of such a large proportion of the national population as is contained in Greater London, and the attraction to the Metropolis of the best industrial, financial, commercial and general ability, represents a serious drain on the rest of the country. (Barlow Commission 1940)

How, then, to 'power up' the economies of the country's Northern cities in order to reduce this dominance of London? What is the scale of the challenge? In the remainder of this chapter we focus particularly on this latter question. We start by showing how a North–South pattern of spatial economic imbalance—of a more prosperous London and South East, and a lagging North and West—was already well established in the nineteenth century. We then move forward to the period since the beginning of the 1970s. Using novel data, we show how major Northern cities have lagged behind in terms of growth of employment, output and productivity over the past 40 years or so. A crucial aspect of the issue is shown to be the dramatic decline in the manufacturing export base of the Northern cities, and, unlike London, their failure to replace this shrinking base on a sufficient scale with new tradable activities (see also Berry's chapter in this volume). This problem is not readily attributed to Northern cities being 'too small' as some observers have claimed. What is arguably more important is the fact that London has long enjoyed the position of hosting all of the key economic, financial and political institutions that govern the economy and determine national economic policy.

Spatial imbalance in the UK is not just an economic issue: it is also one of the major spatial imbalances in the location and operation of the key levers of economic, financial, political and administrative power. The UK is one of the most politically centralised countries in the OCED: it is surely not simply coincidental that it also has one of highest levels of regional economic inequality. What emerges from our brief analysis in this chapter is that spatial economic imbalance is in fact an entrenched, persistent and indeed institutionalised feature of the national economy, and as such is a major challenge for policymakers. Although new policies are being introduced that are aimed at spatially rebalancing the economy—including the creation of a 'Northern Powerhouse' to rival that of London—and even a partial devolution of fiscal powers and policies to cities is underway, we conclude that these will have only a limited impact on what has long been a systemic and deep-seated London-centric bias in Britain's national political economy. We begin our narrative with some economic history.

THE LONG-STANDING NATURE OF BRITAIN'S SPATIALLY UNBALANCED ECONOMY

According to many economic historians and geographers, during the nineteenth century it was the towns and cities of Northern England—in the regions of the North West, North East and Yorkshire–Humberside—that were the country's economic 'powerhouses'. Throughout the long Victorian period, so the argument runs, 'the North' was the most dynamic and prosperous part of the country, centred on the growth of key export-based industries, especially cotton and woollen textiles, shipbuilding, and heavy engineering equipment and manufactured products, associated with the expansion of Empire and Britain's domination of international trade. For example, back in the 1880s, the Lancashire cotton mills ranked as one of wonders of the industrial world. Much of the Victorian industrial economy was located in the Northern towns and regions of the country. Unemployment was primarily a problem of the 'South', with its difficulties of agricultural depression and the decline of old-craft industries, especially in London.

Immediately following the First World War, however, the story continues, adverse shifts in Britain's world trade position imposed severe shocks on the industrial North. The decline of Empire and the rise of new international competitors, such as the USA, Germany and Japan, combined with a lack of technological modernisation in Britain's old staple industries, restrictive domestic economic policies and recurrent deep recessions in the 1920s and early 1930s, resulted in structural decline

Table 2.1   Regional shares of UK GDP 1861–1911

	1861	1881	1911
London	17.1	19.9	20.1
South East	11.2	10.9	13.1
East Anglia	3.1	2.4	2.2
South West	8.1	6.1	5.9
East Midlands	4.7	4.6	5.4
West Midlands	7.1	6.9	6.8
Yorks–Humberside	6.8	7.3	7.7
North West	11.1	13.3	13.7
North	4.1	5.2	5.3
Wales	4.3	4.2	4.4
Scotland	10.3	10.4	9.5
Ireland	12.0	9.3	5.8
UK	100.0	100.0	100.0

Source Geary and Stark (2015)
Note Because of the lack of consistent data for Northern Ireland, Geary and Stark use Ireland to define the UK

and the emergence of acutely high unemployment in many Northern towns and cities. Meanwhile, the 'new growth industries' of the period, based on light engineering, motor vehicles, and a variety of electrical and mass consumer goods, became clustered in London, the South East and the Midlands (Scott 2007). Hence, according to these same economic historians, a major reorientation occurred in the geography of the British economy: 'in terms of many of the basic measures of social inequality, the geography of the country had to a large extent been reversed' (Massey 1986: 31) The old geography of sectoral specialisation and economic organisation, which had favoured the North, was being replaced by a new and different pattern of sectoral specialisation and organisation that favoured the South.

While many aspects of this historical narrative are correct and well-documented, there is also more recent evidence that suggests that some important qualifications and modifications are called for. New analyses by leading economic historians suggest that the argument that the national economy was led by the North up until the interwar years, when the South suddenly took over that role, may be exaggerated, and that in fact even by the middle of the nineteenth-century London had already pulled well ahead of the North of the country in terms of output and prosperity (see Tables 2.1, 2.2; also Crafts 2005; Geary and Stark 2015, 2016).

Table 2.2 Spatial imbalance in the British economy, 1901–1931 Regional GDP per capita relative to the average (GB = 100). Geary–Stark estimates

GB = 100	1901	1911	1921	1931
London	134.2	133.8	137.4	144.3
South East	107.0	104.1	101.2	114.0
East Anglia	83.7	83.5	83.5	82.7
South West	91.7	92.4	91.3	92.3
East Midlands	92.4	97.2	88.6	86.6
West Midlands	86.0	90.5	82.1	95.7
Yorks–Humberside	88.3	90.1	93.6	86.4
North West	103.7	104.8	109.3	88.6
North	85.8	83.0	83.1	81.1
Wales	80.3	82.1	76.5	81.1
Scotland	90.5	86.9	92.3	94.3
Coefficient variation (%)	16.9	16.6	18.5	22.6

Source of data Geary and Stark (2015)
Note Geary and Stark use a Great Britain index base for this set of results, rather than a UK one in their analysis shown in Table 2.1. Again, the lack of consistent data for Northern Ireland precluded inclusion of this region

London was the single largest centre of manufacturing industry in the country, even though for the most part it consisted of small-scale factories and workshops. The city also had the nation's largest port and docks. In addition, and crucial in determining the city's subsequent economic development several decades later, even by the early nineteenth-century London had become firmly established as the nation's trading and financial capital, and indeed one of the world's most important financial centres, having taken over that role from Amsterdam. Up until the middle of the nineteenth century, the British banking system had been a regional and county-based system, but through merger, acquisition and amalgamation, and successive waves of local bank closures, by the close of the century most of the surviving major banks had become headquartered in London, where the primary institutions of the Bank of England, Lloyds Insurance and the main Stock Exchange had been established more than two centuries earlier.

Similarly, the spatial distribution of middle- and upper-class wealth in nineteenth-century Britain was not concentrated in the industrial towns of the North, as is often claimed,[3] but rather was focused on London (Rubenstein 1977, 1981). The importance of Northern trading cities such as Liverpool, Manchester, Leeds and Glasgow notwithstanding, more than 50 per cent of middle-class income in Victorian times was accounted for by London. This was due not just to its larger middle-class population, but also to its higher middle-class per capita income. This brief excursion into economic history is not intended to refute the undoubted industrial success of much of Northern Britain in the nineteenth century, and the crucial role that many Northern towns and cities—such as Manchester, Liverpool, Leeds, Sheffield, Newcastle, Hull and Glasgow—played in the Industrial Revolution, the Victorian economy and the development of empire that took place in that era. They were unquestionably successful and were certainly industrial powerhouses. However, as the new analyses by Crafts (2005) and Geary and Stark (2015, 2016) show, while the North West was certainly the second or third wealthiest region in the country, and while a distinct shift towards London and the South East definitely occurred in the interwar period, the fact of the matter is that London was already in a league of its own by the middle of the nineteenth century. Doubt can thus be cast on the view that it was only in the interwar years that economic advantage 'suddenly shifted' to the South. London and the South East were established as the most prosperous areas of Britain well before the reorientation of the national economy that took place in the 1920s and 1930s. It was precisely because these regions were already positioned as the prosperous core—in which the nation's major financial, political and economic institutions were already well established—that they attracted the bulk of the new industries that emerged in the interwar period. In a certain sense, the 'greater London' region—London and neighbouring parts of the South East—in effect 'reinvented' itself in those years, in as much that this part of Britain led 'the new economy' just as the North experienced the structural upheavals and decline of 'the old economy' inherited from the previous century.

What is clear is that the problem of spatial imbalance in the British economy that has become the focus of political concern and rhetoric since 2010 is in fact hardly new. It has roots that go back well into the nineteenth century, if not earlier. Thus, while our leading politicians have been correct to recognise that the British economy is too spatially unbalanced, with growth too dependent on and concentrated in London and much of the surrounding South East, and although the problem intensified during the long phase of uninterrupted growth between 1992 and 2007, the spatially unbalanced nature of the national economy is of much longer historical standing. This suggests that in explaining the current pattern of spatial economic imbalance it is not sufficient to appeal to contemporary factors and causes, but also necessary to understand how the past has shaped the present: there is a strong degree of path dependence in regional economic development (see Martin and Sunley 2006). Furthermore, and a key element in making for such path dependence, past structures of spatial economic organisation can in effect become institutionalised and reproduced by the national political economy—the geographical configuration of national economic and political power and policy. This is a large part of the problem in the UK. We return to this issue later in the chapter. But first, we look at the economic performance of individual major Northern English cities over the past 40 years to get a sense of how they have fared relative to the rest of the country over this period, and hence the scale of the challenge of reviving the 'Northern Powerhouse' as a route to spatially rebalancing the British economy.

Lagging Behind: The Recent Economic Performance of Major Northern Powerhouse Cities

As Jane Jacobs (1984) famously argued, it is not possible to understand a 'national' economy without reference to the performance of the cities and city-regions of which it is composed. It is in cities and city-regions that the bulk of a nation's wealth is created, its exports are produced, its jobs are located and its incomes are spent. It is perhaps somewhat ironic, therefore, that while national economic policy thinking has come to recognise the crucial role played by cities in shaping the nation's economic fortunes and progress, UK governments have never collected regular or consistent data on the economies or economic performance of our cities. Our understanding of how economic growth has varied across urban Britain is surprisingly poor: we know relatively little about the productivity of our cities, their trade balances or the innovativeness of their economies. There is even a lack of general agreement about how our cities should be meaningfully defined geographically.

Constructing reliable and meaningful economic data series for British cities has been part of a major research programme with which we are involved. This is concerned, *inter alia*, with compiling consistent time series on some key dimensions of city economic performance—particularly employment, output and productivity—back to the 1970s. The complete data set covers some 82 sectors of activity for 85 cities annually over the period 1971–2014. The cities are defined in terms of travel-to-work areas (using 2011 geographical definitions), and hence have a functional character. These are the most complete data series of their kind and enable us to provide some interesting insight into the comparative economic performance of individual cities and how that performance has varied over time.[4]

A useful way of exploring this issue is to compute the cumulative difference between the annual growth rate (for example, of employment and output) in a given city and the corresponding rate for the country as a whole.[5] This allows comparison of cities one against another by reference to their performance relative to a national 'yardstick'. The computed cumulative differential growth series for employment and output for the major Northern cores cities of Manchester, Liverpool, Leeds, Sheffield and Newcastle—the main cities that make up the 'Northern Powerhouse' area—together with London for comparison, are shown in Figs. 2.1 and 2.2. A number of key features are evident. First, it is

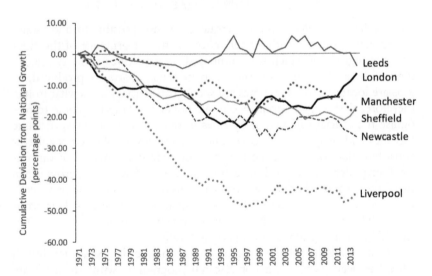

Fig. 2.1   Annual growth of employment in Northern Core Cities and London, 1971–2014: cumulative deviation from Great Britain average. *Source of data* Authors' own data. See also Martin et al. (2016). *Notes* Total employment. Cities defined in terms of 2001 travel-to-work areas

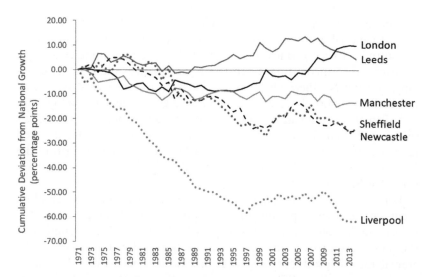

Fig. 2.2 Annual growth of gross value added in Northern Core Cities and London, 1971–2014: cumulative deviation from Great Britain average. *Source of data* Authors' own data. See also Martin et al. (2016). *Notes* Gross value added, workplace-based estimates. Cities defined in terms of 2001 travel-to-work areas

clear that for both employment and output growth, all of the Northern English core cities except Leeds have lagged well behind the national economy as a whole since the beginning of the 1970s, as indicated by their negative growth gaps. This was particularly the case up to the mid-1990s, since when they have tracked national economic growth more closely, but have failed to recover any of their cumulative lost ground to any significant degree. As a result, by 2014, cumulative growth in Manchester, Sheffield and Newcastle had fallen behind the Great Britain average by some 20 percentage points.

Second, the plight of Liverpool is particularly striking: its cumulative growth gaps are well over 40 percentage points on both employment and output. Third, Leeds emerges as the only Northern English core city to have more or less matched the growth record of the national economy as a whole over the 40-year period. In terms of output growth, in fact, from the late 1980s up to the recent recession its growth outstripped that nationally, and kept pace with London. And London's comparative performance is itself of key interest. Up to the early 1990s it too lagged behind national growth, much more so in the case of employment than for output. However, since then it has undergone something of a major 'turnaround', experiencing much faster growth than the national economy, and the Northern cities, except Leeds in output terms, so that by 2014 it had almost eliminated its cumulative growth gap in employment, and turned its cumulative negative growth gap in output into a positive growth lead. What is also striking is that output growth recovered far more strongly in London after the 2008–2010 recession than in the Northern cities, including Leeds, which, like its other Northern counterparts, has been much slower to recover.

For any city, the comparative growth rates of output and employment define a corresponding rate of growth in labour productivity.[6] Considerable concern has been expressed by the UK Government at the poor productivity performance of the national economy. The annual rate of productivity growth has in fact been on a downward trend since the late 1970s, in common with a number of other major advanced economies (Carmody 2013) There is a debate over the causes of this slowdown: whether it is due to the structural shift amongst the advanced economies from high-productivity growth manufacturing to lower productivity growth services, to a failure of advances in technology (especially computing) to show up in productivity, to a slowdown in transformative innovation itself, to a slowdown in investment, to a lack of a skilled workforce or to measurement problems (the argument that productivity in some service activities is possibly underestimated). Whichever of these possible causes has been operative, an additional dimension to the productivity problem in the UK is the low productivity of many Northern cities: most of these have labour productivity levels below the national average, while most Southern cities have levels above the average; and the disparity has a high degree of persistence over time (see Fig. 2.3).[7] Moreover, the labour productivity in the major 'Northern Powerhouse' cities has remained consistently below the national average over the past four decades or more, while in London labour productivity has steadily pulled ahead of that for the national economy as a whole, so that, for example, there is now a 50 percentage point gap between London and Manchester (see Fig. 2.4).

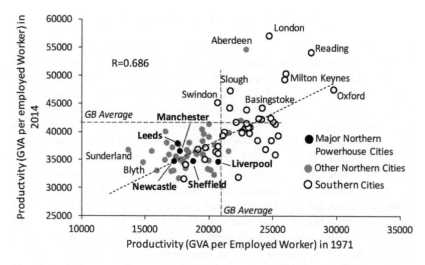

Fig. 2.3 Labour productivity across 85 British cities, 1971 and 2014. *Source of data* Authors' own data. See also Martin et al. (2017)

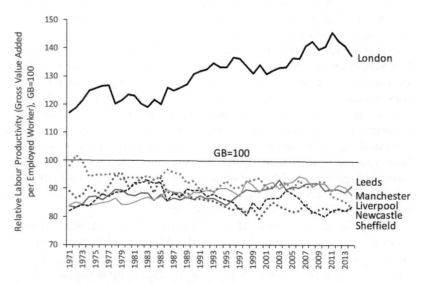

Fig. 2.4 Relative labour productivity (GVA per Employed Worker) in Northern Core Cities and London, 1971–2014, (Great Britain = 100). *Source of data* Authors' own data. See also Martin et al. (2017)

THE COLLAPSE OF AN EXPORT BASE

One of the key arguments in Jane Jacob's discussion of the importance of cities in the national economy is the role cities play in generating exports. This idea links closely of course with export-based theories of economic growth. In Kaldor's (1981) growth model, for example, other things being equal, the more competitive (in terms of productivity) an economy's export sectors, the greater will be the external demand for those exports, the faster will be the growth of output in those sectors (and via multiplier effects, the economy more generally). This growth in its turn will stimulate investment, innovation and labour productivity, which will boost competitiveness still further, which then stimulates additional demand for that economy's exports, and so on, in a circular and cumulative manner (see also Setterfield 1998; Martin 2017). Kaldor himself used this framework to explain regional differences in economic growth. A city's export or tradable base may thus be expected to play a crucial role in determining its growth performance.

Building on these ideas, Rowthorn (2010) argues that, in the absence of actual regional trade data, the 'export base' is a useful proxy because it 'consists of all those activities which bring income into the region by providing a good or service to the outside world, or provide locals with a good or service which they would otherwise have to import'. He therefore suggested that the 'export base' of a region could be approximated by the following sectors: agriculture, manufacturing, extractive industries, finance and business services, and hotels and restaurants. He goes on to argue that the much-debated 'North-South Divide' in the UK's economic landscape can be attributed to the fact that the North has seen a particularly severe decline in its manufacturing export sector while the Southern regions, particularly the Greater South East, have specialised more in high-end tradable services. In relative terms, he estimates that the cumulative decline of employment in the Northern private export base since 1971 has been around 30 per cent.

Using the detailed sectoral employment and output series referred to in the previous section, Martin et al. (2016) employ two definitions of a region's 'export intensity', based on those sectors that nationally export at least 50 and 25 per cent of their output overseas. Using the latter measure to define the export base of the three main regions making up the 'Northern Powerhouse', Fig. 2.5 confirms Rowthorn's general finding: in both Yorkshire–Humberside and the North West

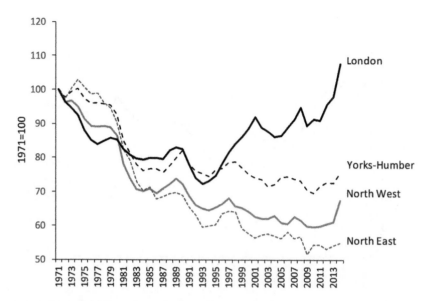

Fig. 2.5 Export base employment in the Northern Powerhouse Regions and London, 1971–2014 (Indexed 1971 = 100). *Source of data* Authors' own data

export-based employment has shrunk by around 25–30 per cent since the beginning of the 1970s, although in the North East region the contraction has been almost 50 per cent. A significant proportion of this decline occurred in the recessions of the early 1980s and early 1990s. In all three of the Northern Powerhouse regions, the erosion in export base employment was particularly rapid during the 1970s and first-half of the 1980s, precisely when these regions experienced pronounced deindustrialization. These trends stand in stark contrast to that for London. While London's export base employment also shrunk up until the early 1990s, it then underwent a major turnaround and increased sharply thereafter so that by 2014 it had more than made up for the previous decline. If we look at the major cities within the Northern Powerhouse regions, only Leeds shows a similar pattern: after witnessing a major fall in export base employment during the 1970s and 1980s, it too then experienced something of a recovery, although since the onset of the financial crisis in 2007 it has failed to keep up with the capital (Fig. 2.6).

A closer look at these trends by broad sector (Table 2.3) indicates that in the 1971–1991 subperiod, in London and all of the major Northern

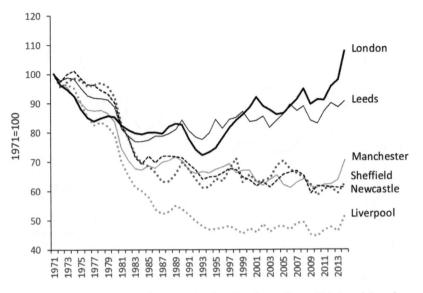

Fig. 2.6 Export base employment in the Northern Core Cities and London, 1971–2014 (Indexed 1971 = 100). *Source of data* Authors' own data

Powerhouse cities the dramatic decline in employment in manufacturing export sectors far outweighed the increase in employment in exporting knowledge-intensive business services (KIBS), which include finance and related activities. While in all cases the scale of the absolute decline of employment in exporting manufacturing activities lessened during the 1991–2014 subperiod, only in three cities—London, Leeds and Manchester—was this loss offset by the increase in employment in exporting KIBS. Taking the period 1971–2014 as a whole, however, only in London had the growth in the KIBS export base more than compensated for the decline of the manufacturing export base in terms of employment.

The problem with using these export base employment estimates is that they assume that a given sector behaves in the same way in the regions and cities as it does nationally. Depending on the sector, this is obviously a questionable assumption. For example, the finance sector in Liverpool or Leeds is assumed to have the same export propensity as that of London, and that all that differs is the relative importance (in employment share terms) of financial services in each city's economy. Thus, while the results

Table 2.3 Export base employment by broad sector, major Powerhouse Cities and London, 1971–2014

	1971–1991	1991–2014	1971–2014
London			
Manufacturing	−607,856	−188,818	−796,674
KIBS	208,492	738,584	947,076
Other sectors	11,031	130,831	141,862
Total	−388,333	680,597	292,264
Leeds			
Manufacturing	−60,085	−36,921	−97,006
KIBS	27,899	50,257	78,156
Other sectors	−759	5559	4800
Total	−32,945	18,895	−14,050
Liverpool			
Manufacturing	−117,211	−24,964	−142,175
KIBS	8808	21,495	30,303
Other sectors	−4772	5570	798
Total	−113,175	2101	−111,074
Manchester			
Manufacturing	−246,875	−107,640	−354,515
KIBS	56,783	121,909	178,692
Other sectors	−8765	11,469	2704
Total	−198,857	25,738	−173,119
Newcastle			
Manufacturing	−70,741	−36,438	−107,179
KIBS	15,496	20,477	35,973
Other sectors	−7341	2433	−4908
Total	−62,586	−13,528	−76,114
Sheffield			
Manufacturing	−73,510	−29,254	−102,764
KIBS	17,260	18,887	36,147
Other sectors	−997	3689	2692
Total	−57,247	−6678	−63,925

Source of data Authors' own data

are interesting, they must be taken in the context of the assumptions on which they are based. As far as actual regional trade is concerned, there are some limited estimates produced by HMRC.[8] Unfortunately, these data only refer to manufactured goods: data for services are patchy and not

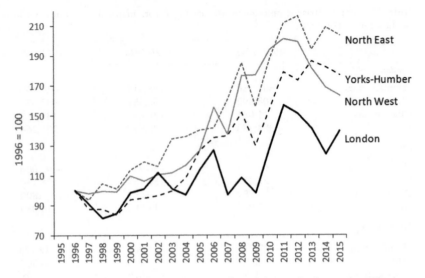

Fig. 2.7 International exports of manufactured goods from the Northern Powerhouse Regions and London, 1995–2015 (Nominal Prices, 1996 = 100). *Source of data* HMRC data on regional (NUTS1) goods exports and imports

reliable. Nevertheless, they provide some insight into certain aspects of the trading position of the Northern regions relative to the rest of the UK.

The results for the three 'Northern Powerhouse' regions as a whole show that the growth in tradable goods exports has outstripped that of the rest of the UK over the 1996–2015 period (Fig. 2.7), which on the surface would seem to give a different picture from that given by the relative growth trends of total output in the major Northern Powerhouse cities (Fig. 2.2). However, this picture relates only to goods exports and excludes trade in high-value services (including finance), in which London has a particular specialisation. Further, it is not just exports that are important. What also matters in the long run is each region's or city's trade balance (Rowthorn 2010). The degree to which a region or city imports goods from overseas contributes to the national trade balance, as well to its own long-run performance. It is well known that the UK as a whole has been running a trade deficit in manufactured goods for some time, and that it has worsened over recent years. The HMRC data contain estimates of the manufactured goods trade balance by region, and these show, perhaps not surprisingly, that in 2015 half of the nation's trade deficit in goods was accounted for by London (Table 2.4).

Table 2.4 Balance of trade in manufactured goods, Northern Powerhouse Regions, London and UK, 1996–2015 (£m)

	1996	2000	2005	2010	2015
North East	2654	2234	2109	1549	761
North West	2945	2099	−313	4369	−790
Yorks–Humberside	1368	−1908	−966	−2488	−6366
Total NPH regions	6968	2425	831	3430	−6394
London	−14,900	−21,228	−16,959	−34,949	−49,816
UK	−2041	−31,034	−60,565	−97,556	−100,086

Source of data HMRC data on regional (NUTS1) goods exports and imports

Table 2.5 Exports per job in the Northern Core Cities and London, 2014

	Total exports (£)	Goods exports (£)	Service exports (£)
Leeds	8260	4470	3790
Liverpool	12,920	6950	5970
Manchester	11,470	5370	6100
Newcastle	8900	5680	3210
Sheffield	8640	5810	2820
London	23,470	5770	17,710
UK average	15,690	8240	7450

Source Centre for Cities (2017) and Centre for Cities Data Tool
Note Total city employment is used as the denominator for both goods and services exports, so that the sum of the two equals the value of total exports per job

However, while the Northern Powerhouse regions' balance of trade in manufactured goods was in surplus in the mid-1990s, this too has turned into a deficit over the past two decades, with only the North East region still showing a small excess of exports over imports. This of course means that the UK and its regions now depend crucially on exportable services to fill the trade gap.

According to TheCityUK (2017), London's financial sector, together with related professional services (legal services, accountancy and management consultancy), generated an estimated trade surplus of some £71 billion in 2014, which more than offset its goods trade deficit of £40 billion for that year. Unfortunately, there are no comparable data for the other UK regions, let alone other cities, so we do not know the contribution of tradable services to the trade balance of the Northern Powerhouse regions or cities. However, the Centre for Cities (2017) has recently estimated the value of exports by tradable services per job by

Table 2.6 Regional gross value added per capita, 1971–2014, indexed to UK = 100

UK = 100	1971	1981	1991	2001	2007	2014
London	153.3	163.7	163.0	165.6	169.3	174.3
South East	105.7	104.3	107.1	110.8	106.0	109.4
East of England	103.8	100.1	98.1	97.4	95.3	92.9
South West	90.9	94.1	92.0	92.3	90.6	89.3
East Midlands	80.7	85.0	84.7	82.9	83.4	82.3
West Midlands	96.4	89.8	90.0	87.4	84.4	83.4
Yorkshire–Humberside	80.7	85.5	84.7	81.4	85.8	80.2
North West	93.9	85.8	85.0	86.1	87.7	85.3
North East	75.3	79.2	75.8	72.0	75.5	73.5
Wales	78.5	78.2	75.3	71.5	73.7	72.0
Scotland	92.2	97.8	103.1	99.2	95.9	94.6
Northern Ireland	80.1	84.6	77.8	80.9	82.8	76.3
CV	21.0	22.9	23.8	25.2	23.3	27.7

Source of data ONS and Cambridge Econometrics
Notes Gross value added per capita in 2011 prices. Workplace (production-based) estimates. Converted to per capita values by dividing resident population not resident workforce. Government Office Regions. CV is the Coefficient of Variation, a measure of the regional 'spread' (disparity) in per capita relativities: the larger the value the more regionally uneven or unbalanced is the economy

city (Table 2.5), and this suggests—not unexpectedly—that the export value per job of London's tradable services sector far outstrips that for the major Northern cities.[9] These estimates also suggest that, with the exception of Manchester, despite the deindustrialisation the city has suffered over recent decades, the major Northern Powerhouse cities still export more manufactured goods than they do services. In this respect, their economies differ markedly from that of London.

A number of key points emerge from this brief analysis of the economic performance of the major Northern Powerhouse cities over the past four decades. In what has been a period of historic change and transformation of the UK economy—most notably the shift from an industrial to a service-based, globalised, and financialised 'post-industrial' mode of growth—the Northern Powerhouse cities have fallen increasingly behind London in terms of employment and output growth, and productivity. Deindustrialisation has seriously eroded their manufacturing export base, but unlike London, they have yet to rebuild that base around tradable, high-value service activities on a scale to compensate for the loss of manufacturing capacity. Another implication is that while London's labour productivity has pulled well ahead of the national average since the mid-1980s, that in the major Northern cities has remained below the national figure, with the result that the 'productivity gap' between London and the Northern cities has widened. Overall, the divide between the more prosperous London and the South East regions on the one hand, and the regions making up the 'Northern Powerhouse'—the North West, Yorkshire–Humberside and the North East—on the other, that, as we have seen, existed back in the nineteenth century, is as pronounced as ever (Table 2.6). Indeed, the lead of London is arguably greater now than it was more than a century ago (cf. Table 2.2).

WHY HAS SPATIAL ECONOMIC IMBALANCE BEEN SO PERSISTENT?

The fact that the pattern and scale of spatial economic disparity across the UK are not much different today than they were more a century ago raises some fundamental questions about the operation of the economy, as well as for policy. After all, according to conventional economic theory, large spatial disparities in economic performance and prosperity should not persist over long periods of time. Market forces—notably the free movement of labour and capital—should automatically operate in a self-correcting way to reduce such gaps. To be sure, there may be short-run frictions to such adjustments, but in the medium to long-term term we should see a convergence across regions and cities in per capita incomes, productivity and the like. The lack of any significant convergence can be given various interpretations.

The first, often advanced by advocates of conventional economic theory, is that there must be major impediments and barriers that are preventing market forces from operating freely. Such 'market failure', they go on to argue, is the only justifiable basis for policy intervention—especially on the 'supply side' of the economy. Yet the UK has had some form of regional and urban policy directed at promoting faster growth and levels of prosperity in economically lagging areas in the country for almost 90 years, since the late 1920s. The second line of argument is thus that these policies have failed. Some are of the view, for example, that the resources devoted to regional and other spatial policy measures have never been adequate to the scale of the task. Others levy the charge that regional policy has never been sufficiently strategic or developmental in its goals. A further interpretation, again one that tends to be preferred by the followers of conventional economic theory, is that the lack of any substantial and lasting positive impact confirms that regional and urban policy can never achieve much since it is trying to work 'against the forces of the market', which in the UK 'naturally' favour the concentration of growth in the already prosperous London and the South East (for an extreme version of this argument, see Leunig and Swaffield 2007). In general, these spatial economists are of the view that there is no case for spatially targeted or selective policies, only general (nationwide) policies aimed at improving the movement of skilled labour (and capital) to where the markets opportunities and rewards are greatest, in combination with the deregulation of land and housing markets (by dismantling planning systems) in and around particular cities—especially London—so that further growth can be more easily accommodated there. This line of reasoning reached its most extreme in the Policy Exchange argument that:

> There is no realistic prospect that our [Northern] regeneration towns and cities can converge with London and the South East. There is, however, a very real prospect of encouraging significant numbers of people to move from those towns to London and the South East. … The implications of economic geography for the South and particularly the South East are clear. Britain will be unambiguously richer if we allow more people to live in London and its hinterland. (Leunig and Swaffield 2007)

A third and quite different conceptual account of the persistent nature of spatial economic imbalance is that market forces, even if allowed free rein, do not tend of themselves to reduce or eliminate spatial imbalance in economic growth and prosperity, but rather tend to perpetuate or even intensify such imbalance. The main process at work in this case is that of the increasing returns associated with spatial agglomeration of economic activity. Spatial agglomeration is seen as conferring various external economies on firms, including 'home market size' effects, the attraction of skilled workers, increased knowledge flows and interactions between firms, backward and forward linkages between firms, and so on, all of which are held to increase productivity, innovation and higher wages. Correspondingly, spatial economic imbalance is not necessarily seen as problematic or inefficient, witness the HM Treasury statement that:

> Theory and evidence suggests that allowing regional concentration of economic activity will increase national growth. As long as economies of scale, knowledge spillovers and a local pool of skilled labour result in

productivity gains that outweigh congestion costs, the economy will benefit from agglomeration... policies that aim to spread growth amongst regions are running counter to the natural growth process and are difficult to justify on efficiency grounds. (HM Treasury 2007)

And the same view seemed to lurk in the Government Paper on *Understanding Local Growth:*

This new understanding [the New Economic Geography] of how economics works across space also alters the expected equilibrium. As both people and firms move to areas of high productivity there will be no simple convergence of productivity levels. Even with fully functioning markets, there can be an uneven distribution of economic performance, and persistent differences that are not necessarily due to market failure. (Department of Business, innovation and Skills 2010, p. 23)

The theory being referred to here—Krugman-style New Economic Geography—has on various occasions been used to promote the idea of an 'equity-efficiency trade-off', as in the quote above, whereby the pursuit of a more spatially balanced economy is believed to be at the cost of national economic efficiency (Martin 2008, 2015). The empirical evidence for such a 'trade-off', however, is far from equivocal. While some studies claim to find a negative relationship between national growth and the degree of spatial agglomeration or regional inequality (Dall'erba and Hewings 2003; Martin 2005; Crozet and Koening 2007), others do not (Sbergami 2002; Bosker 2007; Martin 2008). To add to this ambiguity, Krugman himself (2009) has recently voiced some doubt as to whether increasing returns to spatial agglomeration as important as they once were

There's good reason to believe that the world economy has, over time, actually become less characterised by the kinds of increasing returns effects emphasized by new trade theory and new economic geography. In the case of geography, in fact, the peak of increasing returns occurred long before the theorists arrived on the scene. (2009, p. 569)

So even one of its former leading exponents seems less convinced that spatial agglomeration necessarily promotes faster growth. Nevertheless, the spatial agglomeration argument has proved a powerful discourse. It underpins the contention that one of the reasons that Britain's

Northern cities—especially the major cities making up the 'Northern Powerhouse'—have lagged in economic performance is that they are too small, with the consequence that they do not benefit from the agglomeration economies found in large cities such as London. Thus, according to Overman and Rice (2008), while medium-sized cities in England are, roughly speaking, about the size that Zipf's law would predict given the size of London, the largest city, the major second-tier cities (which include 'core' cities such as Manchester, Birmingham, Sheffield and Newcastle) all lie below the 'Zipf line' and hence are smaller than would be predicted.[10] They go on to state that 'this feature is not a consequence of London being too "large"', but rather that 'second tier cities may be too small' (op cit, p.30). Such an argument would suggest that increasing the size of the core cities, and especially those of the 'Northern Powerhouse', would boost the advantages of agglomeration and hence their economic performance. However, as other authors have cautioned, Zipf's law should not be expected to hold in countries that have a capital that is also the political centre, as is the case with London. As Krugman (1996) himself emphasises in his discussion of Zipf's law, such political centres 'are different creatures from the rest of the urban system'. A similar point is made by Gabaix (1999) who argues that '[i]n most countries Zipf plots usually present an outlier, the capital, which has a bigger size than Zipf's law would warrant. There is nothing surprising there because *the capital is indeed a peculiar object, driven by unique political forces*' (op cit, p.756, emphasis added).[11]

The argument that Northern cities are 'undersized' is thus open to debate; improving their performance is a much more complex issue than simply increasing their size. The fact is that some of the fastest rates of productivity *growth* across Britain's urban system over the past four decades have been recorded among smaller and medium-sized cities, especially those in Southern England (Martin et al. 2016): there is no simple relationship between city size and growth, and the lack of any such relationship appears to be a common feature across most OECD countries (Dijkstra and McCann 2013). A different way of looking at the issue might be to argue that the benefits of agglomeration can be realised not by making Northern cities substantially bigger but by vastly improving the connectivity between them so as to enable them to function as an efficiently interconnected and integrated multi-centric 'super-city regional system', in which the whole could indeed be 'greater than the sum of its parts' (City Growth Commission 2014). Investing in the infrastructures required to achieve that would arguably yield a greater economic dividend for the Northern cities than the High Speed 2 rail connection between London, Birmingham and Manchester, the case for which has never been convincingly proven.

The key question remains: why has spatial economic imbalance in the UK been so persistent? Another way of posing this question is to ask why is it that the London–South East corner of the country has been able to successfully 'reinvent' its economy and its export base twice over the last century—in the 1920s and 1930s, and again since the 1990s—while Northern regions and cities have found it much more difficult to do so? Why is it that the legacies of an industrial past, and what Linkon (2013, 2014) calls the 'half-life of deindustrialization' (see also Strangleman 2016), lingered longer and have been more inhibiting to economic reorientation and diversification in the Northern cities and regions than in London? Part of the answer obviously lies in the different capabilities, specialisms and structures as between the Northern regions and cities on the one hand and London on the other. London suffered deindustrialisation over the 1970 and 1980s no less than many Northern cities. But it also had other key sectors of activities—especially finance, banking and the raft of related services that both support and depend on finance—which had long been established there around which a new phase of growth could be organised. Northern cities did not have the same potential growth sectors 'waiting in the wings'. So, part of the different experiences of London compared to Northern cities undoubtedly resided the inherited scope for economic diversification.

But without question, part also lies in the fact that London has long been the power centre of national economic, financial and political life. As such it has long exerted a dominating influence over the orientation, operation and priorities of those institutions that shape the national economy. While most of the policies followed by those institutions are ostensibly 'non-spatial' and supposedly geographically (and socially) 'neutral', invariably they have profoundly uneven effects, spatially and socially. As Lord Heseltine argued in the mid-1980s, all too often those policies have effectively functioned as 'counter-regional' policies, operating in favour of and serving to protect or reinforce the interests and priorities of London (and even more specifically the financial City) over the conditions and interests of the rest of the country.[12]

CONCLUSION: WHAT IS TO BE DONE?

Although it is certainly the case that in today's globalised economy the notion of 'combined and uneven geographical development' needs to be reworked to reflect the fact that many of our cities and regions are linked as much if not more to global markets, production networks and value chains than they are to one another (see, for example, Baldwin 2016), how they compete and function in those global arenas nevertheless remains strongly influenced by and dependent on national economic policies and interventions. And in the UK, those policies and interventions are shaped by London-centric institutions and priorities. In recent decades, successive Governments have been concerned—one might say obsessed—to enhance and protect the role and competitiveness of London as a global city and global financial centre. Indeed, for many, finance is seen as *the* central role that the UK can and should play in the new global economy, as the primary or perhaps only activity in which it commands a comparative advantage. Hence the attention is given to London. There is little discussion about what other actual or potential competitive strengths the UK has that can also be promoted to help the nation compete in the global economy. Thus, while the banks could not be allowed to fail in the crisis, the threat to the UK steel-making sector by the dumping of cheap Chinese steel, or the loss of domestic manufacturing and technology firms through takeover by foreign competitors, receives no such defensive support. Yet maintaining London's success, and its attractiveness to financial institutions, skilled workers and foreign investment, has become ever more costly: ever more major infrastructural investment is needed just to protect, let alone enhance, London's competitiveness. Though often held up as a beacon of prosperity driven by 'market forces', London's economy is hugely underwritten by the state (Oxford Economics 2007). The attention and support accorded by central government to our major Northern cities, to help them to establish competitive roles in today's global economy, has been marginal by comparison.

But with the Government's new-found concern over spatial economic imbalance, and its new spatial imaginary of the 'Northern Powerhouse' and the 'Midlands Engine', are we now at a policy crossroads? Is the new political credo of 'spatially rebalancing the economy' being translated into policy actions capable of achieving that goal? Over recent years the departments of Government responsible for economic policy—Business,

Energy and Industrial Strategy, Communities and Local Government, and even the Treasury—have all 'discovered geography' and the 'importance of place'. Several new policy initiatives have been introduced and announced with the aim of setting the national economy on a higher productivity growth path, and spatially rebalancing the economy as part of that objective, including new Local Enterprise Partnerships, a Local Growth Agenda, City Deals, a National Infrastructure Commission, a Productivity Commission, a Patient Capital Review, an Industrial Strategy Green Paper, changes to local business rates, and the beginnings of devolution of (limited) fiscal and policy powers to cities and city-regions (conditional on the establishment of 'metro-mayors'). While these and others measures are to be welcomed, it remains unclear whether together they add up to a strategy that is sufficiently radical, bold and coherent to secure the desired outcome, especially as the Government continues at the same time to pursue its programme of fiscal austerity, including cuts in central grants to local government.

Some thirty years ago, Michael Heseltine, a long-time 'one-nation' Conservative, bemoaned the over-centralization of the national political economy in London:

> In a sense we are becoming a rather monopolistic political society. I don't say that in the narrow party sense. I say it in terms of the domination of Britain by the City of London, in terms of ownership and wealth. I say it in terms of the lack of obvious roots of power outside the major political parties and the increasing location of the major corporate headquarters in London, the drift South of the public sector.... (Michael Heseltine, cited in Lloyd 1988: 17)

Even further back, in the 1960s, that journalistic bastion of free market economic thinking, *The Economist*, was moved to argue that what the North of Britain needed was its own 'London'. It has more recently reiterated that view:

> So much of what is wrong with Britain today stems from the fact that it is unusually centralised. Draw a circle with a 60-mile radius centred on Charing Cross. Within that circle, the vast majority of public spending is administered. Also: all major decisions pertaining to foreign policy, defence, the economy, the national debt, interest rates... That circle contains all the major banks, most of the major theatres, the media and arts worlds, the five best universities (according to the Times Higher

Education rankings for 2017), the hubs of all the country's major industries, 70 per cent of the FTSE 100, most of Britain's airport capacity. The divide between Britain inside the circle and Britain outside it concentrates too much power within too few city districts ... So, while moving Britain's capital would not solve every problem, it would go a long way to addressing the complaints that lead to today's divided country. It would contribute hugely to the rebalancing of the economy. It would help drive the urban integration needed to raise productivity and thus living standards outside the charmed South-East. (*The Economist* 2017)

Stimulated in part by Heseltine's (2012) provocative call for a devolution of fiscal and other powers, the UK has begun the first tentative steps in this direction. But just how far down this path the London-based political establishment and financial elites will be willing to go remains to be seen (indeed, the Coalition Government's initial enthusiasm for devolution seems to have lost some momentum under Theresa May's Conservative administration). At the same time, the 'combined authority' model of devolution that has been championed does not readily mesh with the complex two-tier layering of local political power and responsibilities that exist across the country: many local authorities are themselves not yet convinced that the proposed model of devolution will bring much material benefit. Nevertheless, the fact is that other OECD countries have devolved or federalized systems of political–economic governance that seem to work more effectively and productively than the UK's over-centralised model, and most enjoy much greater regional economic balance. A century and a half of spatially unbalanced prosperity and growth in the UK is surely sufficient cause to warrant a fundamental reform of the nation's political economy. At present the changes underway are ad hoc, rather than based on a detailed analysis of what the most beneficial and effective political and geographical configuration across the whole nation would look like. What is clear, however, is that the growing popular disaffection now evident across the cities and regions with the remoteness and self-serving nature of the London establishment is a long-overdue wake-up call that fundamental reform is needed.

NOTES

1. This research for this paper was undertaken as part of a project funded by the ESRC (ES/N006135/1) into 'Structural Transformation, Adaptability and City Economic Evolutions', as part of its Structural

Transformations Programme. We are grateful to the ESRC for its support.

2. The acronym NICE is usually attributed to the former Governor of the Bank of England, Mervyn King.

3. For example, in commenting on the 'North-South Divide' debate that arose in the mid-1980s, Lord Young the then Secretary of State for Trade and Industry under the Thatcher Government ventured to claim that 'Until 70 years ago the North was always the richest part of the country...that is where all the great country houses are because that's where the wealth was. Now some of it is in the South. It's our turn, that's all' (Quoted in *Business* 1987, p. 17). This was a highly simplistic and not altogether accurate reading of the country's historical economic geography, and a dismissive interpretation of the widening gap between the prosperous South and lagging North in the 1980s as some sort of 'natural justice of history'.

4. Details of this ESRC-funded research programme, entitled *Structural Transformation, Adaptability and City Economic Evolutions* (Grant ES/N006135/1), can be found at http://www.cityevolutions.org.uk.

5. Technically, this is measured as $Cumy_{iT} = \sum_{t=1}^{T} (y_{it} - y_{Nt})$, where y_{it} is the per cent change in, say, employment or output in year t, and y_{Nt} is the corresponding per cent change in Great Britain as a whole, and $Cumy_{iT}$ is the cumulative sum of the growth differential for city i from time t up to time T. This simple technique was used to interesting effect by Blanchard and Katz (1992) to chart the disparate economic evolution of US states in the post-war period.

6. Estimating total factor productivity (TFP) by city is not possible because we do not have data on capital stock or investment over time at this spatial scale.

7. Southern are cities defined as those in the following regions: London, South East, East of England, South West and East Midlands. Northern cities are defined as those in the West Midlands, Yorkshire–Humberside, North East, North East, Scotland and Wales. Great Britain averages shown by intersecting pecked lines.

8. It should also be borne in mind that the HMRC trade figures are in current prices, and thus reflect both movements in the volume of trade as well as their prices.

9. The definition of cities used by the Centre for Cities is the Primary Urban Area, essentially the contiguous Local Authority Districts which contain the built-up area of a city. These differ from the Travel-to-Work Area definitions used in our analyses. The Centre for Cities estimates the value of exports per service job by apportioning national service export data to cities on the assumption that each city's service sector has the same export orientation as it does nationally. The estimates should thus be

interpreted with the same caveat that applies to our estimates of city export intensity used above.

10. Zipf's law refers to the relationship between city size and city rank. If cities are ranked by population size and the slope of a plot of the log of city rank (by size) against the log of size is -1, this is referred to as Zipf's law.

11. In an important study of city size distributions in 75 countries, Soo (2005) found that departures of the rank versus size relationship from a slope of -1 are explained by political factors rather than by economic geography factors like economies of scale or agglomeration economies.

12. This argument was set out in a speech that Michael Heseltine gave to the Brick Development Association in London in the mid-1980s. He was Secretary of State for Trade and Industry at the time.

REFERENCES

Baldwin, R. 2016 *The Great Convergence: Information Technology and the New Globalisation*. Cambridge, Mass: Harvard University Press.

Barlow Commission. 1940. *Royal commission on the distribution of the industrial population*. London: H.M. Stationery Office.

Bernanke, B.S. 2004. *The great moderation, remarks at the meeting of the eastern economic association*. Washington, DC, February 20. Available at http://www.federalreserve.gov/boarddocs/speeches/2004/20040220/.

Blanchard, O.J., and L.E. Katz. 1992. *Regional evolutions*. Brookings papers in economic activity, 1, Washington, DC.

Bosker, M. 2007. Growth, agglomeration and convergence: A space-time analysis for the European regions. *Spatial Economic Analysis* 2: 91–100.

Brown, G. 2010. Mansion House speech, The Mansion House, City of London, June 20. Available at http://webarchive.nationalarchives.gov.uk/; http://www.hm-treasury.gov.uk/2014.htm.

Business. 1987. Across the north–south divide, September.

Cable, V. 2013. London draining life out of rest of country. http://www.bbc.co.uk/news/uk-politics-25444981.

Cameron, D. 2010. *Transforming the British economy: Coalition strategy for economic growth*. Speech, 28 May, Prime Minister's Office, London. https://www.gov.uk/government/speeches/transforming-the-british-economy-coalition-strategy-for-economic-growth.

Centre for Cities. 2017. *Cities outlook 2017*. London: Centre for Cities.

City of London Corporation. 2011. *London's competitive place in the UK and global economies*. Research report. London: City of London Corporation.

City of London Corporation. 2014. *London's finances and revenues*. Research report. London: City of London Corporation.

Clegg, N. 2010. Fair shares. *The Northern Echo*, 29 June. http://www.theNorthernecho.co.uk/features/leader/8244486.Fair_shares/.

Carmody, C. 2013. Slowing productivity growth: A developed economy comparison. *Economic Roundup* (2). The Treasury, Australian Government. http://www.treasury.gov.au/PublicationsAndMedia/Publications/2013/Economic-Roundup-Issue-2/Economic-Roundup/Slowing-productivity-growth.

City Growth Commission. 2014. *Unleashing metro growth*. London: The City Growth Commission; London: RSA.

Crafts, N. 2005. Regional GDP in Britain, 1971–1911: Some estimates. *Scottish Journal of Political Economy* 52: 54–64.

Crozet, M., and G.P. Koenig. 2007. *The cohesion-growth trade-off: Evidence from EU regions*. Paris: University of Paris.

Dall'erba, S., and G.J.D. Hewings. 2003. European regional development policies: The trade-off between efficiency-equity revisited. Discussion paper 03-T-2, Regional Economics Applications Laboratory, University of Illinois.

Department of Business, Innovation and Skills. 2010. *Understanding local growth*. BIS Economics Paper, London.

Deutsche Bank. 2013. *London and the UK economy: In for a penny, in for a pound?* Special report. Deutsche Bank Markets Research.

Dijkstra, L., E. Garcilazo, and P. McCann. 2013. The economic performance of European cities: Myths and realities. *European Planning Studies* 21: 334–354.

Gabaix, X. 1999. Zipf's law for cities: An explanation. *Quarterly Journal of Economics* 114: 739–767.

Geary, F., and T. Stark. 2015. Regional GDP in the UK, 1861–1911: New estimates. *Economic History Review* 68: 123–144.

Geary, F., and T. Stark. 2016. What happened to regional inequality in Britain in the twentieth century. *Economic History Review* 69: 216–228.

Heseltine, M. 2012. *No stone unturned: In pursuit of growth*. London: Department for Business, Innovation and Skills.

H.M. Government. 2010. *Local growth: Realising every place's potential*. Cm 7961. London: H.M. Government.

H.M. Treasury. 2007. *Regional disparities and growth in Europe* (author C. Lees). London: H.M. Treasury, Mimeo.

Jacobs, J. 1984. *Cities and the wealth of nations: Principles of economic life*. New York: Random House.

Kaldor, N. 1981. The role of increasing returns, technological progress and cumulative causation in the theory of international trade and economic growth. *Economie Appliquée* XXXIV: 593–617.

Krugman, P. 1996. *The self-organising economy*. Oxford: Blackwell.

Krugman, P. 2009. The new economic geography: Now middle-aged. *Regional Studies* 45: 1–7.

Leunig, T., and J. Swaffield. 2007. *Cities unlimited: Making urban regeneration work*. London: Policy Exchange.

Linkon, S. 2013. Navigating past and present in the deindustrial landscape: Contemporary writers on Detroit and Youngstown. *International Labor and Working-Class History* 84: 38–54.

Linkon, S. 2014. The half-life of deindustrialisation: Twenty-first century narratives of work, place and identity. Paper presented at deindustrialization and its aftermath: Class, culture and resistance, Centre for Oral History, May, Montreal, Quebec.

Lloyd, J. 1988 The Tory opposition, Marxism Today, March, 12–19. Available from: http://208.109.186.237/Pub/MarxismToday-1988mar-00012. Accessed 31 July 2017.

Martin, P. 2005. The geographies of inequality in Europe. *Swedish Economic Policy Review* 12: 85–108.

Martin, R.L. 2008. National growth versus regional equality? A cautionary note on the new trade-off thinking in regional policy discourse. *Regional Science, Policy and Practice* 1: 3–13.

Martin, R.L. 2015. Rebalancing the spatial economy: The challenge for regional theory. *Territory, Politics, Governance* 3: 235–272.

Martin, R.L. 2017. Cumulative causation, endogenous growth and regional development, Chapter 22. In *Encyclopedia of geography: People, the earth, environment and technology*, ed. M. Dunford. New York: Wiley.

Martin, R., and P. Sunley. 2007 Complexity thinking and evolutionary economic geography. *Journal of Economic Geography*, 7 (5): 573–601.

Martin, R.L., P.J. Sunley, P. Tyler, and B. Gardiner. 2016. Divergent cities in post-industrial Britain. *Cambridge Journal of Regions, Economy and Society* 9: 269–299.

Martin, R.L., P.J. Sunley, and B. Gardiner. 2017. Structural change and city productivity growth. Submitted to *Journal of Economic Geography*. Available from author.

Mackinder, H.J. 1919. *Democratic ideals and reality: A study in the politics of reconstruction*. New York: H.H. Holt.

Massey, D. 1986. The Legacy Lingers On: The impact of Britain's international role on its internal geography. In *The geography of deindustrialisation*, ed. R. Martin and B. Rowthorn. London: Macmillan, 31–52.

May, T. 2016. Speech given at the conservative party annual conference, 5 October, Manchester.

Osborne, G. 2014. We need a Northern Powerhouse, speech delivered in Manchester, 23 June. https://www.gov.uk/government/speeches/chancellor-we-need-a-northern-powerhouse.

Overman, H., and P. Rice. 2008. Resurgent cities and regional economic performance. SERC Policy paper 1, June 2008.

Oxford Economics. 2007. *London's place in the UK economy*. Report for the City of London Corporation. London: Oxford Economics.

Rowthorn, R.E. 2010. Combined and uneven development: Reflections on the north–south divide. *Spatial Economic Analysis* 5: 363–388.

Rubenstein, W.D. 1977. The Victorian middle classes: Wealth, occupation and geography. *Economic History Review* 30: 602–623.

Rubenstein, W.D. 1981. *Men of property: The very wealthy in Britain since the industrial revolution*. Beckenham: Croom Helm.

Sbergami, F. 2002. Agglomeration and economic growth: Some puzzles. HEI Working paper 02/2002, Graduate Institute of International Studies, Geneva.

Scott, P. 2007. *The Triumph of the south: A regional economic history of early twentieth century Britain*. Farnham: Ashgate.

Setterfield, M. 1998. *Rapid growth and relative decline*. London: Macmillan.

Soo, T.K. 2005. Zipf's law for cities: A cross country investigation. *Regional Science and Urban Economics* 35: 239–263.

Strangleman, T. 2016. Deindustrialisation and the historical sociological imagination: Making sense of work and industrial change. *Sociology*, http://journals.sagepub.com/doi/abs/10.1177/0038038515622906.

Sturgen, N. 2014. Speech to Scotland's business sector, Glasgow (1 December 2014), reported in *The Herald* (Scotland). http://www.heraldscotland.com/politics/scottish-politics/sturgeon-london-brings-benefits-to-scotlands-economy. 1417439283.

TheCityUK. 2017. UK-based financial and related professional services: Enabling growth across the UK, London. https://www.thecityuk.com/assets/2017/Reports-PDF/UK-based-financial-and-related-professional-Services-Enabling-growth-across-the-UK.pdf.

The Economist. 2017. The pragmatic case for moving Britain's capital north. *The Economist*, London. http://www.economist.com/blogs/bagehot/2017/02/go-north?fsrc=scn/tw/te/bl/ed/.

Authors' Biography

Ron Martin is Professor and Director of Research in Economic Geography in the Department of Geography, and a Research Associate of the Centre for Business Research in the Judge Business School, at the University of Cambridge. He is among the world's leading scholars of regional economic development and focuses in particular on the application of economic theory to understanding regional and city economic growth, adaptation, resilience and evolution. He also studies the geographies of financial systems. He is Fellow of the British Academy, currently the President of the Regional Studies Association, a Leverhulme Emeritus Fellow, and the principal investigator on a major ESRC project on structural transformation and city economic evolutions.

Ben Gardiner is Director of Cambridge Econometrics, an economic consultancy specialising in applied local and regional economic development and policy, and is currently Senior Research Associate on Ron Martin's ESRC city project. His research interests cover regional economic growth, developing econometric methods for regional analysis, and the study of regional and city economic resilience, which is also the focus of PhD research that he is currently undertaking.

CHAPTER 3

Law, Legislation and Rent-Seeking: The Role of the Treasury-Led Developmental State in the Competitive Advantage of the Southern Powerhouse

Simon Lee

Abstract This chapter argues that the political economy of England's 'Northern Powerhouse' cannot be understood in isolation from that of its 'Southern Powerhouse' neighbour. The UK's relative decline, especially manufacturing in the North, is frequently allocated to the absence of a state-led technocratic industrial modernisation programme. This paper challenges that analysis, contending that public policy and governance arrangements in contemporary England are the outcome of the long-term strategic priorities of the English (latterly British) developmental state, fashioned by its pilot agency, the Treasury. George Osborne's 'Northern Powerhouse' should therefore be understood not as something novel or a departure, but as simply the latest political narrative in a long-standing tradition of British statecraft which has subordinated the interests of development in the North of England to those of the global financial and commercial interests of the City of London.

S. Lee (✉)
University of Hull, Hull, UK
e-mail: s.d.lee@hull.ac.uk

© The Author(s) 2018
C. Berry and A. Giovannini (eds.), *Developing England's North*,
Building a Sustainable Political Economy: SPERI Research & Policy,
https://doi.org/10.1007/978-3-319-62560-7_3

Keywords City of London · Developmental state · Economic policy
North–South divide · Northern Powerhouse · The Treasury

A powerhouse by definition is 'a country or organization that has a
lot of power or influence' (Collins English Dictionary 2016). It is a
term which entered the lexicon of economic policy and performance
in the UK as recently as the 23 June 2014 when the then Chancellor
of the Exchequer, George Osborne, identified the need for 'Northern
Powerhouse' to counter the increasing dominance of 'the powerhouse
of London' which he contended was neither healthy for the economy
nor 'good for our country' (Osborne 2014). Although not a country
in their own right, with a combined Gross Value Added (GVA) production of goods and services of more than £627 billion in 2015 (Office
for National Statistics 2016: 4) which would have been sufficient to
rank them among the world's twenty largest economies, London and
the South East can lay claims to constitute the economic and financial 'Southern Powerhouse' of both England and the UK, accounting
for 43.8 per cent of England's and 37.6 per cent of the UK's output
of goods and services in 2015 (Office for National Statistics 2016:
4). Much of this power has been founded upon London's status as
'not just a capital city, but a city of national and global capital' (Lee
2017a). For example, London's $2406 billion and 37 per cent share
of daily global turnover in foreign exchange trading in April 2016
was similar in size to the annual income of the UK as a whole (Bank
for International Settlements 2016: 14). In addition, London, due to
the presence of the Westminster parliament and central government
departments in Whitehall, has retained its status as the political, legislative and administrative powerhouse of what remains one of the most
centralised polities among advanced, industrialised economies. Among
England's cities, London is unique in having its own institutional
and political identity via a directly elected mayor and directly elected
25-member assembly.

For the three northernmost administrative regions of England, that
is, the North West, the North East, and Yorkshire and the Humber, the
term 'Northern Powerhouse' has remained only an aspiration, not least
during Osborne's tenure as Chancellor. In 2015, with an annual GVA of
only £316 billion, the economy of the Northern Powerhouse was barely
half the size of that of the Southern Powerhouse, accounting for only

22 per cent of England's and 19 per cent of the UK's production (Office for National Statistics 2016: 4). Furthermore, the Northern Powerhouse does not possess any institutional or democratic political identity of its own to rival or counterbalance those of London or the devolved elected institutions in Scotland, Wales and Northern Ireland. Indeed, because during the more than 1000 years of its history as a nation, England has never been a federal or a quasi-federal state, with a written constitution or any significant regional tier of directly elected political institutions to challenge the sovereignty of Westminster, the possibility of a Northern Powerhouse has always depended upon the political initiative and ambition of politicians, such as George Osborne, operating at the national level (Lee 2017a, b).

One of the definitive features of the contemporary condition of England is the manifest disparity of economic growth, income and wealth between the Southern Powerhouse and the rest of England, and in particular the putative Northern Powerhouse. This national political economy has not come about by the spontaneous action of the free market. It has been the outcome of laws and legislation and deliberate political choices made over a period of several centuries, but especially during the past half century when the political economy of England has been transformed by parallel processes of market deregulation, liberalisation and privatisation which have entrenched rather than challenged the domination of the Southern Powerhouse (Lee 2017b). The political economy of England's putative Northern Powerhouse therefore cannot be understood in isolation from that of its Southern Powerhouse neighbour. Nor can it be understood without placing recent developments in public policy and the governance of England within a wider historical context. That is the purpose of this chapter.

Contributions from both the left and right have frequently attributed the UK's relative decline, especially the decline of manufacturing in the North of England, to the absence of a state-led technocratic industrial modernisation programme (Lee 1997). Because England was the world's first industrial nation, and the location of the first 'Industrial Revolution' (1770–1830), it has frequently been assumed that England's early industrialization meant that the role of the state was limited to that of a passive nightwatchman, able to stand back in the face of the vigorous entrepreneurial spirit, self-reliance and commitment to free trade of the original industrial Northern Powerhouse manufacturers of the nineteenth century. English and British industrial decline and the frustration of modernization programmes have been attributed to a failure to intervene strategically to pick winners among civilian manufacturing industries (see for example Newton and Porter 1988), and to follow the pattern of administrative guidance and selective supply of patient, long-term credit for investment characteristic of later industrialising East Asian developmental states (see for example Marquand 1988).

This chapter challenges that analysis. Instead, it contends that public policy and governance arrangements in contemporary England are the outcome of the long-term strategic priorities of the English (latterly British) developmental state, led by its pilot agency, HM Treasury. The state in England has picked winners and intervened strategically, but has chosen to back sectors other than civilian manufacturing, notably financial and commercial services, and military industries. Indeed, during the seventeenth century in particular, and around a century before England experienced its Industrial Revolution, it had experienced a 'Financial Revolution' as part of a transformative period in its political economy which witnessed parallel revolutions in politics, warfare, science, commerce and the emergence of political economy itself as a discipline as part of a wider English Enlightenment (Lee 2017b). These revolutions and this pattern of strategic intervention have embedded the dominance of the Southern Powerhouse.

This chapter focuses upon the most recent strategic interventions by the developmental state in England in the period since the 2007–2008 global financial crisis, with particular focus upon the interventions (and non-interventions) of the Treasury during George Osborne's tenure as Chancellor of the Exchequer from May 2010 until July 2016. Salient among Osborne's own interventions was his invention of the Northern Powerhouse political narrative and policy agenda on the 23 June 2014. Osborne's Northern Powerhouse should be understood not as something novel or a departure, but as simply the latest political narrative in a long-standing tradition of British statecraft which has accorded primacy to the global financial and commercial interests of the City of London and its hinterland in the South East, and in so doing subordinated the development of the North of England to the interests of the Southern Powerhouse. That relationship of primacy and subordination has been reflected in a pattern of public expenditure, notably upon vital infrastructure, which has heavily favoured the Southern Powerhouse (Institute for Public Policy Research 2016). It has also, and more importantly, been manifested in the strategic priorities and scale of the ambition of the British state under successive governments.

England as a Developmental State

This is an interesting and important time to be contemplating the political economy of England, and to be doing so through the lens of the developmental state. 'The North' in 'Northern Powerhouse', after all, is not the North of Britain, Great Britain or the UK, since it would constitute but the Midlands of these polities. Missing from the abbreviation 'The North' are the vital words 'of England'. In the wider literature which has addressed comparative economic performance, either between different national economies and/or different historical periods, there has been a proclivity for the self-same conflation, confusion, of failure to diferentiate between England and Britain, Great Britain or the UK which has been so prevalent in other debates about the politics, constitution and identity of England (Lee 2017b). Thus, whether it is through the lens of different varieties of capitalism (Hall and Soskice 2001), models of capitalism (Albert 1993; Coates 2000), cultures of capitalism (Hampden-Turner and Trompenaars 1993), national systems of innovation (Nelson 1993) or developmental states (Johnson 1982; Amsden 2001), England as a distinctive national political economy in its own right has tended not to feature.

Although it has been widely acknowledged as the world's first industrial nation, in the vast literature on British decline in general and the relative economic decline of the UK in particular, the early timing of England's industrialization has been widely held to be a significant competitive disadvantage in terms of her later capacity to develop the appropriate institutional foundation for industrial modernization, especially when compared with the political economy of later industrialising economies. In short, economic growth and development in England (and, latterly, in the UK) has been held to have been frustrated by the absence of an industrial policy, developmental state, national system of innovation or technocratic modernization strategy (Lee 1997).

This is also an important time to be thinking about the developmental state. In recent years, the United Nations has championed the need for a new developmental state with policy space to implement an industrial policy in developing economies. For example, in its 2013 human development report, *The Rise of The South: Human Progress in a Diverse World*, the United Nations Development Program contended that in societies which have brought about transformational human development, a common feature has been 'a strong, proactive state, also referred to as a "developmental state"', that it, 'a state with an activist government and often an apolitical elite that sees rapid economic development as their primary aim', and capable of setting policy priorities for and nurturing the development of selected industries (United Nations Development Program 2013: 55). In a similar vein, and over more than a decade, the United Nations Conference on Trade and Development has championed the virtues of an industrial policy implemented by a developmental state as an alternative blueprint for economic development to the neoliberal 'developmental market' political economy of entrepreneurship, liberalisation, deregulation and privatisation. Thus, in its 2016 Trade and Development Report, UNCTAD has advocated a reassessment of structural transformation and investment in manufacturing via a developmental state-led industrial policy as a curative to both stalled industrialization and premature deindustrialization (UNCTAD 2016).

Historically, political economists have tended to draw a distinction between the late industrialising developmental state model and the Anglo-American 'developmental market' model, characterised by free trade, market-based innovation and entrepreneurial risk-taking (Albert 1993). However, this distinction has been challenged in more recent research. Michael Lind has identified an American developmental state tradition from the work of Alexander Hamilton, George Washington, Abraham Lincoln, Henry Clay and Franklin Roosevelt (Lind 2012). William Novak has exposed the myth of the 'weak' American state, William Lazonick has highlighted the role of the American developmental state in fostering entrepreneurial ventures, and Fred Block has charted the rise of a 'hidden' developmental state in the USA (Novak 2008; Lazonick 2008; Block 2008). More recently, Mariana Mazzucato has challenged both the theory, practice and linguistic narrative of the neoliberal developmental market model by offering up a vision of the 'entrepreneurial state'. Here, the state's role is transformed: 'From an inertial bureaucratic "leviathan" to the very catalyst for new business investment; from market "fixer" to market shaper and creator; from simply "derisking" the private sector, to welcoming and taking on risk due to the opportunities it presents for future growth' (Mazzucato 2013: 9).

If, as according to Block's analysis, the American developmental state has remained 'hidden', the English developmental state has remained buried. Only David Edgerton's thesis of 'liberal militarism', and its identification of England as a profoundly militant and technological nation, has begun the process of uncovering the developmental warfare state in England from 1815 onwards (Edgerton 1991, 2006). However, if attention is focused upon an earlier period of England's history, it is possible to identify the genesis of an English developmental state, primarily during the revolutionary events of the seventeenth-century 'English Enlightenment' (Porter 2000). During this great transformative period, a revolution in political economy, both as a science and in its practical application, was to the fore. England underwent its first Financial Revolution and entrenched a link between the financial interests of the Southern Powerhouse and England's grand strategy to build a global commercial empire, more than a century before the Industrial Revolution forged a new Northern Powerhouse built upon the cotton textile and other manufacturing industries of the North of England (Dickson 1967; Wennerlind 2011; Murphy 2012). But England's 'Age of Revolutions' was not confined to the transformation of finance (Pincus 2009). Parallel revolutions occurred in English politics, public administration, science, commerce and warfare, all of which contributed to and were shaped by a process of state- and empire-building (Braddick 2000; Brewer 1988; Lee 2017b).

At the heart of that English state-building was the Treasury (Roseveare 1991). England became the model for other nations to emulate, not because of any commitment to laissez-faire, non-intervention or free trade, but because England was among the most interventionist states of its age (Reinert 2011). That intervention provided the inspiration for the later political economy of Alexander Hamilton and Friedrich List (Lee 2017b). As Pincus has argued, English liberalism 'was not antagonistic to the state. The liberalism spawned in 1688–1689 was revolutionary and interventionist rather than moderate and antistatist' (Pincus 2009: 8).

Of particular significance for the political economy of modern and contemporary England was that the seventeenth-century revolution in political economy in England, which culminated after 1689 in the triumph of a Whig project of modernization over a rival Tory project (Pincus 2009). This victory of liberalism over conservatism was symbolised by the establishment of the Bank of England in 1694, not as an institution to fund manufacturing, but as a means of enhancing the English state's capacity to borrow to finance the warfare which would enable the expansion of its overseas empire (Dickson 1967). Towards the end of the twentieth century, a counter-revolution in political economy in England once again witnessed the triumph of Whig liberalism over Tory conservatism, when Margaret Thatcher and Sir Keith Joseph's project to restore an entrepreneur-led enterprise culture was victorious over the industrial modernization agenda of One Nation 'Middle Way' conservatism (Lee 2015a).

Although the language and political narrative of Thatcherism and subsequent neoliberal political economy has been one of the virtues of rolling forward the frontiers of the discovery process of the 'developmental market', and rolling back the frontiers of the state, the political economy of England during the past 45 years has witnessed a huge increased in laws, legislation and state intervention to entrench the primacy of the Southern Powerhouse. What has amounted to a second Financial Revolution grew from the seeds of neoliberalism in the Heath government's 1971 Competition and Credit Control Act, through the abolition of exchange controls, and the liberalisation and deregulation of the City of London's 'Big Bang' during the 1980s, to the more recent £1.2 trillion bailout of UK banks in the face of the 2007–2008 global financial crisis (Lee 2017b). Where other states have used selective intervention and administrative guidance to extend support to civilian manufacturing industries, the British state has chosen instead to pick winners in the banking and allied financial and commercial services, which are centred upon the Southern Powerhouse.

THE NORTHERN POWERHOUSE IN CONTEXT

One of the most conspicuous features of the debates about the Northern Powerhouse is that they have been conducted largely in a historical vacuum. Remarkably for a debate around a term which itself incorporates the word 'power', but perhaps reflecting the technocratic bias of many of the expert commissions and think-tank reports whose recommendations have shaped political and media discussion, little attempt has been made to explore the very questions of political power and the role of vested interests which should be at the heart both of the discipline of political economy, and of any meaningful debate about the future of England. Instead, discussion has been dominated by a technocratic, elite-to-elite discourse about economic geography and 're-balancing', which has largely excluded the voice or the participation of the people of England themselves. Such technocratic pragmatism has divided England into functional economic and administrative areas, notably 'regions', 'city-regions' and 'core cities', but of which the Northern Powerhouse has been the most salient ever since George Osborne's use of the term in a speech delivered in Manchester on the 23 June 2014.

This terminology, and the thinking lying behind the Northern Powerhouse and the wider division of England into a number of 'city-regions', has owed much to the work of American economists and commentators (e.g. Florida 2014; Glaeser 2011; Katz and Bradley 2013), but has remained detached from any connection to the history of the English state, and the history and identity of the English people. The focus of debate has been upon the efficient functional management of territory, rather than the questions of democratic citizenship and national identity which have shaped debates in Scotland, Wales and Northern Ireland. In England, questions of economic growth have been placed well ahead or even kept separate from questions of governance. And yet, George Osborne's 'Northern Powerhouse' cannot be understood without placing it within a wider political and historical context that focuses upon the particular pattern that devolution has taken in England.

First, it is important to acknowledge that the most important form of devolution in England during the past 40 years of its second Financial Revolution had been devolution to individuals as market actors—entrepreneurs, consumers, homeowners and rentiers via the policies of liberalisation, deregulation and privatisation rather than as citizens via enhanced opportunities to participate in referendums or new directly elected political institutions (Lee 2017b). Second, London had been the only part of England to have experienced even a limited form of political devolution, involving a referendum followed by direct elections to newly created institutions. However, unlike the devolved institutions elsewhere in the UK, the Greater London Authority, composed of the directly elected Mayor of London and 25 member Greater London Authority, does not control or deliver education, health, social care, arts and culture or environmental protection (Sandford 2016: 7). The governance of the Southern Powerhouse appeared to have been deemed too important for control of policy design and resource allocation affecting these important areas of policy to be devolved by the central government.

Third, since May 2010, devolution in England has taken the form of 'deals', negotiated in two rounds in secrecy between Whitehall and local government leaders. As one parliamentary select committee report has noted, there has been 'a significant lack of public consultation and engagement at all stages in the devolution process' (House of Commons Communities and Local Government Committee 2016: 3). Furthermore, 'the Government's approach to devolution in practice has lacked rigour as to process: there are no clear, measurable objectives for devolution, the timetable is rushed and efforts are not being made to inject openness or transparency into the deal negotiations' (House of Commons Communities and Local Government Committee 2016: 3).

Fourth, this approach to devolution in England enacted since May 2010 has not in any sense challenged the power of the Treasury. Devolution in England, both prior to and after Osborne's 23 June 2014 Northern Powerhouse speech, had done nothing to dilute the impact of fiscal austerity upon local government and public spending bodies throughout England, but especially in the Northern Powerhouse where communities have tended to be more dependent upon the public realm. Thus, the National Audit Office (NAO) had calculated that 'Local authorities' revenue spending power (government grant and council tax) had fallen by 25.2 per cent in real terms from 2010–2011 to 2015–2016 (National Audit Office 2016a: 8).

The amount of additional public funding offered by the Treasury as an inducement for local government elites in England to engage in devolution 'deals' had been equally insignificant. The NAO has calculated that the total amount awarded for investment in economic growth to nine areas of England with a population of 15.5 million in devolution deals was £246.5 million a year. This compared to '£461.5 million a year provided to the Local Enterprise Partnerships in the same nine devolution deal areas under the Local Growth Fund, and £4.4 billion in total capital expenditure by the local authorities involved in these nine devolution deals in 2014–2015' (National Audit Office 2016a: 8). Devolution deals would therefore provide additional public funding amounting to a derisory £11 per head for Greater Manchester, £22 per head for Sheffield City-Region and £20 per head for Liverpool City-Region (National Audit Office 2016a: 23).

This trivial financial commitment to English devolution over a 30-year period contrasted vividly with the Treasury's willingness to sanction a deal with foreign governments to construct the Hinkley Point C nuclear power station project. It would provide no less than £2 billion of taxpayer guarantees to the China General Nuclear Corporation and China General Nuclear Corporation. Moreover, for a duration of 35 years, the

Treasury had agreed to a Strike Price for energy generated by Hinkley Point set at £89.50/MWh (or £92.50 if the final investment decision on the Sizewell C nuclear power station was not taken), more than twice the existing wholesale electricity price, and fully indexed to the Consumer Price Index. The Cameron government had also confirmed that it was not continuing 'the "no public subsidy policy" of the previous administration' (Department of Energy and Climate Change 2015), opening up the possibility of further subsidies to foreign corporations. Thus, while the Treasury has been prepared to grant only a highly limited degree of financial or political autonomy to local government in the North of England, it has been prepared to make a far larger and longer term strategic financial and political investment in a project involving foreign, largely state-owned corporations.

Fifth, devolution had also done nothing before or subsequently to dismantle any of the huge arrays of legislation and central prescription and controls over resource allocation and policy formulation (as opposed to policy implementation and service delivery) which had been institutionalised in the Treasury-led Spending Reviews. Thus, the Northern Powerhouse agenda would do little to dismantle the 1293 duties imposed upon local authorities in England, only 8 per cent of which had existed before the election in May 1979 of the first Thatcher government, and no fewer than 50 per cent had been introduced by the New Labour Blair and Brown governments between May 1997 and 2009 (House of Commons Political and Constitutional Reform Committee 2013: 8–9).

It was equally unclear how Osborne's Northern Powerhouse would address the imbalance between the economic performance of the Southern Powerhouse and the Northern Powerhouse. The primacy of the Southern Powerhouse is reflected in official statistics for Gross Value Added (GVA), i.e. 'a measure of the increase in the value of the economy due to the production of goods and services' which is 'measured at current basic prices, which include the effect of inflation, excluding taxes (less subsidies) on products (for example, Value Added Tax)' (Office for National Statistics 2016: 2). In 2015, England as a nation had a GVA of £1,433,164 million, and a GVA per capita of £26,159. However, London had a GVA per capita of £43,629 or 167 per cent of the average for England, while the South East had GVA per capita of £27,847 or 106 per cent of the average for England. These were the only parts of England to enjoy a GVA per capita above the English average or the £25,351 average for the UK. By comparison, the three constituent administrative regions of the Northern Powerhouse were all well below the average for both England and the UK. In 2015 the North East had a GVA of only £18,927 per capita or 72 per cent of the average for England; the North West had a GVA of £21,867 or 84 per cent of the average for England, while Yorkshire and the Humber had a GVA of £20,351 or 78 per cent of the English average (Office for National Statistics 2016: 4).

The Southern Powerhouse had also grown much faster under both recent Labour and Conservative-Liberal coalition governments. In the period 1997–2014, London's GVA had grown by 143.9 per cent and the South East's by 107.7 per cent, constituting the two fastest grow-ing administrative regions of both England and the UK, and also above the growth performances for both England (107.0 per cent) and the UK (104.7 per cent). By contrast, the GVA of the Northern Powerhouse economies had grown by only 93.5 per cent (the North West), 90.8 per cent (the North East) and 89.7 per cent (Yorkshire and the Humber), all way below the growth performances for England and the UK (Harari 2016: 5). Furthermore, in the aftermath of the 2007–2008 financial cri-sis, London's GVA had grown by 28.9 per cent, and the South East's by 22.6 per cent, once again both well above the growth performances of England (20.9 per cent) and the UK (20.0 per cent). This compared to post-crisis growth rates for 2009–2014 of 15.2 per cent for the North East, 14.2 per cent for the North West, and only 12.2 per cent for Yorkshire and the Humber (Harari 2016: 5).

THE NORTHERN POWERHOUSE: A TOP-DOWN, LONDON-DRIVEN, TREASURY-CENTRIC AGENDA

There could be few clearer indications of the degree to which the governance of the North of England is a quintessentially top-down, London-driven and Treasury-centric exercise than the timing of George Osborne's Northern Powerhouse speech and agenda on the 23 June 2014. While previously there had been mention of the need to rebalance the economy away from an overdependence upon financial services, and London and the South East, towards manufacturing and the economies of other parts of the UK, the notion of a 'Northern Powerhouse' had not featured during the first 4 years of the Cameron–Clegg Coalition government. It was in neither the 2010 Conservative Party nor the Liberal Democrat general election manifestos, not least because nei-ther party (nor the Labour Party) had furnished a separate manifesto for

England. The Northern Powerhouse was not mentioned in the Coalition Agreement, the Programme for Government, the 2010 and 2013 Spending Reviews, or any of Osborne's previous Budget statements. It had also been conspicuous by its absence from other key Treasury documents throughout Osborne's tenure as Chancellor. The overriding mantra of the Coalition, led by Osborne via his Autumn and Budget statements, had been 'we're all in this together', as the government sought to persuade a resolutely sceptical electorate that austerity via expansionary fiscal contraction and deficit reduction was the unavoidable price the public should pay for the reckless lending and speculation of private financial institutions which had culminated in the financial crisis of 2007–2008 and the subsequent recession (Lee 2011a, 2011b, 2015b, 2015c). When austerity had threatened to return the UK economy to recession, and had resulted in rising levels of public debt, Osborne had diluted the pace of his expansionary fiscal contraction. In October 2013, Osborne had also introduced the notion of the 'long-term economic plan', as a convenient political shorthand to signal that the elimination of the annual budget deficit would take 10 years and two parliamentary terms, rather than one as had been promised by the June 2010 Budget and October 2010 Spending Review (Lee 2011b, 2015b).

One of the most conspicuous features of Osborne's 'Northern Powerhouse' speech was what it revealed about his own conception of the Southern Powerhouse. As a 'proud Londoner', Osborne claimed, 'something remarkable has happened to London over these recent decades. It has become a global capital, the home of international finance, attracting the young, the ambitious, the wealthy and the entrepreneurial from around the world in their tens of thousands' (Osborne 2014). Confronted by this 'global city', the cities of the North of England while 'individually strong' had collectively 'not been strong enough'. In short, the whole had been 'less than the sum of its parts', enabling 'the powerhouse of London' to dominate 'more and more' (Osborne 2014). For Osborne, the solution was to 'bring the cities of the North together as a team' because, 'in a services based economy' (and here Osborne chose not to focus upon manufacturing), size mattered 'like never before', because of 'a powerful correlation between the size of a city and the productivity of its inhabitants'. Therefore, to take advantage of such agglomeration effects, there would need to be 'fast and effective communications' because 'all this requires scale. You need a big place, with lots of people. Like London' (Osborne 2014). By replicating global cities such as London and Tokyo, a Northern Powerhouse could be built, but only:

> by joining our Northern cities together – not physically, or into some artificial political construct – but by providing the modern transport connections they need; by backing their science and universities; by backing their creative clusters; and giving them the local power and control that a powerhouse economy needs. (Osborne 2014)

At this juncture, with a general election less than a year away, with the costs of public borrowing for major infrastructure at an historic low, with the International Monetary Fund and Organization for Economic Cooperation and Development advocating increased infrastructure investment, and, above all, given Osborne's own personal political ambitions to succeed David Cameron as Prime Minister and leader of the Conservative Party, Osborne's audience might have been forgiven for expecting a major announcement of urgent, new, additional investment in public transport infrastructure to join together the cities of the Northern Powerhouse. A golden opportunity had presented itself to reset not only government economic policy and priorities but also the Conservative Party political constituency and Osborne's own leadership prospects by announcing the go ahead for a High Speed 3 (HS3) rail line and network linking Hull to Liverpool. What then existed as the second phase of High Speed 2 (HS2) from Birmingham to Manchester and Leeds could have been recast by Osborne so that it would open simultaneously with the first phase from London to Birmingham on the 1 December 2026, and not six years later. A parallel accelerated programme of high-speed Internet connection could have been announced to place the Northern Powerhouse at the forefront of the digital age. In this way, the Treasury could have extended its picking of winners beyond the financial services of the Southern Powerhouse.

Osborne had claimed 'we need to think big', through 'an ambitious plan to make the cities and towns here in this Northern belt radically more connected from East to West—to create the equivalent of travelling around a single global city' (Osborne 2014), but his rhetoric was far from the actual substance of policy. There was to be no departure from the Treasury's priorities of fiscal austerity for public spending bodies in the North of England, and no parallel commitment to infrastructure projects on the scale, ambition and with the urgency of Southern Powerhouse projects such as Crossrail, Crossrail 2 or a new runway for Heathrow airport. On the contrary, Osborne's 'ambitious plan' was limited to three elements. First, the announcement that thinking should be started on a third high-speed railway line between Manchester and Leeds, not across the whole of the Northern Powerhouse from Hull to Liverpool and one using the existing rail route (Osborne 2014). Second, identification of the existing plan for Phase Two of HS2 to reach Manchester, Leeds and Sheffield, as 'the most important investment in the North for a century' (Osborne 2014), but not until 2032—almost two decades in the future, and two years after the opening of Crossrail 2. Third, since 'The final thing you need in a Powerhouse is, of course-Power', and because 'Global cities have powerful city governments', Osborne stated that he was starting a conversation about 'serious devolution of powers and budgets for any city that wants to move to a new model of city government—and have an elected Mayor' (Osborne 2014).

In the week after the Conservative Party's 2015 general election victory, Osborne returned to Manchester to set out what he proclaimed as 'a revolution in the way we govern England', which amounted to 'power to the working people of our country'. The Southern Powerhouse example of the Mayor of London would be Osborne's model for his 'devolution revolution', taking the form of 'a radical new model of city government' via 'new city-wide elected mayors who work with local councils' (Osborne 2015). Osborne claimed 'I will not impose this model on anyone. But nor will I settle for less' (Osborne 2015). However, it was not only a de facto imposition, but a de jure imposition. Cities would not get new devolved powers unless they agreed to have a new, directly elected mayor. The empowerment of working people would not include a prior referendum to allow them to decide if they wanted a mayor.

This may have been because, as recently as the 3 May 2012, in referendums nine out of ten English cities had voted not to have an elected mayor, including Manchester, where more than 53 per cent had voted 'No', and most working people had shown their open indifference to the idea in a lacklustre turnout of only 24.7 per cent. Moreover, and maintaining the theme of the 'devolution revolution' bypassing the English demos, Osborne had used his 14 May 2015 speech to announce that Jim O'Neill, Chair of the City Growth Commission and one of the prime movers behind the Northern Powerhouse, would be joining the Cameron government as Commercial Secretary to the Treasury. However, through the power of Prime Ministerial patronage, on the 28 May 2015 O'Neill was able to join the House of Lords, thereby circumventing the need for any form of democratic election, participation or accountability.

PICKING WINNERS IN THE SOUTHERN POWERHOUSE

The divorce between the ambitious rhetoric of Osborne's Northern Powerhouse, and the actuality of its failure to deflect or dilute the impact of austerity upon public spending bodies, while simultaneously creating a new tier of executive mayors to implement and potentially take the blame for further cuts to services, stands in vivid contrast with the way in which the Treasury has intervened strategically since September 2007 to underwrite the competitive advantage of the Southern Powerhouse. The reward for financial institutions whose reckless lending and speculative trading fostered the financial crisis has been a steady supply of cheap credit from the Treasury to rebuild balance sheets, and a commitment to major infrastructure projects. At its peak, the Treasury had provided a total of £1162 billion of guarantees (£1033 billion) and cash loans (£133 billion) to banks (National Audit Office 2016b). This was a strategic intervention without precedent in peacetime, in terms of the scale of the support provided to a single sector of the economy. No sector in the Northern Powerhouse has ever been the recipient of such largesse from the taxpayer.

This intervention included £256 billion for the recapitalisation of the Royal Bank of Scotland (RBS), in the process acquiring 83 per cent of RBS shares; £276 billion for the recapitalisation of Lloyds Banking Group, acquiring 41 per cent of shares; £106 billion for the nationalisation of Northern Rock and Bradford and Bingley; and £11 billion for loans to insolvent banks for repayment of customer deposits over £50,000. Furthermore, the financial sector as a whole had been provided with £250 billion for the Credit Guarantee Scheme; £200 billion for the Special Liquidity Scheme; £50 billion for the Asset Backed Securities Scheme; and £13 billion for an unused recapitalisation fund (National Audit Office 2016b). In addition, the Treasury had supported the £375 billion programme of Quantitative Easing (subsequently extended to £435 billion in August 2016) administered by the Bank of England which had not only provided financial institutions in the Southern Powerhouse with a further huge supply of cheap credit to rebuild their balance sheets, but also resulted in an increase in asset values, not least property prices in London and the South East (Bank of England 2012), further inflated by a new surge in banking lending to mortgage-holders, especially those operating in the lucrative buy-to-let property market (Lee 2017b).

When students of British decline have written about HM Treasury, it has more often than not been to condemn it for failing to provide the long-term strategic interventions and investment for industrial modernization associated with the role of agencies such as Japan's former Ministry of International Trade (MITI), at the heart of the East Asian developmental state (see for example Pollard 1982). Paradoxically, the Treasury has a history, institutional longevity, resources and powers akin to or much greater than MITI or any of the industrial policy agencies whose absence declinists have held largely responsible for the UK's relative economic decline.

As the UK's economic and finance ministry, the Treasury has a responsibility not only for public expenditure and strategic oversight of the UK's tax system, and ensuring that the economy is 'growing sustainably'. It also is responsible for 'financial services policy: including banking and financial services regulation, financial stability, and ensuring competitiveness in the City', and both the delivery of infrastructure projects across the public sector and the facilitating private sector investment into UK's infrastructure (HM Treasury 2016a). These Treasury powers had enabled it to make a series of strategic interventions to rescue financial institutions between 2007 and 2010.

As a consequence of these strategic interventions which no other sector of the UK economy would ever experience, the Treasury Group of institutions had acquired net assets of £130.5 billion by the end of March 2015 (National Audit Office 2015: 8), as part of its role of manager of the UK government's total financial assets. In 2014–2015, these amounted to £400 billion, 'equivalent to just over a quarter of total assets (£1455 billion), around £14,814 per UK household and around a third of total government borrowing' (National Audit Office 2016c: 6). Moreover, in April 2016, the Cameron government strengthened the capacity of the Treasury to act a strategic asset manager by unifying the functions of the Shareholder Executive (ShEx), which had managed the government's shareholder relationships with businesses owned or part owned by the British state, and UK Financial Investments Limited (UKFI), which had managed the state's shareholdings in rescued banks, to create a new Treasury-owned company, UK Government Investments

(UKGI). This was with a view to the sale by the Treasury of assets valued at £106 billion by the end of April 2020, in what would be an unprecedented privatisation programme (National Audit Office 2016b: 8–9).

The scale and ambition of the Treasury's strategic support for the key financial and commercial interests of the Southern Powerhouse has stood in stark contrast to the relative lack of ambition which has been accorded to strategic infrastructure investment in the Northern Powerhouse. In this regard, the Institute for Public Policy Research (IPPR) has analysed planned government expenditure for investment in transport for the period from 2016–2017 to 2020–2021. It has reported that during this period London has a planned allocation of £17.063 billion, or an average spend of £1869 per person and £4271 per commuter. The South East, London's sister English administrative region in the Southern Powerhouse has a planned allocation of £2.66 billion, or an average spend of £289 per person and £713 per commuter, the second highest regional allocation after London (Institute for Public Policy Research 2016).

By contrast, the three Northern English administrative regions which constitute the 'Northern Powerhouse' have a combined planned allocation of £4.26 billion or £277 per person and £710 per commuter (Institute for Public Policy Research 2016). Individually, the North East has a planned allocation of £806.35 billion, or £304 per person and £802 per commuter; the North West a planned allocation of £2.1 billion, or £289 per person and £740 per commuter; and Yorkshire and the Humber a planned allocation of £1.35 billion, or £247 per person and £629 per commuter (Institute for Public Policy Research 2016). Thus, London has a planned allocation for public investment in transport infrastructure around six times higher than that for the Northern Powerhouse as a whole. Just a single project for the Southern Powerhouse, Crossrail, has a planned allocation of £4.61 billion or £505 per person and £1155 per commuter, which is a larger sum than for the entire Northern Powerhouse (Institute for Public Policy Research 2016).

The primacy of the Southern Powerhouse in the Treasury's plans has been illustrated in its commitment not only to Crossrail, but also to other major infrastructure projects notably Crossrail 2, HS2 and HS3. In his March 2016 Budget statement, George Osborne announced the Cameron government was 'giving the green light' to the Crossrail 2 scheme (whose projected cost is £28 billion), in response to a report from the National Infrastructure Commission. There would be £80 million of public funding to help fund development of Crossrail 2, a request to Transport for London to match that Exchequer commitment, and the aim of bringing forward legislation, in the form of a Hybrid Bill, before the end of the Parliament in 2020 (HM Treasury, 2016a, b, c: 62). By comparison, although Osborne simultaneously gave 'the green light' to the High Speed 3 (HS3) rail link between Manchester and Liverpool, it would not extend to a transpennine HS3 link from Hull to Liverpool across the whole of the Northern Powerhouse) (HM Treasury 2016b: 62). This time, however, there was no pledge of taxpayer funding to develop HS3, even in its limited, truncated form, and no commitment to introduce legislation before the end of the Parliament.

CONCLUSION: THE NORTHERN POWERHOUSE, RIP?

On the 14 July 2016, George Osborne's departure from ministerial office meant that the Northern Powerhouse had lost both its principal champion and prime mover within the UK government. Subsequent developments during the first 6 months of Theresa May's tenure as prime minister have suggested that the principal threats to the interests and competitive advantage of the financial and commercial interests of the Southern Powerhouse are posed by Brexit and the possible loss of unrestricted access to the financial markets of the European Union, rather than by any potential resetting of economic policy or 'rebalancing' of public expenditure towards the Northern Powerhouse. Indeed, little further political capital is likely to be invested in the Northern Powerhouse, possibly because of its close association with George Osborne, her former rival as successor to David Cameron, but more because May has instead chosen to focus upon alternative policy priorities and political narratives. While May has affirmed her government's commitment to the implementation of the Cameron government's 'historic devolution of power from Westminster to cities' via directly elected mayors (May 2016a), the idea of a Northern Powerhouse has been firmly subordinated to May's central national (meaning British and UK-wide) political narrative of 'a country that works for everyone and not just the privileged few' (May, 2017). In economic policy terms, this has meant a new quest for national efficiency and a drive to close the UK's 30 per cent 'productivity gap' with the USA and Germany via a £23 billion National Productivity Investment Fund (HM Treasury 2016c: 2).

Theresa May has sanctioned an administrative reorganisation to create the Department for Business, Energy and Industrial Strategy, instituted and chaired an Economy and Industrial Strategy Cabinet Committee, and promised 'A proper industrial strategy to get the whole economy firing' and to protect important strategic sectors of the economy (May 2016b). However, when confronted with her first potential opportunity to intervene to protect a strategic industry, following the £24.3 billion proposed takeover of ARM Holdings, England's largest technology company and designer of around 95 per cent of the silicon chips used by smartphones, the May government chose not to intervene. It would be 'business as usual' for a strategic sector of greater importance, namely the financial institutions of the Southern Powerhouse which would help to broker the takeover of ARM by SoftBank, a Japanese corporation.

On the 23 November 2016, when the May government published simultaneously *A Northern Powerhouse Strategy* (HM Government 2016) with the Autumn Statement, it consisted of little more than a compilation of the spending commitments previously announced by George Osborne in the 2015 Spending Review and March 2016 Budget. In a similar vein, when writing newspaper articles for the two principal daily newspapers published in the North of England, May's announcement of new initiatives for the North of England was limited to her decision to hold one of two victory parades for Team GB's Olympians and Paralympians in Manchester, and her backing on Yorkshire Day for British Cycling's successful bid to bring the World Racing Championship to Yorkshire in 2019 (May 2016a, c).

Above all, the May government chose not to use the opportunity provided by its 2016 Autumn Statement to reset economic policy in favour of significant increases in public investment in the infrastructure or public services of the putative Northern Powerhouse. On the contrary, while Chancellor of the Exchequer Philip Hammond announced the May government's willingness to borrow an additional £122.2 billion between 2016–2017 and 2021–2022, compared to George Osborne's March 2016 Budget plans (HM Treasury 2016c: 12), this would be for the purpose of preparing the entire UK economy to be resilient during the UK's exit from the European Union, and not for major additional public investment in the North of England to 're-balance' the economy. None of the expenditure cuts affecting communities and services in the Northern Powerhouse proposed by George Osborne in the 2015 Spending Review would be reversed. Moreover, all of the

May government's three major announcements of major infrastructure spending during in its initial months in office—approval of a third runway at Heathrow airport, construction of the Hinckley Point C nuclear power station, and Phase One of the HS2 rail project from London to Birmingham—will affect locations in the South of England, and two out of the three will directly bolster the competitiveness of the Southern Powerhouse. Consequently, there will be continuity rather than change in the primacy of the interests of the Southern Powerhouse over those of the Northern Powerhouse in the political economy of England and the UK.

REFERENCES

Albert, M. 1993. *Capitalism against capitalism*. London: Whurr.
Amsden, A. 2001. *The rise of "The Rest": Challenges to the west from late-industrializing economies*. Oxford: Oxford University Press.
Bank for International Settlements. 2016. *Triennial Central Bank Survey of Foreign Exchange and OTC Derivatives Market in 2016*. Available from: http://www.bis.org/statistics/d11_2.pdf. Accessed 30 Dec 2016.
Bank of England. 2012. *The Distributional Effects of Asset Purchases Bank of England*, July 12. Available from: http://www.bankofengland.co.uk/publications/ Documents/news/2012/nr073.pdf. Accessed 23 Dec 2016.
Block, F. 2008. Swimming against the current: The rise of a hidden developmental state in the United States. *Politics and Society* 36 (2): 1169–1206.
Braddick, M. 2000. *State Formation in early modern England c.1550–1700*. Cambridge: Cambridge University Press.
Brewer, J. 1988. *The sinews of power: War, money and the english state, 1688–1783*. Cambridge, MA: Harvard University Press.
Coates, D. 2000. *Models of Capitalism: Growth and Stagnation in the Modern Era*. Oxford: Wiley.
Collins English Dictionary. 2016. London: Harper Collins. Available from: http://www.collinsdictionary.com/dictionary/english/powerhouse. Accessed 10 Sep 2016.
Department of Energy and Climate Change. 2015. Hinkley point C to power six million homes. October 21 News release.
Dickson, P. 1967. *The financial revolution in England*. London: Macmillan.
Edgerton, D. 1991. *England and the aeroplane: An essay on a militant and technological nation*. London: Macmillan.
Edgerton, D. 2006. *Warfare state Britain, 1920–1970*. Cambridge: Cambridge University Press.
Florida, R. 2014. *The rise of the creative class revisited*. New York: Basic Books.
Glaeser, E. 2011. *Triumph of the city*. London: Macmillan.

Hall, P., and D. Soskice (eds.). 2001. *Varieties of capitalism: The institutional foundations of comparative advantage.* Oxford: Oxford University Press.

Hampden-Turner, C., and F. Trompenaars. 1993. *The seven cultures of capitalism: Value systems for creating wealth in the United States, Britain, Japan, Germany, France, Sweden, and The Netherlands.* London: Piatkus.

Harari. 2016. Regional and local economic growth statistics. Briefing Paper No.05795, 30 August. House of Commons Library, London.

HM Government. 2016. *Northern powerhouse strategy.* Available from: https://www.gov.uk/government/uploads/system/uploads/attachment_data/file/571562/NPH_strategy_web.pdf. Accessed 24 Dec 2016.

HM Treasury. 2016a. *About Us.* Available from: https://www.gov.uk/government/organisations/hm-treasury/about. Accessed 19 Sep 2016.

HM Treasury. 2016b. *Budget 2016,* HC.901. London: The Stationery Office.

HM Treasury. 2016c. *Autumn statement 2016,* Cm.9362. London: HMStationery Office.

House of Commons. 2013. *Prospects for codifying the relationship between central and local government,* HC.656-I. London: The Stationery Office.

House of Commons Communities and Local Government Committee. 2016. *Devolution: The next five years and beyond,* HC.369. London: The Stationery Office.

Institute for Public Policy Research. 2016. *Transport secretary urged to close £1600 per person London-North spending gap.* Available from: http://www.ippr.org/news-and-media/press-releases/transport-secretary-urged-to-close-1-600-per-person-london-north-spending-gap. Accessed 10 Sep 2016.

Johnson, C. 1982. *MITI and the Japanese miracle: The growth of industrial policy, 1925–1975.* Stanford: Stanford University Press.

Katz, B., and J. Bradley. 2013. *The metropolitan revolution: How cities and metros are fixing our broken politics and fragile economy.* Washington, DC: The Brookings Institution.

Lazonick, W. 2008. *Entrepreneurial ventures and the developmental state: Lessons from the advanced economies.* New York: United Nations University World Institute for Development Economics Research Discussion Paper No.2008/01.

Lee, S. 1997. Part B: Explaining Britain's relative economic performance. In *The political economy of modern Britain,* ed. A. Cox, S. Lee, and J. Sanderson, 65–253. Cheltenham: Edward Elgar.

Lee, S. 2011a. No plan B: The coalition agenda for cutting the deficit and rebalancing the economy. In *The Cameron-Clegg government: Coalition politics in an age of austerity,* ed. S. Lee and M. Beech, 59–74. London: Palgrave Macmillan.

Lee, S. 2011b. "We are all in this together": The coalition agenda for British modernization. In *The Cameron-Clegg government: Coalition politics in an age of austerity,* ed. S. Lee and M. Beech, 3–23. London: Palgrave Macmillan.

Lee, S. 2015a. Why Am I a conservative? From one nation technocratic pragmatism to the development market. Unpublished paper delivered to the political studies association conservatives and conservatism specialist group 'Recovering neo-liberalism: From myth to reality?' Panel, 2015 Political Studies Association Conference, Sheffield Town Hall, 30 March.

Lee, S. 2015b. The condition of England under the coalition. In *The conservative-liberal coalition: Examining the Cameron-Clegg government*, ed. M. Beech and S. Lee, 145–161. Basingstoke: Palgrave Macmillan.

Lee, S. 2015c. Indebted and unbalanced: The political economy of the coalition. In *The conservative-liberal coalition: Examining the Cameron-Clegg government*, ed. M. Beech and S. Lee, 16–35. Basingstoke: Palgrave Macmillan.

Lee, S. 2017a. The gathering storm: Federalization and constitutional change in the UK. In *The future of federalism intergovernmental financial relations in an age of austerity*, ed. R. Eccleston and R. Krever. Cheltenham: Edward Elgar, forthcoming.

Lee, S. 2017b. *The state of England: The nation we're in*. London: Palgrave Macmillan, forthcoming.

Lind, M. 2012. *Land of promise: An economic history of the United States*. New York: HarperCollins.

Marquand, D. 1988. *The unprincipled society: New demands and old politics*. London: Fontana Press.

May, T. 2016a. Prime Minister Theresa May: Why the Olympic parade deserves to be in Manchester'. *Manchester Evening News*, September 20. Available from: http://www.manchestereveningnews.co.uk/news/greater-manchester-news/prime-minister-theresa-may-olympic-11909364. Accessed 30 Dec 2016.

May, T. 2016b. 'We can make Britain a country that works for everyone', speech delivered on July 11. Available from: http://www.itv.com/news/2016-07-11/what-are-theresa-mays-key-pledges-home-secretary-outlines-her-plan-for-the-future/. Accessed 2 Aug 2016.

May, T. 2016c. Theresa May: My vision for Yorkshire's bright future, *Yorkshire Post*, August 18. Available from: http://www.yorkshirepost.co.uk/news/opinion/theresa-may-my-vision-for-yorkshire-s-bright-future-1-8074726 Accessed 30 Dec 2016.

May, T. 2017. 'We will create a fairer society', The Sun, 19 January. Available from: https://www.gov.uk/government/speeches/we-will-create-a-fairer-society-article-by-theresa-may. Accessed 31 July 2017.

Mazzucato, M. 2013. *The entrepreneurial state: Debunking public vs. private sector myths*. London: Anthem Press.

Murphy, A. 2012. *The origins of english financial markets: Investment and speculation before the South Sea Bubble*. Cambridge: Cambridge University Press.

National Audit Office. 2015. *The report of the comptroller and auditor general to the house of commons: Report on Accounts: HM Treasury 2014–2015 17 July 2015*. London: National Audit Office.

National Audit Office. 2016a. *English devolution deals*, HC.948. London: National Audit Office.

National Audit Office. 2016b. *Taxpayer support for UK banks: FAQs*. Available from: https://www.nao.org.uk/highlights/taxpayer-support-for-uk-banks-faqs/. Accessed 10 Sep 2016.

National Audit Office. 2016c. *Evaluating the government balance sheet: Financial assets and investments HC.463 Session 2016–17 30 June 2016*. London: National Audit Office.

Nelson, R. (ed.). 1993. *National innovation systems: A comparative analysis*. New York: Oxford University Press.

Newton, S., and D. Porter. 1988. *Modernization frustrated: The politics of industrial decline since 1900*. London: Routledge.

Novak, W. 2008. The myth of the "Weak" American state. *American Historical Review* 113 (3): 752–772.

Office for National Statistics. 2016. *Regional gross added value (income approach), UK: 1997 to 2015*. Available from: https://www.ons.gov.uk/economy/grossvalueaddedgva/bulletins/regionalgrossvalueaddedincomeapproach/december2016 Accessed 30 Dec 2016.

Osborne, G. 2014. 'We need a Northern powerhouse' speech, Museum of Science and Industry, Manchester, 23 June.

Osborne, G. 2015. 'On building a Northern powerhouse' speech, Victora Warehouse, Manchester, 14 May.

Pincus, S. 2009. *1688 the first modern revolution*. New Haven: Yale University Press.

Pollard, S. 1982. *The wasting of British economy*. London: Croom Helm.

Porter, R. 2000. *Enlightenment: Britain and the creation of the modern world*. London: Penguin.

Reinert, S. 2011. *Translating Empire: Emulation and the Origins of Political Economy*. Cambridge, MA: Harvard University Press.

Roseveare, H. 1991. *The Financial Revolution, 1660-1760*. New York: Longman.

Sandford, M. 2016. The greater London authority. House of commons library briefing paper number 05817, 12 August 2016. House of Commons Library, London. Available from: http://researchbriefings.parliament.uk/ResearchBriefing/Summary/SN05817. Accessed 12 Sep 2016.

United Nations Conference on Trade and Development. 2016. *Structural transformation for inclusive and sustained growth: Trade and development report, 2016*. New York: United Nations Conference on Trade and Development.

United Nations Development Programme. 2013. *The rise of the south: Human progress in a diverse world. human development report 2013*. New York: United Nations Human Development Programme.

Wennerlind, C. 2011. *Casualties of credit: The english financial revolution, 1620–1720*. Cambridge: Harvard University Press.

AUTHOR BIOGRAPHY

Simon Lee is Senior Lecturer in Political Economy at the University of Hull. He published *Boom and Bust: The Politics of Legacy of Gordon Brown* in 2009, and has recently co-edited two books (with Matt Beech) on the Conservative–Liberal Democrat coalition. He has also published in leading academic journals such as *Local Economy, Policy Studies* and *New Political Economy.*

CHAPTER 4

'D is for Dangerous': Devolution and the Ongoing Decline of Manufacturing in Northern England

Craig Berry

Abstract This chapter considers the recent history, and likely future, of manufacturing in Northern England, with reference to the potential impact of initiatives related to the Northern Powerhouse agenda in this area. The chapter is structured around 'the three Ds' of the Northern Powerhouse: deindustrialisation, devolution and de-development. Contesting the view that the Northern Powerhouse can be understood primarily as a process of institutional or constitutional reform, it instead locates the agenda within the long (but limited) history of UK industrial policy. It argues that regional policy has always substituted for industrial policy in the UK state's 'horizontal' support for manufacturing, and that devolution to Northern city-regions is therefore the ultimate expression of *laissez-faire* industrial policy. However, the agenda touches upon post-crisis concerns around place and empowerment, even while it serves to

C. Berry (✉)
Sheffield Political Economy Research Institute, University of Sheffield,
Sheffield, UK
e-mail: craig.berry@sheffield.ac.uk

© The Author(s) 2018
C. Berry and A. Giovannini (eds.), *Developing England's North*,
Building a Sustainable Political Economy: SPERI Research & Policy,
https://doi.org/10.1007/978-3-319-62560-7_4

reduce the control of Northern citizens over their own local economies by offering only a narrow understanding of how economies develop.

Keywords Deindustrialisation · Development · Devolution
Industrial policy · Manufacturing · Northern Powerhouse

The notion that Northern England represents—or may represent—a 'powerhouse' within the British economy clearly connotes the North's industrial past, as well as intimating an industrial renaissance in the not-too-distant future. But now for the bad news: connotations and intimations are probably as good as it is going to get. There would appear to be very few reasons to believe that the Northern Powerhouse agenda, as promulgated by then Chancellor of the Exchequer George Osborne, foretold the kind of radical shift in economic statecraft that would in all likelihood be required to transform the prospects for manufacturing industries in the North (and indeed elsewhere in the UK). This is despite the clear resonance between the possibility of a manufacturing resurgence and the wider economic 'rebalancing' agenda, which new Conservative Prime Minister Theresa May appears to have revived despite initially distancing her government from the Northern Powerhouse moniker. Most obviously, 'imbalances' between Northern and Southern England, and manufacturing and financial services industries, are identified as key dimensions of the UK's economic malaise. The discourse around rebalancing has also repeatedly cited imbalances between exports and imports, and investment and consumption—both of which imply that manufacturing (and therefore the North, at least to some extent) will be more important to the UK's economic future than it has been to the recent past. Devolution—to Northern city-regions, although not exclusively so—has been presented as part of the solution to these problems. Yet it seems the content of the devolution 'deals' agreed between central and local government since 2010 (as well as the ways in which the Conservatives have paradoxically sought to *strengthen* central government) reinforces industrial policy traditions which have served to marginalise manufacturing within the UK political economy.

This chapter considers recent policy practice in these areas—emanating from both the Conservative/Liberal Democrat coalition government of 2010–2015 and the Conservative government of 2015 onwards—in historical context, in terms of both industrial policy traditions and trends in manufacturing performance in the UK. It is organised around 'the three Ds' of manufacturing decline in Northern England. The chapter looks first at *deindustrialisation* and its implications for economic activity in the North, including the more recent consequences of the financial crisis and 'Brexit', that is, the UK's withdrawal from the European Union (EU). It then looks more closely at the *devolution* agenda as a dimension of industrial policy and economic statecraft more generally. Finally, the chapter reflects on the notion of economic development in relation to manufacturing in Northern England, advancing a specific argument about the *de-development* of the Northern economy (which has been reinforced by Brexit). The third section therefore seeks to situate what is happening *in* and *to* the North within a broader understanding of capitalism and uneven development, suggesting that Northern England is largely absent from a refurbished global capitalist 'core', and instead largely resides in the periphery or semi-periphery of the global economic order. The North's more peripheral status may in fact create new opportunities for growth, but on subservient terms, and accompanied by greater inequality within the North.

DEINDUSTRIALISATION AND THE NORTH/SOUTH DIVIDE

Manufacturing and Economic Decline

By any measure, the UK's manufacturing sector has been experiencing a long-run decline. Arguably, decline has been relative rather than absolute, insofar as manufacturing output continued to grow in the UK even as it grew (much) faster elsewhere, particularly in Germany, Japan and the USA from the mid–late nineteenth century to the early–mid-twentieth century. However, it is clear that from at least the Second World War onwards, manufacturing output growth has noticeably slowed in the UK. This began to translate from the 1970s onwards into enormous job losses, especially under the Margaret Thatcher and Tony Blair governments, as the UK economy in general dipped several times into recession, and manufacturing industries in particular began to face competition from non-OECD countries (Froud et al. 2011; Matthews 2007). There has of course been no single moment of crisis within UK manufacturing throughout this period, and generally speaking the value of manufacturing output has remained constant in recent decades even as manufacturing employment has plummeted, and the share of manufacturing within the UK's overall economic output has shrunk (PricewaterhouseCoopers 2009). This may help to explain why the UK policy elites have been relatively indifferent to manufacturing decline—yet their complacency is misplaced.

That said, manufacturing does feature, albeit sometimes only implicitly, in some of the main 'declinist' accounts that have been upheld by UK elites at various times, which focus primarily on how the UK's economic decline in relative terms had reduced its influence on world affairs in absolute terms. In these accounts, decline is said to be a product of the failure of the UK's 'gentlemanly' economic culture (and/or the absence of a bourgeois revolution) to instil an entrepreneurial flair among *nouveau-riche* industrialists, or of how the success of the UK's industrial revolution—propelled by the access to natural resources and consumer markets enabled by British imperialism, as well as technological ingenuity—led to complacency among elites regarding the construction of a continental-style developmental state (English and Kenny 2000; Gamble 2000). It was, however, the more critically focused decline theorists, however, who focused most directly on the ailments of manufacturing in the UK, with scholars such as Geoffrey Ingham and Karel Williams identifying the nature and role (and political power) of the finance sector in both starving the manufacturing sector of capital, but also, crucially, instilling among manufacturers a short-termist business model that made industry unusually vulnerable to overseas competition (Ingham 1984; Williams et al. 1983).

However, the 1970s 'stagflation' crisis undermined the notion of an activist, manufacturing-centred industrial policy, even if it had never really been tried in the UK (as discussed further below). The most influential decline account, offered by W.D. Rubinstein (1993)—one to which Margaret Thatcher adhered—identified the same circumstances as Ingham and Williams, but reached the opposite conclusions. The finance sector, in this account, was not holding UK industry back; rather, the finance sector *is* UK industry, and should be protected and promoted as the UK's key industrial speciality. This is one of the reasons that the Thatcher government sought to maintain a high value of sterling, making the City of London more attractive, but manufacturing exports less attractive. There is of course little doubt that declinism abated in the 1990s as a finance-led growth model appeared to be responsible for delivering sustained economic growth (and tax revenues which enabled high levels of public sector investment under the Blair government). The development of the European single market probably helped in this regard, in terms of providing consumers for financial services exports, and indeed in helping to sustain (but not necessarily revive) some manufacturing industries.

The 2008 crisis problematised this model, and led to greater elite-level attention on some of the problems that tend to mount when ostensibly highly developed economies see their manufacturing base shrink. First, insofar as a smaller manufacturing base made the UK more dependent on finance, the country was seemingly afflicted by 'the finance curse' whereby productive activity is handicapped by financial rent extraction, and the growth path mirrors the inherent volatility of the finance sector (Christensen et al. 2016). Second, the UK's current account balance deteriorated significantly during this period, reaching a deficit of around £15 billion (3.5 per cent of GDP) by 2008 with a trade deficit of around £13 billion, resulting from a decline in manufacturing exports, the main culprit (Office for National Statistics 2016a; see also Rowthorn and Coutts 2013). Third, manufacturing's demise is the central explanation for the UK's productivity problem, insofar as manufacturing is at root the application of technology to natural resources, and therefore the motor of innovation within capitalist economies (irrespective of how the manufacturing sector is categorised statistically) (Chang 2014: 256–267).

The Economic Geography of Deindustrialisation

Manufacturing decline clearly has an impact on the UK economy at the aggregate level. Yet its impact has not been felt evenly across the country. The concentration of manufacturing in Northern England is perhaps the most important explanation for elite indifference to manufacturing decline—which might be characterised more cynically therefore as *complicity* rather than, as suggested above, merely *complacency*. Although manufacturing output has traditionally been fairly even spread across UK regions since the 1970s, the sector has clearly been a more important part of some regional economies than others. As late as 1997, manufacturing represented around 25 per cent of regional GVA for the North East, 24 per cent for the North West and 24 per cent for Yorkshire and Humberside. The proportion was comparable in Wales, slightly higher for the Midlands regions, but significantly lower for Southern regions (only 7 per cent in London) and Scotland. A similar pattern is evident for 2014 (the latest available data), although the gap between the Northern regions (the share of manufacturing is 15–16 per cent in all three regions) and the East and the South West has narrowed, while grown significantly larger between the Northern regions and London and the South East (Office for National Statistics 2015).

An important caveat to the notion of manufacturing decline is that it is not unique to the UK. Deindustrialisation, which Andy Pike defines as 'the contraction and rationalisation of manufacturing industry' (Pike 2009: 51), is a process common to the vast majority of advanced capitalist economies, and indeed is often seen as a hallmark of development rather than an economic problem or dilemma. However, as suggested above, it has certainly been steeper in the UK than most, or indeed all, comparable countries (Rowthorn and Coutts 2013). Moreover, it is important to be clear about the precise implications of deindustrialisation; crucially, it acquires most meaning in relation to particular local economies, invariably described as 'deindustrialised regions'. Deindustrialisation typically refers to declining manufacturing employment; this usually accompanies a lower share of manufacturing within overall output, but not necessarily. It certainly does not mean that manufacturing output declines in absolute terms, as the process is generally characterised by a shift towards higher value, capital-intense manufacturing industries, with lower value, labour-intense industries migrating to 'newly industrialising countries' as part of the proliferation of transnational production networks.

As such, it is from the UK's apparent embrace of a 'post-industrial' economy, largely eschewing the opportunity to move towards higher value manufacturing in place of mass industry, that deindustrialisation acquires most meaning in the UK context. While some Northern cities have, eventually, developed economies that might broadly be conceived as post-industrial—obviously, services sector employment has grown in all parts of the UK in both relative and absolute terms—many places remain scarred by the loss of manufacturing (Hudson 2013). Employment rates and earnings have invariably been significantly lower in the Northern regions (and, generally speaking, the Midlands) than in the South as a result (although it is worth noting that earnings in London and the South East have surged ahead of the rest of the South in the last 10–15 years) (Office for National Statistics 2016c). While the picture is inevitably complex, geographers such as Danny Dorling (2010) have argued persistently and persuasively that the so-called North/ South divide in England is therefore widening rather than narrowing, as embodied in differing outcomes for deprivation and life expectancy, as well as the labour market, across the divide. Interestingly, Dorling has of course always included the Midlands within the divide, rather than conveniently leaving these regions out of the overly parsimonious North/South framework. He generally argues that a jagged, diagonal line from Gloucester in the West to Grimsby in the East marks the border between North and South in England, in terms of understanding geographical inequalities.

There are of course Northern cities which buck these trends—York, for instance, consistently scores highly on the measures deployed by Dorling and others (it is of course not a coincidence that York's economy was never as heavily industrialised as most other local economies in the North). Furthermore, Manchester is often lauded as a post-industrial success story, but perhaps serves as an ideal reminder that the apparent success of some Northern cities in adapting to the services economy has not eradicated problems associated with deprivation. The City of Manchester is among the local authority areas with the highest deprivation problem, with 40 per cent of its wards in the most deprived decile of wards across England (Bullen 2015). The volume *City of Revolution*, edited by Jamie Peck and Kevin Ward, on the post-industrial 'restructuring' of Greater Manchester offers an illuminating account in this regard. Peter Dicken (2002) charts Manchester's transition 'from globaliser to globalised', noting its subservient role in global production networks that it once sat at the apex of, and the coalescence of prosperity and vulnerability. Benito Giordano and Laura Twomey (2002) identify an 'intractable' joblessness result as one of the consequences, as the 'hype' around post-industrial growth is challenged through evidence of the ephemerality of high-value services industries in Manchester since the 1970s, and Dean Herd and Terry Patterson (2002) note the failure of recent welfare-to-work programmes to address the structural sources of such problems. Rosemary Mellor charts the development of Manchester's city centre, noting 'the scale of the poverty-belt enveloping the urban playground' (2002: 217). Manchester's poor are both more dependent on the city centre as inner-city neighbourhoods decay, and more excluded from it. Nevertheless, more recent work by Ward, with others, demonstrates the extent to which Manchester is seen as an exemplar of city-regional governance—and indeed the extent to which its own leaders have carefully cultivated this 'mythic' image (Haughton et al. 2016; see also the chapter by Blakeley and Evans in this volume).

This story is not—or is no longer—unique to Manchester, as the contradictory dynamics of post-industrialism have been evident in many parts of the North to a greater or lesser extent, and indeed other parts of the UK. Many parts of Southern England, especially parts of the Greater London area, were also of course dependent on manufacturing, even if the regional economy was overall more diverse. Yet these economies have been more able to build upon their diversity to grow financial services and other knowledge-intense service industries, and indeed retain and grow some high-value manufacturing industries such as pharmaceuticals and computing which are heavily intertwined with higher education institutions in the South East, in part due to their proximity to London (Elledge 2016; Pike 2009: 54). Peck's work, with Nik Theodore, on 'variegated capitalism' provides an important step towards understanding such dynamics. For Peck and Theodore (2007), the process of capitalist restructuring—essentially, the opening of new sites of globally chained production as the West deindustrialises—is both spatially bound, emerging from and relying upon specific economic geographies (such as the City of London's global role) *and* exhibits common underlying logics, as large cities within the West develop new relationships with each other and the industrialising semi-periphery.

We can perhaps think of such shifts as emblematic of the regrouping of the core within the global capitalist economy, a process known more innocently as 'globalisation', whereby cities demonstrating leadership in knowledge-intense industries become increasingly interconnected (with connections spreading into elite cities within the so-called developing world) while becoming partially detached from their domestic political and economic environment. Yet we must not forget that post-industrialism is a British story as well as a global story. Variegated capitalism may have served as a useful rejoinder to the methodological nationalism inherent in Peter Hall and David Soskice's (2001) 'varieties of capitalism' thesis, but the condition of Northern England is evidently a product of a very British variety of deindustrialisation (see Pike 2009). The need to eschew methodological nationalism need not simultaneously require us to overlook the abiding force of industrial practices reinforced by national-level institutions. The varieties of capitalism literature is also useful (as Peck and Theodore acknowledge), insofar it emphasises the role of institutional and evolutionary dynamics in explaining political–economic outcomes—an analytical approach embraced by Ray Hudson (2005), for instance, in accounting for the particularities of Northern demise.

The Impact of the 2008 Crisis

It would be incorrect to presume that 2008 represented a significant rupture within the manufacturing sector in the UK, as it did for the rest of the economy—because manufacturing had not shared in the pre-crisis boom. Unlike other sectors, there had been no upturn in manufacturing output between 2002 and 2007, and stagnation in manufacturing pay helped to hold back general earnings growth even as the economy soared (Berry 2015; Froud et al. 2011). The impact of the recession on manufacturing output was of course significant: output in manufacturing remains more than 6 per cent below its pre-crisis peak in 2007, and around half a million jobs have been lost in the sector (Office for National Statistics 2016b). This helps to explain how output per head has fallen across the Northern regions since 2008, while rising elsewhere, particularly London and the South East (Berry and Hay 2016: 4–5). Interestingly, however, job losses in manufacturing have been comparable to those in other regions. The North East, North West and Yorkshire and Humberside have experienced, respectively, a 13, 11 and 6 per cent decline in manufacturing employment since their pre-crisis peaks, yet these figures are lower than a decline of 18 per cent in London, 19 per cent in the South East, and comparable to the East of England (12 per cent), the South West (10 per cent), East Midlands (10 per cent) and West Midlands (8 per cent) (Office for National Statistics 2016d).

As such, we can perhaps conclude that the 2008 crisis has not had a disproportionate impact on manufacturing in the North in any direct sense, notwithstanding the greater reliance of Northern regions on manufacturing employment. The issue is more one of the North's abilities to adapt to such shocks, and whether greater barriers to developing a genuinely post-industrial economy in the North means its development will be held back by the non-reversal of manufacturing decline. It seems likely, however, that Brexit will have a more direct, targeted impact on manufacturing in the North, insofar as exporting manufactured goods to Europe (as opposed to selling to the rest of the world, or to domestic customers) is more central to the business model of manufacturers in the North (Berry et al. 2016). Moreover, the products of the industries to which the EU imposes the highest tariffs—generally speaking, cars and chemicals—are significantly more likely to be located in the North and the Midlands, particularly the North East. Conventional wisdom suggests that the enormous fall in the value of sterling that immediately followed the Brexit vote should have boosted manufacturing exports, but UK manufacturing is now heavily dependent on the import of components due to 'broken' domestic supply chains (Pike et al. 2012: 32–34)—something which particularly muddies the ostensible post-crisis success story of car manufacturing in the North East, which is reliant on both finance and components from Japan (Berry 2015: 183). Crucially, even if the UK were to negotiate entry into the European Economic Area along the lines of Norway—which at the time of writing is far from certain—it would not be part of the EU's customs union, meaning that 'rules of origin' provisions would apply. Goods that the UK exports to the EU would have to be substantially composed of content produced domestically, or indeed within the EU itself, to qualify for tariff-free single market access (Piris 2016: 8).

Devolution and the Northern Powerhouse in the British Industrial Policy Tradition

Industrial Policy in the UK

Any exploration of manufacturing decline requires an understanding of the UK's industrial policy tradition, not least because the line between industrial and regional policy in the UK has always been a blurry one. By conflating a desired industrial renaissance with an agenda around local government reform, the Northern Powerhouse agenda arguably served to intensify this inheritance. Industrial policy involves the state deliberately favouring manufacturing industries over others, irrespective of market signals. Essentially, through industrial policy the state intervenes 'vertically' in parts of the economy in order to ensure that private economic actors are properly incentivised to pursue the public good of enhanced productivity (for the benefit of the entire economy). This definition is of course a contested one—and the contest has a direct bearing upon the British industrial policy tradition. UK policymakers would generally claim that Britain has long upheld a functional industrial policy regime, albeit one that operates 'horizontally' to improve the general environment for all business activity, rather than vertically in support of manufacturing and related industries. This chapter is based on the assumption that industrial policy, by definition, has to be in part vertical in nature. Yet this debate is of little consequence for our present purposes. It is more important to note that manufacturing benefits, by design, from vertical industrial policy. That the UK favours a horizontal approach signals the British state's long-standing indifference to manufacturing (and by extension, the regions most reliant on manufacturing industries) (Berry 2017).

As such, direct support for manufacturers has generally taken the form of 'soft' interventions such as advice services and the dissemination of best practice and tax allowances for R&D or capital investment (Buigues and Sekkat 2009). It should be noted that in the 1970s, Harold Wilson's Labour government introduced a more interventionist approach, involving direct subsidies and planning agreements, although the agenda became largely focused on defensive interventions to rescue unproductive firms and industries (Coates 2015). The 2008 crisis, however, appeared to reignite an interest among policy elites in industrial policy, and indeed seemed to endorse vertical interventions in support of manufacturing, insofar as the Conservative–Liberal Democrat coalition promised to 'rebalance' the economy from finance (or services in general) towards manufacturing, and from London and the South East (or the South in general) towards the North. This narrative had already been present to some extent in the Labour government's post-2008 agenda— as represented in the *New Industry, New Jobs* (HM Government 2009) strategy—but it was only from 2010 onwards that more explicit references to the geographical dimension of supporting manufacturing through industrial policy firmly re-entered the lexicon of the UK policy elite. The 2010 coalition agreement stated that:

> We want to create a fairer and more balanced economy, where we are not so dependent on a narrow range of economic sectors, and where new businesses and economic opportunities are more evenly shared between regions and industries. (HM Government 2010: 9)

An accompanying speech by new Prime Minister, David Cameron (2010) argued that 'our economy has become more and more unbalanced, with our fortunes hitched to a few industries in one corner of the country, while we let other sectors like manufacturing slide', and in 2011 the coalition's 'plan for growth' repeated:

Sustainable growth requires a rebalancing of the UK economy away from a reliance on a narrow range of sectors and regions, to one built on investment and exports, with strong growth more fairly shared across the UK. (HM Treasury and Department for Business, Innovation and Skills 2011: 28)

The 'plan for growth' was of course launched by George Osborne's now infamous 'march of the makers' speech (Osborne 2011). But what kinds of policies were actually associated with this agenda? Access to finance— primarily a horizontal issue, focused on small- and medium-sized enterprises (SMEs) in general rather than any particular industry—has been a core concern. The government has issued loan guarantees that could amount to around £2 billion, in addition to the Bank of England's Funding for Lending scheme, although this scheme was initially used predominantly to support mortgage lending. The British Business Bank enabled a more direct form of lending to SMEs, albeit with funds of only around £1.5 billion. Other measures focused on SMEs include better targeting of government procurement, increased apprenticeship funding, and tax and planning incentives within 'enterprise zones'. There were more vertical forms of support for manufacturing industries. Perhaps what is most interesting, however, is that policymakers (especially elected politicians) were content to create the impression that industrial policy was being targeted on particular, strategically significant industries; for example, in the coalition's 2012 industrial strategy, outlining the eleven key sectors as the focus of government action (many of which were manufacturing and related industries) (HM Government 2014). Yet arguments in 'the plan for growth' that might support a more interventionist industrial policy run alongside support for fiscal conservatism, lower taxes and deregulation, and flexible labour markets (albeit with a higher skilled workforce). This might help to explain the conservatism of the government's agenda in this regard. The creation of a series of 'catapult centres' related to particular sectors or industries was probably the most significant policy, although the centres were not all entirely new. The centres enable firms and universities to collaborate on R&D and access common, publicly funded resources (they are expected to become profitable and attract private funding in the medium term). The Advanced Manufacturing Supply Chain Initiative (at a cost of around £240 million) is also worth noting, as is the coalition's extension of tax allowances related to capital investment, which primarily benefit manufacturers.

Vince Cable, Liberal Democrat MP and Business Secretary within the coalition government, clearly wanted to have gone further, especially in terms of advanced manufacturing. He openly criticised the government's 'piecemeal' approach to industrial policy, and argued that greater state intervention was legitimate and necessary, because public investment was more efficient than private investment from the perspective of boosting productive capacity over the long term (Cable 2011, 2012). He enjoyed support from both the Confederation of British Industry and the Trades Union Congress for his position, as well as his departmental colleague, science minister and Conservative MP, David Willets (see Willets 2012). But we must not exaggerate Cable's radicalism in this regard. Indeed, in 'sector analysis' published by his department in 2012, it was stressed that '[h]orizontal policies, such as setting the legal and regulatory frameworks in which businesses across the economy operate, form the bedrock of industrial strategy'. The momentum behind the coalition's industrial strategy appeared to have waned significantly by 2015, before disappearing in all but name following the Conservative Party's 2015 general election victory (Berry 2017). Intriguingly, during Theresa May's campaign for the Conservative Party leadership, after the Brexit vote, she signalled her support for a 'proper industrial strategy' and 'economic reform', echoing remarks from 2013 in favour of 'a more strategic role for the state in our economy' (May 2013, 2016c). However, there are as yet few genuine signs that she intends to transform UK industrial policy (Berry 2017). Furthermore, insofar as May's words can be taken at face value, she appears less keen than her former colleagues in the Conservative Party to explicitly associate industrial strategy with support for either manufacturing or Northern England.

Regional Policy and the Emergence of the Northern Powerhouse

In recent decades, regional policy has in the UK effectively functioned as industrial policy by proxy—and it was at the regional level that the state apparatus appeared during this period to take on a more interventionist or vertical pose. This applied most to the New Labour era, with the Blair government clearly more inclined to take an interest in its depressed 'heartland' constitutions in the North, but it was also, to a lesser extent, a feature of the Thatcher and especially Major governments' agenda. This was again often limited, however, to defensive moves, in recognition of the particular economic geography of hardships associated with deindustrialisation. In general, the regional layer simply replicated the horizontal approach of national government, and indeed probably reinforced it, by encouraging all regions to pursue similar economic objectives, often in competition with each other and paradoxically with little sense that strategies were genuinely 'place-based' (Bailey and Driffield 2007; Bailey et al. 2015). As suggested above, one of the interesting paradoxes of post-crisis industrial policy in the UK is that those most in favour of a more vertical approach at the national level seem least concerned about the geographical dimension to supporting manufacturing. Vince Cable, for instance, appears not to have bought into Northern Powerhouse to any extent, despite the fact that his party leader, then Deputy Prime Minister Nick Clegg, arguably initiated the coalition's interest in this area, albeit in a rather nebulous manner through his Northern Futures initiative. Incredibly, among Cable's flagship catapult centres, only two of eleven current centres have a Northern footprint: the medicines discovery centre is based in Cheshire, and the high-value manufacturing centre has seven bases, one of which is in Redcar, with a further two in Rotherham (connected to the University of Sheffield).

Shortly before becoming Prime Minister, Theresa May appeared to signal that her government would not champion the North above other areas, arguing that she would initiate 'a plan to help not one or even two of our great regional cities, but every single one of them' (May 2016c). This implied rebuke to Osborne's focus on the North has subsequently softened, although it is probably significant that she first resuscitated the Northern Powerhouse moniker when speaking directly to a Northern audience, writing in *The Yorkshire Post* that 'Yorkshire is a key part of our vision for a Northern Powerhouse—our plan to help the great cities and towns of the North pool their strengths and take on the world' (May 2016a). The Northern Powerhouse is perhaps understood by May as a policy agenda (or branding) relevant to the North, but not necessarily the UK economy in general. Comically, a similar article endorsing 'the Midlands Engine' (a later Osborne concoction) appeared in *The Birmingham Mail* on the same day (May 2016b). Ultimately, of course, the fact that politicians such as George Osborne (who represents a constituency in Cheshire) were keen to promulgate the idea of a Northern manufacturing revival does not mean they upheld a more genuinely place-based approach to industrial policy than espoused now by Theresa May. The memoirs of former Liberal Democrat minister David Laws revealed that, after Clegg lobbied Osborne to include Sheffield (where

Clegg's constituency is) rather than Leeds in the first wave of announcements related to the Northern Powerhouse, Clegg told him that 'George is hilarious. He immediately suggested including Sheffield and just dropping Leeds' (cited in Chakrabortty 2016).

The coalition government's interest in local growth started somewhat inauspiciously when it abolished Labour's Regional Development Agencies (RDAs) immediately after coming to office. RDAs were New Labour's attempt to revolutionise the governance of local economic development in England, using central government budgets more effectively to support new and growing industries, not least to enable post-industrial transition and engender more balanced growth. While Scotland and Wales began the path to political and constitutional devolution in Labour's first term, RDAs were explicitly designed as arms-length, apolitical bodies (the Labour government quickly aborted half-hearted efforts democratise regional policy in England during its second term following a referendum defeat in the North East). Defined by their regional location rather than any particular vision for industrial policy, there were few natural limits to the scope of their responsibilities. The resources, of course, seldom matched the policy ambition. While many RDAs lobbied for further devolution, for others it was rather unwelcome. Transplanted on top of a historically messy governance hierarchy in England, RDAs ultimately became a new institutional repository for the mess (although this does not mean they were entirely unsuccessful, judged on their own terms). Although RDAs were pitched by Labour as the solution to the malaise of deindustrialisation, they were largely place-blind in practice, arguably more so than the minimal regional economic development structures created by the Conservatives in the 1980s and early 1990s (although they were less explicitly market-oriented). Every part of England was covered by an RDA, including London, in contrast to the European norm of focusing regional policy initiatives on the areas most in need (Pike et al. 2016a; Pike and Tomaney 2009).

RDAs were replaced by Local Enterprise Partnerships (LEPs), semi-autonomous bodies, organised loosely on a city-regional basis, led by representatives of both local government and local business communities working in partnership. It is worth noting that RDAs had themselves become more local- or city-based over time, particularly during Labour's third term when they were instructed to deliver interventions via local authorities as far as possible, and (unelected) regional supervisory chambers were abolished (Pike et al. 2016a, b). LEPs were established by the central government, but were given miniscule resources to fund a small core staff and organisational administration. LEPs do not themselves invest, but are expected to encourage investment by public and private actors in self-defined priority areas. LEPs hold few, if any, actual policy powers. While conceived as an attempt to instil a genuinely (business-defined) localism, LEPs' lack of power and resources is compounded by the problem of multiple and blurred lines of accountability (enabling reinvented forms of centralisation), gerrymandered and overlapping political boundaries, and a constitutive inability to address market failure (Jones 2013; Pike et al. 2015).

The non-statutory and unincorporated nature of LEPs means the initiative has functioned in parallel with, but only loosely connected to (limited) funding streams for local economic development, such as the Regional Growth Fund (RGF; a £2.4 billion pot for regeneration projects, available from 2011 to 2015). Many LEPs controlled some RGF funds designed for very small projects, but most of the RGFs is administered by central government, with LEPs required to work with local firms to apply to the centre. The devolution of power to local government encapsulated by 'city deals' has also been organised in parallel with LEPs. City deals are the mechanism through which central government has sought to devolve powers to combined authorities (consortia of local authorities, typically organised on a city-regional basis). City deals have to date also focused rather too much on devolving the responsibility to *deliver* national policy, rather than the responsibility to *decide* on how best to support local economies. The most significant move towards decentralisation to date involves Greater Manchester taking control of the region's health and social care budgets. However, 'at the moment, "devo-health" is more akin to delegation than devolution' (Quilter-Pinner 2016: 1). Furthermore, and more significantly, very few economic policy powers being devolved to Northern local authorities constitute a meaningful opportunity to develop industrial policy at the local level. Many local authorities are likely to end up with some new powers over transport, although generally not powers to decide on major infrastructure projects. Some planning powers and housing budgets will be devolved, alongside some aspects of central government's training, skills, employment support and business support services—with all recent and future spending cuts devolved too. Limited central government budgets for direct investment in productive activity will remain exactly where they are. And too often, delivery powers require local authorities to outsource the actual administration of, for example, employment support programmes, relying on many of the same firms hitherto contracted by central government (Berry 2016a: 42–43). It is revealing that the Treasury has been almost solely responsible for the devolution agenda within central government; this has led to a deal-making process typical of Treasury statecraft (see the chapter by Lee in this volume for a longer discussion of the Treasury). Tellingly, the announcement of new or updated city deals is often accompanied by announcements around new investment in infrastructure or regeneration—yet these initiatives typically remain under central government's control.

It would be interesting at this point to note the contribution of veteran Conservative cabinet minister (and rival to Margaret Thatcher), Michael Heseltine, to coalition thinking around local growthand industrial policy. Heseltine's 2012 report *No Stone Unturned in Pursuit of Growth*, commissioned—but not necessarily enthusiastically—by George Osborne, offered a fairly lavish vision for the state in coordinating an economy-wide growth plan, joining up all both national and local governments, and public and private sectors, initiatives to improve UK productivity and competitiveness Heseltine (2012). His key recommendation was that all public spending relevant to economic growth (he identified around £50 billion in relevant spending per year) should be devolved. More precisely, he recommended that this expenditure should be amalgamated into a single fund, enabling LEPs to apply to central government for access to these funds. As such, Heseltine offered a somewhat surreal approach, with little grounding in how central government budgets actually function, or indeed any understanding of how LEPs operate in practice. Nevertheless, while Osborne rejected the notion of devolving budgets on this scale to local government in any form, we can trace similarities in the sentiments of both men, insofar as Osborne viewed the city deal process as one in which local government could be refashioned in the image of Heseltine, with local authorities themselves becoming more LEP-like, seeking primarily to attract exogenous investment rather than playing a meaningful role in governing the local economy. Heseltine may support a stronger role for the state, but it is nevertheless a technocratic, depoliticised state.

Interestingly, *No Stone Unturned* includes very few references to manufacturing, or any particular manufacturing industry. Manufacturing may have resurfaced in the Conservative approach to localised industrial policy, but perhaps only as something that local government must itself find ways of supporting, without a substantive strategy at the national level. In the Conservative approach, cities, rather than industries or governments, are the new agents of economic history, but only insofar as cities are conceived as the ideal incubator of market dynamics. This approach is heavily influenced by the 'new urban economics' and 'new economic geography', forms of spatial economics drawing substantially upon neoclassical theory, which emphasise urban 'agglomeration' as a more perfect form of market dynamics, creating sustainable economic equilibria—and explaining disequilibrium with reference to public interventions to protect unecomonic forms or spatial organisation (Engelen et al. 2016; Martin 2015; Martin et al. 2015; see also the chapters by Martin and Gardiner, and Gray, Pugalis and Dickinson in this volume) (These perspectives had of course influenced New Labour's approach to regional governance, and the evolution of the RDAs (Pike et al. 2016a, b)). There is even a catapult centre devoted to 'future cities' (based in London) which, apparently, 'accelerate[s] urban ideas to market, to grow the economy and make cities better' (Future Cities Catapult 2016).

In Heseltine's vision, the fixation on cities equates to enriching business-led LEPs. For Osborne, far more attuned to the intricacies of political power and symbolism, it equates to the establishment of so-called 'metro-mayors', directly elected to oversee combined authorities within city-regions. The scope of powers to be allocated to metro-mayors remains far from certain—this is seemingly not a primary consideration for national policymakers—beyond chairing existing or new combined authority boards. The Northern Powerhouse therefore takes on greatest significance insofar as the North of England is deemed to be home to a handful of large cities, whose interests will be promoted by this agenda. The focus on the region's metropolitanism, rather than any other socio-economic characteristics, helps to explain the prominence of transport investment and planning rules in growth plans. When the Treasury replaced the 2011 growth plan with 'the productivity plan', following the 2015 general election, the associated document *Fixing the Foundations* listed 'Resurgent cities, a rebalanced economy and a thriving Northern Powerhouse' as one of the key ambitions towards delivering 'a dynamic economy', which was identified alongside 'long term investment' as one of two drivers of national productivity. It is interesting perhaps that there were no explicit references to the North in relation to the long-term investment driver, and that the key ambition in relation to a dynamic economy was labour market deregulation (HM Treasury 2015b). Despite the focus on productivity, *Fixing the Foundations* does not contain a single reference to manufacturing.

Despite its implicit, yet deliberate, allusion to the UK's past manufacturing glories, the Northern Powerhouse, and its partial embodiment in the city deals process, essentially represents a form of 'bottom-up horizontalism' within UK industrial policy. While the valorisation of city-led growth alludes to the possibility of vertical intervention at the local level to support local industries, in actual fact the transposition of responsibility for industrial policy to the local level probably serves to dilute even the horizontal forms of intervention traditional favoured by UK policymakers. The Northern Powerhouse is a largely place-blind agenda in which cities are asked to improve the attractiveness of their areas to business, but not primarily to assist firms in improving their performance once situated within the their jurisdiction. The key tax change related to devolution (relevant to all local authorities) fits the notion of bottom-up horizontalism well. Amid ongoing city deal negotiations between the Treasury and local authorities in 2015, the government announced the wholesale devolution of business rates (a tax on the physical footprint of private companies), alongside the phased withdrawal of central government grants to local authorities. The move (which is discussed by both Bailey, and Muldoon-Smith and Greenhalgh, at greater length in their chapters in this volume) is ostensibly designed to enable city-regions to exercise greater control over their finances, yet clearly benefits those areas with strong, existing private sector bases, which of course already tend to be more affluent than those lacking this characteristic. Moreover, while the simultaneous withdrawal of central grants inherently disincentivises local authorities from increasing business rates, just to be on the safe side, the government prohibited increases at the local level without the prior approval the private sector appointees on the relevant LEP board, and even then increases must take the form of a capped surcharge to fund a specific, local infrastructure project (HM Treasury 2015a).

THE DE-DEVELOPMENT OF NORTHERN ENGLAND

Development and Unevenness

As intimated above, the North or the manufacturing industries located within Northern regions cannot be understood in isolation, from either the rest of the UK or the global economy. The notion of 'uneven development' has become increasingly important to critically minded social scientists interested in the fortunes of areas such as the North of England. The concept implies not simply that different areas have different levels of affluence (or are at different stages of development) but, furthermore, that the economic experience of different areas are related and in interaction with each other (Peck and Theodore 2007). In this vein, Ron Martin (2015) challenges regional studies to adopt both a 'total national system' framework (in which scholars assess 'a nationwide evolving pattern of combined and uneven geographical development, set in the context of that national economy's changing external linkages and interactions and its evolving internal institutional and political structures') and a 'total place' framework (assessing a 'region's or city's economy in all its multi-scalar detail, as a complex open system set within the relevant national and international networks and structures to which it relates and with which in interacts') (Martin 2015: 262–263). Accordingly, Martin finds little evidence that efforts to rebalance the UK economy towards the North and manufacturing are transformative of the basic structures and relationships upheld at the national level, and supported internationally, which provide for uneven development within the UK economy (Martin 2015: 264).

The links between seemingly local development projects are central to Ray Hudson and Dan Swanton's (2012) report on the fascinating case of the decline in steel production in both Teesside and Dortmund, Germany, alongside the simultaneous expansion of production in China. Somewhat remarkably, after ending production in Dortmund, German steel producer ThyssenKrupp dismantled the bulk of the relevant steelworks, and sold and shipped it to a Chinese producer for reassembly in Jiangsu Province. In contrast, the British equivalent had little resale value given the lack of investment in modernisation. While steel-making capacity was therefore retained in the North temporarily, with the plant eventually reopened under the ownership of Indian conglomerate Tata (to service, primarily, Indian demand) paradoxically this put the UK in competition with Chinese producers, with little evidence of capacity within the UK to develop more advanced production techniques (domestic steel demand in the UK, in areas such as defence and transport infrastructure, is generally met through imports). The recent turmoil around the likely closure of the Tata plant in Teesside, due in part to price manipulation by the Chinese government (which the UK government sought to *prevent* European authorities challenging—signifying that the UK policy elite is probably more concerned with the country's political and economic relations with China than prosperity in the North), is as predictable as it is devastating for those directly affected. While Dortmund has evolved into an important urban economy within the global, post-industrial core, benefiting from high-value manufacturing activity in neighbouring cities, Teesside, largely isolated from post-industrial prosperity in some Northern cities, has become increasingly vulnerable to shifting hierarchies within global production networks.

As important as this literature (spanning regional studies and economic geography) is, it probably takes for granted too readily what it means for an economy to develop or become 'more developed'. Recognising that development is an uneven process, and that processes such as deindustrialisation create new hardships, is not quite the same as arguing that deindustrialisation may actually represent a form of 'de-development'. There remains a strong sense in UK public discourse (and within parts of the academic community) that post-industrialism represents a 'higher' stage of economic development (see Davis 2012; Kay 2016). Two sets of responses to this are possible. The first concerns the role, noted above, of a strong manufacturing sector in the prospects for sustainable growth, and particularly productivity improvements. Manufacturing is the motor of innovation, and acts to support and propel other sectors in an infinite number of ways (Chang 2014; Pike et al. 2012). Of course, in theory the North needs not necessarily itself house a large manufacturing sector in order to benefit from the fruits of manufacturing—and nor can we assume that, even if it were able to revive its manufacturing base, the North would necessarily capture the bulk of the benefits, or indeed create large numbers of new manufacturing jobs. However, the more salient point is that manufacturing matters to more than elite discourses tend to recognise, and that by building upon its traditional strength in manufacturing, the North will be able to more effectively control its own destiny.

The second set of related responses, best represented in the critical international political economy literature, concerns a complementary narrowing *and* broadening of the notion of development, enabled by distinguishing clearly between development and (capitalist) growth. Accordingly, the notion that development must take a particular economic form is eschewed, with the development concept redeployed more narrowly in terms of a development 'model' which crystallises a particular approach to securing growth (and which may be a flawed approach, or partial to the interests of some groups over others). At the same time, this literature shows that all (political) economies are constantly 'developing' in a broader sense. Development is not a process with an endpoint, but rather a way describing multi-dimensional processes of economic change. From this perspective, what is most important to understand is whether a given polity is able to exercise meaningful control over these processes (Bishop 2016; Payne 2005; Payne and Phillips 2009). Although this perspective has to date been largely agnostic about manufacturing, and is concerned mainly with national economies (and the relationships between them) rather than local economies, its application to the North does not require too great an intellectual leap. Irrespective of the centrality of manufacturing to sustainable growth in general terms, the North's particular experience of deindustrialisation has been accompanied by a decentring of Northern regions from the UK's prevailing development model (in narrow terms), but also, relatedly, the increased vulnerability of development processes (in broad terms) within the North to exogenous forces.

De-Development in the Northern Periphery?

The question of whether the North is in fact de-developing may therefore offer an important framing for future research. This concept has a relatively limited genealogy in social science. It has been applied in a fairly conventional manner—with de-development understood as a reversal of upward trends in quantitative indicators of improvements in living standards and economic growth—to countries transitioning to liberal democracy following the collapse of the Soviet Union (Meurs and Ranasinghe 2003). More prominently, and more interestingly, it has been applied to the case of Palestine, following Sara Roy's work on the economy of the Gaza Strip, which showed that Gaza was de-developing despite having experienced relatively strong output growth since the 1960s, because Israeli rule 'weakens the ability of [Gaza's] economy to grow and expand by preventing it from accessing and utilizing critical inputs needed to promote internal growth beyond a specific structural level' (Roy 1987). Eventual economic collapse in Palestine perhaps indicates Roy's view—that this collapse was a consequence of Israel security policy, rather than any economic weakness, strengthens rather than undermines this point, assuming we accept the broader understanding of development suggested above. Foreign aid now sustains the Palestinian economy, but in a way, argues Hani Mahmoud (2014), that also reinforces de-development. The concept has even been applied recently to the UK, in a polemical book by economics journalists Larry Elliott and Dan Atkinson (2012) on what they see as the imminent *absolute* decline of the UK economy, compounding post-war *relative* decline. The loss of UK manufacturing features heavily in Elliott and Atkinson's account, although they frustratingly understand development in rather crude terms, insofar as they see the de-development process as one in which the UK will start to resemble 'a third world economy'. This is clearly an overstatement, and probably misses the real significance of what might be happening in different parts of the UK. Northern England is clearly not becoming what would be understood in conventional parlance as an under-developed economy, but it may be losing what power it has over its own fate. That this might not apply uniformly to the North is a rather mundane inevitability, but could also underline the fact that in order to achieve growth, Northern cities and/or regions must compete with each other for the favour of external entities.

Agglomeration-based dogma about the importance of cities reinforces this situation, insofar as it reduces the Northern economic space to a set of discrete urban centres (legitimising their political separation at the same as stronger transport links between Northern cities are advocated). This is of course not to suggest that the North can only develop *qua* the North, or that cities are economically insignificant. The first section of this chapter endorsed the view that some (post-industrial) cities are to some extent transcending national borders to form a new global economic core. The question is whether an economic strategy which privileges urban centres (including, furthermore, the North's relatively miniscule urban centres) is likely to benefit the Northern economy. This is a particularly important issue given that it is a strategy which also underpins the process of devolution to the North. Calvin Jones' (2015) response to Ron Martin's challenge to regional studies advocates a world-systems approach to studying local and regional economic developments, following the approach to international relations and the global economic order developed by Immanuel Wallerstein. Wallerstein understood the global political economy in terms of core and peripheral (and semi-peripheral) nation-states, with variable levels of development across the world not simply transitory, but rather a structural product of the governance of the global order by core countries. Jones seeks to introduce this approach to the study of uneven development within countries, which he sees in parallel to, and in part a function of, global unevenness. Crucially, it is within countries that we can see more precisely how complex circuits of capital are shaped by institutions of political governance *external* to the economic spaces in question—Jones argues this is central to understanding the uneven spatiality of capitalist organisation (Jones 2015; see also Engelen et al. 2016).

The lesson, perhaps, is that the North has to be understood as a peripheral part of the British economy (we can speculate that it occupies a semi-peripheral status within the global economy, despite its location within a traditional core economy), notwithstanding the possibility that some parts of the North are more peripheral than others, and that other parts of the UK may belong in the same category. Simply trying to replicate in the North what has (apparently) enabled London—and other Southern cities, to a lesser extent—to proper within an emerging global core of transnational cities may be a fallacious strategy. Moreover, because the city-based strategy is a product of the same national-level governance procedures that act to sustain unevenness within the UK, it may be that the privileging of the larger Northern cities, at the expense of Northern regions as a whole, enables them to prosper as satellite cities of the transnational core, without challenging the structures that ultimately underline their subservience. As such, the North's recent successes tend to be built upon the location of regional outposts of London-centred financial and business service industries within city centres, coupled with the coterminous expansion of retail, leisure and hospitality industries. The conflation of industrial and regional policy characterised here as bottom-up horizontalism allows for a degree of prosperity among the strongest post-industrial cities, but not for large-scale upgrades in manufacturing capacity, nor for any systematic strategy to address inequality. Moreover, while some parts of the North may be growing, this does not mean they are not stuck in the same de-development trap, because their prosperity depends on the persistence of political–economic structures within which the North is inherently subservient. The ongoing failure of the North to systematically renew its manufacturing capacity illustrates well that the North lacks the authority to adopt a development model which builds upon its own endogenous strength in manufacturing—reinforced by a focus of regeneration initiatives on city centres at the expense of the range of geographies in which contemporary, high-value production might actually be located.

Even the apparent exceptions to this trend (no historical process is unidirectional) are quite revealing. Sheffield city-region, for instance, has been successful in retaining and reviving some high-value dimensions of engineering related to steel production, albeit with only a limited role for native (or even British) enterprises. Similarly, the discovery of 'miracle material' graphene in Manchester has not led to the establishment of new graphene-based industries in the local economy on any significant scale, in part due to the UK's broken high-value manufacturing supply chains (Institute of Mechanical Engineers 2013; Froud et al. 2011)— the graphene experience is at the time of writing subject to an inquiry by the science and technology select committee in the UK parliament. Furthermore, the relocation of old manufacturing industries, such as car manufacturing, to parts of the North East where it had not traditionally been strong is consistently lauded as a rebalancing success story, yet it is paradoxically only possible because deindustrialisation in the North East has made its economy more amenable to lower skill assembly processes. (And there are already signs that Brexit problematises this arrangement in disrupting the business model of foreign producers based in the North.) No parts of the North can be said to have been successful in developing industries connected to computers and consumer electronics. The focus of post-crisis industrial policy on supporting science and R&D may, or may not, be the correct focus for the UK economy as a whole, but even if this were the case, we can conclude that few parts of the North are in a position to take advantage of the new resources associated with this strategy (an issue further explored in Kieron Flanagan and James Wilsdon's contribution to this volume).

A 2016 report by think-tank Centre for Cities, comparing UK cities with European counterparts across a wide range of economic indicators, underlines the problems facing the cities of the North, as they have fallen significantly below the European average in terms of productivity, in a domestic economy more dominated by its capital city than any comparable country. The report implicitly underlines the peripheral nature of the North in international terms. Interestingly, the report also notes that successful German cities appear to be accounted for not by any particular industrial composition, but rather the co-location of cities with varying industrial strengths—including several medium-sized cities where output is dominated by manufacturing—within the same administrative region. The intellectual barriers to addressing the North's developmental dilemmas are evident, however, in the fact that the report's conclusions appear to ignore its own evidence. The report simply (and glibly) instead presses for the UK's underperforming cities to simply focus on attracting foreign investment into knowledge-based industries, and invest in transport links to 'better link jobs in city centres... to residential areas in suburbs and hinterlands' (Bessis 2016: 23–24). Even among the most vociferous advocates and students of local economic development, concerns that the North's development cannot simply replicate London and other Southern cities, and indeed that the North's developmental interests might conflict with the wider UK developmental model, are thoroughly marginalised.

Too often, such analysis presents cities, domestically and internationally, as either in competition with each other, or at the very least relatively isolated from each other economically. In practice, and quite obviously, city economies are highly integrated across transnational networks. As noted above, withdrawal from the EU is likely to make a manufacturing revival in the North more difficult, if not impossible. One of the few prominent academic economists who supported the leave campaign, Patrick Minford, argued in *The Sun* that Brexit would 'eliminate' manufacturing in the UK over the long term. He added, however, that 'this should not scare us.... It is time for Britain to focus on our services and design skills, to start producing more of what we're good at' (Minford 2016). Nevertheless, the North voted decisively to leave in the referendum of 23 June 2016 (by 56 to 44 per cent, compared to the national result of 52 to 48 per cent). There is insufficient space here to explore why Northerners voted the way they did, and we of course cannot be certain what the very long-term implications for manufacturing will be, not least because the remaining EU continues to struggle with several existential challenges. Nevertheless, it is possible to speculate that the North's support for Brexit is related to its de-development dilemma. Encased in a development model in which it is inherently subservient, and becoming increasingly stratified, many Northerners took the opportunity to register their opposition to the UK status quo, even though the implications are highly likely to cause further hardship in the North, and undermine the case for a more vertical, place-based industrial policy. (This is not to discount the influence of anti-immigration sentiment within the North—but we should not assume that this sentiment can be satisfactorily disentangled from views about the UK's economic order.)

CONCLUSION

The Northern Powerhouse agenda epitomises many of the challenges facing Northern England, summarised here with reference to three very dangerous Ds: deindustrialisation, devolution and de-development. The chapter's most provocative suggestion is of course that the North may be de-developing or, more precisely, stuck in a de-development trap. Yet we need not accept the efficacy of this term in full in order to recognise the bevy of development dilemmas it seeks to crystallise conceptually. All economies are of course always 'developing', that is, experiencing over-lapping, multi-dimensional and contradictory processes of development. The problem, first, is that development in the North is largely governed under the rubric of a UK development model within which the interests of Northern regions are marginal. Second, the North is seemingly unable to establish an endogenous approach to achieving prosperity without further entrenching its subservience to this London-centred model and/or acquiescing to the deepening of inequalities *within* the North. The North may arguably have been more central in the past to the UK development model, and indeed part of the global economic core, but it is now firmly peripheral within the UK economy, and semi-peripheral, at best, in a global economic order within which London and its hinterland are the only British representative in the core.

The ongoing stutters of UK manufacturing illustrate the North's status well. A substantive revival of manufacturing in the North would empower the North, but given the long-standing indifference to manufacturing among the UK policy elite, the North would require more power to shape the UK economy in order to bring such a revival about. There should be no suggestion that a manufacturing revival would directly create a large number of new jobs in the North, given technological change within the sector, yet the fact that the productivity/jobs trade-off barely registers within public discourses around manufacturing demonstrates the extent of elite indifference to the North's economic prospects. It is not necessary to adjudicate here on whether the coalition and Conservative governments have genuinely sought to revive UK manufacturing, as the discourse around rebalancing and the Northern Powerhouse would suggest, since the financial crisis. The more salient point is that, even if this were the case, it was always very unlikely to have been achieved without seriously challenging the UK's industrial policy traditions. There are no firm reasons to believe that the May government intends to initiate this challenge, despite rediscovering the coalition's early rhetoric around industrial strategy. The notion that the North may become a 'powerhouse' of course explicitly invokes the North's historical prowess in manufacturing, but in a rather infantilising way. A sustainable manufacturing revival requires a holistic approach to economic development (and its political foundations) in places such as Northern England; simply reducing the (prospective) Northern economy to its industrial past will paradoxically inhibit the restoration of this supposedly glorious past. As it stands, the process of devolution to English city-regions—the main policy dimension of the Northern Powerhouse agenda—reinforces rather than challenges the UK's industrial policy orientation, offering little more than 'bottom-up horizontalism'. Devolution is an attempt by national politicians to address evident post-crisis concerns around place, identity and local control among the electorate, yet in dividing places such as the North politically into city-regions, arguably the process will serve to reduce the control that Northern citizens exercise over their local economies (Berry 2016b).

However, there are some grounds for optimism for the North. While the Northern Powerhouse and plans for devolution might have been devised as a way to modify rather than transform the UK's pre-crisis development model, the fact that associated discourses explicitly recognise, albeit partially, the value of the North and the manufacturing sector to the UK economy may over time prove to be a significant political opening. Clearly, the UK economy, even if it is technically recovering, is struggling to resume the path of stable growth. And crucially, while Brexit will in all likelihood prove to be a self-inflicted wound for the North, not least due to the negative implications for manufacturing industries, London's finance-led economy may also be significantly impeded by the UK's withdrawal from the EU. It is not inconceivable that a more significant rupture in the UK's pre-crisis economic order will occur, enabling an enhanced role for the North in national prosperity. At the moment, however, civic leaders in the North generally remain wedded to George Osborne's vision for local growth, while national leaders of the Labour Party and the trade unions—organisations through which the North is normally represented in national politics—appear not to be focused on the North's specific development dilemmas. The fact that these two groups of leaders have become effectively estranged in recent years may help to explain the inadequacies of each group's strategies for Northern development. That said, the establishment of metro-mayors may ironically provide a platform for both reconciliation and radicalism in Northern politics—as long as the new mayors' agenda involves the denunciation of the city-based vision for economic development to which they will owe their positions.

REFERENCES

Bailey, D., and N. Driffield. 2007. Industrial strategy, FDI and employment: Still missing a strategy. *Journal of Industry, Competition and Trade* 7 (3): 189–211.

Bailey, D., P. Hildreth, and L. De Propris. 2015. Mind the gap! What might a place-based industrial and regional policy look like? In *New perspectives on industrial policy for a modern Britain*, ed. D. Bailey, K. Cowling, and P.R. Tomlinson, 263–286. Oxford: Oxford University Press.

Berry, C. 2015. The final nail in the coffin? Crisis, manufacturing decline, and why it matters. In *The British growth crisis: The search for a new model*, ed. J. Green, C. Hay, and P. Taylor-Gooby, 174–197. Palgrave: Basingstoke.

Berry, C. 2016a. *Austerity politics and UK economic policy*. Basingstoke: Palgrave.

Berry, C. 2016b. The resurrected right and disoriented left: Growth model failure and the nascent politics of a transformative narrative. *SPERI Paper #27*. Available from: http://speri.dept.shef.ac.uk/wp-content/uploads/2016/02/SPERI-Paper-27-The-Resurrected-Right-and-Disoriented-Left.pdf. Accessed 23 Sept 2016.

Berry, C. 2017. Industrial policy change in Britain's post-crisis economy: Policy innovation in an incomplete institutional and ideational environment. *British Journal of Politics and International Relations*, 18(4), 829–847.

Berry, C., and C. Hay. 2016. The Great British "rebalancing" act: The construction and implementation of an economic imperative for exceptional times. *British Journal of Politics and International Relations* 18 (1): 3–25.

Berry, C., S. Lavery, T. Hunt, and C. Kirkland. 2016. UK regions, the European Union and manufacturing exports. Available from: http://speri.dept.shef.ac.uk/wp-content/uploads/2016/05/Brief23-UK-regions-the-EU-and-manufacturing-exports.pdf. Accessed 12 Aug 2016.

Bessis, H. 2016. *Competing with the continent: How UK cities compare with their European counterparts*. Centre for Cities. Available from: http://www.centreforcities.org/wp-content/uploads/2016/09/16-09-21-Competing-with-the-continent.pdf. Accessed 22 Sept 2016.

Bishop, M. 2016. Rethinking the political economy of development beyond "the rise of the BRICS". *SPERI Paper #30*. Available from: http://speri.dept.shef.ac.uk/wp-content/uploads/2016/07/Beyond-the-Rise-of-the-BRICS.pdf. Accessed 18 Sept 2016.

Bullen, E. 2015. Indices of deprivation 2015, Manchester City Council Briefing Note. Available from: http://www.manchester.gov.uk/downloads/download/ 414/research_and_intelligence_population_publications_deprivation. Accessed 11 Aug 2016.

Buigues, P.-A., and K. Sekkat. 2009. *Industrial policy in Europe, Japan and the United States: Amounts, mechanisms and effectiveness*. Basingstoke: Palgrave Macmillan.

Cable, V. 2011. 'Speech on industrial strategy', speech delivered on 26 October. Available from: https://www.gov.uk/government/speeches/business-secretary-speech-on-industrial-strategy-at-policy-exchange. Accessed 3 May 2016.

Cable, V. 2012. Vince Cable's letter on industrial policy in full. *The Telegraph*, 6 March. Available from: http://www.telegraph.co.uk/news/politics/9126795/ Vince-Cables-letter-on-industrial-policy-in-full.html. Accessed 3 May 2016.

Cameron, D. 2010. 'Transforming the British economy: coalition strategy for economic growth', speech delivered on 28 May. Available from: https://www. gov.uk/government/speeches/transforming-the-british-economy-coalition-strategy-for-economic-growth. Accessed 3 May 2016.

Chakrabortty, A. 2016. The case against Osborne is clear. But Corbyn has to provide an alternative. *The Guardian*, March 15. Available from: https:// www.theguardian.com/commentisfree/2016/mar/15/budget-2016-jeremy-corbyn-alternative-osborne. Accessed 22 Aug 2016.

Chang, H.-J. 2014. *Economics: The user's guide*. London: Penguin.

Christensen, J., N. Shaxson, and D. Wigan. 2016. *The finance curse: Britain and the World Economy* 18 (1): 255–269.

Coates, D. 2015. Industrial policy: International experiences. In *New perspectives on industrial policy for a modern Britain*, ed. D. Bailey, K. Cowling, and P.R. Tomlinson, 41–59. Oxford: Oxford University Press.

Davis, E. 2012. *Made in Britain: Why our economy is more successful than you think*. London: Abacus.

Dicken, P. 2002. Global Manchester: From globaliser to globalised. In *City of revolution: Restructuring Manchester*, ed. J. Peck and K. Ward, 1–33. Manchester: Manchester University Press.

Dorling, D. 2010. Persistent north-south divides. In *The economic geography of the UK*, ed. N.M. Coe and A. Jones, 12–28. London: SAGE.

Elledge, J. 2016. Have southern English cities grown faster than northern ones? The answer may surprise you. *CityMetric*, August 11. Available from: http:// www.citymetric.com/politics/have-southern-english-cities-grown-faster-northern-ones-answer-may-surprise-you-2340. Accessed 11 Aug 2016.

Elliott, L., and D. Atkinson. 2012. *Why Britain will have a third world economy by 2014*. Basingstoke: Palgrave.

Engelen, E., J. Froud, S. Johal, A. Salento, and K. Williams. 2016. How cities work: A policy agenda for the grounded city. CRESC Working Paper No. 141.

Available from: http://www.cresc.ac.uk/medialibrary/workingpapers/wp141. pdf. Accessed 1 Sept 2016.

English, R., and M. Kenny. 2000. Decline or declinism? In *Rethinking British decline*, ed. R. English and M. Kenny, 279–299. Basingstoke: Macmillan.

Froud, J., S. Johal, J. Law, A. Leaver, and K. Williams. 2011. Rebalancing the economy (or buyer's remorse). CRESC Working Paper No. 87. Available from: http://www.cresc.ac.uk/publications/rebalancing-the-economy-or-buyers-remorse. Accessed 28 Feb 2014.

Future Cities Catapult. 2016. Who we are. Available from: https://futurecities. catapult.org.uk/about/. Accessed 5 Sept 2016.

Gamble, A. 2000. Theories and explanations of British decline. In *Rethinking British decline*, ed. R. English and M. Kenny, 1–22. Basingstoke: Macmillan.

Giordano, B., and L. Twomey. 2002. Economic transitions: Restructuring local labour markets. In *City of revolution: Restructuring Manchester*, ed. J. Peck and K. Ward, 50–75. Manchester: Manchester University Press.

Hall Peter, A., and D. Soskice (eds.). 2001. *Varieties of capitalism: The institutional foundations of comparative advantage*. Oxford: Oxford University Press.

Haughton, G., I. Deas, S. Hincks, and K. Ward. 2016. Mythic Manchester: Devo Manc, the Northern Powerhouse and rebalancing the English economy. *Cambridge Journal of Regions, Economy and Society*, forthcoming. Available from: http://cjres.oxfordjournals.org/content/early/2016/04/07/cjres.rsw004. abstract. Accessed 19 Sept 2016.

Herd, D., and T. Petterson. 2002. Poor Manchester: Old problems and new deals. In *City of revolution: Restructuring Manchester*, ed. J. Peck and K. Ward, 190–213. Manchester: Manchester University Press.

Heseltine, M. 2012. No stone unturned in pursuit of growth. Available from: https://www.gov.uk/government/uploads/system/uploads/attachment_data/file/34648/12-1213-no-stone-unturned-in-pursuit-of-growth.pdf. Accessed 19 Aug 2016.

HM Government. 2009. New industry, new jobs. Available from: http://webarchive.nationalarchives.gov.uk/20100430155636/, http://www.bis.gov. uk/files/file51023.pdf. Accessed 3 May 2016.

HM Government. 2010. *The coalition: Our programme for government*. London: The Stationery Office.

HM Government. 2014. Industrial strategy: Government and industry in partnership—Progress report. Available from: https://www.gov.uk/government/uploads/system/uploads/attachment_data/file/306854/bis-14-707-industrial-strategy-progress-report.pdf. Accessed 3 May 2016.

HM Treasury. 2015a. Chancellor unveils "devolution revolution", press release issued on 5 October 2015. Available from: https://www.gov.uk/government/news/chancellor-unveils-devolution-revolution. Accessed 8 Nov 2015.

HM Treasury. 2015b. *Fixing the foundations: Creating a more prosperous nation.* Available from: https://www.gov.uk/government/uploads/system/uploads/attachment_data/file/443898/Productivity_Plan_web.pdf. Accessed 19 Aug 2016.

HM Treasury, and Department for Business, Innovation and Skills. 2011. The plan for growth. Available from: https://www.gov.uk/government/uploads/system/uploads/attachment_data/file/31584/2011budget_growth.pdf. Accessed 3 May 2016.

Hudson, R. 2005. Rethinking change in old industrial regions: Reflecting on the experiences of North East England. *Environment and Planning A* 37 (4): 581–596.

Hudson, R. 2013. Thatcherism and its geographical legacies: The new map of socio-spatial inequality in the Divided Kingdom. *The Geographical Journal* 179 (4): 377–381.

Hudson, R., and D. Swanton. 2012. Global shifts in contemporary times: The changing trajectories of steel towns in China, Germany and the United Kingdom. *European Urban and Regional Studies* 19 (1): 6–19.

Ingham, G. 1984. *Capitalism divided? The city and industry in British social development.* London: Macmillan.

Institute of Mechanical Engineers. 2013. Graphene: Small wonders, slow progress. Available from: http://www.imeche.org/docs/default-source/public-affairs/imeche-graphene-ps.pdf?sfvrsn=0. Accessed 18 Sept 2016.

Jones, C. 2015. On capital, space and the world system: A response to Ron Martin. *Territory, Politics, Governance* 3 (3): 273–293.

Jones, M. 2013. It's like déjà vu, all over again. In *Where next for local enterprise partnerships?* ed. M. Ward and S. Hardy, 86–95. London: The Smith Institute.

Kay, J. 2016. The economics and politics of manufacturing fetishism. John Kay's personal website, 29 August 2016. Available from: http://www.johnkay.com/2016/08/29/the-economics-and-politics-of-manufacturing-fetishism/. Accessed 30 Aug 2016.

Mahmoud, H. 2014. Foreign aid: development or "de-development"? *Open Democracy*, April 13. Available from: https://www.opendemocracy.net/arab-awakening/hani-mahmoud/foreign-aid-development-or-dedevelopment. Accessed 18 Sept 2016.

Martin, R. 2015. Rebalancing the spatial economy: The challenge for regional theory. *Territory, Politics, Governance* 3 (3): 236–272.

Martin, R., A. Pike, P. Tyler, and B. Gardiner. 2015. *Spatially rebalancing the UK economy: The need for a new policy model.* London: Regional Studies Association. Available from: http://www.regionalstudies.org/uploads/documents/SRTUKE_v16_PRINT.pdf. Accessed 1 Sept 2016.

Matthews, D. 2007. The performance of British manufacturing in the post-war long boom. *Business History* 49 (6): 763–779.

May, T. 2013. 'We will win by being the party for all', speech delivered on 9 March. Available from: http://www.conservativehome.com/platform/2016/07/full-text-of-theresa-mays-speech-we-will-win-by-being-the-party-for-all.html. Accessed 2 Aug 2016.

May, T. 2016a. My vision for Yorkshire's bright future. *Yorkshire Post*, 18 August. Available from: http://www.yorkshirepost.co.uk/news/opinion/theresa-may-my-vision-for-yorkshire-s-bright-future-1-8074726. Accessed 23 Aug 2016.

May, T. 2016b. My plan to build a "Midlands Engine" and create more good jobs in Birmingham and beyond. *The Birmingham Mail*, August 18. Available from: http://www.birminghammail.co.uk/news/midlands-news/theresa-may-plan-build-midlands-11763399. Accessed 23 Aug 2016.

May, T. 2016c. 'We can make Britain a country that works for everyone', speech delivered on 11 July. Available from: http://www.itv.com/news/2016-07-11/what-are-theresa-mays-key-pledges-home-secretary-outlines-her-plan-for-the-future/. Accessed 2 Aug 2016.

Mellor, R. 2002. Hypocritical city: Cycles of urban exclusion. In *City of revolution: Restructuring Manchester*, ed. J. Peck and K. Ward, 214–235. Manchester: Manchester University Press.

Meurs, M., and R. Ranasinghe. 2003. De-development in post-socialism: Conceptual and measurement issues. *Politics and Society* 31 (1): 31–53.

Minford, P. 2016. Brexit will boost our economy and cut the cost of BMWs and even brie. *The Sun*, March 15. Available from: https://www.thesun.co.uk/archives/politics/1086319/brexit-will-boost-our-economy-and-cut-the-cost-of-bmws-and-even-brie/. Accessed 17 Sept 2016.

Office for National Statistics. 2015. Regional gross value added (income approach): December 2015. Available from: http://www.ons.gov.uk/economy/grossvalueaddedgva/bulletins/regionalgrossvalueaddedincomeapproach/december2015#industrial-analysis. Accessed 11 Aug 2016.

Office for National Statistics. 2016a. *UK balance of payments: The pink book, 2016.* Available from: https://www.ons.gov.uk/economy/nationalaccounts/balanceofpayments/bulletins/unitedkingdombalanceofpaymentsthepinkbook/2016. Accessed 11 Aug 2016.

Office for National Statistics. 2016b. *UK index of production: June 2016.* Available from: http://www.ons.gov.uk/economy/economicoutputandproductivity/output/bulletins/indexofproduction/june2016. Accessed 11 Aug 2016.

Office for National Statistics. 2016c. *UK labour market: July 2016.* Available from: https://www.ons.gov.uk/employmentandlabourmarket/peopleinwork/employmentandemployeetypes/bulletins/uklabourmarket/july2016. Accessed 11 Aug 2016.

Office for National Statistics. 2016d. *Workforce jobs by region and industry.* Available from: https://www.ons.gov.uk/employmentandlabourmarket/peopleinwork/employmentandemployeetypes/datasets/workforcejobsbyregionandindustryjobs05. Accessed 12 Aug 2016.

Osborne, G. 2011. 'Budget speech', speech delivered on 23 March. Available from: http://webarchive.nationalarchives.gov.uk/20130129110402/, http://www.hmtreasury.gov.uk/2011budget_speech.htm. Accessed 3 May 2016.

Payne, A. 2005. *The global politics of unequal development.* Palgrave: Basingstoke.

Payne, A., and N. Phillips. 2009. *Development.* London: Polity.

Peck, J., and N. Theodore. 2007. Variegated capitalism. *Human Geography* 31 (6): 731–772.

Pike, A. 2009. De-Industrialization. In *International encyclopaedia of human geography*, ed. R. Kitchin and N. Thrifts, 51–59. Amsterdam: Elsevier.

Pike, A., S. Dawley, and J. Tomaney. 2012. How does manufacturing contribute to UK resilience? Foresight/Government Office for Science Future of Manufacturing Project Evidence Paper 28. Available from: http://www.ncl.ac.uk/curds/documents/PikeDawleyandTomaney2013HowDoesManufacturingContributetoUKResilience-ReportforForesightProgr.pdf. Accessed 11 Aug 2008.

Pike, A., D. Marlow, A. McCarthy, P. O'Brien, and J. Tomaney. 2015. Local institutions and local economic development: The Local Enterprise Partnerships in England, 2010–. *Cambridge Journal of Regions, Economy and Society* 8 (2): 185–204.

Pike, A., M. Coombes, P. O'Brien, and J. Tomaney. 2016a. Austerity states, institutional dismantling and the governance of sub-national economic development: The demise of the Regional Development Agencies in England. *Territory, Politics, Governance*, forthcoming. Available from: http://eprint.ncl.ac.uk/file_store/production/226186/0FAAE69A-66B8-4042-AE09-7F1C83CF5F2E.pdf. Accessed 2 Sept 2016.

Pike, A., A. Rodriguez-Pose, and J. Tomaney. 2016b. Shifting horizons in local and regional development. *Regional Studies*, forthcoming. Available from: http://eprints.lse.ac.uk/67542/. Accessed 7 Sept 2016.

Pike, A., and J. Tomaney. 2009. The state and uneven development: The governance of economic development in England in the post-devolution UK. *Cambridge Journal of Regions, Economy and Society* 2 (1): 13–34.

Piris, J.-C. 2016. *If the UK votes to leave: Seven alternatives to EU membership.* Centre for European Reform. Available from: http://www.cer.org.uk/sites/default/files/pb_piris_brexit_12jan16.pdf. Accessed 12 Aug 2016.

PricewaterhouseCoopers. 2009. *The future of UK manufacturing: Reports of its death are greatly exaggerated.* Available from: https://www.pwc.co.uk/assets/pdf/ukmanufacturing-300309.pdf. Accessed 28 Feb 2014.

Quilter-Pinner, H. 2016. *Devo-health: What and why?* Institute for Public Policy Research. Available from: http://www.ippr.org/files/publications/pdf/devo-health_whatwhy_Aug%202016_spreads.pdf?noredirect=1. Accessed 1 Sept 2016.

Roy, S. 1987. The Gaza Strip: A case of economic de-development. *Journal of Palestine Studies* 17 (1): 56–88.

Rowthorn, R., and K. Coutts. 2013. Deindustrialisation and the balance of payments in advanced economies, Foresight/Government Office for Science Future of Manufacturing Project Evidence Paper 31. Available from: https://www.gov.uk/government/uploads/system/uploads/attachment_data/file/283905/ep31-de-industrialisation-and-balance-of-payments.pdf. Accessed 11 Aug 2016.

Rubinstein, W.D. 1993. *Capitalism, culture and decline in Britain, 1750–1990.* London: Routledge.

Willets, D. 2012. 'Our hi-tech future', speech delivered on 4 January. Available from: https://www.gov.uk/government/speeches/our-hi-tech-future-2. Accessed 3 May 2016.

Williams, K., J. Williams, and D. Thomas. 1983. *Why are the British bad at manufacturing?* London: Routledge.

AUTHOR BIOGRAPHY

Craig Berry is Deputy Director of the Sheffield Political Economy Research Institute at the University of Sheffield. His previous roles include Policy Advisor at HM Treasury, Pensions Policy Officer at the Trades Union Congress, and Head of Policy and Senior Researcher at the International Longevity Centre-UK, and he has taught at the University of Warwick and University of Manchester. He published *Globalisation and Ideology in Britain* in 2011 and *Austerity Politics and UK Economic Policy* in 2015.

CHAPTER 5

Powerhouse of Science? Prospects and Pitfalls of Place-Based Science and Innovation Policies in Northern England

Kieron Flanagan and James Wilsdon

Abstract Science and innovation are increasingly seen by the UK government as central to regional economic development policy, with a new emphasis on 'place' a prominent feature of related policy initiatives. This is reflected in debates over the 'Northern Powerhouse', most visibly through the £235 million investment in the 'Crick of the North' Royce Institute for Advanced Materials Research and Innovation, which is the largest single investment in science in the North of England in a generation. At the same time, public investment in science and innovation is ever more focused within the South-East 'Golden Triangle', with concentration driven by the Research Excellence Framework and by the pulling power of the labour market in London and the South East. This chapter teases apart the rhetoric from the reality of science and innovation investment in the North, ask what decision makers in the North can do to harness science and innovation in support of economic

K. Flanagan (✉)
Alliance Manchester Business School, Manchester, UK
e-mail: kieron.flanagan@manchester.ac.uk

J. Wilsdon
Department of Politics, University of Sheffield, Sheffield, UK
e-mail: J.Wilsdon@sheffield.ac.uk

© The Author(s) 2018
C. Berry and A. Giovannini (eds.), *Developing England's North,*
Building a Sustainable Political Economy: SPERI Research & Policy,
https://doi.org/10.1007/978-3-319-62560-7_5

121

development, and examining the changing role of universities in local political economies.

Keywords Advanced manufacturing · Investment · Northern Powerhouse · Place · Science and innovation · Universities

> We've got an incredible opportunity to change the landscape of British science. I look at London and I see the largest research institute in Europe—the Crick Institute—being built. What's the Crick of the North going to be? Materials science? Nuclear technology? Something else? You tell me. Today I call on the Northern universities to rise to the challenge, and come up with radical, transformative long term ideas for doing even more outstanding science in the North—and we will back you. (George Osborne, 23 June 2014)

Science and innovation are increasingly seen by the UK government as central to regional economic development policy, with a new emphasis on 'place' a prominent feature of related policy initiatives. Accordingly, science and innovation feature strongly in the discourse around the Northern Powerhouse. In this chapter, we unpick the rhetoric from the reality of science and innovation investment in the Northern Powerhouse. We ask whether policymakers will have the appetite to reverse the concentration of investment over recent decades in the London-Oxford-Cambridge 'Golden Triangle', and what decision makers in the North can do to harness science and innovation in support of wider development goals. And we look at the Northern Powerhouse science agenda through the prism of changing scholarly and policy thinking about the roles universities play as hubs for research and innovation, delivery agents for economic development and industrial strategy and as powerful actors in their local political economies.

From the launch of the Northern Powerhouse concept, science and innovation took centre stage. Then Chancellor of the Exchequer George Osborne's speech in June 2014, from which the quote above is taken, was delivered at the Museum of Science and Industry in Manchester, and peppered with references to technologies, old and new. Osborne drew attention to the techno-industrial heritage surrounding him, and went on to identify science and universities as one of four ingredients of his vision for the North's renaissance—alongside transport; creativity and culture; and the devolution of power.

After a decade in which 'impact' has risen in prominence to join 'excellence' as an explicit objective of UK science and innovation policy, 'place' now looks set to do the same (Greenhalgh et al. 2016; HMT/BIS 2014). This shift was signalled in the December 2014 HM Treasury/BIS strategy (*Our Plan for Growth*), developed by Greg Clark MP—in his then combined role as minister for universities, cities and science—and Sir Mark Walport, as Government Chief Scientific Adviser. Money began to follow: most visibly through a £235 million commitment to the Manchester-based Royce Institute for Advanced Materials Research and Innovation, the largest capital investment in science in the North of England in a generation. This was followed by a series of regional science and innovation audits, and further targeted investments.

The resignation of David Cameron as Prime Minister—and the departure of George Osborne—has raised uncertainties about the level of continued government enthusiasm for the Northern Powerhouse. But the inclusion in the November 2016 autumn budget statement of a new £2 billion Industrial Strategy Challenges Fund suggests that place-based research and innovation policy is here to stay under May (Wilsdon et al. 2016). The purposes to which the new fund will be directed forms part of the government's January 2017 consultation on its industrial strategy. But the aspiration to support local and regional economic developments, alongside research excellence and priority technologies, is clear. As the consultation notes:

At present 46 per cent of Research Council and Higher Education Funding Council for England (HEFCE) funding is spent in Oxford, Cambridge and London...We could create new funding streams to support world-class clusters of research and innovation in all parts of the UK....In this way we will use some of the additional R&D funding to help boost growth across the economy, as well as growing it overall. (HM Government 2017)

At the time of writing, Greg Clark is back at the helm as secretary of state in a renamed Department for Business, Energy and Industrial Strategy (BEIS). Sir Mark Walport has recently been announced as the inaugural chief executive of the new £6 billion per annum mega-funding agency UK Research and Innovation. And the release of a new Northern Powerhouse strategy, with 'enterprise and innovation' as one of its five themes, suggests that this aspect of George Osborne's legacy may outlast him (HM Treasury 2016).

THE ROLE OF PLACE IN SCIENCE AND INNOVATION POLICY

Placeless Excellence

To understand the evolution of thinking about the role of place in science and innovation policy, we need to go back several decades. Research and higher education have often played an important part in the narrative and branding of redevelopment plans in several cities—examples include the partially realised Manchester Higher Education Precinct of the 1960s, or the current interest in Knowledge Quarters and Innovation Corridors in cities such as Liverpool, Manchester and Newcastle. But prior to the 2000s, neither cities nor regions were a visible focus of national science and innovation policy (Perry 2008).

One might expect innovation policy to have been more spatially aware, but until recently that has not been the case. In formal terms, policies and funding for science, research and technological innovation have historically been blind to geography. The focus has instead been on allocating public investment to curiosity-driven and problem-oriented research alike on the basis of 'excellence'. This criterion has been enacted through the prospective peer review of project proposals by the research councils, and by the retrospective review of published outputs submitted by universities through the regular cycle of research assessment exercises. The resulting geographical concentration of funds has not historically been seen as a matter for public debate (although private grumbles have of course been expressed).

From the 1980s, the UK government gradually withdrew from direct support for 'near-market' R&D, for largely ideological reasons. Prime Minister Margaret Thatcher (with her own background in industrial research) believed strongly that it was important for the taxpayer to continue to support so-called 'basic' research, but that it was the role of industry to fund 'applied' R&D. Technology policy seen as a subset of industrial policy largely gave way to sector- and place-blind innovation policy, focused on efforts to promote technology transfer and the commercialisation of research findings through the encouragement of academic-industry links and increased patenting, licensing and spin-off activity. This implicit view of universities as factories of potentially exploitable knowledge also reflected the belief—widely held by politicians, funders and university leaders—that research universities had played a decisive role in the development of innovation superclusters in the USA, including Silicon Valley and Boston's Route 128 (Flanagan and Keenan 1998; Nightingale and Coad 2014; Uyarra 2010).

The UK's asymmetric governance has meant that Scotland, Wales and Northern Ireland have had some leeway with regard to science and innovation funding. They were able to establish their own economic development agencies and, after 1992, gained higher education funding bodies. New Labour's devolution accelerated this trend, granting elected assemblies and governments to the devolved nations and introducing administrative regionalism to England.

From its inception, New Labour's regional policy in England ascribed a central role to universities in the delivery of policies for economic and social development (Charles and Benneworth 2001; Smith 2007; Warren et al. 2010). The English Regional Development Agencies (RDAs) became the main delivery vehicle for subnational economic development policies, including responsibility for the regional development funding mechanisms of the European Union. Incentives and funding for knowledge transfer and commercialisation strengthened over the same period, and some RDAs began to promote collaboration and strategic partnerships between universities, businesses and other organisations, aligned to regional social and economic development goals (Kitagawa 2004).

From Regions to City-Regions

The trajectory of this developing 'territorialisation' of English universities was deflected by two developments in the 2000s. First, a controversial ministerial decision in 2000 politicised the spatial distribution of science spending in an unprecedented way. Second, the *city-region* emerged as a competing focus of attention to the larger RDA regions, and became the major focus following the demise of the English RDAs in 2010.

The controversy related to the decision to build a new 'fourth generation' synchrotron source—an advanced radiation source for investigating the structure of biological and non-biological samples—at Harwell in Oxfordshire, rather than replacing the existing national synchrotron facility at Daresbury in Cheshire (midway between Manchester and

Liverpool), where the human and technical capability to design and run such a facility was located. The anger of local and regional stakeholders at this announcement caught the government by surprise, and as Perry (2007) notes, galvanised a new awareness of the uneven pattern of science spending across England. The decision was not reversed, but ministers felt forced to offer a consolation prize, in the shape of a modest regional science and innovation fund, and the creation of a North West Science Council, to develop proposals for future science and innovation activities. Following the North West's lead, and encouraged by the subsequent House of Lords report on 'Science and the RDAs' (House of Lords S&T Committee 2003), the other English RDAs set up similar councils, and the Northern RDAs in particular became active investors in science and innovation activities. Perhaps because resources were limited, or perhaps because of a lack of imagination, much of this activity followed the familiar science park and commercialisation route that the UK had already trod for decades. Meanwhile, the concentration of investment in the Golden Triangle continued through the 2000s.

At the same time, the notion of the *city-region* as a relevant unit of analysis and action was increasingly coming to the fore. The 'knowledge economy' thinking of the time lent itself particularly well to the notion: see for example the influential 2006 Work Foundation report *Ideopolis: Knowledge City-Regions*, and the influence at that time in the UK—as elsewhere—of the work of urban theorists such as Richard Florida (Nathan 2015). This new focus on city-regions gave rise to the 'Science City' initiative (Perry 2008; Wray and Charles 2009). In 2005, six cities across England (Birmingham, Bristol, Manchester, Newcastle, Nottingham and York) were named 'Science Cities'. The intention was to emphasise the potential for science to contribute to local economic growth, but there were no resources attached to this appellation, and it was completely delinked from any other aspect of national research funding.

The incoming coalition government announced the abolition of the English RDAs in 2010. Instead they promoted the formation of Local Enterprise Partnerships (LEPs), typically focused on smaller (often city-regional) geographies. Unlike the RDAs, with their large devolved budget and staff, LEPs were to be bottom-up, private-sector-led partnerships, with no core resources, but an ability to bid for grants from modest central funds (Bentley and Pugalis 2013). Whatever science and innovation policy capacity the RDAs had managed to build up was quickly dispersed. Meanwhile, central government support for applied technologies and innovation, channelled since the late 2000s through the Technology Strategy Board (later renamed Innovate UK), was also coming under criticism, for being geographically skewed towards the South of England. The initial geography of the new network of 'Catapult Centres' (inspired by the application-oriented network of Fraunhofer Institutes in Germany) did little to dispel this perception (see the chapter by Berry in this volume).

In the intervening period, academic and policy thinking about the roles of university and research organisations in the knowledge economy had evolved beyond a simple view of universities as 'knowledge factories' or sources of entrepreneurial spin-off activity, towards more nuanced notions of universities as active engagers, brokers and intermediaries, able to connect different actors across local, national and global networks (Uyarra 2010). Local and regional policymakers and analysts increasingly saw universities as powerful 'anchor organizations', by virtue of their local rootedness (CLES 2015; Ehlenz 2015; Lowe and Feldman 2008). For their part, universities were quick to play up to such expectations, particularly when they came hand-in-hand with public funds or political support—but were sometimes subject to local criticism for failing to live up to their promises (Flanagan et al. forthcoming).

WILL THE REAL POWERHOUSE OF SCIENCE PLEASE STAND UP?

Northern England is home to twenty-three universities, including eight self-professed 'research-intensives' and other more teaching-oriented institutions. The histories of these institutions are often closely entwined with the civic, industrial and commercial development of their cities (Centre for Cities 2015). In 2007, the eight research-intensive universities (Durham, Lancaster, Leeds, Liverpool, Manchester, Newcastle, Sheffield and York) set up the N8 group, to promote strategic collaboration in research.

While it is certainly the case that the N8 universities are globally competitive research institutions, the results of the 2014 Research Excellence Framework show how comprehensively they are outperformed by Golden Triangle institutions in terms of research scale and critical mass (Else 2015). Largely as a result of successive RAE/REF block funding allocations, the share of research funding going to universities in London, Oxford and Cambridge is still increasing: from 42.8 per cent

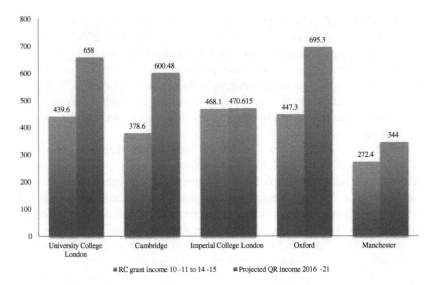

Fig. 5.1   Research Council income (£m) versus HEFCE QR income (£m) for four 'Golden Triangle' institutions plus the University of Manchester. *Data Sources* Times Higher Education survey for 5 year RC data; author's projection based on current HEFCE grant letter for QR

of all government funding allocated in England in 1997–1998 to just over 46 per cent by 2013–2014 (BIS 2015: 9). The main driver of this growing gap is the increased selectivity in quality-related (QR) funding allocations over time. Figure 5.1 compares 5 years of research council allocations and the projected 5-year allocation of QR funding (based on REF results) to four 'golden triangle' institutions and the University of Manchester (as an example of a leading Northern research university).

Sociologist Robert Merton (1968) famously noted that a 'Matthew effect' operates in science, so that prestige attracts rewards, which further increase prestige, and so on. The selectivity in QR funding seems to be out-pacing even the 'natural' Matthew effect that emerges from the decentralised process of peer review involved in the allocation of competitive research council grants. This is unsurprising, as increasing the concentration of university research funding has been an aim of national research assessment since it was first introduced in 1986 (Flanagan and Keenan 1998).

Golden Triangle institutions benefit both from a positive feedback between funding and reputation, and from a geographical agglomeration of research activity, which makes them magnets for the best and brightest from all over the world. In particular, London and Cambridge offer an intensity of opportunities across a single scientific labour market (now labelled the 'London-Stansted-Cambridge Corridor'), which cannot be matched by any city in the North.

The labour market effects of agglomeration are such that, for a potentially mobile upcoming scientist from Barcelona, Boston or Bangalore, it will appear a much smaller personal and professional risk to uproot her career and family to move to one of the best known and most productive clusters of scientific and technological activity in the world, than it would to move to an apparently peripheral Northern city with a single research-intensive university. This calculation may remain the same even when the scientist is fully aware that the quality of her colleagues and facilities will be broadly similar, and that the cost of living will be lower and quality of life higher in the North. The accelerated Matthew effect driven by the selectivity of English QR funding and the labour market effects of agglomeration in the golden triangle are mutually reinforcing. The outcome is that the North's research universities must run harder and harder simply to limit the ground they are losing, as the golden triangle institutions continue to pull away from the pack. One-off initiatives, even on the scale of the Royce Institute (which remains the largest science investment to date under the Northern Powerhouse agenda) barely make a dent, let alone reverse such trends.

A further setback to Northern hopes of a science-driven industrial renaissance has been the decision of the Anglo-Swedish pharmaceutical company AstraZeneca to relocate its main UK R&D facility from its historical base at Alderley Park, just South of Manchester, to a new combined global R&D centre and HQ in Cambridge (Rankin 2013). Local leaders understandably tend to feel great pride and satisfaction in the achievements of 'their university'. However, this thinking can lead to complacency with regard to the relative lack of critical mass in research. So the shock that the supposed 'critical mass' of biomedical research and advanced training in Manchester was not in fact sufficient to retain AstraZeneca has had a similar effect on city-regional actors in the North West to that of the decision a decade earlier to site the Diamond Light Source synchrotron at Harwell, rather than Daresbury.

Furthermore, the Royce Institute typifies the persistent challenges that the North faces with regard to science and innovation. Although presented publicly—and regarded in Whitehall—as the collective response of the N8 universities to Osborne's June 2014 challenge, there have been complaints from other Northern universities that Manchester broke ranks with its fellow N8 institutions to promote the Royce proposal, and that the decision bypassed input from the Research Councils and normal processes of peer review (McLeish 2015). This has dented the trust that has been built painstakingly over recent years, between institutions that have traditionally seen each other as direct competitors.

Another interesting contrast can be drawn with flagship science investments in London, such as the Sir Francis Crick Institute for biomedical research, which opened in 2016. Although the government's commitments to constructing and equipping the Royce and the Crick are in the same ballpark, the Crick's total capital budget, including contributions from charitable funders such as the Wellcome Trust and Cancer Research UK, is around £700 million, so three times larger (Callaway 2015). Furthermore, the Royce will have its main 'hub' in Manchester supplemented by Northern 'spokes' at the Universities of Sheffield, Leeds and Liverpool, and additional golden triangle 'spokes' at Cambridge, Oxford and Imperial College. Perhaps because the latter aspect sits so uneasily with its Northern Powerhouse rhetoric, George Osborne omitted to mention the golden triangle spokes in his initial announcement about the Royce to the House of Commons, in his 2014 autumn budget statement. It is also worth noting that Crick Institute has no spokes at all, let alone in the North. Indeed, when Sir Paul Nurse, the Crick's director, was asked by the *Financial Times* how the new institute would play a 'national' role, he argued that only by being based in London could the Crick play an effective national role (Cookson 2013). His clear implication was that to be located anywhere else would be to accept provincial status.

PLACE-BASED POLICY REDUX

So the picture remains mixed. However, as we shall show, there are signs that the government may be ready to rethink the effects of decades of intensifying concentration in research and innovation funding. We have already noted that the most striking feature of the Coalition's science and innovation strategy, published at the end of 2014 (HMT/BIS 2014), was the emphasis it placed on the role of science and technology in 'place-making'. The subsequent 2015 budget (HMT 2015) went further in identifying a role for science in regional economic development, and inviting 'universities, cities, LEPs [local enterprise partnerships] and businesses to map strengths and identify potential areas of strategic focus for different regions' through a series of 'science and innovation audits'.

The short-lived tenure of Sajid Javid as Secretary of State for Business, Innovation and Skills, following the 2015 election, seemed to herald a retreat from industrial strategy and a tentative interest in the connections between science, innovation and place. The prevailing rhetoric reverted to emphasise sector- and space-neutral innovation policy and an industrial 'approach', over proactive strategy (Rigby 2015). Javid's most visible enthusiasm was for cost cutting, and he called in the consultancy firm McKinsey to develop a 'BIS 2020' plan to slash budgets, staff numbers and the number of BIS-funded public bodies (Wilsdon 2015). This included the closure of the BIS office in Sheffield, its largest anywhere outside London, with a loss of 250 skilled civil service jobs—hardly a vote of confidence in the Northern Powerhouse (Perraudin 2016). Following the post-EU referendum changes at the top of government in summer 2016, however, which saw the return of Greg Clark as Secretary of State to the renamed Department for Business, Energy and Industrial Strategy (BEIS), the agenda that he set out in the *Our Plan for Growth* strategy has been dusted off. Place-based policymaking is once again in the ascendant.

One of the commitments in that 2014 strategy—for an initial series of regional 'science and innovation audits'—has now been delivered (BEIS 2016), and a second wave is on the way. It remains to be seen how these audits will inform future science and innovation spending. The LEPs appear to have interpreted the task primarily as producing a brochure listing their science and innovation assets, rather than of conducting a detailed warts-and-all analysis of strengths, weaknesses and opportunities (McKenzie 2016). The audits come at the same time as a new wave of devolution deals for metro cities, raising the possibility that science and innovation may become an area of focus for emerging city-regional authorities. And the January 2017 industrial strategy Green Paper consultation (HM Government 2017) seems open to the possibility of some tentative regionalisation of science and innovation spending in England.

However, the policy of geography-blind, excellence-based science policy and funding remains dominant. The imminent reorganisation of the UK Research Councils, Innovate UK and the research functions of HEFCE into a single, powerful body called UK Research and Innovation complicates the picture (BIS 2016; Wilsdon 2016), not least because ministers have had to make assurances about autonomy and excellence in order to smooth the passage of the enabling legislation (still under debate in the House of Lords, at the time of writing). Assuming all is well UKRI will formally come into existence on 1 April 2018. It will be led by the other architect of the 2014 *Our plan for growth* strategy—Sir

Mark Walport—who will move from his current role as chief scientific adviser, to become UKRI's inaugural CEO (Flanagan 2017).

QR funding will also fall under the new UKRI structure, and debates are now intensifying about the design of the next Research Excellence Framework (scheduled for 2021). Following a review by Lord Stern, a consultation is underway about reforms intended to reduce the burdens of the REF and minimise its unintended effects (HEFCE 2016). But while the consultation raises lots of important issues around the design and operation of a national assessment exercise, it does not question the philosophy behind how the REF scores are used to drive increasing concentration of funding in London and the South East. So far, there has been surprisingly little public debate about the QR formula and whether selectivity may have gone too far.

How decision-making will operate across the new consolidated funding body is not yet clear. One of the strongest arguments that government has made in favour of UKRI's creation is that it will enable more strategic, system-wide analysis of the opportunities for closer alignment between research strengths and economic, industrial and social priorities—with the new industrial strategy one prominent strand of this (BIS 2016; Kingman 2016). At the same time, the notional arms-length relationship between ministers and the UKRI board and chief executive means that some decisions (for example, over the QR formula) will be made a step further away from wider government policymaking on industrial strategy and spatial rebalancing. Meanwhile, rumoured discord within the N8 group of research universities, the resistance of some local authorities to joining forces in combined authorities and the continued tendency for some local leaders to be captured by the interests of 'their universities' all pose significant challenges to the development of a distinctive Northern agenda for science and innovation.

Conclusion: Taking Back Control?

The centrality of science and innovation to the original vision of the Northern Powerhouse illustrates both Osborne's genuine enthusiasm, and a significant body of empirical evidence in support of the linkages between universities, research, innovation and regional economic growth. Science and innovation investment is rarely seen through a party-political lens: it is typically presented as a straightforward investment in the future. It also delivers newsworthy announcements and photography opportunities at a fraction of the cost of transforming local or regional transport infrastructure.

The emerging industrial strategy (and its linked £2 billion challenge fund), the creation of UKRI, and the active support of ministers such as Greg Clark, suggests that place-based policies for science and innovation will continue to garner political attention and focus. Whether there will be any significant shift in investment patterns across England is harder to predict. The design of UKRI certainly gives Walport and his board the scope to make such changes, either through further large capital investments or through tweaks to the QR formula in the next REF. At the same time, wider uncertainties in the research landscape—particularly linked to Brexit and a potential reduction in European sources of funding (which currently amount to around £850m of research grants to the UK each year, not to mention science and innovation projects supported with EU regional development funds)—may overwhelm modest moves towards a place-based rebalancing of investment. The additional investment promised through the Industrial Strategy Challenges Fund may end up simply plugging a hole created elsewhere in research budgets by a 'hard' Brexit.

In the North, greater critical mass is required for science and innovation to deliver substantial change. Worsening regional disparities in terms of science activity need to be addressed, and this cannot be done through one-off initiatives such as the Royce; however, impressive these are on their own terms. Instead, serious reforms are required to the funding policies that underlie these disparities. This means actively reversing, or at the very least halting, the explicit drive for greater concentration of research funding that has characterised English research policy for decades. Will UKRI really have the appetite to take resources from the Golden Triangle, and give them to the North? As Dame Athene Donald wrote recently, 'squaring politics, geography and excellence, in a way that satisfies both politicians and the wider research community, will be no mean feat' (Donald 2017).

Other crucial success factors for science and innovation are common to all elements of the Northern Powerhouse. Endlessly discussed but slow-to-progress inter-Northern public transport improvements hold some potential to replicate the labour market effects generated by the Golden Triangle agglomeration of research activity, at least between some cities. At the same time, regional and local leaders in the North need to be more realistic about what investment in research can and cannot buy them. The persistent yet misguided belief that the growth of superclusters such as Silicon Valley and Route 128 is the direct result of the exploitation of research done in top universities has resulted in what we might call the 'closed system fallacy'. This suggests that, because scientific discovery A takes place in country/region/city/university A, it follows that it should be commercialised in the same place. Yet, however strong Northern science is, there will always be far more scientific and technological R&D going on elsewhere. Though scientific and technological knowledge is often 'sticky', it is produced in complex global collaborations, and flows rapidly from node to node. Proximity is important—but there are other kinds of proximity, in addition to spatial proximity. There is no reason to suppose that discovery, commercialisation and innovation should normally happen in the same place. Indeed the odds are against it.

What research strengths buy for any region is the capacity to understand, evaluate, absorb and use knowledge that has been developed elsewhere (Bhidé 2010). But these strengths come with no guarantee of economic, industrial or commercial success: they are primarily an entry ticket into global science and technology networks. The North needs to attract and retain more talented researchers from across the UK and beyond, Brexit notwithstanding. The lower cost of living is not going to be enough to counter the Golden Triangle effect—even as costs soar there. If the funding formula that drives the Golden Triangle effect is not loosened, then critical mass must be built in other ways. Improving transport links between Northern university cities could help, but political leaders must also avoid letting their understandable pride in the local research university lead to their capture by that institution.

Courageous leaders could, for instance, work to attract top foreign universities to open research and teaching facilities in their cities. Legitimate concerns have been raised about the changes being introduced through the current Higher Education & Research Bill (Curry 2016). But the government's interest in allowing 'new entrants' into English higher education need not start and stop at private, for-profit degree mills. This may be made more difficult by Brexit—but surely not impossible. EU universities, US universities and even Scottish universities might all be enticed to invest in research and teaching activities in the

North with the right incentives. This could be one step towards building a genuine powerhouse of science in the North.

References

BEIS. 2016. *Science and innovation audits: Wave 1 summary reports*. London: Department for Business, Energy and Industrial Strategy.

Bentley, G., and L. Pugalis. 2013. New directions in economic development: Localist policy discourses and the Localism Act. *Local Economy* 28 (3): 257–274.

Bhidé, A. 2010. *The venturesome economy: How innovation sustains prosperity in a more connected world*. New York: Princeton University Press.

BIS. 2015. *Public research and innovation expenditure: Geographic breakdown of public research and innovation expenditure*. London: Department for Business, Innovation and Skills.

BIS. 2016. *Case for the creation of UK research and innovation*. London: Department for Business, Innovation and Skills.

Callaway, E. 2015. Sir Paul's Cathedral: Europe's superlab. *Nature* 552 (7557): 406–408.

Centre for Cities. 2015. *Northern powerhouse factsheet: Key figures on the city regions in the Northern Powerhouse*. London: Centre for Cities.

Charles, D.R., and P. Benneworth. 2001. Are we realizing our potential? Joining up science and technology policy in English regions. *Regional Studies* 35 (1): 73–79.

CLES. 2015. *Creating a good local economy: The role of anchor institutions*. Manchester: Centre for Local Economic Strategies.

Cookson, C. 2013. Building on London's scientific tradition. *Financial Times*, December 4, 2013. https://www.ft.com/content/9b1b2222-55bb-11e3-96f5-00144feabdc0. Accessed 7 Mar 2017.

Curry, S. 2016. Why the Higher Education and Research Bill must be amended. *The Guardian*, October 18, 2016. https://www.theguardian.com/science/occams-corner/2016/oct/18/higher-education-research-bill-needs-amended Accessed 7 Mar 2017.

Donald, A. 2017. All eyes are on Sir Mark Walport, the new supremo of UK science. *The Guardian*, February 9, 2017. https://www.theguardian.com/science/political-science/2017/feb/09/all-eyes-are-on-sir-mark-walport-the-new-supremo-of-uk-science. Accessed 7 March 2017.

Ehlenz, M.M. 2015. Neighborhood revitalization and the anchor institution. *Urban Affairs Review* 52 (5): 714–50.

Else, H. 2015. N8 remains optimistic despite REF slide. *Times Higher Education*, April 9, 2015. https://www.timeshighereducation.com/news/n8-remains-optimistic-despite-ref-slide/2019541.article. Accessed 7 Mar 2017.

Flanagan, K., and M.P. Keenan. 1998. Trends in UK science policy. In *Science and technology in the United Kingdom*, ed. P.N. Cunningham. London: Cartermill. https://www.research.manchester.ac.uk/portal/files/32298306/ FULL_TEXT.PDF. Accessed 7 Mar 2017.

Flanagan, K. 2017. The six billion dollar man. *Research Fortnight*, February 15, 2017. http://www.researchresearch.com/news/article/?articleId=1365986. Accessed 7 Mar 2017.

Flanagan, K., E. Uyarra, and F. Kitagawa. 2017[Forthcoming]. The university as a city-regional governance actor: The case of the University of Manchester in Greater Manchester. In *The urban university and the knowledge economy: New spaces of interaction*, ed. P. Ingallina and D. Charles. London: Routledge.

Greenhalgh, T., J. Raftery, S. Hanney, and M. Glover. 2016. Research impact: a narrative review. *BMC Medicine* 14 (1): 78. doi:10.1186/s12916-016-0620-8.

HEFCE. 2016. *Consultation on the second research excellence framework*. Bristol: Higher Education Funding Council for England.

HM Government. 2017. *Building our industrial strategy*. London: HM Government.

HM Treasury. 2016. *Northern Powerhouse Strategy*. London: HM Treasury.

HM Treasury and BIS. 2014. *Our plan for growth: Science and innovation*. London: HM Treasury and Department for Business, Innovation and Skills.

HM Treasury. 2015. *Summer budget*. London: HM Treasury.

House of Lords. 2003. *Science and the RDAs: Setting the regional agenda: Fifth report of the house of lords select committee on science and technology*. London: House of Lords Select Committee on Science and Technology.

Kingman, J. 2016. UK research and innovation: "nine brains in one body". *Times Higher Education*, June 2, 2016. https://www.timeshighereduca-tion.com/comment/uk-research-and-innovation-nine-brains-in-one-body. Accessed 7 Mar 2017.

Kitagawa, F. 2004. Universities and regional advantage: Higher education and innovation policies in English regions. *European Planning Studies* 12 (6): 835–852.

Lowe, N., and M. Feldman. 2008. Constructing entrepreneurial advantage: Consensus building, technological uncertainty and emerging industries. *Cambridge Journal of Regions, Economy Society* 1 (2): 265–284.

McKenzie, L. 2016. Regional science audits "lacking in hard data". *Research Fortnight*, November 23, 2016.

McLeish, T. 2015. New science policy initiatives threaten to destroy UK's research excellence. *The Conversation*, January 13, 2015. https://theconver-sation.com/new-science-policy-initiatives-threaten-to-destroy-uks-research-excellence-36147. Accessed 14 Feb 2017.

Merton, R.K. 1968. The Matthew effect in science. *Science* 159: 56–62.

Nathan, M. 2015. After Florida: Towards an economics of diversity. *European Urban and Regional Studies* 22 (1): 3–19.

Nightingale, P., and A. Coad. 2014. The myth of the science park economy. *DEMOS Quarterly*, April 23, 2014. https://quarterly.demos.co.uk/article/issue-2/innovation-and-growth/. Accessed 7 Mar 2017.

Osborne, G. 2014. We need a Northern Powerhouse. Speech delivered in Manchester on June 23, 2014. https://www.gov.uk/government/speeches/chancellor-we-need-a-northern-powerhouse. Accessed 21 Feb 2017.

Perraudin, F. 2016. BIS confirms Sheffield office will close with jobs moving to London. *The Guardian*, May 26, 2016. https://www.theguardian.com/politics/2016/may/26/department-business-innovation-skills-confirms-sheffield-office-close-jobs-moving-london. Accessed 7 Mar 2017.

Perry, B. 2007. The multi-level governance of science policy in England. *Regional Studies* 41: 1051–1067.

Perry, B. 2008. Academic knowledge and urban development: Theory, policy and practice. In *Knowledge-Based Urban Development: Planning and Applications in the Information Era*, ed. T. Yigitcanlar, K. Velibeyoglu, and S. Baum, 21–41. London: IGI Global.

Rankin, J. 2013. AstraZeneca's move south will leave the north-west without a vital element. *The Observer*, March 31, 2013. https://www.theguardian.com/business/2013/mar/31/astra-zeneca-move-south-north-west-vital-element. Accessed 7 Mar 2017.

Rigby, E. 2015. Sajid Javid raises doubts over industrial policy. *Financial Times*. July 1, 2015. https://www.ft.com/content/eda7ebb6-1f44-11e5-aa5a-398b2169cf79. Accessed 7 Mar 2017.

Smith, H.L. 2007. Universities, innovation, and territorial development: A review of the evidence. *Environment and Planning C: Government and Policy* 25: 98–114.

Uyarra, E. 2010. Conceptualizing the regional roles of universities, implications and contradictions. *European Planning Studies* 18: 1227–1246.

Warren, L., F. Kitagawa, and M. Eatough. 2010. Developing the knowledge economy through university linkages: An exploration of RDA strategies through case studies of two English regions. *International Journal of Entrepreneurship and Innovation* 11 (4): 293–306.

Wilsdon, J. 2015. Sajid Javid's blueprint for BIS heightens fears for research funding. *The Guardian*, October 1, 2015. https://www.theguardian.com/science/political-science/2015/oct/01/sajid-javids-blueprint-for-bis-heightens-fears-for-research-funding. Accessed 7 Mar 2013.

Wilsdon, J. 2016. UKRI if you want to: How to read the new research landscape. *Wonkhe*, May 18, 2016. http://wonkhe.com/blogs/analysis-ukri-if-you-want-to-how-to-read-the-new-research-funding-landscape/. Accessed 15 Feb 2017.

Wilsdon, J., K. Flanagan, and S. Westlake. 2016. What will an extra £4.7 billion do for UK science and innovation? *The Guardian*, November 24, 2016.

https://www.theguardian.com/science/political-science/2016/nov/24/autumn-statement-what-will-an-extra-47-billion-do-for-uk-science-and-innovation. Accessed 7 Mar 2017.
Work Foundation. 2006. *Ideopolis: Manchester Case Study.* London: Work Foundation.
Wray, F., and D. Charles. 2009. *Science Fiction? Science Cities in an International Context: Report to NESTA.* Newcastle: KITE, Newcastle University.

Authors' Biography

Kieron Flanagan is Senior Lecturer in Science and Technology Policy at the University of Manchester's Manchester Business School. He has published widely on regional development, innovation and science policy, in leading academic journals such as *Science and Public Policy, Environment and Planning C: Government and Policy,* and *European Planning Studies.*

James Wilsdon is Professor of Research Policy in the University of Sheffield's Department of Politics, where he also serves as Faculty Director of Impact and Engagement. His research interests include research and innovation policy, and the role of evidence and expertise in policymaking, particularly the politics and practice of scientific advice. His previous roles include Professor of Science and Democracy at the University of Sussex's Science Policy Research Unit, Director of Science Policy at the Royal Society, and Head of Science and Innovation at Demos. He is also Director of the Nexus Network, an ESRC-funded initiative to link research and policy across food, energy, water and the environment.

PART II

Place, City-Regional Governance and Local Politics

CHAPTER 6

The Northern Powerhouse Meets the Cities and Local Growth Agenda: Local Economic Policymaking and Agglomeration in Practice

Nick Gray, Lee Pugalis and Danny Dickinson

Abstract A policy canon has emerged over recent years which contends that decentralised arrangements are a primary means to address long-standing spatial inequalities. This new conventional wisdom, which frequently portrays cities and metropolitan areas as 'economic engines', has gained substantial national and international traction. Often encapsulated by the UK Government's amorphous Cities and Local Growth agenda, but sometimes positioned as a standalone approach, the Northern Powerhouse is the most high-profile policy episode in a fast-developing

N. Gray (✉)
Newcastle Business School, Northumbria University, Newcastle, UK
e-mail: n.gray@northumbria.ac.uk

L. Pugalis
Institute for Public Policy and Governance, University of Technology Sydney, Sydney, Australia
e-mail: Lee.Pugalis@uts.edu.au

D. Dickinson
Newcastle City Council, Newcastle, UK
e-mail: daniel.dickinson@newcastle.gov.uk

© The Author(s) 2018   141
C. Berry and A. Giovannini (eds.), *Developing England's North*,
Building a Sustainable Political Economy: SPERI Research & Policy,
https://doi.org/10.1007/978-3-319-62560-7_6

story of decentralisation in pursuit of (city-centric) economic growth. This chapter draws upon empirical work to consider whether the current approach to subnational development represents a serious, coherent and sustained attempt to begin to close the economic gap between the North and the South. We examine the recent evolution of Cities and Local Growth and the Northern Powerhouse in the context of current debates around agglomeration economics, looking specifically at ambiguities of scale around the Northern Powerhouse, the kind of policies emergent at the local level, and local perceptions of central government intentions for subnational development policy.

Keywords Agglomeration · City-region · Devolution · Economic growth · Governance · Northern Powerhouse

The slow recovery from the 2008 economic downturn has highlighted (growing) spatial disparities in the UK, with the North falling further behind the South. This has been accompanied by renewed popular interest in subnational development policy (albeit often referred to as 'localism'), heighted further by the UK referendum decision to leave the EU and subsequent debates around 'left behind' places (Goodwin and Heath 2016). A policy canon has emerged, which contends that decentralised arrangements are a primary means to address long-standing spatial inequalities alongside increasing democratic participation and accountability (Goodwin et al. 2012; Gray and Pugalis 2016). This new conventional wisdom, which frequently portrays cities and metropolitan areas as 'economic engines', has gained substantial national and international traction (see for example World Bank 2009; Glaeser 2011). Often encapsulated by the UK Government's amorphous cities and local growth agenda (hereafter referred to as CLOG), but sometimes positioned as a standalone (and presumably complimentary) approach, the 'Northern Powerhouse' is the most high-profile policy episode in a fast-developing story of decentralisation in pursuit of (city-centric) economic growth. First mentioned by the Chancellor George Osborne in 2014, the Northern Powerhouse is framed as *the* meta-strategy that will begin to resolve the long-standing, entrenched and growing spatial economic imbalance in England. The central narrative, we suggest, rests upon the notions of agglomeration economics and locally designed policies. The premise of policymakers is that this will 'unleash' economic growth potential in the North of England and, consequently, engender economic 'rebalancing' between the North and South (Pugalis and Townsend 2012).

In this chapter we consider whether the current approach to subnational development represents a serious, coherent and sustained attempt to begin to close the economic gap between the North and the South. In doing so, we investigate the evolution of CLOG in the context of cities/city-regions in the North of England and, more specifically, we examine the somewhat nebulous concept of the Northern Powerhouse and its relationship with the broader CLOG policy 'framework'. In order to do so, we analyse current scholarly debates concerned with agglomeration economics that appear to influence the contours and character of CLOG and the Northern Powerhouse policies (see also the chapter by Martin and Gardiner in this volume). To achieve this, we draw upon empirical work to explore local and national actors' experiences and understanding of CLOG and the Northern Powerhouse (and their interrelationships). In the course of the research we conducted 40 semi-structured interviews with stakeholders in the North of England and with Whitehall civil servants. Interviewees included local councillors and officers, Local Enterprise Partnership board members and executives, leaders of Combined Authorities and senior officers, university representatives, and Chambers of Commerce officers.

We find a degree of confusion and wariness among local and national policymakers particularly in terms of central government's objectives and political motives around the Northern Powerhouse. Our research findings also highlight that, while there is significant enthusiasm for what is perceived as a city-focused agenda to boost the economy of Northern England, there is no explicit 'Northern' focus, spatial sensitivity or geographic granularity emanating from the CLOG policy framework. Moreover, the notion of the Northern Powerhouse has limited substance in the formal workings of government, and we draw attention to the notable lack of institutional substance and coherence of this initiative. Therefore, we characterise the Northern Powerhouse as a *piggyback initiative* that has to a large extent (and rather effectively) sponged a variety of related, partially relevant and, even, unrelated policies, interventions and funding announcements. We conclude that subnational policy, as manifest in CLOG and the Northern Powerhouse, is distinctively disorderly in its approach which, together with relatively austere funding, limits the development of place-specific governance and policy and is unlikely to make a significant impact on rebalancing the economy.

The chapter is organised into three sections. First, we examine the policy background to the emergence of CLOG and the Northern Powerhouse, drawing out some of their distinctive themes and highlighting key points in their development. Second, we explore the objective of rebalancing in the context of the key idea of agglomeration, looking specifically at ambiguities of scale, the kind of policy emergent at the local level, and local perceptions of central government's intentions for CLOG and the Northern Powerhouse. We conclude with some remarks on the tensions and confusion within current subnational policy and suggest some future avenues for research.

THE EMERGENCE OF CITIES AND LOCAL GROWTH POLICY AND THE NORTHERN POWERHOUSE

Spatial economic inequalities in the UK are exceptionally pronounced and exacerbating (Martin et al. 2016; McCann 2016). Successive UK governments have attempted to devise 'regionalised' structures and regional development policies to promote growth outside of London and the greater South East (Pugalis and Townsend 2012; Pugalis et al. 2016), the most recent being the CLOG policy agenda incorporating or running alongside the Northern Powerhouse initiative (and other mooted 'engines' and 'powerhouses'), and intended to incorporate the place-based characteristics of 'localism' and 'regionalism'. However, despite a period of relatively strong growth in Northern regions and approaching a century of regional development policy, spatial economic imbalances in the UK remain significant and in recent decades have increased more quickly than in other major European Countries (Martin et al. 2016). Associated with these economic imbalances, the UK is one of the most politically and fiscally centralised countries within the OECD. In the UK, just 1.7 per cent of tax as percentage of GDP is set at the local or regional level, compared with an OECD average of 8.9 per cent (O'Brien et al. 2014). UK spatial disparities in the UK have long been notable for (although not restricted to) the English North–South divide, with the economic gap between London and the South East, and the North of England stretching back until at least the 1920's. Persistent imbalances in terms of GVA and employment growth have accumulated over time, which tend to widen during recoveries and booms and have a North–South pattern (Gardiner et al. 2013).

CLOG and the Northern Powerhouse follow nearly a century of regional development policy in the UK. The post-war years were dominated by redistributive 'spatial Keynesian' regional policy with government seeking to actively disperse employment throughout the country. Since this period, regional development policy has continued to evolve in geohistorically distinct ways, but the UK, such as many advanced economies, has seen a broad shift away from central planning with one characteristic being the 'entrepreneurial turn' (Harvey 1989) in urban and regional development wherein territorial governments and public–private partnerships assume responsibility for generating employment and investment. The long period of growth during the 1990s until the mid-2000s saw a focus on city and urban regeneration and talk of a Northern 'urban renaissance' alongside the emergence of policies around skills, business formation and innovation aimed to boost endogenous growth in regions. Central to this were the Regional Development Agencies (RDAs) alongside the pan-Northern initiative known as the 'Northern Way' (Goodchild and Hickman 2006). There were also attempts to build partnerships at functional geographies in multi-area agreements which were often associated with early efforts to establish 'city-regions', often matching the geography of current combined authorities. Regional Development Agencies were subject to contested criticisms from the 2010–2015 Conservative/Liberal Democrat coalition government, who lamented them for being inflexible, overambitious, expensive, unaccountable, top-down, bureaucratic, configured to inappropriate geographies, and failed in their objectives, particularly the aim of reducing regional economic imbalances (Pike et al. 2016a; Pugalis 2011a). Based on this reading, we suggest that CLOG and the Northern Powerhouse, in part, developed out of this critique but, as we will make the case later in this chapter, it is questionable whether they are more likely to achieve the key objective of reducing spatial imbalance.

The Cities and Local Growth Policy Agenda

CLOG emerged from 2010 onwards (Business Innovation and Skills (BIS) and Communities and Local Government (CLG) 2010; Cable and Pickles 2010; Clarke 2010; HM Government 2010b, 2011) amidst an economic distressed global context and national austerity, in what can be viewed as a restless search to 'fix' spatial disparities in England, most strikingly between the North of England and London/the greater South

East. The approach remains characteristically ad hoc (Pike et al. 2016b; Pugalis 2010, 2011a, b), with key ideas and initiatives dispersed over numerous documents, memos, letters, articles and ministerial statements (Table 6.1 for a timeline of key developments), but a key mechanism appears to be a preference for deal-making (exemplified by City, Growth and Devolution Deals). The deals, which can be conceptualised as 'place-based' deals (Pugalis 2015), are conditional agreements to devolve funding and power to subnational governance institutions, including Local Enterprise Partnerships (LEPs), combined authorities and, more recently, combined authorities led by an elected mayor. Deal-making, particularly devolution deals, is often promoted as a key policy means of 'rebalancing' and accelerating local growth.

One of the first acts in implementing CLOG involved inviting local areas to form LEPs. There was initially very little guidance, with one of the few prescriptions being that the private sector should take the lead. Since then, guidance, funding and responsibilities have slowly increased and LEPs began to solidify with a small, but significant, number of staff and growing resources (Pike et al. 2013; Pugalis et al. 2015). From the outset, Government favoured cities in the applications of CLOG initiatives with, for example, the eight English Core Cities taking priority in the first wave of City Deals (HM Government 2011), with a second wave and a number of one-off deals taking the total to 30. The deals offered packages of funding and decision-making powers, such as transport infrastructure investment and fiscal incentives to promote development in return for cities agreeing to specific targets, typically around jobs or new businesses.

In 2014, LEPs submitted their strategic economic plans to Government to come into effect from April 2015 (and which have subsequently been updated). In theory, these plans have the potential to provide a long-term local development strategy, but were also intended to provide the basis for negotiating growth deals with central government and interviews with LEP representatives revealed that the strategic aspirations codified in plans were side-lined during 'negotiations' with central government preoccupied with 'shovel ready' capital infrastructure projects (Pugalis et al. 2016). At the same time, new local government arrangements, including combined authorities, began to emerge in parallel with LEPs (or in some cases subsuming or incorporating the LEP into their institutional arrangements as an advisory body). In some places, city deals were also evolving; in some cases tessellating with

Table 6.1 Key points in the evolution of the CLOG and Northern Powerhouse agendas

2010	Publication of the Local Growth white paper (*Local growth: Realising every place's potential*) which confirmed the first wave of LEPs
2011	Localism Act passed
	Government instigates a number of loosely related ad hoc growth initiatives: Regional Growth Fund, Growing Places Fund, Enterprise Zones
	Greater Manchester Combined Authority created
	Cross-departmental Cities Policy Unit created
	The Government publishes *Unlocking Growth in Cities*, introducing proposals for city deals (initially constrained to the eight 'core cities' of England)
2012	City deals for the eight core cities agreed; elements of some of the deals apply to the wider LEP areas of which the core cities are part
2013	City deals wave 2 begins
	RDAs operationally closed
	The Government publishes "Growth Deals Initial Guidance for Local Enterprise Partnerships" with a deadline of March 2014 for the submission of proposals
2014	All 39 LEPs submit their Strategic Economic Plans to Government
	Combined Authorities are established in Liverpool City-Region, Sheffield City-Region, North East and West Yorkshire
	Chancellor George Osborne makes "Northern Powerhouse" speech in Manchester
	The last of 18 second wave City Deals completed
	First allocations of Local Growth Deals announced
	Greater Manchester Combined Authority devolution agreement—new powers and responsibilities and a directly elected mayor for the metropolitan area
2015	An additional £1 billion for growth deals over the period 2016–2021
	General election: Election of a Conservative Government
	Chancellor announced city-centric devolution plan for England
	Chancellor's Comprehensive Spending Review; by then virtually all English Local Authorities have to formed groups which have applied to central government for a devolution agreement
	Provisional devolution deals announced for Cornwall, Sheffield, North East, Tees Valley, West Midlands, and Liverpool
2016	Provisional devolution deals announced for East Anglia, Greater Lincolnshire, and West of England
	Cities and Local Government Devolution Act passed
	Third Round of Local Growth Fund announced
	UK votes to leave the European Union; George Osborne leaves post as Chancellor
	LEPs produce revised Strategic Economic Plans
	Autumn Statement 2016 sees publication of a Northern Powerhouse Strategy
2017	The third round of Local Growth Fund allocates more money per head to Northern LEP areas with confirmed mayoral devolution deals

(continued)

Table 6.1   (continued)

Several devolution deals remain stalled with notable delays in Northern 'core city' areas; Leeds remains on the drawing board, Sheffield is delayed because of legal action, and the North East deal has been withdrawn and possibly negotiated at a new geography

other institutional geographies, such as LEPs (for example, in Greater Manchester), whereas in other cases new or alternative institutional geographies were preferred (for example, in Newcastle and Gateshead).

In May 2015, the newly elected Conservative government announced legislation related to cities and devolution, which was subsequently enacted as the Cities and Local Government Devolution Act 2016; providing the legislative scope to decentralise responsibilities to cities and local authority areas, or more specifically, city-regions in the form of Combined Authorities led by a directly elected 'metro-mayors' (Gains 2016). This built, at least, rhetorically, on the metropolitan focus of the decentralisation agenda evident in initiatives such as city deals, although the purported benefits of devolution would be theoretically available to any part of England. The strong cities focus in UK subnational development policy is influenced by work in the field of New Economic Geography and New Urban Economic exemplified in work by, for example, Krugman (1998) and Glaeser (2011). The notion of a Cities and Local Government Devolution Act is a continuation of a theme visible in CLOG since 2010 (Hildreth and Bailey 2013), although the ongoing interest in urban agglomeration has been, in part, promoted by individual and groupings of city-regions, think-tanks and commissions (see for example Manchester Independent Economic Review 2009; City Growth Commission 2014) invoking boosterist tones and claims, such as 'Unleashing Metro Growth' (City Growth Commission 2014; see also Haughton et al. 2014).

The Northern Powerhouse Initiative

Whilst 'rebalancing' was deployed as a key political trope immediately after the 2010 general election (Pugalis and Townsend 2012), there was a lack of specificity and spatial awareness in many of the Government's initiatives related to CLOG; a prime example being the Regional Growth

Fund. It was not until 2014, that policy vocabulary referring to a 'Northern Powerhouse' began to gain traction. This was given impetus by a speech by the then Chancellor of the Exchequer, George Osborne (2014), in which he posited the idea of a major agglomeration in the North of England:

> The last census found that the average commute of someone who travels into London from outside is 40 miles. If you make a circle of the same distance, and *centre it here on Manchester*, you'd have a catchment area that takes in Leeds, Sheffield and Liverpool, Lancashire, Cheshire and Yorkshire, and contains ten million people – more than Tokyo, New York or London. An area containing nearly two million graduates. A huge pool of talent. (Osborne 2014, *emphasis added*)

Over subsequent years, the Northern Powerhouse has remained prominent in national policy rhetoric, including a green paper on UK industrial strategy (BEIS 2017), a Northern Powerhouse Strategy (HMT 2016) and an independent review of 'Northern education' (Weller 2016). In a timely paper, Lee (2016) argues that the notion of a Northern Powerhouse has a solid theoretical and empirical base in new economic geography and urban economics (what Martin (2015) has collectively termed the new spatial economics), which provides a rationale for public intervention to facilitate agglomeration in the North. Identifying the key 'ingredients' of the Northern Powerhouse to include transport, science and innovation, political decentralisation, and art and culture, Lee questions the substance of the Northern Powerhouse, arguing that it risks being more of a brand than a concerted development strategy. Interestingly, Lee identifies the Northern Way as an institutional antecedent of the Northern Powerhouse. It is a point that finds some support through our own empirical investigations, which reveals that the principles of a pan-northern strategy to address distinct 'Northern' issues (and also exploit distinct 'Northern' opportunities, strengths and capabilities) retains some advocates among Northern policymakers.

> I think we can cooperate. We've shown that we can ... It is happening more and more but we need to make sure it happens within a structure that is a Northern structure. (Councillor, Yorkshire)

In summary, CLOG emerged under the coalition government as the latest approach purporting to address long-standing regional economic disparities in England, couched in terms of 'rebalancing'. Place-based deals, with a state spatial focus on core city/city-regions framed as key 'drivers' of growth, are a primary element of CLOG. The Northern Powerhouse emerged later, generating enthusiasm with its Northern and urban focus, despite some reservations about it substance as a development strategy. In the next section we will analyse how scholarly debates concerned with agglomeration economics appear to influence the contours and character of CLOG and Northern Powerhouse policies.

AGGLOMERATION ECONOMICS AND THE CITIES AGENDA

The spatial selectivity of central government has tended to favour cities and city-regions (which are often referred to in policy documents in an interchangeable manner) in promoting subnational growth, particularly in the form of the 'core cities' of local authorities. The core cities, and in some cases their partner local authorities, were the first to be invited to negotiate city deals as part of the 'first wave'. As such, we can situate the urban focus of CLOG and the Northern Powerhouse in the context of the important contemporary policy debate between place-based and space-neutral development paradigms, and their approach to agglomeration economies (Barca et al. 2012). In its purest form, an agglomeration-orientated, space-neutral approach considers the spatial targeting of policy support and services in lagging regions to be an inefficient option (Gill 2010), suggesting that such policies have failed in the past to resolve problems of spatial inequality and, in fact, are likely to be economically inefficient at the level of the whole (national) economy (World Bank 2009). Instead, it is prescribed that policies should be generally applicable and broadly supply-side–typically involving investment in skills and infrastructure–intended to enhance mobility and connectivity in order to improve access to economic opportunities wherever they are located.

Building upon ideas of new economic geography (Fujita et al. 1999; Krugman 1998) and echoing critical geographers, such as, Harvey (1996), the role of place, in the form of urban centres, is more rather than less important in a globalised economy. Physical proximity and large metropolitan areas are increasingly important in an economic sense and that, further, there are market-driven concentrations (agglomerations) of economic activity across the world. The space-neutral approach favours policy that works with, builds upon and facilitates the expansion of these 'natural' agglomerations. In this sense, the 'space-neutral' label can provide an impression that place is unimportant, which is clearly not the case. Importantly, the approach assumes or expects a high degree of labour mobility from weaker economic areas to economically stronger agglomerations. Thus, major cities, city-regions and metropolitan areas represent the core units of spatial selectivity through a space-neutral policy lens. These ideas have proved to be extremely influential and contemporary debates around development policy and metropolitan governance have been said to be dominated by an emergent orthodoxy built around this presumed desirability and uncontested efficiency of large-scale urban agglomerations (Deas 2014; Haughton et al. 2014; Tomaney 2014).

Critics have argued that an implicit trade-off between efficiency—such as maximising national growth—and spatial equity is not convincingly supported by theory or evidence (Martin 2015). Moreover, evidence suggests that cities in England do not demonstrate the economic productivity advantages that the spatial economics theory suggests they should (McCann 2016). Importantly, agglomerations are in part the result of public as well as private decisions and are shaped by policy decisions around, for example, land use and public investment in research and development that are often closely tied to place and tend to promote the interest of capital/major cities under the influence of urban elites (McCann and Rodriquez-Pose 2011).

In contrast to space-neutral predispositions, a place-based approach would aim to facilitate growth in all places, whether cities, regions or rural areas, growing or lagging, by first recognising the importance of current and historical decisions that promote 'natural' agglomerations, and by building institutional capacity in economically lagging regions in an effort to stimulate endogenous growth. Critics of an agglomeration-first approach point to evidence that smaller cities are often the site of highly productive economies (Centre for Cities 2016). In addition, policies that seek to nurture large urban agglomerations and accompanying (explicitly or implicitly) large-scale labour migration and spatial adjustment are questioned from a place-based perspective on the basis that they are likely to involve significant social and cultural cost about which relativity little is known (Barca et al. 2012).

The Ambiguous Scale of CLOG and the Northern Powerhouse: Agglomeration or Agglomerations?

In the context of CLOG and the Northern Powerhouse, debates around the importance of agglomeration are, in part, manifest in an implicit tension in applying a theoretical approach that assumes spatial disparity to be an *equilibrium* outcome (Martin 2015) in a policy context where the stated *desired* outcome is the reduction of spatial disparity. This is to some extent evident in confusion or 'fuzziness' around the geography at which it is assumed agglomeration effects are seen to apply in the Northern Powerhouse (Lee 2016). These tensions apply to the CLOG policy framework more broadly and perhaps reflect the, at times confused, mix of assumptions that underpin the economics of the approach, which Hildreth and Bailey (2013) identify as a mix of place-based and space-neutral. In the first instance, an agglomeration approach might imply prioritising a policy that follows market signals and aims to facilitate greater density around London by, for example, transport investment and encouraging increased housing supply through planning deregulation (Cheshire et al. 2014). At the same time, Manchester has been portrayed as the centre of a Northern Powerhouse, interpreted as a counter agglomeration to London, as well as a much-cited exemplar in Whitehall (Haughton et al. 2016). This has contributed to political tensions around the perceived favouring of particular territories and a fear in some Northern cities and non-metro areas that 'the rest' may miss out (on an often ill-defined policy opportunity or potential funding 'windfall'):

> the risks are that not all of the Northern cities are near to each other... particularly for the cities of the North East; Middlesbrough and Newcastle, we are quite a long way from the rest and I think there's a bit of a risk that it almost ends up leading to more resource in the North, but only for certain bits of the North. *So it creates new winners and losers.* (Senior Local Authority Officer, North East, *emphasis added*)

However, while Manchester has featured heavily in the notion of what could be described as a counterweight agglomeration to complement London, Osborne (2014) was careful to also emphasise a polycentric approach:

Not one city, but a collection of Northern cities – sufficiently close to each other that combined they can take on the world. (Osborne 2014)

The ambiguous approach from government, including subsequent discussion of a 'Midlands Engine', together with bottom-up manoeuvring amongst local leadership teams have helped reinforce the polycentric strand that was already present in CLOG and a prominent feature of the Northern Way. Perhaps more pragmatically and importantly, the Northern Powerhouse, to a large extent, relies upon sponging policy mechanisms from CLOG, the clearest example being the place-based deal mechanism including the ongoing devolution deal process and the growth deals, which predate the Northern Powerhouse and are available to all parts of England.

Locally Designed Policy and Its Financing

Notions of devolved governance and locally designed policy are at the heart of CLOG and the Northern Powerhouse rhetoric:

> Policy should...recognise that the situation will be different for each place and is likely to be particularly affected by factors such as the inherent skills mix or entrepreneurial tradition of the population; business confidence; quality of infrastructure provision; and proximity to trading markets. (HM Government 2010a, b: 7)

While the government has, to a degree, both formally and informally prioritised cities and city-regions, it is not always clear that emergent policies and interventions at the local level reflect an agglomeration agenda. In the first instance, while transport projects feature heavily in the various place-based deals, there is comparatively little specific policy designed to facilitate connections between urban centres in the North. It is notable that perhaps the most ambitious plan with this explicit focus, Transport for the North, was in large part instigated by a collaboration of local authorities and LEPs, although to date, the plans' ambitions have not been matched with similarly ambitious investment.

Within territories, local politics continue to perform a significant role in the manner that combined authorities and LEPs devise spatial priorities. Interviewees suggested a degree of 'jam spreading' in operation to appease all local authorities:

There's a lot of horse-trading does go on in terms of if everyone didn't get something out of it, it wouldn't work. So if all of the technical appraisal showed really good projects and two areas that don't get anything, it wouldn't work. So there's an element of realism. (Senior Local Authority Officer, Yorkshire)

In practice much of the thinking and policy to emerge under CLOG and the Northern Powerhouse conforms with orthodox economic development tools; typically infrastructure, skills and property-led development. Emergent plans have been somewhat light on innovation policy and there has been limited discussion of, for example, smart specialisation characteristic of a place-based approach (Barca 2009; Foray 2015). Indeed, most LEPs have struggled to agree upon spatial priorities, which are either 'smart' or 'specialised':

Devolution deals are just a minor evolution. In fact, they're probably narrower than the growth deals and the strategic economic plans, because they're focused on… a relatively limited number of funding domains. So it's low level skills, transport, something about business development… there's very little innovation in them at all. It's doing more of what we've done in the past. Building more roads, more science parks, putting more grants into businesses. (Recently retired civil servant, London)

Much has been made of the finance aspect of the nascent devolution deals, particularly the almost ubiquitous investment funds of £30 million per annum. However, the deals are intended to be much more than funding agreements, with a greater focus on devolved decision-making powers ('freedoms and flexibilities'). In this sense, they might be seen as a step forward towards greater local influence in shaping development policy. Alternatively, the powers 'on offer' are sometimes rather limited and it will be necessary to observe how (or *if*) the deals unfold in practice. For example, the West of England Devolution Agreement makes the somewhat vague statement that the government will 'work towards closer cooperation…on trade and investment' (2016: 6).

In the context of ongoing austerity where local government budgets in Northern urban areas have been dramatically reduced, 'additional' money for local growth is difficult to identify or differentiate from investment that may have happened in any case. Furthermore, the sums of money involved in CLOG are relatively marginal and with a tendency to be announced on multiple occasions, as well as also being badged as Northern Powerhouse initiatives (Lee 2016). More recently, the January 2017 subregional allocations of the third round of the Local Growth Fund saw the funding announced for the third time, having been previously announced in the 2016 Budget and again in that year's Autumn Statement. The money was, of course, billed as a £556 million 'boost' for the Northern Powerhouse, despite all regions of England, including London, receiving a share of the available funds. In the latest round of Local Growth Fund, Northern subregions (still LEP areas despite recurring predictions of LEPs' demise) were allocated 31 per cent of the near £1.8 billion available for England, slightly more than if the fund were weighted by regional population size. While this is an increase on previous rounds, where Northern LEP area allocated 22 per cent of the total growth deal funding, it is perhaps less than clear to pitch the money as a £556 million boost for the Northern Powerhouse when all parts of England are to receive a share of the fund. Furthermore, the disparate and conditional funding streams under the control of local institutions should be viewed in the context of the combined budgets of the three Northern RDAs at their peak, which exceeded £900 million.

Boosterism is pronounced in the relatively marginal funding opportunities that are regularly celebrated as 'transformative' and 'path-defining'. In this sense, local policymakers are party to the 'fuzzy financing' of local growth (Lee 2016), motivated, in part, by a local boosterist approach of 'talking up' local economic prospects (or sending 'a signal to the market' in the words of one interviewee) and, in part, by a desire to remain 'on message' with Whitehall in the hope of benefiting in some unknown way in the future.

> There's a bit of a political game to it. We need to be seen to be playing our part in delivering the growth deal, otherwise we're not going to get success in future growth deals or devolution [deals]. (Senior Local Authority Officer, Yorkshire)

Outside of the traditional infrastructure and skills approaches to subnational development, public funding for research and development, focussed as it is on the 'golden triangle' of London, Cambridge and Oxford, remains an area of contention and civil servants are clear that public funding for research and development is there to support 'excellence' rather than support regional development and that excellence tends to be concentrated in these areas (see also the chapter by Flanagan and Wilsdon in this volume).

The View from 'the North'

Our research finds an enthusiasm for a Northern-focussed agenda coupled with a lack of clarity over what distinguishes the Northern Powerhouse and scepticism around central government intentions. Interviews with stakeholders in Northern cities reveal a definite perception of political motivations underpinning the pushing of the Northern Powerhouse concept, and this can lead to hostility among some in Labour areas in the North which perceive it as being in large part a Conservative electoral strategy:

> The ethos that supposedly sits behind it, I can't imagine that anyone in the region would argue with, apart from the people who argue with everything. But so long as you've got...a Northern Powerhouse brand... that is so clearly identified with the Conservative Party in general and this Conservative Chancellor in particular, it's going to be perceived as a negative thing by a lot of people. (Private sector stakeholder, North East)

This is in part raw party politics, and in part a wariness born out the large-scale funding cuts to local government that have hit Northern urban areas hardest; in plain terms, there is a question of a lack of trust (see also the chapter by Giovannini in this volume). This wariness of central government motivations runs parallel with a view that the available policy levers are insufficient for the job in hand. At the same time, while there is a recognition amongst many stakeholders in Northern cities that rebalancing from the South to the North in any serious sense is well beyond the scope of CLOG there is a determination to make the most of the policy levers available. This genuine belief that places can begin to make some progress alongside a tendency toward boosterism and 'talking up' local development policy means local leadership teams are happy to employ the Northern Powerhouse brand.

Perhaps the clearest aspect in which CLOG could be said to have a Northern focus is the exalted status of Greater Manchester as a leader, exemplar and role model for decentralisation and local economic growth for England (despite the persistence of intra-city-regional disparities); a status carefully cultivated by local leaders over a number of years

(Haughton et al. 2016; see also Blakeley and Evans in this volume). At the same time, much that has been described as 'Northern Powerhouse' was already present in CLOG. In those areas where Northern Powerhouse activities can be distinguished from CLOG, they tend to be top-down interventions, such as the £150 million directed to the Henry Royce Centre in Greater Manchester or work by UK Trade and Industry to direct property investment out of London. In this context, Lee (2016) identifies a substantive policy tool of the Northern Powerhouse as the centralised political overruling of technocratic decisions such as cost–benefit analysis of transport projects that might otherwise lead to more investment in the South East of England, or science and innovation funding mechanism that favour and reinforce the 'golden triangle'. Again, there is an element of confusion in the approach with top-down interventions being the antitheses of the localist rhetoric of decentralised governance and locally designed policy that characterise CLOG and Northern Powerhouse.

In this sense the Northern Powerhouse can be seen as an example of politicised regional development and the need for the Conservative Government to boost its standing in the Northern cities of England; a theme that consistently emerged in our own fieldwork and that reiterates local scepticism:

> They need to persuade us in the North they love us, so how do we go about it? That's it, we create a Northern Powerhouse cause that sounds like very Northern and it sounds like you're serious about giving the locals some powers. (Councillor, Yorkshire)

This scepticism perhaps in part reflects a cynicism born of local leaders' experiences of austerity together with a sense of confusion around subnational policy in England. The final section of this chapter highlights this incoherence and draws together some conclusions on the relationship between CLOG and the Northern Powerhouse.

Concluding Remarks

Through this chapter we have sought to highlight the confusion and tensions of the CLOG policy framework as it intersects with the Northern Powerhouse. We identify a policy style and approach that generates enthusiasm and some creative thinking, but suffers from an incoherence which, along with limited funding, hampers the objective to reduce spatial economic disparities in England. Such policy incoherence is reflected in stakeholders' perceptions, wariness and sometimes confusion over the Government's intentions and motivations for devolution policy, local growth and the Northern Powerhouse.

The notion of a Northern Powerhouse evolved relatively quickly from the idea of a mega-agglomeration (with Manchester as the core) to ideas influenced by polycentricity and a pan-northern approach (with Manchester as one of multiple key nodes). Partly because, first, favouring particular places on a large scale is politically divisive. Second, resources constraints prevented the funding of a bespoke package of Northern Powerhouse programmes and interventions. Consequently, in order to retain policy appeal, the Northern Powerhouse initiative has deployed a political strategy that has piggybacked on anything that could be conceivably 'claimed' to support the growth and development of the North. In this sense, we refer to the policy notion of the Northern Powerhouse as a policy sponge. Indeed, a spurious list of Government support for interventions in the North of England has typically been badged as Northern Powerhouse activity. Hence, we find the Northern Powerhouse initiative to be a nebulous creation that applies to a fuzzy geography has limited formal institutional structure in the workings of national or local government and, employing few policy interventions of its own, regularly applies the Northern Powerhouse brand to spending decisions or policy interventions that were likely to have happened in any case. This sponging of policy from other agendas applies particularly to CLOG where, for example, Devolution Deals, billed as the centrepiece of the Northern Powerhouse, follow and are linked to the earlier Growth Deals and City Deals with most involving the same CLOG institutional actors (particularly LEPs and Combined Authorities) and often building upon policy and funding streams set out in these earlier deals. Furthermore, these decentralised governance deals, which have developed under CLOG since 2010, do not have an explicit Northern focus and are available to any part of England.

In the context of limited resources, there is a shared boosterist agenda around CLOG and the Northern Powerhouse with local and national policymakers keen to talk up the scale and impact of interventions; in part because the austerity context limits their options. Just as a narrative of failure developed around the previous regional policy approach and RDAs in particular (Pike et al. 2016a), all stakeholders, including ambitious local leaders keen to be seen to deliver growth and jobs, have some interest in a narrative of success around cities, local growth and a Northern Powerhouse—exemplified by the celebration of Greater Manchester as a model of decentralised governance and economic growth policy (Houghton et al. 2016).

Recent research suggests that, such as the scale and longevity of geographical imbalance, state-sponsored subnational development, whether affiliated with CLOG, the Northern Powerhouse or any other policy initiative, will not come close to spatially rebalancing the economy (e.g. Gardiner et al. 2013; McCann 2016). Despite the political narrative of success and boosterist agenda, many local and national policymakers are candid about the limits of what they can achieve with the available policy tools and, in the words of one interviewee, significant economic rebalancing towards the North of England would likely take 'a fundamental change over a generation'. For example, while as Lee (2016) observes, central government is seeking new and sometimes 'creative' ways to allocate funding for infrastructure and innovation, the level of investment available the 'golden triangle' is huge in comparison with the relatively meagre resources directed at subnational development either from the centre or via combined authorities and LEPs.

More positively, any policy that aims, as CLOG does in theory, to reduce spatial disparities in the UK by boosting the economy in slower growing cities and regions must arguably take a more place-based approach and consider the gap between the North and South of England. In addition, our research raises the question of whether there is an appetite for pan-northern cooperation of even some kind of formal institution to address what Hildreth and Bailey (2014) refer to as the 'missing middle' and, among some local leaders, there remains a degree of enthusiasm for formal pan-northern cooperation. Other future research might trace the evolution of 'rebalancing' policies in the wake of the vote to leave the EU and as the process of leaving the union moves forwards. In the months following the referendum there has been a new focus on 'left behind' places that were more prone to vote for Brexit (Goodwin and Heath 2016). Observers have queried the potential impact on subnational policy (Swinney 2016) and the possibility of the UK seeing the return of a more ameliorative or compensatory industrial and regional policy, which challenges more recent flirtations with agglomeration-infused growth policy. Whatever the policies ultimately taken forward, the decision to leave the EU may have a decisive influence on subnational development policy. On the one hand, the removal of EU structural funds could mean subnational development policy could become less important or at least further under-resourced. Alternatively, Brexit could push subnational development policy even further up the political agenda as politicians grapple with the problem of how to deal with regional disparities in the face of an angry and influential section of the electorate; a factor that perhaps overshadows the earlier concerns amongst local leaders in the North of England that former Chancellor Osborne was in large part concerned with the question of how to secure a long-term stable electoral majority for the Conservative Party.

REFERENCES

Barca, F. (2009). An agenda for a reformed cohesion policy a place-based approach to meeting European Union challenges and expectations. Available from http://ec.europa.eu/regional_policy/archive/policy/future/barca_en.htm. Accessed 27 Feb 2017.

Barca, F., P. McCann, and A. Rodríguez-Pose. 2012. The case for regional development intervention: Place-based versus place-neutral approaches. *Journal of Regional Science* 52 (1): 134–152.

Business, Energy and Industrial Strategy (BEIS). 2017. *Building our industrial strategy*. London: HMSO.

Business Innovation and Skills (BIS), and Communities and Local Government (CLG). 2010. *Understanding local growth*. BIS Economics Paper No. 7. London: HMSO.

Cable, V., and E. Pickles. 2010. *'Local enterprise partnerships', open letter to local authority leaders and business leaders*. London: HM Government.

Centre for Cities. 2016. Cities outlook 2016. Available from http://www.centreforcities.org/publication/cities-outlook-2016/. Accessed 27 Feb 2017.

Cheshire, P.C., M. Nathan, and H.G. Overman. 2014. *Urban economics and urban policy challenging conventional policy wisdom*. Cheltenham: Edward Elgar.

City Growth Commission. 2014. *Unleashing metro growth: Final recommendations of the city growth commission*. London: City Growth Commission.

Clarke, G. 2010. Driving local growth. Local Enterprise Partnerships Conference, Local Government Association, Local Government House, London, 28 October.

Deas, I. 2014. The search for territorial fixes in subnational governance: City-regions and the disputed emergence of post-political consensus in Manchester, England. *Urban Studies* 51 (11): 2285–2314.

Foray, D. 2015. *Smart specialisation: Opportunities and challenges for regional innovation policy.* Abingdon: Routledge.

Fujita, M., A. Venables, and P.R. Krugman. 1999. *The spatial economy: Cities, regions and international trade.* Cambridge, MA: MIT Press.

Gains, F. 2016. Metro Mayors: Devolution, democracy and the importance of getting the 'Devo Manc' design right. *Representation* 51 (4): 1–13.

Gardiner, B., R. Martin, P. Sunley, and P. Tyler. 2013. Spatially unbalanced growth in the British economy. *Journal of Economic Geography* 13 (6): 889–928.

Gill, I. 2010. Regional development policies: Place-based or people-centred? *VOX online article.* Available from http://www.voxeu.org/article/regional-development-policies-place-based-or-people-centred. Accessed 27 Feb 2017.

Glaeser, E.L. 2011. *Triumph of the city: How our greatest invention makes us richer, smarter, greener, healthier, and happier.* London: Penguin.

Goodchild, B., and P. Hickman. 2006. Towards a regional strategy for the North of England? An assessment of 'The Northern Way'. *Regional Studies* 40 (1): 121–133.

Goodwin, M., M. Jones, and R. Jones. 2012. *Rescaling the state: Devolution and the geographies of economic governance.* Manchester: Manchester University Press.

Goodwin, M.J., and O. Heath. 2016. The 2016 referendum, Brexit and the left behind: An aggregate-level analysis of the result. *The Political Quarterly* 87 (3): 323–332.

Gray, N., and L. Pugalis. 2016. Place-based subnational development: Unpacking some of the key conceptual strands and normative dispositions. In *The handbook of research on subnational governance and development,* ed. E.D. Schoburgh and R. Ryan. Hershey, PA: IGI Global.

Harvey, D. 1989. From managerialism to entrepreneurialism: The transformation in urban governance in late capitalism. Geografiska Annaler. Series B. *Human Geography* 71 (1): 3–17.

Harvey, D. 1996. *Justice, nature and the geography of difference.* Oxford: Blackwell.

Haughton, G., I. Deas, and S. Hincks. 2014. Making an impact: When agglomeration boosterism meets antiplanning rhetoric. *Environment and Planning A* 46 (2): 265–270.

Haughton, G., I. Deas, S. Hincks, and K. Ward. 2016. Mythic Manchester: Devo Manc, the Northern Powerhouse and rebalancing the English economy. *Cambridge Journal of Regions, Economy and Society* 9: 355–370.

HM Government. 2010a. *The coalition: Our programme for government.* London: HMSO.

HM Government. 2010b. *Local growth: Realising every place's potential.* London: HMSO.

HM Government. 2011. *Unlocking growth in cities.* London: HMSO.

HM Treasury. 2016. *Northern Powerhouse strategy.* London: HMSO.

Hildreth, P., and D. Bailey. 2013. The economics behind the move to 'localism' in England. *Cambridge Journal of Regions, Economy and Society* 6 (2): 233–249.

Hildreth, P., and D. Bailey. 2014. Place-based economic development strategy in England: Filling the missing space. *Local Economy* 29 (4–5): 363–377.

Krugman, P.R. 1998. What's new about the new economic geography? *Oxford Review of Economic Policy* 14 (2): 7–17.

Lee, N. 2016. Powerhouse of cards? Understanding the 'Northern Powerhouse'. *Regional Studies* 51 (3): 478–489.

Manchester Independent Economic Review. 2009. Reviewers report. Available from http://www.manchester-review.org.uk/. Accessed 27 Feb 2017.

Martin, R. 2015. Rebalancing the spatial economy: The challenge for regional theory. *Territory, Politics, Governance* 3 (3): 235–272.

Martin, R., A. Pike, P. Tyler, and B. Gardiner. 2016. Spatially rebalancing the UK economy: Towards a new policy model? *Regional Studies* 50 (2): 342–357.

McCann, P. 2016. *The UK regional-national economic problem: Geography, globalisation and governance regions and cities 96.* London: Routledge.

McCann, P., and A. Rodríguez-Pose. 2011. Why and when development policy should be place-based. In *OECD regional outlook 2011: Building resilient regions for stronger economies,* ed. OECD, 203–213. Paris: OECD Publishing.

O'Brien, P., A. Pike, D. Mackinnon, D. Marlow, and E. Robson. 2014. Written evidence submitted by Centre for Urban and Regional Development Studies (CURDS), Newcastle University to Communities and Local Government Select Committee Inquiry into the 'Fiscal Devolution to Cities and City Regions'.

Osborne, G. 2014. We need a Northern Powerhouse. Speech given to the Museum of Science and Industry, Manchester, UK, June 23, 2014. Available from   https://www.gov.uk/government/speeches/chancellor-we-need-a-northern-powerhouse. Accessed 27 Feb 2017.

Pike, A., M. Coombes, P. O'Brien, and J. Tomaney. 2016a. *Austerity states, institutional dismantling and the governance of sub-national economic development: The demise of the regional development agencies in England.* Spatial Economics Research Centre Discussion Paper 206. Available from: http://www.spatialeconomics.ac.uk/textonly/SERC/publications/download/sercdp0206.pdf.

Pike, A., L. Kempton, D. Marlow, P. O'Brien, and J. Tomaney. 2016b. Decentralisation: Issues, principles and practice. Available from http://www.ncl.ac.uk/media/wwwnclacuk/curds/files/decentralisation.pdf. Accessed 27 Feb 2017.

Pike, A., D. Marlow, A. McCarthy, P. O'Brien, and J. Tomaney. 2013. Local institutions and local economic development: The local enterprise partnerships in England, 2010–. *Cambridge Journal of Regions Economy and Society* *2015* 8 (2): 185–204.

Pugalis, L. 2010. Looking back in order to move forward: The politics of evolving sub-national economic policy architecture. *Local Economy* 25 (5–6): 397–405.

Pugalis, L. 2011a. The regional lacuna: A preliminary map of the transition from regional development agencies to local economic partnerships. *Regions* 281: 6–9.

Pugalis, L. 2011b. Sub-national economic development: Where do we go from here? *Journal of Urban Regeneration and Renewal* 4 (3): 255–268.

Pugalis, L. 2015. Place-based deal-making: New modes of city and regional development. Rethinking the region & regionalism in Australasia: Challenges & opportunities for the 21st century. Inaugural Australasian Conference, RMIT University, Melbourne, 31 August–2 September, 25.

Pugalis, L., and A.R. Townsend. 2012. Rebalancing England: Sub-national development (once again) at the crossroads. *Urban Research & Practice* 5 (1): 159–176.

Pugalis, L., A.R. Townsend, N. Gray, and A. Ankowska. 2015. *Planning for Growth: The role of local enterprise partnerships in England, Final report.* London: Royal Town Planning Institute (RTPI).

Pugalis, L., A.R. Townsend, N. Gray, and A. Ankowska. 2016. New approaches to growth planning at larger-than-local scales. *Journal of Urban Regeneration & Renewal* 10 (1): 89–99.

Swinney, P. 2016. What the EU referendum tells us about economic development policy. Available from http://www.centreforcities.org/blog/eu-referendum-tells-us-economic-development-policy/. Accessed 27 Feb 2017.

Tomaney, J. 2014. Region and place I: Institutions. *Progress in Human Geography* 38 (1): 131–140.

Weller, N. 2016. *A Northern Powerhouse schools strategy: An independent review by Sir Nick Weller.* London: HMSO.

West of England Combined Authority/HM Government. 2016. West of England devolution agreement. Available from https://www.gov.uk/government/uploads/system/uploads/attachment_data/file/508112/160315_West_of_England_Devolution_Agreement_Draft_-_FINAL.pdf. Accessed 27 Feb 2017.

World Bank. 2009. World development report 2009: Reshaping economic geography. Retrieved from Washington DC: Available from http://web.worldbank.org/WBSITE/EXTERNAL/EXTDEC/EXTRESEARCH/EXTWDRS/0,,contentMDK:23080183~pagePK:478093~piPK:477627~theSitePK:477624,00.html. Accessed 27 Feb 2017.

AUTHORS' BIOGRAPHY

Nick Gray is Doctoral Researcher and Research Associate at Newcastle Business School, Northumbria University. Previously, he was a Policy Advisor in local government, specialising in local and regional economies, social inclusion, and migration.

Lee Pugalis is Professor at the Institute for Public Policy and Governance at the University of Technology Sydney. His research traverses local and regional economic development, urban regeneration, and strategic planning. He has published in a wide range of academic journals, currently edits the journals *Regional Studies, Regional Science* and *Local Economy,* and has experience of working in local, regional and national government in the UK.

Danny Dickinson is Policy Officer in Newcastle City Council's Economic Development team. His research interests include social mobility, inclusive growth, skills development and city-regional devolution. His current role includes supporting the development of Newcastle's approach devolution and public service reform approaches.

CHAPTER 7

The Uneven Governance of Devolution Deals in Yorkshire: Opportunities, Challenges and Local (Di)Visions

Arianna Giovannini

Abstract The Devolution Deals and Northern Powerhouse agenda were presented by George Osborne as the making of a 'devolution revolution' in the North of England. But while the signing of the 'Devo Manc' agreement has followed a rather smooth path, the Chancellor's plan is developing in an uneven way across other parts of the North. In Yorkshire the situation seems to be particularly complex, and local authorities are taking very different approaches to devolution deals—none of which is without controversy. Drawing on the findings of interviews with key stakeholders, this chapter seeks to explore the emerging, complex and uneven governance of devolution deals in Yorkshire, assessing the prospects and challenges of the model of devolution currently on offer, and the implications this could have for the Northern Powerhouse.

A. Giovannini (✉)
Department of Politics and Public Policy, De Montfort University,
Leicester, UK
e-mail: arianna.giovannini@dmu.ac.uk

© The Author(s) 2018
C. Berry and A. Giovannini (eds.), *Developing England's North,*
Building a Sustainable Political Economy: SPERI Research & Policy,
https://doi.org/10.1007/978-3-319-62560-7_7

Keywords Democracy · Devolution · Governance · Local government · Northern Powerhouse · Yorkshire

INTRODUCTION

When introduced by the former Chancellor George Osborne in 2014/2015, the devolution deals and Northern Powerhouse agenda were presented as the making of a 'devolution revolution' in the North of England. While the signing of the 'Devo Manc' agreement has followed a relatively smooth path, the Chancellor's plan is developing in an uneven way across other parts of the North.

In Yorkshire the situation seems to be particularly complex: different areas across the region are taking very different approaches to devolution deals—none of which is without controversy. Sheffield was the first city-region to sign a deal in principle, but the path leading to its completion is proving more difficult than expected. A number of issues, including the role of the mayor and the boundaries of the deal, have slowed down the process. Leeds city-region, on the other hand, did put in a deal proposal, but this has not yet been agreed and tensions seem to be growing, showing incongruence between what the city-region wants (i.e. an ambitious deal) and what the government is prepared to offer. Meanwhile, in the East part of Yorkshire the situation is even more ambiguous: Hull and the East Riding called for a 'Greater Yorkshire deal' with West Yorkshire, so as to avoid being relegated to the 'deal-have-nots' camp and thus missing out on the opportunities offered by devolution. So far, local leaders in the area have received very little reassurance both within the region and from the UK government about the feasibility of this option. At the same time, the South Bank of the Humber went for a deal with Greater Lincolnshire (which eventually collapsed in November 2016), fracturing, in practice, the areas covered by the Humber Local Enterprise Partnership. Thus, the path of devolution deals in Yorkshire is still unfinished and far from being settled—casting doubts as to whether the present piecemeal approach will be successful, and what its endpoint will be.

Against this complex background, this chapter seeks to map out and make sense of the emerging architecture of devolution deals in Yorkshire, assessing the prospects and challenges inherent in the model of devolution currently on offer. From this angle, the first aim is to understand if devolution deals, as envisaged by the present government, could lead to a sustainable system of governance in Yorkshire. The second aim is to explore if and how the current plans fit into, and could allow pursuing, the wider Northern Powerhouse agenda. To achieve this, the chapter opens with an evaluation of the process underpinning the proposals for devolution deals in Yorkshire. This is followed by an analysis 'on the ground' aimed at identifying the key issues and opportunities connected with devolution deals, based on the findings of interviews conducted with key stakeholders (i.e. local authorities, city-regions, and LEPs representatives) in Yorkshire between June and September 2016.[1] Finally, the chapter closes with a critical assessment of the emerging uneven governance of devolution deals in Yorkshire, and the implications this could have for the Northern Powerhouse.

THE PATH TO DEVOLUTION: REVOLUTION OR CHAOS?

The debate on devolution in England dates back decades, and rests on the widespread idea that England is a highly centralised country (Tomaney 2016; Hazell 2006). In this context, the North of England (and, within it, Yorkshire) has been the focus of several attempts by successive governments to tackle over-centralisation and economic disparities by means of devolution—none of which, to date, has proven particularly successful (Giovannini 2016; Willett and Giovannini 2014; Sandford 2009).

Between the 1980s and 2010, it was the Labour Party that led the agenda on devolution in the North, conceived as a strategy to address the North–South economic divide. This process culminated with the establishment of Regional Development Agencies (RDAs) in the aftermath of Labour's landslide victory in 1997, but came to a halt after the failure of the referendum for directly elected regional assemblies (which were meant to attach democratic accountability to RDAs) held in the North East in 2004. Afterwards, the Labour government concentrated primarily on addressing economic inequalities through RDAs, city-regions and the Northern Way strategy (Giovannini 2016).

The election of the Conservative–Liberal Democrats coalition government in 2010 saw the disbandment of many institutions created by the Labour party, and opened the way to a new phase of devolution focussing on a narrative of 'localism' and 'community empowerment'. The Localism Act 2011 was a clear sign in this direction, changing the role of local government in England, in order to facilitate the devolution of decision-making and powers from central government to individual local authorities and communities (Localism Act 2011). Labour's RDAs were soon replaced by Local Enterprise Partnerships (LEPs) consisting of local authorities and businesses. Building on the premises of the Localism Act, the coalition government started to promote a series of 'partnership' deals with cities and following Lord Heseltine's report (2012), *No Stone Unturned,* a Local Growth Fund was created. Subsequently, in 2012 and 2014, the government introduced City Deals with 'core cities', and in 2014 and 2015 two rounds of Growth Deals were signed with LEPs. City-regions and LEPs in Yorkshire (as in other parts of the North) were included in these, and secured funding aimed at fostering economic growth in their areas. The process of devolving powers to the local level gained new impetus towards the end of 2014, when the government announced the first Devolution Deal with the Greater Manchester Combined Authority. This was followed by two more Devolution Agreements with Sheffield City-Region (December 2014) and West Yorkshire (March 2015), ahead of the 2015 general election (Sandford 2016a).

The formation of a new Conservative government in May 2015 gave further momentum to the devolution agenda. In his inaugural statement, the Prime Minister called for further decentralisation of powers in England (Cameron 2015), and two weeks after the election in a speech in Manchester the then Chancellor George Osborne called for "a radical new model of city government" based on handing down "power from the centre to cities, to give [them] greater control over transport, housing, skills and healthcare ... [heralding] a revolution in the way we govern England" (HM Treasury 2015). In the same speech, Osborne also emphasised the need to see devolution as a key means to achieve economic development both for cities and towns and counties, and called for new 'deals' to be submitted to the Treasury by September 2015. In addition, he reiterated his commitment to the Northern Powerhouse, linking this firmly to devolution deals, and discussed the introduction of new elected mayors as figureheads to drive and give accountability to the process.

In short, he laid the ground for a new agenda, presented as bold and innovative, to change the economic future of the North of England by passing powers down to the local level: a 'devolution revolution', to borrow Osborne's catchphrase. Subsequently, the Cities and Local Government Devolution Bill was introduced in Parliament at the end of May 2015, and received Royal Assent in January 2016. The Act provides the legal framework for the implementation of devolution deals with Combined Authorities and other areas such as counties (LGA 2016), and realises the government's ambition of putting devolution into practice.

This reconstruction of the path that led to devolution deals helps to assess the extent to which they introduced any real radical change in the North, and specifically in Yorkshire. The current proposals may have been presented as revolutionary but, in practice, they are the outcome of a process of devolution that has developed incrementally and in spurts, following the ebb and flow of different governments' political visions for the North. Today we may see devolution to the North of England as branded in a novel manner, but the way in which it is conceived and the purposes it is meant to serve share similarities with past initiative which aimed to address economic development issues in the North, bridge the North–South divide, and relieve central government from the burdens connected with the two previous points.

Thus, the narrative of devolution deals and the Northern Powerhouse continues to be strongly economic, top-down and centre driven, and with very limited real powers attached to it (Giovannini 2016; Sandford 2016b). The idea of 'empowerment' is portrayed as a key feature of this new wave of devolution—yet, any 'power' passed down comes from the centre on its own terms and conditions, without any substantial bottom-up inputs. All of the negotiations that led to the submission of deal proposals in Yorkshire (and elsewhere) were conducted behind closed doors, with no public consultation prior to the signing of agreements (Blunkett et al. 2016). The government was keen to implement its devolution agenda quickly, and it maintained a strong lead—often imposing key provisions, such as the introduction of elected mayors, despite the widespread disquiet on this point across most local authorities (Giovannini and Mycock 2016; Prosser et al. 2017). Some local leaders did manage to secure a few veto powers in the negotiations, but the powers devolved (transport, skills, business and houses, in most cases) are not only limited, but have also to meet a range of standards and requirements set by the centre.

As Richards and Smith (2015) note, the government's approach to devolution grafts onto the British political tradition, with a focus on maintaining central power and control on the process of devolution—as underlined by the absence of any subsidiarity informed democratic settlement. This approach strips out any democratic meaning and political empowerment from the notion of devolution—reducing it to a simple set of 'partnerships' between elites, based on a 'messy' geography, whereby certain areas are recipient of devolution deals, whilst others are excluded. Yorkshire is a case in point here: the deal proposals submitted in September 2015 were the result of discussions between CAs' representatives with the Government and did not entail any measure of public consultation on the powers, scale and purpose of devolution (Prosser et al. 2017). Furthermore, the fact that Sheffield City-Region has agreed a deal, while Leeds is in stand-by mode and the East part of Yorkshire is left in a limbo, suggests that we are moving towards an idiosyncratic, competitive, uneven, highly centralised form of multilevel government (Tomaney 2016). Within this, devolution is a 'concession' rather than an opportunity that can be freely called upon by local areas to meet the needs of their communities. Tomaney (2016: 550) summarises this point arguing that in the current context 'devolved policy-making is approved only if it meets the criteria of central government (or precisely the Treasury) and often individual ministerial approval and selected business interests'.

From a rational institutionalist perspective, some may claim that the creation of new spaces of governance requires a degree of central government control/guidance, and that lack of public involvement is the price to pay for the new structures to be put in place smoothly and effectively. This could perhaps be true if the current system of devolution had a clear blueprint, a defined endpoint and was designed to cover all the areas of England, endowing them with similar powers. However, the case of Yorkshire helps to illustrate that this is not what is happening. Thus, the introduction of devolution deals is likely to lead to the creation of a patchwork of governance arrangements and 'fixes'. This places many stresses both on a shrinking central government that seeks to manage in an ad hoc manner a number of local deals (Tomaney 2016) with different shapes, sizes, powers and remit; as well as on local authorities, as they enter a system of competition to get their deals approved before other regional players (Giovannini 2015). All in all, rather than a 'revolution' this seems to equate more to a simple, and far from unproblematic, 'evolution' of devolution (Blunkett et al. 2016) as a policy instrument(ally) driven by the centre.

The aim of the next section will be to test these claims against empirical evidence, drawing on an analysis of data collected across Yorkshire. This will allow an examination of the opportunities and challenges that devolution deals offer to Yorkshire, how these fit into the broader Northern Powerhouse project, and assess what could be the outcome of devolution.

Deal or no Deal? Devolution and Governance Restructuring in the Eyes of Local Actors

This section maps out the path of devolution deals in Yorkshire from its inception until the present time.[2] To achieve this, it focuses on the areas that have played a key role in the debate on devolution deals (i.e. Sheffield City-Region, West Yorkshire Combined Authority, and Hull and the East Riding). The analysis is organised around three broad themes: the devolution deals process, the opportunities offered by present arrangements and the challenges of the current devolution settlement—as envisaged by local authorities' representatives.

Sheffield City-Region Combined Authority

As outlined in the previous section, the debate on devolution deals in Yorkshire started in late 2014, soon after the signing of the 'Devo Manc' agreement. The Sheffield City-Region Combined Authority (SCRCA) was created in April 2014 and comprises nine councils,[3] some of which extend outside Yorkshire into areas of Derbyshire and Nottinghamshire. The devolution deal process was set in motion over the summer in 2015. Interestingly, the government started discussions at two different ends: they suggested that more devolution would be on offer soon, and advised the Local Enterprise Partnership (LEP) to propose new ideas in this respect, whilst the Treasury targeted directly the city-region (SCR), and entered a discussion on the actual content of the deal. As explained by a senior local figure:

> In June 2015 the government announced that there was scope for further devolution and asked the LEP to come forward with ideas (...) so the LEP submitted a set of proposals which spanned from business, housing, transport, skills, employment (...) and we corralled these with ours [SCR's]. We used our LEP as a sounding board for the CA (...) so there was a fairly bottom up process from our governance structure and then corporately we pulled the proposal together. (SCR representative, June 2016)

At the same time, the same interviewee pointed out that:

> while this was going on Treasury got in touch with us [SCR] (...), with the indication that they wanted to close deals quite fast and that there would be a fast timeline for places that got their act together. So while we were doing the formal bit, (...) we'd already started discussions with Treasury about what was in the deal (...), so almost the day we submitted on the 4th of September we were down in Treasury talking about our deal. (...) We were told that there was a prize for going first: (...) more money, first mover status. (SCR representative, June 2016)

This approach allowed the development of a fast and effective process: in practice, by the time the deal proposal was submitted, SCR was already in a position to know that it would be accepted. However, evidence seems also to indicate that the Treasury had a strategic aim: pushing Sheffield into the deal at a fast pace (by promising 'extras' for being the first area to sign a deal), in order to maximise control over the terms and conditions of the agreement.

> The Treasury...were quite keen that the process was private, so they didn't want us to talk to other places [in Yorkshire] about what was in our deal. (...) I guess it was easier for them to have private conversations. Part of it was...they wanted to force some of their departments to go further than they had gone before...on housing or planning or skills funding. Part of it was also because they like the idea of competition and it's easier for them to get us to agree to stuff if we didn't know what other places got. (SCR representative, June 2016)

This suggests that the Treasury was keen to move quickly in implementing its devolution agenda in the area: it had a clear view on the way in which it wanted this to happen, and wanted to 'drive' the process. The same respondent reinforced this point by further arguing that:

> There were criticisms that's all been back doors deals...but there isn't such thing as doing deals that isn't behind the scenes, private. We had a lot of Treasury access, senior officials...it was all done through Treasury, we weren't in talks with any other department. (SCR representative, June 2016)

These extracts emphasise how the Treasury played a key role in orchestrating the deals with local authorities, keeping control of the process both within the cabinet and at the local level. On the one hand, this approach seems to be driven by a desire to attach powers (as well as liabilities) to the deals on policy areas previously held at the centre. On the other, it shows that the Treasury favoured a 'divide and rule' strategy, deliberately drawing on the idea of competition, and making a clear appeal to the benefits of doing deals fast and privately. Thus, they entered into private negotiations only with individual regional actors, so as to make sure they could not talk to each other, and come up with alternative (and perhaps more ambitious) proposals—leaving central government's leverage on the process unchallenged. From this perspective, it could be argued that the SCR adopted a 'pragmatic approach' to devolution deals: they followed the path set by the Treasury without any particular resistance, in order to grab the opportunity on offer ahead of other areas. Indeed, it was also a question of competition and 'prestige', so as to gain the status of the first city-region to sign a devolution deal regionally and nationally (after Manchester). This is an important point to note. The fast pace of the process meant not only that SCRCA could not open dialogue with other combined authorities, but also that, beyond council leaders, a large part of local politicians (and in particular councillors) did not get to know about the deal until it was agreed at the beginning of October 2015. As underlined by a local councillor:

> We had absolutely no idea of what was going on. Our leader was involved, sure, but did we discuss the implications of this [i.e. devolution deal] collectively? No, we didn't. Many of us got to know about it only once the agreement was signed! (Sheffield City Council representative, June 2016)

So, SCRCA signed a deal in principle in October 2015 quite swiftly. Interview data indicate that the fact that most councils within the CA are Labour-led was key to generate consensus over the devolution deal at local level. The government recognised and valued the presence of a strong partnership across local authorities as a good basis on which to build a devolution agreement, and this was key in giving the 'green light' to the SCRCA deal.

From the point of view of local actors, the devolution deal offers a wide range of opportunities for SCR. Economic development emerged as the main theme underpinning the rationale for the deal. Indeed, local authorities felt that this wave of devolution would be instrumental to gain control over key sectors to boost the economy. The opening line of the SCR website dedicated to the deal makes this point very clear, claiming that the devolution deal 'marks another step in the journey that the Sheffield City-Region has taken over the last five years in securing greater control over its own economic affairs' (SCR 2016). This position is reflected in the views of local actors:

> The main opportunities are...powers over transport...the ability of the mayor to control the transport system...through bus devolution or single transport budget. (...) Control over the adult skills budget...we've been asking for it for ages and suddenly it's offered to us. The ability to retain business rate growth, so actually finally receiving rewards for being part of growing your economy. (SCR representative, June 2016)

> The skills agenda...that's a big area to drive productivity...the business support agenda, and getting some proper investment to drive some of the infrastructure change we need to do. (...) Bus franchising is a great opportunity...and it's something which I think is a real win because it's very close to the public's heart. (Sheffield City Council representative, August 2016)

Here the interviewees emphasise how the offer to get access to powers that directly affect local politics but were previously held at the centre was perceived as the main 'asset' of the SCRCA devolution deal. In their words:

> The point is not about the powers that we didn't get this time; the point is about the *powers we didn't have before* locally to do this sort of stuff. We never had any kind of revenue generating powers, we never had the ability to generate capital through infrastructure levies...or to define what our transport network looks like. So those are quite compelling, even if they may compare not particularly favourably to other city-regions. (SCR representative, June 2016)

> This is just the next step along where we want to be, bearing in mind how centralised we are as a country...if you believe that devolution is the right thing and therefore letting cities off the leash a bit more because they generate growth...[with the deal we can] reshape the skills policy around the needs of the City-Region's economy to grab hold of that nine hundred million pound over thirty years and start investing in the things that actually matter to our economy and not having to wait for Whitehall to sign off decisions. (Sheffield City Council representative, August 2016)

In a context in which local government has had to operate under strong central government restrictions for a long time, the offer of new powers over key policy areas was seen as an opportunity not to be missed for local authorities. Interestingly, local actors do recognise that there are limitations to the deal, but at the same time they felt that, as underlined by a local leader, 'it would be irresponsible to reject devolution' (SCC 2016). As explained by local actors:

> The government departments letting go of their budgets is still a tricky one. Local growth fund is still predominantly Department for Transport cash with a few other departments chipping in. DfT don't like that very much because they are relinquishing control over their national budget so I think there will be challenges in implementing and giving local areas freedom to shift budgets around and plan...it means re-writing relationships between central and local government. (SCR representative, June 2016).

> There's challenges: the first is delivering...we've worked hard to get the policy change and secure some of the finances and the levers to actually do it, we've now got to get on and do it because if we don't you end up in that period in five years where Government say 'well you haven't delivered it so we'll just take it back', and the Government have still got the levers to do that. (Sheffield City Council representative, August 2016)

Local representatives are aware that the powers on offer are not extensive, that the budget attached to the deal is far from ideal and that the government will maintain a strong hold over the latter, as devolved competences (and responsibilities) will have to meet requirements and standards set centrally to maintain the promised funding. In short, there are a number of liabilities and risks implicit in the deal; nonetheless signing the agreement was seen as the right thing to do at that point in time. This was a question of responsibility towards local communities (i.e. rejecting the offer could jeopardise opportunities for economic development and policy and infrastructures improvement), but local actors also perceived that, despite its limitations, the deal could open up opportunities for further devolution in the future.

> Ministers were clear throughout the process that this is 'devo stage two' in what will likely be a whole series of devolution deals...this isn't the end point of devolution...and we were always clear that...we should get the deal and then you'll get more next, and that's been the lesson from Manchester. (SCR representative, June 2016)

It's an iterative development because...there's no big piece of legislation that says we're going to devolve everything...they're not re-carving up the state...it will have to happen step by step, and this is a step in the right direction. (Sheffield City Council representative, August 2016)

We know there's not enough money, not enough powers...but this was the only deal on the table, so it is the best deal and we had to grab it...it's in the best interest of the people of Sheffield. (...)Economic development through devolution is the only game in town. And if we start with this now, we will get more in the future. (Sheffield City Council representative, September 2016)

Local representatives in the SCRCA seized the opportunity offered by the devolution deal because they are confident that, if they deliver, they will get more autonomy in the future. This is certainly a big challenge. One of the main shortcomings of the devolution process heralded by Osborne is that it does not seem to have a clear roadmap or endpoint (Giovannini and Mycock 2016)—thus, the idea that there will be more devolution to follow this wave of deals is a matter of speculation. This has been thrown into further relief following the vote for Brexit in June 2016, and the subsequent changes at the helm of the government. The new Prime Minister Theresa May has never given any clear indication of where she stands on devolution. Her focus on developing an industrial strategy for the whole country has led some to question her commitment both to devolution deals and to the Northern Powerhouse agenda, and only recently she has offered some (if still vague) reassurance on the latter (see Berry in this volume).

Finally, two other key themes that emerged in the fieldwork concern the figure of the elected mayor and democratic accountability. Throughout the deal negotiations, members of the SCRCA made several public statements on how, in principle, they were against the introduction of an elected mayor. However, the government was not prepared to give way on this key provision. In the end, SCRCA members agreed on this and by making slight changes to the SCRCA constitution they could introduce measures to ensure the new figurehead would not be able to overrule the CA (SCR 2016). In the view of local actors:

The mayor...we didn't want it, but it was part of the deal...it was deal with mayor or no deal, so we had to take it." (SCR representative, June 2016)

I'm not an advocate for mayors...but I can see the logic. (...) The mayor...obviously it was a government policy line and if we wanted to get the deal then that was part of the package. (...) But actually it creates a new bit of direct accountability over a geography which currently has kind of semi-accountability through the Combined Authority...you'd have somebody who can be held to account by the public through the ballot box for making decisions. (Sheffield City Council representative, August 2016)

Overall, SCRCA representatives were pragmatic and accepted the idea of mayors imposed by the government in spite of criticism, because the prize (i.e. the deal) was considered to be too big to be missed. Some local actors have even changed their mind throughout the negotiations and, as emphasised in the last extract above, came to see the new figurehead as a means to add more accountability to the new devolved structures. Others, however, simply gave into the pressure, but continue to be against the idea of a 'metro-mayor'—especially in areas, such as Doncaster, that have their own directly elected mayor.

Beyond this, there are other issues connected with issues of democratic accountability attached to the devolution deal. Following a statutory requirement by the government to finalise the deal (Sandford 2016a), SCR commissioned two rounds of public consultation through a survey on their website. Crucially, these returned a very small number of responses (see SCR 2016), and the questions posed did not allow respondent to express their views on the decision to have a deal, or in relation to its content (i.e. powers, mayor; for a discussion, see Prosser et al. 2017). There is also a sense that the local population is largely unaware of the fact that there could be a devolution deal in the SCRCA, or that they could have an elected 'metro-mayor' in the future. This raises questions about the democratic accountability of the new structures of governance introduced with the deal, which are particularly pressing in the current context when we regularly see low turnout at local elections (Giovannini and Mycock 2016). This has been further compounded by the growing sense of disillusionment towards politics underlined by the results of the EU membership referendum in the SCR area, which voted decidedly for Brexit (see BBC 2016). Interestingly, local actors seem to be aware of these issues—but, at the same time, they also view democracy as something that can be 'fabricated', and adjusted around the new governance architecture.

> We will invest money in promotion for the mayor and the opportunities that devolution provides...the public is still unaware of this, and if they are aware they lack the details. We have to do far better at promoting what is happening, and challenge some of the preconceptions about 'it's another layer of government, it's another expensive politician'. (...) There is a sort of issue, but we can fix it... you can run communication programmes and marketing stuff. The online consultation is our first stab at this. (...) First we'll create the new structures and then we'll put democracy around it. (SCR representative, July 2016)

This extract suggests that democracy and public engagement are seen as issues that can be 'fixed', and as something that can be easily steered, or somehow mustered by local authorities. This is an interesting point to note, especially because it seems to be based more on wishful thinking than on evidence. Indeed, the literature on democratic engagement suggests that gaining public support is not an easy task, especially at times of anti-politics (Jennings and Stoker 2016).

Overall, the picture emerging in the SCR shows that economic development and growth are the key drivers behind the devolution deal. There is an awareness of the potential issues (especially in terms of finances, central control over budgets, delivery and democracy) connected with the deal, but local authorities are prepared to take these on-board, and press ahead. In autumn 2016, all the documentation concerning the SCRCA devolution deal was sent to the Secretary of State. Local leaders were therefore expecting the order for the devolution deal to go through parliament within a short period of time, with the first mayoral election to be held in May 2017. However, in December 2016, issues related to boundaries and insufficient consultation have led to delay—and, indeed, doubts—in the SCRCA. Interestingly, these questions were seen as 'unproblematic' or 'easy to address' by the interviewees—showing how some local actors may have underestimated their relevance.

At the outset, the SCRCA had four constituent members (Sheffield, Doncaster, Barnsley and Rotherham), and five non-constituent members (Derbyshire Dales, North East Derbyshire, Chesterfield, Bolsover and Bassetlaw). The Local Devolution Act 2016 introduced key changes that allowed Chesterfield and Bassetlaw to join the SCR Combined Authority as constituent members (SCR 2016), settling—at least initially—potential issues over the boundaries of the deal. In June 2016, the SCRCA launched a self-contained consultation concerning whether two areas in neighbouring county councils (Bassetlaw, in Nottinghamshire; and Chesterfield, in Derbyshire) should become full members. Following this, Bassetlaw and Chesterfield gained 'constituent members status' within the SCRCA, as well as the right to vote in the forthcoming mayoral election, which is not granted to non-constituent members. However, in fear of losing the assets of the largest town in the county, Derbyshire County Council applied for a judicial review of Chesterfield's decision to join the SCRCA as a statutory member. In December 2016, the High Court found that the process should be rerun due to lack of appropriate public consultation and omission of most controversial proposals from consultation materials (Perraudin 2016).

Interestingly, the controversies that have emerged around the SCR deal shed light on one of the main, although often underestimated, limits of the current approach to devolution deals. Their artificial nature—based on city-regions' functional economic geographies that do not map onto local communities and identities—can generate critical tensions among bordering authorities as well as grievances among local populations, hampering the whole process from within. Indeed, at the time of writing the SCRCA deal seems to have hit stalemate, and the mayoral election has been delayed for 12 months. This hiatus has encouraged the re-emergence of proposals for a 'pan-Yorkshire' devolution deal among some local leaders in other parts of the region.

WEST YORKSHIRE COMBINED AUTHORITY

In West Yorkshire a Combined Authority (WYCA) was formed in April 2014 and the first devolution agreement was formulated in March 2015, building on the previous Growth and City Deals. Thus, in principle, similar to SCRCA, West Yorkshire had both the governance structures in place and an agreement with the government to provide a basis for getting a devolution deal in 2015. However, the process that should have led to this turned out to be much more complex. As a senior figure within the combined authority explained:

In March 2015 we signed a devolution agreement with the government. (...)It gave us some devolved powers without an elected mayor. Then... we get a general election and the Tories win! So they saw that as the green light to take the lead, to say 'we're not going to agree to any devolution deal without a mayor', so we got stuck there. (...) As soon as they said this people here started talking about the way forward and there were differences of opinion. (WYCA representative, June 2016)

The election of a new Conservative government in May 2015 was instrumental in changing the direction of the devolution deal in West Yorkshire (WY), especially in terms of content and boundaries. George Osborne, as Chancellor at the time, led the process imposing the introduction of 'metro-mayors' as a requirement for any new deal to be signed. The fact that the SCR accepted this element, in spite of general scepticism, set a precedent in the region. However, for WY the elected mayor triggered new controversies, creating frictions between the local level and national politicians elected in the area, based on the geography of the deal. Ideally, the City-Region geography should have been the most suitable one for WY. But the fact that the Leeds City-Region (LCR) does include parts of North Yorkshire—a Conservative stronghold—meant that party-political interests got in the way, impinging on the devolution deal process.

The new Tory government coming in last year was a game changer. Manchester had agreed to have a mayor, and that became the benchmark. Sheffield went for it too. They were not 100 per cent convinced, but they went for it. But for us the geography of the deal...it's a real problem. (Leeds City Council representative, July 2016)

Osborne said he wants devolution to be about economic growth around cities and their regions. (...)We already got an economic footprint which was the LCR and LEP. So WY leaders agreed that was the best geography. (...)We put in our bid...and that's where it all started to get messy because if it's a LCR deal that means the five WY councils plus Harrogate, Craven, Selby and York. So North Yorkshire County Council said 'hang on, we don't want these districts going off' and then North Yorkshire MPs got in too saying 'we don't support the LCR model because it splits North Yorkshire'. Then WY Conservative MPs decided they didn't want a WY model either because it would deliver a Labour mayor – so they went to see Osborne while we were discussing a deal...and somebody had the bright idea 'ooh, now Sheffield's gone, let's put all the rest in the same pot and call it Greater Yorkshire'! (WYCA representative, June 2016)

We've hit stalemate because North Yorkshire have talked to Conservative MPs...and then Conservative MPs in North Yorkshire and WY went to see Osborne and said they wouldn't accept any deal that would deliver a Labour mayor. Osborne couldn't afford to upset so many Tory MPs. (Leeds City Council representative, August 2016)

The lack of a clear footprint by the government on the size, shape and remit of devolution deals has opened a space for unexpected controversies. Whilst in the view of the Treasury, devolution should prompt economic growth, foster local synergies and improve decision-making at the local level, party-political interests have been thrust to the centre stage. Local authorities in WY want a deal that works for their 'economic area' (i.e. the city-region), but at the same time, arguably, they also want to maintain current leadership structures. However, Conservative MPs see this as a threat to their authority especially because, based on the political geography of the area, a WY mayor would most likely be Labour. Neither the previous nor the current government have managed to address this issue, and the data collected suggest that Whitehall is engaging in multiple conversations with local authorities and MPs, giving mixed and often conflicting answers. This is a major, unexpected shortcoming of devolution, which explains why the LCR deal has not been signed yet. In addition, this situation has prompted further frictions about geography between WY and the Eastern part of the region. Conservatives MPs would prefer a 'Greater Yorkshire Deal', which would include West and North Yorkshire, the East Riding and Hull—as this would give more chances to elect a Conservative mayor. However, WY authorities do not buy into this plan, and see it as unfeasible.

Greater Yorkshire? If a bit of it [SCR] leaves what's left is Lesser Yorkshire, not Greater. If you had devo deals based on that geography it would not be focussed. (...)I'm not bothered about fishermen in Bridlington. I'm responsible for this area, and my job is to grow the economy *here*. (...)There isn't a Yorkshire economy, but there is a WY economy. They [Humberside] should be doing a deal based on their economic footprint, not try to gain from ours. (WYCA representative, June 2016)

[The city-region] scale is what the government prefers because there is already a deal, really. But it can't be signed off because of the Tory MPs. And then you get Hull saying they want to be involved as well. Well, that's nonsense, because Hull should be creating a Combined Authority based on the Humberside. (...) But they've not being able to do it because over there they fall out like ferrets in a sack. (…) So they want to join WY. Well, they're not part of WY, they've got a different economy…devolution is not about local government reorganisation, it's about growing our cities. (…) I'm told by Conservatives that I'm being political because I don't want a Greater Yorkshire model. That's nonsense. (WYCA representative, June 2016)

These extracts show that beyond tensions between local leaders in WY and Conservative MPs, the geography of the deal has also triggered frictions with other parts of Yorkshire. WY does not see the proposal for a 'Greater Yorkshire Deal' as palatable, and they use the economic argument (i.e. the fact that WY and the Humberside rely on very different sectors and have different assets) to support their claims. However, this could perhaps also be seen as a way to cover up local political interest. In WY Labour has a strong hold on most of the local authorities, and opening the deal towards the Humberside could challenge this. Interestingly, the two areas managed to work together under the Regional Development Agency (RDA, Yorkshire Forward) that was set in place by the Labour government—at the time, no one claimed that there was not a Yorkshire economy. But RDAs had no directly elected figurehead attached to them. Thus, it could be argued that the approach adopted by the government for devolution deals has set local authorities to compete against each other, for economic and political reasons. This seems to be generating a sort of 'local tribalism' and a vicious circle of 'blame games' both across the region and towards national politicians that could prove problematic to handle in the long term, and seem also to run counter the principles underpinning the Northern Powerhouse agenda.

WY sees a host of opportunities for economic development in the devolution deal and, despite the issues outlined above, they are still determined to sign an agreement. Similar to SCR, the idea of gaining decision-making powers on key sectors such as transport, skills and housing based on the view that the local level can make better decisions for their communities in these policy areas is seen as a key prospect:

These are key planks of the public sector and if we had more control over them we could do a much better job. (…) Being able to make decisions without having to get into a bidding war, going to Westminster and prove who's more in need than others, but also if we get the ability to raise money then there's a much more sustainable model rather than always waiting for the next statement from the government. (Leeds City Council representative, August 2016)

Can devolution be a good thing? Can it benefit our residents? Yes, it can, because decisions are best made locally...it can make a difference, but devolution has to mean *real* devolution, it has to have real money and powers. (WYCA representative, June 2016)

This links to another theme that has emerged from the interviews. WY does want a deal, but at the same time it is not prepared to settle for anything that is not ambitious in scope and resources. Interestingly, LCR sees itself as a powerhouse in its own right and, drawing on its alleged status as economic engine of Yorkshire, local leaders believe that the government could not realise its Northern Powerhouse agenda if they were not on-board, and will have to find a compromise with them. As emphasised by local actors:

Leeds has already got one of the biggest Growth Deals in the country, so why should we settle for something that's less than what we've already got? (...) LCR has the strongest economic footprint [in Yorkshire], we are a powerhouse (...) and we're not going to settle for *any* deal. (...)There is no Northern Powerhouse if Leeds does not get a good deal. (Leeds City Council representative, August 2016)

There's an argument to say we should get this deal as the precursor to something stronger down the line. (...) I'm a hardliner...I think we've got to play real tough and get the government to accept our asks because the better deal we can get now, the more likely we can get something further down the line. (WYCA representative, June 2016)

The main priority for LCR is to maintain its role as economic driver of the region, and get a deal that matches such position. Thus, if the government was prepared to offer an ambitious deal to LCR, leaders would also accept the institution of an elected mayor—even though, similarly to SCRCA, there is widespread scepticism about this point.

The mayor...there's scepticism about it, but we could live with it if our asks were accepted. People in this city voted against a mayor a few years ago...but this time it was imposed by Osborne, which is blackmail...saying you can't have devolution without a mayor! But that's where we're at. (WYCA representative, June 2016)

The mayor...I guess it depends on who then comes through and what they actually do with it, and if they make it into a success that people can see...

that actually has a material impact on the quality of their lives for the better...then it will generate more interest, but if it doesn't work...if there's a
low turnout... And they will have to work well with the existing governance structures, with the CA...so you have to build in safeguards, like veto
for CA members, so that it's actually a democratic model that reflects the
view of the members and their populations. (Leeds City Council representative, August 2016)

These extracts suggest that local leaders are aware of the problems that
could be generated by the introduction of a 'metro-mayor', especially for
what concerns their powers and the extent to which they could resonate
among the public. Local actors feel that they could work around these
issues. Yet, there seems to be a paradox in the way in which they frame
public engagement and democracy. On the one hand, local authorities recognise the need to have citizens' support for the new structures.
For example, a low turnout at mayoral elections could impinge on the
accountability of the figurehead and of the whole deal. On the other,
however, the fact that the public has not had any voice over the devolution deal debate in WY does not seem to be a matter of concern, as local
leaders see themselves as better placed to make this kind of decisions.

Democratic engagement? I'm not bothered. The thing about leadership
is that sometimes you've got to lead. (...)When the public are asked that
kind of question that they actually don't understand because it's compli-
cated, it's about economies...how are they supposed to know what's best?
(...)We know our people, and we know what's best for them. If people
understand the real impact, they would be behind it. (...)So we should
lead on this. (WYCA representative, June 2016)

Like in SCRCA, in WY there seems to be an assumption that public
engagement is something that can be easily 'steered', and that political
leaders have both the ability to make the best decisions for their citizens
and to make them understand the value of the deal. Whilst the first part
of the argument builds on a question of accountability and representation which can be seen as rational and coherent, the second one is less
straightforward—and it remains to be seen whether the local citizenry
would turn up to vote for a new set of governance structures they know
very little about. Ironically, by adopting this approach local leaders seem
to replicate the impositions made on them by central government and
apply them to their local populations. This also emphasises how the very

idea of 'localism', which, in theory, should be meant to 'empower local communities', is being interpreted and implemented in a controversial manner.

As of autumn 2016, the LCR devolution deal was still at a standstill. Local politicians seemed to be hopeful, but they were also aware that things could change under the new government. Most local leaders emphasised that it was important to keep an eye on developments in neighbouring areas, such as SCR, before making the next step. Interestingly, soon after the SCRCA deal hit stalemate in December 2016, WY council leaders released an official statement on devolution (WYCA 2017a). In the document, they reinforce the view that LCR provides the best basis for devolution, but they also emphasise that, so far, their ambitions to gain a devolution deal have been thwarted by the lack of response from the government, and that they are "determined LCR cannot be left behind" (WYCA 2017a). For this reason, they are now willing to consider other options for devolution. Remarkably, in the face of the government's lack of support for their proposed deal, WY local leaders seem to have changed their views on the geography of the deal. They now suggest that a pan-Yorkshire deal 'underpinned by the existing combined authorities is one of the options that could unlock our LCR deal, along with those of our colleagues in SCR, and the North and East of Yorkshire' (WYCA 2017a). This idea was further developed in a WYCA meeting held in February 2017, where leaders fleshed out a devolution deal model for Yorkshire based on (i) a single Mayor with multiple combined authorities (including existing and potential new ones) representing distinct functional economic areas across the region; (ii) a cabinet (made of LEPs and Unions representatives); and (iii) an Assembly (to ensure local members' and other partners' involvement, and to hold the Mayor and the CAs into account) similar to the London model (WYCA 2017b).

In essence, this proposal seems to resemble a calculated compromise: a pan-Yorkshire scale with a single figurehead could appeal to Conservative representatives at local and national levels; but it would also allow the WYCA to get a devolution deal whilst maintaining a degree of political and economic autonomy. WY is determined not to be left in the 'deal have-nots' camp, and has therefore adopted a strategic approach to secure devolution for its city-region, even if this comes as part of a wider pan-Yorkshire settlement. This also shows that local leaders in WY are trying to exert agency, and reverse the government's top-down approach to devolution by coming up with their own, alternative proposal. It is also interesting to note that the WYCA proposal would involve the introduction of yet another model (and geographic footprint) of devolution deals—complicating further the map of governance across the North of England, as well as the architecture of the Northern Powerhouse.

However, in a recent interview, the Northern Powerhouse Minister Andrew Percy has defined WY proposals as a mere 'distraction', and claimed that the SCR deal will go ahead, whilst WY and Hull and the East Riding should work towards a 'Greater Yorkshire Deal' so as to ensure that no one in the region is left out (Young 2017). Thus, for the time being, the WYCA proposal is still in flux, and it is not clear whether other areas in the region (especially SCR) and the government will be willing to agree to it.

HULL AND THE EAST RIDING

In many respects, the Eastern part of Yorkshire can be seen as the outlier in the devolution deals debate. First, the South Bank of the Humber—i.e. North and North East Lincolnshire—did initially decide to join the Greater Lincolnshire deal (although this eventually collapsed in November 2016). In short, long-standing local rivalries between the two banks of the river are 'splitting' the geography of the Humber. Second, and related to this, there is no Combined Authority or city-region in the area, and the Humber LEP is the only 'joint body' that brings together local leaders and business. Thus, there is a lack of the structures that are in place in LCR and SCR, on which to build a deal.

As explained in the previous sections, SCRCA and WYCA have developed a clear strategy for themselves, which focuses on the interests of their own areas and, at least until recently, they did not seem to be a prepared to engage with the East Riding and Hull. The data collected in these locations are particularly interesting, especially because they shed light on issues that did not emerge in SCR and WY. For instance, interviewees underlined how other regional actors have marginalised them. Allegedly, in summer 2015, talks were held between representatives of Yorkshire authorities to devise a 'regional' devolution deal proposal. Initially, Hull and the East Riding were assured that this would go ahead, but then SCR and WY put in their own proposals, without informing them.

About 15 months ago I went to Leeds to broach this idea of a wider Yorkshire concept, almost going back to the Yorkshire Forward days. But Sheffield didn't like it because they were down the road with their deal. (...) So we looked at 'Greater Yorkshire'. But then it became clear that Leeds did not like the idea (...) because with that geography there would have been more Conservatives. (...)They [WY] said 'if Sheffield comes in, we're in'. So they blame it on Sheffield...and went their own way too. (...) There was a disastrous meeting with the government where the WY people bad-mouthed us and it was really unpleasant. (Humber LEP representative, July 2016)

We had informal meetings with WY, everybody seemed happy about a Greater Yorkshire deal. (...) This takes us to July 2015, the LGA conference...we're all there, we were going to announce this...but the District Councils of North Yorkshire were called into a meeting with WY leaders... and we were never asked, we didn't know...that whatever we said in the past, they didn't want to be part of it anymore. (...)The reason given was that there's no economic geography...but the truth is that it was decided politically. They'd worked out the political formulation to return a Labour mayor. (Hull City Council representative, Sept 2016)

These extracts suggest that Hull and the East Riding were left in the cold for political reasons, and local authorities in WY used economic arguments to justify their choices. This is an interesting point because it indicates that, as previously argued, the introduction of devolution deals have triggered a dangerous type of competition across Yorkshire, rather than fostering synergies at the local level. The idea of 'local tribalism' and intra-regional 'peripheralisation' surfaces again here. This casts doubts not only about the system of governance that could emerge from any devolution deal in Yorkshire but also on how such fragmented scenario, characterised by rivalries and inequalities, could feed into the notion of a Northern Powerhouse.

Hull and the East Riding see many opportunities in getting a devolution deal either for Greater Yorkshire or for the whole of Yorkshire, especially in term of economic development. Unlike other areas, from their perspective the economic diversity of Yorkshire is a strength rather than a weakness. They also believe that, to be effective, devolution deals have to have a sufficient size. Covering a population of just over a million people, their area is too small to go alone and succeed, whilst a Yorkshire deal could have the right mass and economic footprint, and more leverage at Westminster. As emphasised by a local actor:

> Yorkshire would have been a fantastic Combined Authority for a deal... it could have had so much power...five million people, it's the size of Scotland...it would have had a real place on the national stage, and one of the strengths is that we have a diverse economy...and the Yorkshire brand, that really resonates among the population and in the national and international stage...but we're going to be split off into separate little chunks that actually give us nothing. (East Riding Council representative, Sept 2016)

Once SCR agreed its deal in 2015, Hull and the East Riding saw Greater Yorkshire as the best alternative scale for devolution. Thus, they pushed for this option, accepting in full also the introduction of a mayor. To this end, local authorities in the area were working with representatives of North Yorkshire to put together a 'spatial plan'. This was going to be used in the first place to vouch for a deal with WY—failing this, the only alternative was for the three areas to try and create their own Combined Authority.

> We're working on a joint spatial plan, but it isn't a natural economic geography and if we were to have a Combined Authority it would have to reflect different interests...the city interests of York and Hull...and the rural aspect of that bigger area, then you have the coastal strip's interests...so it would be a fairly complicated deal to achieve...and Craven and Harrogate's aspiration to go with WY...there's also that issue. (...) We're doing that, but we're also still pushing for a Greater Yorkshire Deal... but the economic geography has got contaminated by politics. (Hull City Council representative, Sept 2016)

> We said 'look, if [LCR deal] is happening we don't want to miss out because we feel we ought to be part of the CA, this could go on for years and we need to get somewhere'. So we're looking at forming a North Yorkshire, York, East Riding and Hull Combined Authority. (...) We would have two separate CAs, us and WY, but actually demonstrating how we work together and then at some point you would hope that it would come together as one CA. (East Riding Council representative, Sept 2016)

The creation of a separate combined authority is clearly proving problematic and, as of autumn 2016, the area did hang on the hope of convincing WY to take them on-board—although, as shown in the previous section, the climate in Leeds was not particularly supportive of a Greater

Yorkshire option. The risk here is that Hull and the East Riding could be left out, and could not get any devolution deal. Local leaders are aware of the fact that this could have disastrous consequences for their area, deepening issues of economic development and inequality in a part of the region that is already facing substantial issues.

> Our fear is that we'll get left behind, economically, socially...so we're using every possible tactic we can to come to some compromise. (Hull City Council representative, Sept 2016)

> If you look a powers and funding attached to the deals, there's not much there...but it would make a difference for us...we all know the issues we have in this area...but also, being left behind would have a psychological effect...that we're going to be bypassed in terms of economic development...leaving behind an area that's already been left behind. This would affect local authorities and the people...the idea that we're not good or worth enough. (Humber LEP representative, June 2016)

Local leaders are conscious of the limits of the current devolution deals. Nonetheless, there is a real concern that being excluded from devolution could engender a negative reaction among local authorities and across the population. This links to issues of democratic participation and engagement. On this question, all the local representatives interviewed were aware of the fact that, on the one hand, devolution would not work if the people are not behind it and, on the other, that there is a lesson to be learnt from Brexit—i.e. that the local population here is disillusioned with traditional politics and politicians. So leaving them out, or including them in a deal which would lead to the creation of new structures they know very little about, could end up engendering further alienation and dissatisfaction with politics—compromising the whole idea of devolution. Interestingly, interviewees in Hull and the East Riding were the only one to mention the role of identity and regional pride in the devolution process, beyond the economic argument—underlining how a 'Yorkshire option' is the only way to engage people, because the citizenry does recognise and identify with the regional dimension. Although there is only limited evidence to support this view (see Flinders et al. 2016), it is remarkable that only leaders in the Eastern part of Yorkshire see regional culture and identity as elements that could (and should) play a key role in the debate on devolution. However, the other CAs and the government have shown no sign of interest in this respect, and devolution continues to be framed primarily in economic terms.

Up until autumn 2016, with the inception of a new government and the uncertainties related to Brexit, but also due to the resistances of WY, the debate on devolution in the Eastern part of Yorkshire had stalled. Recent developments in WY have provided new hopes for local leaders. This shows that the future of devolution for Hull and the East Riding is still highly dependent on decision made by existing CAs and by the government. It also emphasises their relatively marginal status, suggesting that 'weaker economic poles' struggle to have any real voice in the devolution debate.

CONCLUSION

The analysis developed in this chapter shows that devolution deals in Yorkshire could open up new opportunities for local authorities, especially for policy areas such as transport, skills, housing and business which are key to local economies. At the same time, however, it has also highlighted that the approach of the government has many shortcomings.

In the first place, there is a clear fear that what is on offer may not be 'real devolution': it is a partnership plan with a distinctively economic focus, yet based on a loose definition of the parameters that this should follow. Economic theories of agglomeration (Overman 2012, 2013) have been used to sustain the idea of 'city-region deals', in spite of the fact that there is scant evidence (see Berry 2016; Harrison and Heley 2015) as to whether this may actually be the only viable solution, especially for a region that has a diverse economic and social outlook such as Yorkshire. Indeed, scholars have suggested that in the context of devolution deals perhaps there is a need to contest such taken-for-granted assumptions about how economies work, looking instead at how particular models of economies and markets come to be inserted into policy debates in ways that end up privileging certain groups of areas and actors over others (Haughton et al. 2016: 359).

In addition, the powers on offer are limited, Whitehall departments continue to show resistance towards relinquishing control, and the funding attached to the deals is not only small, but also still tightly controlled by the centre and restrained by its austerity agenda (CLES and SPERI 2016). Local authorities will be able to 'raise their own money' through business rates retention—this is welcomed by those areas that could get a devolution deal, and is likely to become the backbone of how local government is funded. And yet, this could create further problems in

Yorkshire, as most councils at the moment are not in financial surplus. Local leaders are aware of these limits: yet, they would be willing to take the risk of embarking in this venture, because they know that the price for being left out would be high for their communities. They also hope that the deals could pave the way to a more ambitious form of devolution in the future, although there is no clear assurance on this point, especially within the new government. Indeed, recent developments in SCR suggest that even the limited powers 'promised' in 2015 could be not be relinquished.

Second, and related to this, in the view of the government devolution is solely about improving economic growth. Yet, the lack of a clear economic and geographical blueprint for the deals have led to a paradox: devolution could end up benefitting the areas that already perform well on balance, such as SCR and WYCA, but it could also see the areas that need real improvement, such as Hull and the East Riding, being excluded. This is an important point to acknowledge because it shows a lack of 'long term thinking' on the part of the government on the effects that intra-regional competition can create, and how these could affect the wider Northern Powerhouse plan. If this latter is, as claimed, about bridging the North/South divide and give the North the means to foster its own economic development (Osborne 2015), then the picture emerging from Yorkshire suggests that such a goal may not be achieved. Indeed, far from creating new synergies across the region and close economic and social cleavages, devolution deals have spurred local divisions, and could engender new dynamics of peripheralisation—where the areas already lagging behind could end up being placed further at the margins, widening the gap between 'deals haves' and 'have nots', and creating 'winners and losers of devolution' (see also Muldoon-Smith and Greenhalgh in this volume).

Findings in this chapter shed light on how linking the discourse of devolution to economic development could also have other perverse effects. It has created an unhealthy climate of competition among local authorities, and it has generated a space for new political frictions, across local governments and between them and regional MPs, especially on issues of leadership and authority connected with the introduction of new elected mayors—showing a gross miscalculation on the part of the government. As illustrated, economic motives have overlapped with or have been used to defend political ones, exacerbating 'local tribalism', and vicious 'blame games' between actors. In this context, existing CAs are pressing ahead concentrating on the immediate benefits for their own city-regions, whilst the areas that do not have any formal architecture in place struggle to keep up with what has become, in practice, a race for devolution deals. This is still true even in light of the recent proposals for a pan-Yorkshire deal developed by the WYCA. As shown in the analysis of this case, the primary goal for local leaders is still to unlock the best possible deal for LCR, and maintain some degree of economic and political autonomy even within a wider regional footprint.

As a result, a region in which local authorities used to work well under the aegis of RDAs, which secured a single regional vision and programme of development (Yorkshire and the Humber Regional Committee Report 2010; Roberts and Benneworth 2001), is now divided, and cut across by rivalries, suspicions and antagonisms. Interviewees in the three areas analysed have described current relationships between CAs as 'problematic' and 'nowhere near where they should be'—which underlines further the issue of regional cohesion. Local leaders in Yorkshire do recognise the need to work together, and several of them have indicated that perhaps there should be three or four CAs working under a 'strategic umbrella'—but the way in which the debate on devolution deals has been developed by the government has narrowed, rather than promoted, space for these collaborations. The WYCA pan-Yorkshire deal proposal could be seen as a step in this direction. Yet, the proposed model—based on a single elected mayor for Yorkshire with multiple combined authorities—implies that local interests still play a predominant role in the debate. Furthermore, as already emphasised, it remains to be seen whether all local authorities and the central government will be prepared to take this forward.

This piecemeal approach to devolution—based on elites' partnerships and driven by a variety of national and local interests—is further highlighted by the lack of public engagement and awareness. Whilst local leaders have been busy discussing among themselves and with the government what is the 'best deal' for their areas, the local population has a very limited understanding of what is happening. A Survation poll commissioned by the Yorkshire Devolution movement in August 2016 showed that nearly 55 per cent of the population had never heard of devolution deals plans, and less than 9 per cent felt at all informed about it (Survation Poll 2016).

This begs the question of whether devolution in Yorkshire (as elsewhere) could work without public support. Local leaders seem to assume they can 'steer' democratic engagement at their will, but local election results and the outcome of the EU membership referendum give strong signals in the opposite direction. Similar to markets, new state spaces such as city-regions and combined authorities led by mayors or the Northern Powerhouse can be devised by politician based on 'rational economic strategies'—but they do not operate in the void (Brenner et al. 2003; Jessop 2012). On the contrary, their success, in political and economic terms, is tightly connected with the social spaces they are part of and help shape (Haughton et al. 2016). From this angle, if devolution deals and the institutional architecture that underpins them do not resonate with, influence or help mobilising public opinion and imaginaries, they risk to become 'dry branches'—i.e. new structures with little traction and accountability, which would in turn struggle to achieve their alleged goal of empowering localities and boost the economy from the bottom-up. Democracy may not be the ultimate goal of devolution in the current context, but considering it as a 'non-issue' could create problems in the long term, delegitimising the devolution agenda—and, with it, the Northern Powerhouse—from within.

Overall, the case of Yorkshire shows that the system of governance emerging from devolution deals is profoundly fragmented and problematic in political, economic and democratic terms. Far from delivering a much-heralded 'revolution' and providing a sustainable system of territorial reform, the government's approach to devolution seems to resemble a patchwork of ad hoc 'spatial fixes' that will not necessarily improve economic development or local politics and democracy, and lack a clear endpoint. Crucially, this could end up playing against the wider Northern Powerhouse narrative, as the current path of devolution is creating new, unexpected issues across Yorkshire which add to, rather than address, existing gaps.

The standstill in the SCR deal and the uncertainties over the proposals for a pan-Yorkshire deal mean that no local authority in the region will get any devolution in the near future. Thus, for the time being, Yorkshire will be left at the margins of the devolution agenda and, as results of this, it could become the 'hole in the middle' of the Northern Powerhouse—putting into question its rationale, geographic footprint and economic prospects. If the situation in Yorkshire gives a measure of what is happening in the context of devolution deals in the North, outside Greater Manchester, the road ahead both for devolution and the Northern Powerhouse could be much rockier than the previous Chancellor had envisaged.

NOTES

1. The fieldwork consisted of 12 semi-structured interviews conducted by the author in South Yorkshire, West Yorkshire, Hull and the East Riding of Yorkshire. In this chapter the personal details of the interviewees have been anonymised in order to protect their privacy. I am indebted to all the interviewees who gave up their time to talk to me for their invaluable contributions.
2. It should be noted that, at the time of writing, events are unfolding in a fast and often unpredictable way. For obvious reasons, the analysis can only cover developments until February 2017, when this chapter was completed.
3. Initially, SCRCA included four constituent councils (Sheffield City Council and the Metropolitan Borough Councils of Barnsley, Doncaster and Rotherham) and five non-constituents councils (Chesterfield Borough Council and the District Councils of Bassetlaw, Bolsover, Derbyshire Dale and North East Derbyshire). From the outset, the 'geography' and boundaries of the SCRCA have proved a problematic, and will be discussed later on in this chapter.

REFERENCES

BBC. 2016. EU referendum: South Yorkshire backs Brexit campaign. *BBC News*, June 24. Available from: http://www.bbc.co.uk/news/uk-england-south-yorkshire-36617899. Accessed 3 Oct 2016.

Berry, C. 2016. Osborne's Legacy is arguably one of centralisation: So what would real devolution look like? *CityMetric*, July 26. Available from: http://www.citymetric.com/politics/osborne-s-legacy-arguably-one-centralisation-so-what-would-real-devolution-look-2287. Accessed 19 Sept 2016.

Blunkett, D., M. Flinders, and B. Prosser. 2016. Devolution, evolution, revolution...democracy? What's really happening to English local governance? *Political Quarterly* 87 (4): 553–564.

Brenner, N., B. Jessop, M. Jones, and G. McLeod (eds.). 2003. *State/space: A reader*. London: Blackwell.

Cameron, D. 2015. Election 2015: Prime Minister's speech. Available from: https://www.gov.uk/government/speeches/election-2015-prime-ministers-speech. Accessed 20 Sept 2016.

CLES and SPERI. 2016. *The real deal: Pushing the parameters of devolution deals*. Report. Available from: http://speri.dept.shef.ac.uk/wp-content/uploads/2016/07/The-Real-Deal-SPERI-CLES.pdf. Accessed 3 Oct 2016.

Flinders, M., K. Ghose, W. Jennings, E. Molloy, B. Prosser, A. Renwick, G. Smith, and P. Spada. 2016. *Democracy Matters. Lessons from the 2015 Citizens' Assemblies on English Devolution*. Report, UK Citizens' Assemblies Project.

Available from: http://citizensassembly.co.uk/wp-content/uploads/2016/04/Democracy-Matters-2015-Citizens-Assemblies-Report.pdf. Accessed 20 Sept 2016.

Giovannini, A. 2015. The Scottish Indyref, one year on: Devolution in England ignores the key lessons from Scotland's referendum. *SPERI Comment*, 22 Sept 2015. Available from: http://speri.dept.shef.ac.uk/2015/09/22/the-scottish-indyref-one-year-on/. Accessed 19 Sept 2016.

Giovannini, A. 2016. Towards a 'new English regionalism' in the North? The case of Yorkshire First. *Political Quarterly* 87 (4): 590–600.

Giovannini, A., and A. Mycock. 2016. The Northern Powerhouse needs to be more than a slogan. *The Conversation*, 10 May 2016. Available from: http://theconversation.com/the-northern-powerhouse-needs-to-be-more-than-a-slogan-59043. Accessed 19 Sept 2016.

Harrison, J., and J. Heley. 2015. Governing beyond the metropolis: Placing the rural in city region development. *Urban Studies* 52: 1113–1133.

Haughton, G., I. Deas, S. Hincks, and K. Ward. 2016. Mythic Manchester: Devo Manc, the Northern Powerhouse and rebalancing the English economy. *Cambridge Journal of Regions, Economy and Society* 9: 355–370.

Hazell, R. 2006. *The English question*. Manchester: Manchester University Press.

HM Treasury. 2015. *Chancellor on building a Northern powerhouse*. May 14. Available from: https://www.gov.uk/government/speeches/chancellor-on-building-a-northern-powerhouse. Accessed 20 Sept 2016.

Heseltine, M. (Lord). 2012. *No stone unturned: In pursuit of growth. Independent report*. London: Department for Business, Innovation & Skills. Available from: https://www.gov.uk/government/uploads/system/uploads/attachment_data/file/34648/12-1213-no-stone-unturned-in-pursuit-of-growth.pdf. Accessed 20 Sept 2016.

Jennings, W., and G. Stoker. 2016. The Bifurcation of politics: Two Englands. *Political Quarterly* 87 (3): 372–382.

Jessop, B. 2012. *Cultural political economy, spatial imaginaries, regional economic dynamics, CPERC working paper*. Lancaster: University of Lancaster.

Local Government Association. 2016. *Get in on the Act: Cities and Local Government Devolution Act 2016*. London: LGA.

Localism Act 2011. (c. 20). London: HMSO.

Osborne, G. 2015. Building a Northern Powerhouse: Chancellor speech. Available from: https://www.gov.uk/government/speeches/chancellor-on-building-a-northern-powerhouse. Accessed Sept 2016.

Overman, H. 2012. Investing in the UK's most successful cities is the surest recipe for national growth. *LSE Politics and Policy Blog*, 26 January 2012. Available from: http://blogs.lse.ac.uk/politicsandpolicy/2012/01/26/investment-cities-national-growth/. Accessed 26 Sept 2016

Overman, H. 2013. The economic future of British cities. *CentrePiece, Centre for Economic Performance, LSE.* Available from: http://cep.lse.ac.uk/pubs/download/cp389.pdf. Accessed 16 Sept 2016.

Perraudin, F. 2016. Sheffield region's bid to absorb Chesterfield faces legal setback after ruling. *The Guardian,* December 22. Available from: https://www.theguardian.com/politics/2016/dec/22/sheffield-city-regions-bid-to-absorb-chesterfield-faces-legal-setback. Accessed 17 Jan 2017.

Prosser, B., A. Renwick, A. Giovannini, M. Sandford, M. Flinders, W. Jennings, G. Smith, P. Spada, G. Stoker, and K. Ghose. 2017. Citizen participation and changing governance: Cases of devolution in England. *Policy & Politics* 45 (2): 251–269.

Richards, D., and M.J. Smith. 2015. Devolution in England, the british political tradition and the absence of consultation, consensus and consideration. *Representation* 51 (4): 385–401.

Roberts, P., and P. Benneworth. 2001. Pathways to the future? An initial assessment of RDA strategies and their contribution to integrated regional development. *Local Economy* 16 (2): 142–159.

Sandford, M. 2016a. *Devolution to local government in England.* House of Commons Library Briefing Paper N. 07029, 19 July 2016.

Sandford, M. 2016b. Signing up to devolution: The prevalence of contract over governance in English devolution policy. *Regional & Federal Studies* 27 (1): 63–82.

Sanford, M. (ed.). 2009. *The Northern Veto.* Manchester: Manchester University Press.

Sheffield City Council. 2016. *Extraordinary meeting—Chief executive report: Sheffield city region devolution agreement: Ratification of the Proposal.* Sheffield: SCC.

Sheffield City Region. 2016. *SCR devolution consultation: Results summary.* Sheffield: SCR. Available from: http://sheffieldcityregiondevolution.org.uk/wp-content/uploads/2016/02/Appendix-C_SCR-Devolution-Consultation-summary-report.pdf. Accessed 20 Sept 2016.

Survation Poll. 2016. Views on devolution in Yorkshire, August 16. Available from: http://survation.com/archive/2016-2/. Accessed 19 Sept 2016.

Tomaney, J. 2016. Limits of devolution: Localism, economics and post-democracy. *Political Quarterly* 87 (4): 546–552.

West Yorkshire Combined Authority (WYCA). 2017a. West Yorkshire Council Leaders' statement on devolution', January 17. Available from: http://west-yorks-ca.gov.uk/News/Articles/Leaders-devolution-statement/. Accessed 17 Jan 2017.

West Yorkshire Combined Authority (WYCA). 2017b. Devolution discussion paper, February 2. Available from: http://westyorks-ca.gov.uk/WorkArea/DownloadAsset.aspx?id=4294970685. Accessed 3 Feb 2017.

Willett, J., and A. Giovannini. 2014. The uneven path of English devolution. Top down vs. bottom up regionalism in England—Cornwall and the North East compared. *Political Studies* 62 (2): 343–360.

Yorkshire and the Humber Regional Committee. 2010. *The work of Yorkshire forward. First report of session 2009–10. House of Commons Report.* London: The Stationery Office Limited.

Young, A. 2017. Andrew Percy MP calls for greater Yorkshire devolution deal, *Hull Mail,* January 9. Available from: http://www.hulldailymail.co.uk/andrew-percy-mp-calls-for-greater-yorkshire-devolution-deal/story-30042807-detail/story.html. Accessed 10 Jan 2017.

AUTHOR BIOGRAPHY

Arianna Giovannini is Senior Lecturer in Local Politics at the Department of Politics and Public Policy, De Montfort University (DMU), where she is also a member of the Local Governance Research Unit (LGRU) and the Centre for Urban Research on Austerity (CURA). Before joining DMU she was a researcher at the Sheffield Political Economy Research Institute (SPERI), University of Sheffield, where she is now an Honorary Research Fellow, and a research assistant for the White Rose Consortium for the North of England project at POLIS, University of Leeds. Her research focuses on devolution, territorial and political identity, regionalism and democracy—with a particular emphasis on the 'English Question' and the North of England. She has published widely on these themes in leading academic journals such as *Political Studies, Policy & Politics* and *The Political Quarterly.*

CHAPTER 8

Leading the Way? The Relationship Between 'Devo-Manc', Combined Authorities and the Northern Powerhouse

Georgina Blakeley and Brendan Evans

Abstract The proposal for a Northern Powerhouse and the development of combined authorities are inextricably connected. In both cases, Manchester plays a pivotal role which is not challenged by the May Government's focus on national rather than simply Northern regeneration. Manchester's leadership of the Combined Authorities initiative is based on its institutional maturity and its central role in the promotion of the Independent Economic Review to develop an economic strategy for the Northern Powerhouse. There is evidence that in the existing governance vacuum of the Northern Powerhouse, the leadership of the GMCA will provide a fulcrum, although there remains uncertainty about the long-term sustainability of both combined authorities and the Northern Powerhouse, until both are tested by the decisions to be taken

G. Blakeley (✉)
The Open University, Milton Keynes, UK
e-mail: georgina.blakeley@open.ac.uk

B. Evans
University of Huddersfield, Huddersfield, UK
e-mail: b.j.evans@hud.ac.uk

© The Author(s) 2018   199
C. Berry and A. Giovannini (eds.), *Developing England's North*,
Building a Sustainable Political Economy: SPERI Research & Policy,
https://doi.org/10.1007/978-3-319-62560-7_8

about Northern transport interconnectivity and the impact of the metro-mayoral elections.

Keyword Combined Authorities · Devolution · Governance Manchester · Northern Powerhouse

INTRODUCTION

The devolution of power and resources to Combined Authorities (CAs) and the invention of the Northern Powerhouse are distinct policy initiatives which have become 'strongly interconnected and overlapping political projects' (Giovanni and Mycock 2016). A case study of Manchester sheds light on these interconnections. Manchester is the benchmark for devolution deals and the creation of CAs and is the fulcrum of the NP. Manchester's council leaders provide a link between CAs and the NP through their leadership.

Manchester has long been in the vanguard of devolution. It was George Osborne, when Chancellor of the Exchequer, who 'hitched together' the NP and CAs. Tellingly he chose Manchester as the venue to deliver his 'Northern Powerhouse speech' in June 2014. Manchester had already appropriated the label 'economic powerhouse' to describe its own ability to 'generate and spread wealth within the city-region and positively impact regional and UK growth' (AGMA 2009: 8). While the NP label is often indiscriminately attached to any Northern initiative, the concept describes the need to power up the Northern economy by increasing its economic productivity until it reaches the levels of the rest of the UK. HM Treasury under Osborne's leadership belatedly responded to the economic recession of 2008–2009 with a proposal to grow and rebalance the economy. This led to a focus upon the North and to the gap between its expenditure and productivity. Northern political leaders aware of the economic and social problems which an under-powered Northern economy produced were instrumental in developing, initially at the region, then at the city-region and increasingly with a pan-northern perspective, a plan to address the problem.

Through a focus on Manchester, the chapter debates whether there is much that is original in either the CA or NP initiatives, explores the economic strategies for the NP developed within the North, considers the new elements in the plans for governance and, after examining the early impact of Brexit, draws conclusions about a rapidly changing scene.

The research for this chapter rests on extensive, semi-structured elite interviews with such stakeholders as Sir Howard Bernstein, eight Council leaders, two backbench councillors, three parliamentarians in the North of England and three leading members of Research Institutes and builds on our 12-year research project on the regeneration of East Manchester. Our elite sample included voices from all three main political parties and representatives from Greater Manchester and West Yorkshire. The interviews took place over an 18-month period culminating in September 2016.

OLD WINE IN NEW BOTTLES?

Manchester's leadership of city devolution is not new. A special status was granted to Manchester as the hub of a city-region when in 2010 the New Labour Government formalised the role of the Association of Greater Manchester Authorities (AGMA), originally established in 1986. While this type of city-region status created a 'light touch' system of governance it was a step towards Northern devolution.

The concepts of CAs and the NP are not new and each is a response to long-standing problems of economic decline and regional imbalance. In the case of the NP precedents include the Special Areas Act of 1934 (HC Deb. 3rd December, 1934, Vol. 295, Cols. 1251–1377) and Lord Hailsham's specific responsibility for regenerating the North-East in 1963 (HC Deb. 11th July 1963, Vol. 680, Cols. 1410–1412). The New Labour Government established Regional Development Agencies (RDAs) in 1998 and these structures combined to engage in the Northern Way in 2008 to promote Northern economic growth. This was a significant innovation in setting up an institutional arrangement for the entire North (SQW 2011: 7). While the Coalition Government abandoned RDAs they soon recognised the need for properly resourced, locally run initiatives to address economic imbalances and the economic domination of London (Prosser 2015).

CAs are a vindication of the Metropolitan District Councils abandoned by the Thatcher Government in 1986. Under New Labour CAs existed in embryo and policy trajectories pursue an independent path regardless of the Government in power (Scott 2001; Gains et al. 2005). Although the formal establishment of CAs derived from the Cities and

Local Government Act of 2016, it was the Local Democracy, Economic Development and Construction Act of 2009, especially Sect. 106, which introduced them. The coalition government reinforced the existence of the city-region as the key spatial structure and perceived cities to be motors of economic growth. The Localism Act of 2011 included an amendment which allowed local councils to argue for new powers and to set their own City Deals (Centre for Cities 2014). Manchester was in the first wave of eight cities to do so in 2012 and enjoyed further grants of power such as responsibilities for health and social care in December 2014, and other examples announced in the Autumn Statement of November 2015 (HM Treasury 2016).

Manchester has long sought greater independence. For example, in 1858 it secured an Improvement Act to clean the rivers and rejected existing legislation as overly interfering. The business groups which now work with the Greater Manchester Combined Authority (GMCA) had their nineteenth-century precursors in promoting wealth creation (Hunt 2004: 202). Current attitudes are embedded. In 1875, Manchester's Town Clerk, foreshadowing Sir Howard Bernstein, complained of a 'want of confidence' by central government in limiting 'independent action' (Redford 1940: 298). A decision in the 1920s resulted in one of Manchester City Council's (MCC) current strengths—its ownership of the airport which is shared across all ten local authorities in Greater Manchester. The historic decision was itself a continuation of the civic initiatives which had led to the city helping fund the Manchester Ship Canal to benefit the city's commerce and industry. Council leaders at the time presciently predicted the airport's 'elaborate expansion' (Redford 1940: 376, 385). The demographic changes in the Manchester region led to a far-sighted proposal in the late 1930s which foresaw the emergence of an enlarged authority as a rational solution to local governance. The advocate of the proposal justified it with reference to the thickly populated nature of the region necessitating a new machinery of governance for 'the district round Manchester where the towns are so closely commercially and industrially linked' and where the then existing municipal boundaries 'seem to be void of any economic or social significance' (Redford 1940: 388–389). The problems of the coordination of services to a metropolitan area and of maximising the economic benefits of a Greater Manchester authority have long been on the agenda.

More recently, is MCC's turn to realism in 1987, following a period of confrontation with Thatcher's Government, involving increased collaboration with Michael Heseltine and the award of such urban regeneration initiatives as City Challenge, the Single Regeneration Budget and Urban Development Corporations. Manchester also attracted international attention with its Olympic Games bid which laid the foundations for the hosting of the Commonwealth Games in 2002. Collaboration with central government intensified under New Labour as Manchester became the 'regeneration capital' with the flagship New East Manchester Urban Regeneration Company.

In short, the case of Greater Manchester suggests that there is little new wine in the new bottle. CAs and the NP are new only in their depth and their greater entrenchment as it will be difficult to 'unpick' what has been accomplished. The reason for the novel elements is explained by Down's (1972 cited in John et al. 2015) 'issue attention cycle' which explains the appearance of problems on the policy agenda as a result of external events or crises which attract the public's and elite's attention. The Scottish referendum and its aftermath, the case for city devolution and city-based economic agglomeration, the ambitions of Manchester and other city politicians and the coincidence of the economic and political cycles with austerity and an imminent general election in 2014 are some of the causes for the arrival of these issues near the top of the domestic political agenda. The issue attention cycle's potency is illustrated by the recurrent concerns with regional economics as in the Depression of the 1930s, the sense of comparative economic decline in the early 1960s and the aftermath of the 2008 recession.

While previous exemplars of regional development derived mainly from ministerial initiatives at the central government level, these more recent developments have been produced by Northern political and economic leaders in collaboration with the central state. There is increasing evidence of the desire of some Northern leaders to own the devolution agenda rather than allowing central government to set the terms. This ownership has its roots in a solid evidence base.

Northern Powerhouse Independent Economic Review

The GMCA took the lead in commissioning an Independent Economic Review (IER) to provide a research base to assist the implementation of the NP. The report was sponsored by Transport for the North (TfN) the statutory body charged with overseeing investment in transport, but it built upon the model of the Manchester Independent Economic Review

(MIER) of 2009, which had made the economic case for the GMCA (AGMA 2009) and 'was a real turning point in removing political obstacles from the planned trajectory of the city. The purpose of the IER was exactly the same, to remove political tensions and to help the private sector to understand' (Research Institute Leader Interview 2016).

The purpose of the Northern Powerhouse IER is to set a transformational target, which some considered insufficiently stretching, of raising Northern productivity to the level of the UK as a whole. Manchester's leadership of this initiative is demonstrated by Sir Richard Leese chairing four meetings with Northern CA leaders in Manchester Town Hall to oversee the report's production (Council Leader Interview 2016).

The report provided evidence for the relative lack of productivity in the North as defined by the measure which compares interregional performance and prosperity, that of Gross Value Added (GVA) per capita. It demonstrated that the North's GVA per capita 'has been consistently about 25 per cent below the average for the rest of England' (SQW 2016: 6) and advanced strategies to transform the Northern economy by 2030. The report's target reflected the Office for Budgetary Responsibility's growth assumptions. If this scenario was to succeed, the economic output of the North would be £37bn higher in real terms by 2030 (SQW 2016: 1) It emphasised four 'Prime Capabilities' across the North, Advanced Manufacturing, Energy, Health Innovation and Digital plus three 'Enabling Capabilities', Financial and Professional Services, Logistics and Education. Together, these capabilities offered 'a distinctive and coherent offer for the Northern region' (SQW 2016: 14–15).

The report argued that the NP should build upon areas of high productivity across the North, such as Advanced Manufacturing, Advanced Materials and Energy, together with those currently concentrated in specific areas, for example, Life Sciences and Pharmaceuticals, Healthcare Technologies, Digital, Logistics and Tourism. The report's recommendation is that the exploitation of specific economic capabilities in subregions should rest with particular city-regions. For example, Hull can maximise the benefits from its port, Cumbria its nuclear and offshore wind energy production and the North-East its life sciences and automotive manufacturing. The report argues the economic effects of accumulation are necessary, but stresses economic growth will be the greater than 'if each part of the North acted independently' (SQW 2016: 9).

The IER advances proposals which offer solutions to the problem of promoting economic growth and provides credibility for a pan-northern approach. Yet Northern economic underperformance is entrenched and the solutions are not straightforward. There is criticism, for example, of the IER's advocacy of 'Smart specialisation' on the grounds that the North is 'genuinely differentiated and distinctive' (SQW 2016: 11). It is argued to the contrary that the 'lessons of history are that you shouldn't create "one-horse towns"' and that each city-region is an economic entity (Research Institute Member Interview 2016). The IER approaches the issue with political sensitivity to smooth over conflicts of interest. Council leaders consider that progress towards pan-northern agreement is obtainable and draw inspiration from their having gained the buy-in of over fifty Individual Transport Authorities in Transport for the North (TfN). Manchester's leaders assert that the IER 'gives inherent credibility' if, as the MIER suggests, it can overcome parochialism and remove political obstacles (Senior Official Interview 2016). As one council leader expressed it: 'The IER evidence helps to take politics out of decision-making' (Council Leader Interview 2016).

Second, there is also criticism that the IER places excessive emphasis upon pan-northern transport. Council leaders argue that an East–West rail link in particular will be crucial in linking the functional economic geographies of the North and that connectivity will drive agglomeration. This is why the IER promotes such pan-northern infrastructural improvements as ports and airports, road building and city centre to city centre rail links to reduce travel times for highly skilled commuters (SQW 2016: 22–23). This orthodoxy has been challenged with the argument that intra-city-region transport improvements are the most cost effective, based upon an analysis of the Rhine-Ruhr and Randstad regions of Germany and Holland. Since commuting is as uncommon and as expensive between the constituent cities of these European regions as it is between Manchester and Sheffield, this challenges the priority of HS2 and HS3 because a focus on individual cities could make them economic powerhouses in their own right (Swinney 2016). Other groups urge an improved capillary network to connect firms and customers across the region rather than HS2 and HS3 (Smedley 2016). While the IER envisages both pan-northern and individual city-region transport initiatives as complementary there are, in an era of straitened finances, resource constraints which pose unresolved demands for those charged with advancing the NP. In any event, transport policy is a pre-requisite not a panacea for achieving the NP.

The third area of controversy is skills. The IER advocates skills training (SQW 2016: 24) and most commercial supporters of the NP regard skills as equal in importance to devolution as transport improvements (Smedley 2016). Brexit intensifies the case for investment in skills training as those areas which voted against the EU had benefited little from the 'replicators' which replaced coal mining with call centres and provided money for buildings and new roads, but had not up-skilled local populations to enable them to access new employment opportunities (Cox 2016). Central government has devolved responsibility for skills to CAs. The report welcomes this because an effective strategy depends upon 'local needs and circumstances' (SQW 2016: 24).

GMCA council leaders assert that metro-mayors will provide the leadership to solve skills shortages, a view strengthened by the suggestion that 'local control of adult skills training will facilitate coherence between local labour markets and the suppliers of skills training' (Research Institute Leader 2016). It is unlikely that simply bringing employers, providers and back to work programmes together, however, will suffice. Even the IER suggests that the skills gap is an aspect of a wider problem requiring a more holistic strategy including 'investment in jobs, infrastructures, and innovation to create an environment in which the highly skilled want to live and work' (SQW 2016: 9).

Such debates are real and some economists warn that there is ambiguous support for the assumption that city-based economic organisations are best, and that in political practice administrative convenience wins over rational economic boundaries (Gardiner et al. 2011). Yet there is a consensus amongst experts, business leaders and politicians, that cities are the key to growth, that city centres can attract the best jobs and that improved transport to allow residents in outer towns in CAs to avail themselves of new opportunities is required.

The main motivation behind both CAs and the NP has been the economic need to improve productivity. Townsend and Champion (2014: 48) attribute their linked development to a consequence of 'slow faltering growth' in the economy after 2010. As one council leader expressed economic development is the one universal function which all CAs share and 'after May 2017, you will get five or six strong leaders who will take forward the NP hopefully using the IER as the evidence base' (Council Leader Interview 2016).

GOVERNANCE

CAs are the governance mechanisms which provide the building blocks for the NP, yet the GMCA is an exception in its history of collaboration between its ten local authorities and its institutional maturity, characteristics not easily replicable elsewhere (for an in-depth account, see Kenealy 2016). The NP is not a government for the North: other than TfN, there are no pan-northern governance structures. Instead the NP project relies on informal networks of council leaders and executives whose collaborative work constitutes soft power.

The metro-mayor is a new feature in the governance arrangements of CAs. As yet, they have not been democratically endorsed by voters: the metro-mayor was a condition imposed by Osborne in return for the devolution deals negotiated with city-regions. The Treasury-led nature of devolution is contained in Osborne's statement (HM Treasury 2015) that 'I will not impose this model on anyone. But nor will I settle for less'. Yet 'conurbation-wide' mayors were originally a recommendation of the Heseltine Review, No Stone Unturned (2012).

The Cities and Local Government Act of 2016 is non-descriptive about the powers of the Mayor which depend on each devolution deal. The Manchester model is consensual and involves shared powers between the Mayor and the GMCA Board as unanimity is required for approving the strategic plan (HM Treasury/GMCA 2015: 1) and a two-thirds vote can overrule the Mayor's budgetary proposals (HM Treasury/GMCA 2015: 8) Sheffield, and Liverpool are similar in that the mayor's spending plans 'can be amended' if two-thirds agree (HM Treasury/Sheffield City-Region 2015; HM Treasury/Liverpool City-Region 2015). Leaders from the West Yorkshire CA, on the other hand, welcomed indications from Theresa May that she would abandon Osborne's policy of directly elected city-region mayors as this proved a stumbling block to securing agreement although DCLG quashed rumours that they had abandoned the idea of mayors. Sajid Javid has removed the North-East deal after the opposition within parts of Tyne and Wear to the devolution proposals from government although the neighbouring Tees Valley is pushing ahead with a devolution deal and a mayoral election (Parker 2016). This remains a complex and moving picture which diminishes the prospect for pan-northern collaboration (see Giovanni's chapter in this volume).

Metro-mayors could gain in 'soft power and informal governance skills' what they might lack in the hard power of 'formal proceedings and votes' (Sandford 2016: 19) both at the CA level and at a pan-northern level if they come together as an effective group to lobby central government. There are already signs that key figures in the NP are organising as a collective force. In the wake of Brexit, Greater Manchester's interim mayor, Tony Lloyd, wrote to Theresa May on behalf of leaders of the Liverpool, North East, Sheffield and West Yorkshire CAs inviting Theresa May to a meeting in Greater Manchester 'to discuss our role within the Brexit negotiations' (BBC News 2016). In September 2016, Andy Burnham and Steve Rotherham, the Labour candidates for Manchester and Liverpool, respectively, argued for the need to join forces to pressure Theresa May to commit to improve rail links across the North (Murphy 2016).

Tensions between CAs and metro-mayors are likely. The case of Manchester is revealing. The cabinet style of the Manchester model of mayoralty could lead to a future mayor lobbying government to increase powers should the CAs frustrate the mayor's proposals. A sign of the weakness of the model comes from Leese's rejection of standing as a candidate arguing that he sees the mayoralty as a 'step backwards, a step down even' from his current role as MCC leader (Williams 2016). Leese is an established leader across Greater Manchester and is unused to challenge so a power struggle might ensue. Yet one advocate of the Manchester mayoral model explicitly rejected the London model and argued that 'two-thirds consensual support isn't weak, we would call it democratic' (Senior GM Official Interview 2016) while another argued that the 'logic' for the Manchester model is 'the history of Greater Manchester and its consensual politics' (Council Leader Interview 2016).

There seems to be no appetite among Greater Manchester politicians for replicating the London structure of an elected Assembly but rather to enhance the capacity of Councillors to challenge the Mayor by an improved version of the existing Scrutiny Pool. There is recognition that scrutiny needs to be strengthened: 'scrutiny needs to be more effective and transparent' and 'if councillors are to feel part of the system, they need to have a clear role within combined authorities' (Senior Council Official 2016).

It is true that the city may shape the mayor. In London's case Boris Johnson was more conciliatory than the tone he adopted as a Brexit campaigner and Ken Livingstone was more pro-capitalist and upheld financial interests when he was responsible for the City of London. The reverse also applies as mayors can extend their powers as happened in London with mayoral pressure for the Olympic Games and the construction of Crossrail. Even modest success in the first term of office can open doors for the award of additional powers thereafter (Clarke 2016). This optimism fails to recognise the 'trap', however, that metro-mayors in satisfying central government are pivoting their accountability from the people to Ministers.

The accountability of metro-mayors is a key question. One consideration for potential mayoral candidates might be the suggestion that 'the mayor may face being held accountable for things that s/he does not control; (Sandford 2016: 20). Although the mayor may be held accountable for health and social care issues in practice, formally the responsibility for integrating health and social care is vested in the Greater Manchester Health and Social Care Partnership Board as 'the elected mayor will not have any executive or budgetary control over the integration of health and social care' (Sandford 2016: 11).

The concept of metro-mayors also has to be sold to a public which have had this constitutional change imposed upon them. Three Greater Manchester leaders argue that the democratic moment to mobilise local people will be the election of a Greater Manchester Mayor in 2017. One GMCA leader (2016) hopes that a simultaneous election day in 2017 across a group of cities will enhance the democratic moment. This is doubtful given that in the North only Manchester, Sheffield, Liverpool and Tees Valley are likely to now hold elections at this time. There are also criticisms of the lack of women as key figures in the CAs and as potential mayoral candidates. Only 28 per cent of leadership roles in the CAs are occupied by women and only one of the seven chairs of the established and proposed CAs in the NP is female (Trenow and Olchawski 2016: 3). One response to this in Greater Manchester has been the emergence of groups in civil society such as 'DivaManc', part of a wider People's Plan (2016) to raise public awareness of the devolution process and to engage the public ahead of the mayoral elections.

Burnham (2016) stresses his desire to adopt a more 'bottom-up' approach to policymaking including a willingness to consult the existing 600 elected councillors in Greater Manchester. Yet Centre for Cities argues that the mayors' strength lie in being the 'single figurehead' and numerical and participatory democracy do not sit together effectively.

Others point to a contradiction between strong problem-solving leadership and a discursive style (Centre for Cities 2016).

The directly elected component of the office may guarantee that the Mayor cannot simply float free. Burnham (2016) stresses that the nature of the office ensures that the mayor is not accountable to either a political party or to the Council but to the electorate. These are inherent tensions: much will depend upon the mayor's capacity to develop relationships.

Support for the mayoralty and the NP has come from business leaders. When Andrew Percy, Minister responsible for the NP, visited Manchester in July 2016, business leaders urged him to maintain the NP. Acknowledging that the North does not pay its way in taxation and productivity, they urged transport investment, and significantly asserted that the powers of the Mayor be increased so that the NP agenda be driven forward. For the business interest the NP and the CAs are indissolubly linked and the purpose of the CAs is to guarantee the NP's success (Chapman 2016a) The Local Economic Partnership (LEP) promotes this priority as does the Manchester Chamber of Commerce (Memmott, 2016) for whom the purpose of the GMCA is to get the NP moving by investments.

The Brexit Effect?

As an enthusiast from IPPR North for the NP, and for Manchester's devolution deal, argues in the aftermath of the referendum, 'Our obsession with the big cities and aggregate growth must take a new turn and wake up to the cries of those on the margins' (Cox 2016). Agglomeration means little to people in Burnley or Wakefield as the political capital which some cities have nurtured has merely 'delivered some small dollops of yellow amidst the sea of blue on the referendum map' (Cox 2016). The inadequacies of intra-regional transport and the skills deficit of large sections of the population should question the easy assumptions about the relationship between cities and the NP (Centre for Cities 2015).

Core–periphery tensions are apparent both within and between city-regions. One suspicion voiced by some CA leaders is that city-region devolution benefits Manchester alone. North-Eastern authorities are most prone to this view. Yet tensions are also apparent between core and peripheral areas within the North East. According to Harrison (2016), the North East is not a city-region in the way that Greater Manchester is but a region which encompasses a far greater distance than either Greater Manchester or Greater London. Much of it is rural and it includes 'many more individual towns and major cities, each with their own distinct identities and far fewer economic links' (Harrison 2016). The rejection of the devolution deal by Sunderland, Durham, South Tyneside and Gateshead in September 2016 should therefore not have been surprising. As Elcock (2014) argues, although the North-East has made progress, there is continuing grievance about the peripheral geography of the region.

The interaction between the Brexit process and the future of the CAs and the NP complicates devolution, but one council leader argues that a seat at the negotiations matters less than that the Government replaces the European Structural Funds with an increased Local Government Growth Fund, and to seize the opportunity to bring about a major change in the way in which powers are exercised in the UK generally (Council Leader Interview 2016). Rotherham and Burnham argued that 'the right response to Brexit is to deepen the commitment to the Northern Powerhouse, not abandon it' (Murphy 2016).

This ambition also differentiates the NP from previous pan-northern initiatives which have 'all previously been led centrally. What's different this time is that we're leading it locally, we're taking ownership and responsibility' (Council Leader Interview 2016). Yet there is ambiguity at the level of central government. On the one hand, Theresa May appeared to weaken both the NP and Manchester's central role within it by arguing that there has been an excessive focus on the North-West of England and that her hope is 'to help not one or even two of our great regional cities but every single one of them' (The Guardian 2016). On the other hand, although 'Manchester is not an easily transferable model', it is still likely to remain central given its institutional maturity: 'it has taken Manchester thirty years to do the groundwork' in contrast to other more hastily constructed CAs (Council Leader Interview 2016). Both the NP and CAs are susceptible to a withdrawal of support and their status remains conditional, but despite the risk posed by the problems in the North-East, local government should seize what is on offer as government 'easily defaults to centralism' (Parker 2016).

CONCLUSION

The litmus test for both the CAs and NP has to be their ability to address the long-standing economic imbalances which previous similar policy initiatives have failed to alter. Until now, the focus of pan-northern initiatives has been on big infrastructural projects such as HS2 to link the North to the South and HS3 to link cities across the North and the transpennine motorway between Manchester and Sheffield. For some, the certainty of HS3 occurring will be decisive in judging whether the North is to achieve 'powerhouse' economic status. Yet it will be in 2017 before the Government has investigated the economic costs of both HS3 and the construction of a new tunnel to reduce the journey times between Manchester and Sheffield by 30 min (Chapman 2016b). If both projects go forward then it will provide a 'kick-start' for the NP.

CAs, with Manchester the prime example, are the enablers of the NP and enjoy support from the business sector. It is a paradox that as May casts doubt upon a Manchester-centric perspective its deal represents 'the high water-mark of the devolution process' (Parker 2016). As one council leader asserted 'Manchester already has the necessary legislation so the departure of George Osborne is less dramatic for us in its consequences' (Council Leader Interview 2016).

There is hyperbolic branding given that there is little that is novel about the NP except for the strong technocratic backing from publications such as the IER, the plans of TfN and the political innovation of the metro-mayor. A key test is whether productivity improves and the specific output targets for 2030 achieved. There will also be the visible test of whether improved cross-northern and intra-city transport connectivity is established. The intangible 'wicked' issue of a skills revolution will be harder to measure and achieve and the current focus on locally based solutions has not yet advanced beyond rhetorical assertion. As one council leader (2016) expressed it 'Transport is relatively easy, it's capital investment, it's visible and tangible and people understand it. In terms of skills you're asking for systemic change—it's much harder'. It is a moot point whether there will be substantial public engagement with CAs and the NP. In any event, the ultimate question is who benefits? Northern Council leaders aspire to inclusivity through the correction of regional economic imbalances and local inequalities. This will prove the hardest problem to solve.

REFERENCES

AGMA. 2009. *Prosperity for all: The Greater Manchester Strategy*. http://www.agma.gov.uk/cms_media/files/final_gms_august_20091.pdf?static=1. Accessed 30 Sept 2014.

BBC News. 2016. North England council leaders demand Brexit talks, 18 July. http://www.bbc.co.uk/news/uk-england-manchester-36825187. Accessed 4 Sept 2016.

Burnham, A. 2016. The first 100 days of the Greater Manchester Mayor. Public Event, Centre for Cities, Manchester Town Hall, 11th July.

Centre for Cities. 2014. *Cities policy briefing: Setting out coalition government policies across a common framework*. http://www.centreforcities.org/wp-content/uploads/2014/10/14-09-22-Cities-Policy-Briefing.pdf. Accessed 4 Sept 2015.

Centre for Cities. 2015. *The changing geography of the UK economy*. http://www.centreforcities.org/wp-content/uploads/2015/12/15-12-17-The-changing-geography-of-the-uk-economy.pdf. Accessed 21 Sept 2016.

Centre for Cities. 2016. The first 100 days of the Greater Manchester Mayor. Public Event, Centre for Cities, Manchester Town Hall, 11th July.

Chapman, S. 2016a. The Northern Powerhouse promised growth, it's now time for big businesses to create it. *Prolific North*, 16th December 2016. https://www.prolificnorth.co.uk/2016/12/the-northern-powerhouse-promised-growth-its-now-time-for-bigbusinesses-to-create-it/. Accessed 3 August 2017.

Chapman, S. 2016b. Will Trans-Pennine tunnel kickstart Northern Powerhouse? Prolific North, 19 August 2016. https://www.prolificnorth.co.uk/2016/08/will-trans-pennine-tunnel-kickstart-northern-powerhouse/. Accessed 3 August 2017.

Clarke, E. 2016. Will the new metro mayors be able to take the tough decisions their cities need? 17 August. http://www.centreforcities.org/blog/metro-mayors-executive-power-take-tough-decisions-cities-need/. Accessed 13 Sept 2016.

Cox, E. 2016. Leaving the North behind led to Brexit. Here's what has to happen next. *The New Statesman*, 24 June. http://www.newstatesman.com/politics/devolution/2016/06/leaving-north-behind-led-brexit-heres-what-has-happen-next. Accessed 14 Sept 2016.

Elcock, H. 2014. Multi-level governance and peripheral places: The North-East of England. *Local Economy* 29 (4–5): 323–333.

Gains, P., P. John, and G. Stoker. 2005. Path-dependency and the reform of English local government. *Public Administration* 83: 553–572.

Gardiner, B., R. Martin, and P. Tyler. 2011. Does spatial agglomeration increase national growth? Some evidence from Europe. *Journal of Economic Geography* 11 (6): 979–1006.

Giovanni, A., and A. Mycock. 2016. The Northern Powerhouse needs to be more than a slogan. *The Conversation*, 10 May. https://theconversation. com/the-northern-powerhouse-needs-to-be-more-than-a-slogan-59043. Accessed 04 Sept 2016.

Harrison, B. 2016. Picking up the pieces as North East rejects devolution deal, 7th September. http://www.centreforcities.org/blog/picking-up-pieces-after-north-east-rejects-devolution-deal/. Accessed 14 Sept 2016.

HC Deb. 3rd December, 1934, Vol. 295, Cols. 1251–1377.

HC Deb. 11th July 1963, Vol. 680, Cols. 1410–1412.

Heseltine, M. (Lord). 2012. *No stone unturned: In pursuit of growth*. London: Department for Business, Innovation and Skills.

HM Treasury. 2015. Chancellor on building a Northern Powerhouse, 14 May. Available   at: https://www.gov.uk/government/speeches/chancellor-on-building-a-northern-powerhouse. Accessed 4 Sept 2015.

HM Treasury. 2016. Devolution to the Greater Manchester combined authority and transition to a directly elected mayor. https://www.gov.uk/government/ publications/devolution-to-the-greater-manchester-combined-authority-and-transition-to-a-directly-elected-mayor. Accessed 13 Sept 2016.

HM Treasury/GMCA. 2015. *Greater Manchester agreement: Devolution to the GMCA & transition to directly elected mayor.* https://www.gov.uk/govern-ment/uploads/system/uploads/attachment_data/file/369858/Greater_ Manchester_Agreement_i.pdf. Accessed 20 Aug 2015.

HM Treasury/Sheffield City Region. 2015. *Sheffield city region devolution agreement.*   https://www.gov.uk/government/uploads/system/uploads/ attachment_data/file/466616/Sheffield_devolution_deal_October_2015_ with_signatures.pdf. Accessed 21 Sept 2016.

HM Treasury/Liverpool City Region. 2015. *Liverpool city region devolution agreement.*   https://www.gov.uk/government/uploads/system/uploads/ attachment_data/file/477385/Liverpool_devolution_deal_unsigned.pdf. Accessed 21 Sept 2016.

Hunt, T. 2004. *Building Jerusalem: The rise and fall of the Victorian city*. London: Phoenix.

John, P., A. Bertelli, W. Jennings, and S. Bevan. 2015. *Policy agendas in British politics*. Basingstoke: Palgrave Macmillan.

Kenealy, D. 2016. A tale of one city: The Devo Manc deal and its implications for English devolution. *The Political Quarterly* 87 (4): 572–581.

Murphy, L. 2016. http://www.liverpoolecho.co.uk/news/must-better-railways-say-steve-11828809.

Parker, S. 2016. Councils must grab devolved powers. *The Guardian*, 14th September.

People's Plan. 2016. People's plan Greater Manchester. http://www.people-splangm.org.uk/. Accessed 31 Oct 2016.

Prosser, D. 2015. Small talk: The effects of killing off regional development agencies are showing. *The Independent*, 2nd February. http://www.independent. co.uk/news/business/sme/small-talk-the-effects-of-killing-off-regional-development-agencies-are-showing-10017041.html. Accessed 13 Sept 2016.

Redford, A., and R.I. Stafford. 1940. *The history of local government in Manchester*. London: Longman Green.

Sandford, M. 2016. *Devolution to local government in England*. Briefing paper 07029, London: House of Commons Library.

Scott, W.R. 2001. *Institutions and organisations, ideas, institutions and identities*. Thousand Oaks: Sage.

Smedley, T. 2016. What practical difference will the Government's vision of a Northern Powerhouse make to SMEs? 13th May. http://www.fsb.org.uk/first-voice/what-practical-difference-will-the-governments-vision-of-a-northern-powerhouse-make-to-smes. Accessed 13 Sept 2016.

SQW. 2011. *The evaluation of the Northern Way 2008–2011, The final report—Full report*. http://www.sqw.co.uk/files/4313/8694/8743/25.pdf. Accessed 13 Sept 2016.

SQW. 2016. The Northern Powerhouse independent economic review: Final executive summary report, 24 June.

Swinney, P. 2016. *Building the Northern Powerhouse. Lessons from the Rhine, Ruhr and Randstad*. http://www.centreforcities.org/wp-content/uploads/2016/06/16-05-31-Building-the-Northern-Powerhouse-Lessons-from-the-Rhine-Ruhr-and-Randstad.pdf. Accessed 21 Sept 2016.

The Guardian. 2016. *Theresa May says she will make success of Brexit as Prime Minister—as it happened*. https://www.theguardian.com/politics/blog/live/2016/jul/11/andrea-leadsom-apologises-to-theresa-may-politics-live? page=with:block-5783a105e4b0ea445f0fe2bf#block-5783a105e4b0 ea445f0fe2bf. Accessed 21 Sept 2016.

Townsend, A., and J. Champion. 2014. The impact of recession on city regions: The British experience 2008–2013. *Local Economy* 29 (1–2): 38–51.

Trenow, P., and J. Olchawski. 2016. *The Northern Powerhouse: An analysis of women's representation*. London: The Fawcett Society. http://www.fawcett-society.org.uk/wp-content/uploads/2016/05/The-Northern-Powerhouse-Report-Fawcett.pdf. Accessed 13 Sept 2016.

Williams, J. 2016. Sir Richard Leese won't be running for Greater Manchester mayor—because it would be a "step down". *Manchester Evening News*, 23 February.

AUTHORS' BIOGRAPHY

Georgina Blakeley is Senior Lecturer in Politics at the Open University. She has published widely on citizen participation and local governance with a specific focus on case studies of Manchester, UK and Barcelona, Spain in several leading academic journals, including *International Journal of Urban and Regional Research*, *Social Policy and Administration*, *Representation* and *Public Policy and Administration*. She is the co-author (with Brendan Evans) of *The Regeneration of East Manchester. A political Analysis.*

Brendan Evans is Emeritus Professor of Politics at the University of Huddersfield. He has published numerous books and journal articles on British party politics, ideology, labour market and skills policy-making, devolution, and on the politics and economic development of Manchester in several leading academic journals, including *Social Policy and Administration*, *Representation* and *Public Policy and Administration*. He is the co-author (with Georgina Blakeley) of *The Regeneration of East Manchester. A political Analysis.*

CHAPTER 9

From Problems in the North to the Problematic North: Northern Devolution Through the Lens of History

Daryl Martin, Alex Schafran and Zac Taylor

Abstract Current debates about Northern English cities and their role in national economic strategies cannot be read simply through the lens of contemporary politics. We therefore take the Northern Powerhouse as our starting point to trace a long history of policy and planning discourses about the North of England. We use Russell's chronology of key historical moments in which Northern English cities hold a particular charge in cultural narratives of the nation to guide our analysis of contemporaneous tensions in debates about planning and governance. A focus on representations about the North of England over the last two centuries reveals four interlocking themes: the role of London in directing debates about

D. Martin (✉)
University of York, York, UK
e-mail: daryl.martin@york.ac.uk

A. Schafran · Z. Taylor
University of Leeds, Leeds, UK
e-mail: A.Schafran@leeds.ac.uk

Z. Taylor
e-mail: gyzjt@leeds.ac.uk

© The Author(s) 2018   217
C. Berry and A. Giovannini (eds.), *Developing England's North*,
Building a Sustainable Political Economy: SPERI Research & Policy,
https://doi.org/10.1007/978-3-319-62560-7_9

the North; a tension between political and spatial approaches to planning; the characterisation of cities in the North as intrinsically problematic; and the continued issue of poverty in these cities.

Keywords Devolution · History · North of England · Planning Poverty · Urbanism

INTRODUCTION

It is significant that in his first speech after the 2015 general election, the then Conservative chancellor George Osborne focused on the idea of a Northern Powerhouse (2015) and its model of partial devolution of budgetary responsibility for transport, housing and health care in city-regions governed by elected mayors. Speaking in Manchester, and presenting this model of governance as an answer to imbalances in the national economy, Osborne based his analysis of the present and prognosis for the future on the capacity of large urban conurbations to drive processes of wider regional growth. Osborne's speech added aspirational detail to an earlier speech, again in Manchester, where the term was introduced into contemporary political debates (2014). This earlier speech offered speculative and unfunded ideas about transport and infrastructure across the North of England, such as a high-speed train link between Manchester and Leeds, HS3, to complement the HS2 project of connecting these cities to London via faster routes. Such ideas drew in large part on proposals by then Commercial Secretary to the Treasury Jim O'Neill, his City Growth Commission, and the 'One North' report (2014) authored by political leaders in Leeds, Liverpool, Manchester, Newcastle and Sheffield. 'One North' articulates the argument, consolidated in Osborne's speeches, that large Northern English cities are not fulfilling their economic potential, not only relative to London, but compared to similarly sized city-regions in mainland Europe, such as the Randstad in the Netherlands and the Rhein-Ruhr Valley in Germany.

This type of benchmarking exercise will be familiar to historians of urban and regional policy. Similar ground was covered in Michael Parkinson's 'Competitive European Cities: where do the Core Cities stand?' report for the New Labour administration 10 years earlier (2004). Indeed, the prescriptions in the 'One North' report for greater connectivity and transport infrastructure (as well as its imaginative geography, tied to large cities and thus missing large parts of Cumbria and

Northumberland) echo those of the Northern Way reports (ODPM 2004) and the speculative contributions of the architect Will Alsop (2005), both from the previous decade. The deeper one digs historically, the greater the sense of déjà vu. The historical echoes careening around the caverns of British decentralisation politics show that the Northern Powerhouse and its immediate policy hinterland must be seen as part of a long legacy of thinking about the North in problematic terms. For more than 150 years, the North has been bandied about in various ways as both a place with problems, and as a problem in and of itself. Despite the national penchant for new schemes, and for new governments to imagine themselves erasing history—and the governance structures and plans of previous administrations—the internal geographic struggles of the UK epitomises Faulkner's (1951: 80) maxim that the 'past is never dead. It's not even past'. The current period and its orthodoxies about Northern cities and their role in national economic strategies cannot be understood simply through the lens of contemporary politics, the power of austerity, neoliberal restructuring and globalisation notwithstanding (Martin 2015).[1]

Situating the prevalent rhetoric—ostensibly that of empowered regional economies, driven by business and political urban elites—within the long history of corrective interventions in Northern English cities elucidates a series of four interwoven themes which reverberate throughout this convoluted history, which are vital to understanding the current devolution discourse. The first is the outsized role of London, in a story ostensibly about the North. The second is the question of spatial planning, and its bricks and mortar interventions, versus a power politics of jurisdictions, authorities and assemblies. The third is the tendency by those in power to slip discursively between the North as a place with problems and as a problem unto itself. Finally, there is the omnipresent question of poverty, entrenched in reality long before Engels ingrained it in the global imagination of the original industrial region (1892). In this chapter, we trace these themes in order to highlight how negative images, embedded historically in cultural representations and through the interventions of successive generations of politicians, retain their potency in shaping the articulation and enactment of policy today in the regions that comprise the North of England. Our chapter draws on Russell's timeline of representations of Northern England in popular culture (2004), and his identification of four moments in which the towns and cities of the North held a particular importance in larger national narratives: the 1840s to early 1850s, the 1930s, the late 1950s to early 1960s and the 1980s. We use a similar chronological frame to situate the role of cities in Northern England within wider debates and developments in the field of planning in the country, but then extend this history in order to transition through to the policies of New Labour and Conservative/Liberal Democrat Coalition governments, before returning once again to present-day proposals for the Northern Powerhouse. We conclude by revisiting our four interrelated themes in order to argue that these are issues which at times get obscured by the politics of the contemporary moment, but which never truly go away.

A Genealogy of the North as a 'Problem'

Victorian Origins

In his Northern Powerhouse pronouncements, George Osborne positioned his neoliberal economic impulses within his party's tradition of One Nation Conservatism, with his latter speech building to its crescendo on precisely the argument that the Northern Powerhouse resolves the question of regional imbalances within the nation (2015). In so doing, Osborne ventriloquised the rhetoric of Disraeli, whose first political articulation of the One Nation trope came in a public address in Manchester's Free Trade Hall in 1872 (Wyke 1996). Disraeli's arguments were rehearsed earlier in fictional writings such as 'Sybil, or the Two Nations' (1845), a novel about the lack of understanding between different social classes which falls within a lineage of 'condition of England novels' (Simmons 2005). In contemporaneous industrial novels, including Dickens's 'Hard Times' (1854) and Gaskell's 'North and South' (1855), one finds imaginative recreations of cities such as Preston and Manchester at a time when their economic power was at its height (Hunt 2004), but with political power still firmly located in London.

Notwithstanding their fictional form, the landscapes described in novels such as those by Dickens and Gaskell are crucial to the fixing of national perceptions and popular understandings of Northern England. They make manifest representations of its cities as repositories of social problems, and as problematic places in themselves (Cockin 2012); threaded through these novels are spatially determined representations of industrialists of these cities as unable to manage capitalism appropriately and equitably. These tropes were substantively seeded alongside the movements towards public health reforms in the early nineteenth century, as in the reports of Edwin Chadwick on sanitation (1842) and James Kay-Shuttleworth on the poverty of living conditions (1832), as well as Engels's famous analysis of the working classes in the Northern Powerhouses of their day (1892). In these writings, we have arguments for greater degrees of responsibility amongst political leaders for the populations of newly emerging cities, in terms of health, employment and housing; separately and together, these texts comprise a recognisable form of a planning imagination, albeit in its nascent state.

Interwar Interventions

By the 1930s, Russell's second period of an 'intensified interest' in the North (2004: 33), Victorian tropes of the problematic North have hardened into hegemonic understandings, reinforced by investigations into the effects of economic depression. These are found equally in novels, such as Greenwood's 'Love on the Dole' (1933), and journalism, such as Orwell's 'The Road to Wigan Pier' (1937), both characterised by their forensic portraits of deep poverty. We also sense deepening cultural differences between Northern and Southern England, in which the North is deviant from the national narratives legitimated through the South's cultural and political institutions (Rawnsley 2000); despite the reflexivity of his account, we should not forget that Orwell's commission from his London-based publisher was to explore this other England in terms that suggest the industrial North's implicit status as an internal colony. An event such as the Jarrow March offers a vivid example of the depth of economic, social and cultural disjuncture between the institutions of the North and the South at that time (Pilmott 1981).

Within the political histories of Northern English cities, by the early decades of the twentieth century entering a period of economic decline, there is a newly articulated role of the city in addressing systemic problems of employment and poverty through major planning projects, held at a tensed distance to national government in London. Housing was often the most visible mechanism by which wider social issues are addressed locally, with councils responding to the national 1919 Housing Act that placed responsibility with them for clearing slums and building new accommodation as a social service to their citizens (Malpass 2005). Thus there came the development of large housing estates in city centres, such as Quarry Hill in Leeds (Ravetz 1974), and in its garden suburbs, as in Wythenshawe in Manchester (Kidd 2006: 221–223). In Liverpool, the 1931 census marked the peak of the city's population, but also a realisation of its economic vulnerability in light of changing trade routes and tourism trends (Belchem 2000). Thus, in the 1930s a tranche of initiatives, including a new airport at Speke to combat the decline of cruise shipping (Sykes et al. 2013), culminate in the Liverpool Corporation Act of 1936, which paved the way for the development of industrial estates outside the city centre (Wilks-Heeg 2003). As has been noted, the powers gifted to Liverpool through the 1936 Act were 'unprecedented for a British Local Authority and gave the city a unique role in the sponsorship of regional economic adaptation' (Lister, 1983, in Wilks-Heeg 2003: 48). Notwithstanding Martin et al.'s recent suggestion that modern 'British regional policy really began in 1945' (2016: 345), Liverpool in the 1930s was the test bed for approaches to regeneration that oscillated between national and local scales and that anticipated mainstream policies in the following decades.

Post-War Planning

Such initiatives did little to stem underlying processes of economic and population decline in the post-war period in Liverpool, and ranged from the poorly conceived to those with only temporary ameliorative effects. The enticement of multi-national companies such as Dunlop, Ford and Kodak to industrial estates on the edge of the city was accompanied by clearances of inner-city populations to overspill estates (Sykes et al. 2013). Liverpool became a 'branch-plant economy' vulnerable to the relocation of capital to geographies of lower labour costs (Wilks-Heeg 2003: 49). Strategies of encouraging inward investment were not unique to Liverpool, being driven not purely by the city but also by national government, through the regional policies of the Labour administration of the mid-1960s. These policies occur around the time of Russell's next era in his focus on Northernness within narratives of national identity (2004), in which many significant representations of youth culture in theatre and film, such as the 'New Wave' or 'Kitchen Sink' dramas (Hill 1986), play out against the impoverished industrial cityscapes of the North.

At the heart of regional policies and national strategies was the short-lived Department of Economic Affairs (DEA) under Harold Wilson's 1964 government, which served as a modernising counterweight to the Treasury and helped to drive forward the UK's 'National Plan', along the lines of the French 'Commissariat au Plan' (Clifford 1997). In its 5-year life, the DEA worked with an economic geography that is more or less familiar to us still, in a series of reports dividing the North of England into the North-West Region, comprising Lancashire, Cheshire and Derbyshire's High Peak District (DEA 1965); Yorkshire and Humberside, encompassing West Yorkshire, South Yorkshire and its Coalfield, the city of York and coastal towns from Filey to Skegness (DEA 1966a), and the Northern Region, including the mostly non-urbanised North Yorkshire, Teesside, Durham, Northumberland, Cumberland and Westmoreland (DEA 1966b). Running through these reports is an underlying anxiety that speaks to similar themes of productivity found in contemporary Northern Powerhouse discourses.

The Northern Region report begins with a comprehensive summary of its problems in the fields of industrial strategy, technological development, commerce and housing, with explicit recommendations for national government interventions. As an example with contemporary resonance,[2] Teesside is identified in the 1960s as an area whose problems transcend regional scales and require intervention from national government (DEA 1966b: 4). The North West report details a region characterised by sluggish employment and with a dilapidated physical fabric. Poverty is a recurrent trope, especially in the cities of Liverpool and Manchester, where:

There is probably no other comparable part of Britain where the influence of bad housing is so all-pervasive and depressing and affects so many people. The first – and lasting – impression of a visitor to the region is one of astonishment that the housing conditions he sees around him can still exist in a relatively prosperous part of an advanced industrial country. (DEA 1965: 108)

The most sanguine of the Northern English reports, that for Yorkshire and Humberside, ruminates phlegmatically on market failure in large areas within the region. Thus, the prospects of Bradford, Halifax and Wilson's own birthplace of Huddersfield are unsentimentally questioned, and towns in the Pennine valleys have their futures repositioned as residential areas with little economic life (DEA 1966a: 72). Taken together, we have in these reports portraits of cities characterised as slums, towns to be wound down and downgraded to dormitories and entire regions in need of intense redevelopment and state intervention. Although the comparison of problems faced by deindustrialising cities and rural areas facing shifts in agricultural production is examined with a degree of complexity, nonetheless these regional portraits are underscored by descriptions of many economic and social problems. This, it can be said that the trope of the North as a problematic place coloured perceptions in all reports and fed into obdurate policy scripts of the North as somehow dependent on intervention by London-based elites.

From Thatcher to the Northern Way

By the 1980s, a period in Russell's cultural history where Northern England is increasingly marked in film and music as a place of anxiousness and 'grit', spatial policy would be restructured in and on the towns and cities with industries on the wrong side of national government priorities. The early 1980s saw a moment of policy change in the move towards a more entrepreneurial form of urbanism (Raco 2007), in which Margaret Thatcher's Conservative administrations broke with the post-war working consensus on the need for regional agencies to direct and shape local employment markets. Instead, Whitehall advocated a less pronounced role in encouraging employers to develop their businesses wherever they wished. Issues of regional inequalities were of secondary concern in the boosterish drive towards building a knowledge economy premised on the mobility of highly skilled labour. The Miners' Strike of 1984–1985 is perhaps the most notable example of such economic policies at a national level and how they impacted on local communities on the ground, especially in the North of England, with miners and their representatives characterised by Thatcher herself as the UK's 'enemy within' (Milne 1994). Such charged political contexts contributed to a wider sense of the North as 'England's "foreign country" within' (1993). As Jones and MacLeod (2004: 438) suggest, the 'election of Thatcher's Conservative Party—a government unsympathetic to regional economic decline and bereft of a regionalist sensibility beyond the wealthy South East—left English regionalism to be virtually silenced for the next decade'. This resulted in a sequence of Northern English cities led by Labour councillors at odds politically, economically and ideologically with national government, as in Sheffield (Payling 2014), Manchester (Robson 2002) and Liverpool (Frost and North 2013).

The positioning of Liverpool as a repository of social problems was prominent throughout the 1980s. In the wake of 1981's Toxteth Riots, Margaret Thatcher's ostensibly non-interventionist administration intervened with plans for the economic refashioning of the city centre.[3] With a regional Tate gallery alongside shops, cafes and bars, the Albert Dock's redevelopment exemplified a regeneration model which involved the pump-priming of public money to leverage in private sector investment (Williams 2004). Under the aegis of Michael Heseltine, a Merseyside Task Force was set up, which eventually morphed into the Merseyside Development Corporation (MDC), the first in a string of Urban Development Corporations (UDCs) in other cities. The UDCs were forerunners of the Regional Development Agencies, quasi-governmental bodies that were charged with smoothing the path of regeneration processes during New Labour's tenure in office (Robson et al. 2000). Once again Liverpool was in the vanguard of changing regeneration strategies authored by London governing elites, which would be rolled out elsewhere in successive decades.

Fostered in Thatcher's administrations and continued by New Labour are pronounced cultures of competition between cities, in line with neoliberalised modes of governance (Peck and Tickell 2007). The curtailment of local government's role in public finance started by Conservative governments in the 1980s 'on ideological grounds, both to shrink the state and curb... the socialist policies of Labour-controlled local authorities' (Martin 2015: 263) continued when a Labour government was next elected nationally, although the rhetoric around localism shifted, as did the scaling of governance strategies. For the North of England, perhaps the most striking examples of New Labour's early regionally directed policy drives were its Sustainable Communities and New Deals for Communities plans (Goodchild and Hickman 2006), although even the word 'community' was problematically conceptualised (Wallace 2010). That is, too often this word obscured governance strategies that abdicated responsibilities for impoverished places and populations at neighbourhood level and masked intensified practices of competitiveness between individual cities and regions (Raco and Imrie 2003).

Strategies of urban competitiveness were subject to critique (Ward and Jonas 2004), and sometimes from unexpected quarters, as in the work of architect Will Alsop. At this time, Alsop was employed on a suite of master plans for numerous deindustrialising urban centres in the North of England typically characterised in policy and cultural terms by economic inertia and poverty. He reimagined Barnsley as a Tuscan hill town; in Bradford he suggested the flooding of a large area in front of its Victorian Town hall; he envisaged a riverside complex in Middlesbrough with buildings in the shape of board games and toys; and in the New

Millennium Community development in East Manchester he designed an apartment block called 'Chips', so-named because it resembled three chipped potatoes laid on top of each other (Porter 2010). Alsop's flamboyant schemes received much media attention at the time, and some of his ideas, such as the 'Chips' building, were eventually built according to his designs. Leaving aside questions of his signature style, more important for our purposes is the place his individual plans held within Alsop's wider proposals for the North of England, which was to reimagine its towns and cities as part of a linear urban network or stretched city, facilitated by the M62 motorway (Alsop 2005; Martin 2010). His most cogent ideas treated cities in the North of England as potential partners in cooperative and collaborative region building (Hatherley 2010), rather than individualised economic units.

Will Alsop's plans parallel those driving the Northern Way initiative endorsed by the Office of the Deputy Prime Minister (ODPM 2004; Martin 2010), which entailed a dovetailing of modernist spatial planning and the political restructuring traditions. Both Alsop and the Northern Way took the motorway network as a spur to economic growth, and both are articulations of an infrastructural imaginary, or what Goodchild and Hickman define as 'the type of "vision"-based planning' relatively rare in explicit governmental thinking (2006: 123). The idea of using transport corridors as engines of economic growth was not new, with existing links through the Pennines, between Leeds and Manchester, being the subject of intermittent academic planning debates in the decade before Alsop and ODPM initiatives (Hebbert 2000). What was novel in the Northern Way plan was its supra-regional scale, so much so that it offered a 'spatial tier that has no other official recognition' (Goodchild and Hickman 2006: 129). Such novelty of scale perhaps places it within a lineage of regionally directed planning in Labour administrations (Martin et al. 2016: 346), but awkwardly so, not least because the Northern Way itself needs to be understood in relation to the failed attempts to institute regional assemblies earlier in the New Labour period of government (see Willett and Giovannini 2014).

If the Northern Way was the most high-profile strand of spatially directed policy initiatives for the North of England in the first two New Labour administrations, by the third administration, the political weather was being made by Conservative politicians and their favourite think-tanks. Most infamous, with respect to debates about Northern England, were the arguments in a series of reports by Policy Exchange, co-founded by future ministers Nicholas Boles, Michael Gove and Francis Maude. In particular, its 'Cities unlimited: making urban regeneration work' report (Leunig and Swaffield 2008) argued that area-based regeneration projects in Northern English cities such as Bradford, Hull and Sunderland would be certain to fail given their position geographically and historically on the wrong side of economic trends and flows. Better, the authors seemed to suggest, to initiate a process of managed decline than throw good investment after bad in such cities and to encourage their working-age populations to migrate to new technological industrial hubs in London and the South East of the country. Although the soon-to-be Prime Minister David Cameron sought to distance himself quickly from the report at the time (Watt 2008), in retrospect one can observe its cold logics in the geographical consequences of his subsequent austerity governments.

Back to the Future: The Northern Powerhouse

Two years prior to George Osborne's first Northern Powerhouse speech in Manchester, now Lord Heseltine's 'No Stone Unturned in Pursuit of Growth' report (2012) was released, refocusing the Northern question on cities and their economies. At the heart of the Heseltine Review (2012) were two related, if recurring, contentions: that the economies of cities and regions beyond London—and the cities of the North of England in particular—are still not performing as well as they should, and that economic growth in these cities could be 'unlocked' by strengthening local governments partnerships with business and by streamlining the ways in which Whitehall funds local economic development-related services and programmes. 'It is not the relative difference between the GVA (Gross Value Added) contributions of different regions that matters most', Heseltine argued (2012: 127), 'but the ability of all regions to grow their wealth and prosperity'.

Heseltine's findings largely dovetailed with the Conservative/Liberal Democrat Coalition Government's (2010–2015) patchwork of city and regional planning strategies, plans which tilted away from spatial regeneration but did not push far from the shadow of London. The Coalition's approach also represented a partial, though not insignificant departure from the previous New Labour government's Northern Way initiative (2004–2011). The Northern Way was envisioned to provide a strategic level of research, coordination and investment across the North, with an overarching mandate to address the GVA output gap between the North and the rest of the UK through a two-pronged emphasis on building a 'world-class economy' and improving place-making efforts and quality of life in the North, to be enacted through institutions such as the unrealised Regional Assemblies, three Regional Development Agencies (RDAs) and City-Region partnerships (2004 Growth Strategy; González 2006). In 2011, the Coalition abolished the Northern Way and the constituent RDAs (Department for Business, Innovation & Skills 2012), yet in many ways carried through and built upon New Labour's emphasis on more city-centred economic development strategies.

The Coalition years thus witnessed a significant formalisation and investment in the capacity and responsibilities of city-regions and Combined Authorities—both New Labour concoctions—as in a series of growth-focused 'City Deals' (2011, 2013) to the former, and through the 2011 Localism Act, which granted the 'power of competence' to the latter, respectively. Equally notable was the creation of Local Enterprise Partnerships (LEPs), voluntary public–private partnerships intended to bring local government and business interests together to identify public investment priorities at the city-regional scale, and in part fill the void left in the wake of the abolition of RDAs in their function as quasi-regional economic development agencies (Department for Communities and Local Government 2010).

The Heseltine Review also served as a key touchstone in the work of the City Growth Commission (2013–2014), led by a select cadre of economists, bankers, real estate developers and policy elites. Although both the Review and the Commission shared many of the same concerns over national economic output—with the problematic cities of the North serving as a key referent—the latter's work played a central role in developing a contemporary Westminster consensus around a more practicable set of devolution interventions. The conclusions of the Commission were further massaged by inputs from a handful of London-based policy think-tanks and membership organisations (e.g. IPPR, Centre for Cities) and the Core Cities (along with strong salesmanship from their respective LEPs). Once again, it is curious to note the ways in which London is centred in this particular round of policy design, both in terms of the way its robust civil society furnished the venue for much of debate, and in the various ways in which conversations ostensibly about Northern cities find their way back to the 'Brightest Star', as one Centre for London report (2014) branded its own manifesto for London devolution. This is not to argue against the further devolution of powers to London, but rather to suggest that recurring southerly turns in recent debate perhaps have the effect of displacing other voices, other places and other questions from the making of the Northern Powerhouse agenda.

This seemingly bi-partisan and business elite-centred consensus overwhelmingly coalesced around a decentralisation agenda focused on the growth-related 'levers' of public service delivery, as in programmes and policies related to skills and education, welfare and housing, transport and connectivity. At the same time, the more prised fiscal powers like increased local control over finance and taxation were often promised as future rewards for the city-regions exhibiting good behaviour (see Centre for Cities 2014; IPPR-North 2014b; Core Cities 2013; Northern Economic Futures Commission 2012). Devolution talk also carried forward the promise of reforms in governance at the city-region level and at the interface between local and national government, including a mayoral system that was universally opposed but nevertheless ultimately accepted by Northern cities (Cities and Local Government Devolution Bill 2015).

If this consensus sounds familiar, that's because it is, building on and borrowing from a lineage of initiatives and agendas that reach well beyond the contemporary horizon of debate. These most recent of echoes, which are now coming so rapidly that any attempt to write about English devolution in the present tense is immediately rendered passé, can at times mask the larger themes that continue to resonate across this long history. Nevertheless, the four themes of London, the tension between political and spatial planning, characterisations of the North as problematic and questions of poverty all ring true today, some front and centre, others submerged in a layer of brand-conscious discourse and boosterish rhetoric.

The Ghosts of Northern Pasts: London, Planning, Problem Space and Poverty

What has the South of Britain got that the North really wants? Short answer: the economic and social stimulus of a London. What has the South got that it could well be rid of? Short answer: the inefficiency of a congested central London. (Economist 1962, in Burnet 2002)

Originally drafted for an *Economist* magazine editorial over half a century ago, the quote above demonstrates that the more times change, the more things stay the same. It is fitting to frame our concluding discussion with London, given the ways in which London today foregrounds the fortunes and futures of the North. Arguments persist within the North that whilst one hand of Whitehall is seemingly gifting cities such as Sheffield and Manchester increased economic autonomy, the other hand is building a spatial and economic plan tacitly placing Northern cities as post-industrial hinterlands for the London economy which already drives the allocation of infrastructure funding disproportionately to its advantage (IPPR-North 2014a, 2015). As Martin et al. argue, despite the rhetoric of cities in the North of England acting as a counterweight to London's hegemony, Osborne's Powerhouse speeches need to be read alongside the contemporaneous Treasury anxiety that 'the growth of London is not hindered or compromised in any way' (2016: 343).

London has also played an outsized role in the development and distribution of devolution in the first place, much as it did in earlier eras. While cries and demands from various Northern voices have always been present, the current version of devolution was crafted in the formal and informal spaces of power in London, not in Manchester or Leeds or Newcastle. The Northern Powerhouse, such as so many efforts that have come before it, is thus always as much about London as it is about the North. When the satirical *Daily Mash* (2015) ran a headline announcing 'Northern Powerhouse relocated to London', the true irony is that it was never not there. London is more present in the North than ever, with their intertwined politics and populations engaged in 'a kind of relational embrace' that is social, cultural and economic in profound ways (Savage et al. 2015: 297).

Second, current plans for a Northern Powerhouse represent a deepening reliance on a political rather than spatial fix for the problems of the North. This long history reveals a constant toggling between solutions rooted in spatial planning—new infrastructure, regenerated neighbourhoods, bricks and mortar and pipes and wires—and those rooted in political power—new jurisdictions, new governance structures and new alliances of institutions operating at different scales. The Northern Powerhouse in this sense is generally part of the latter, a successor to the Northern Way, RDAs and Government Offices, representing a line of thinking and intervening that is linked but overall very different from physical and infrastructural investments in the fabric of this cross-Pennine Randstad. While HS2 and the imagined HS3 connecting Liverpool to Newcastle/Hull is now discussed in conjunction with the Northern Powerhouse, they remain institutionally and imaginatively distinct. Even Transport for the North—the newest of statutory institutions one would think would be at the centre of a Northern Powerhouse, as it is the only institution operating at the same scale—is not part of formal devolution debates, which are focused on city-region deals.

Third, if one thing has changed in the relationship between the North as a place with problems and the North as a problem space unto itself, it is the emergence of deeper divisions internal to the North as the dominant spatial ontology of problem spaces. Internal divisions once centred on identity, sport and economic rivalry (Caunce 2003) are at risk of morphing into something deeper, accelerated through devolution deals that are uneven, varying fundamentally from one to another. Thus we can glimpse increasing gaps between the increasingly wealthy, connected and globalised spaces of the Core Cities (Liverpool, Manchester, Leeds, Sheffield Newcastle) and their regional economic hinterlands, and a lack of even-handedness in how city-regions are being incorporated within this agenda. Although we do not dispute appetite for new regionalism in polities on the ground in the North (Giovannini 2016), the fragmented, London-centric, deal-making nature of the current version of devolution risks allowing narrowly interested elites–including many Southern-based property owners heavily invested in an increasingly glass and steel core of Core Cities—to 'solve' the problem of the North by rendering certain places elite and other places permanently obsolete (see Giovannini, this collection). Fiscal devolution, as Martin suggests, 'could end up favouring the very largest cities' only (2015: 264), and those advocates of the current Powerhouse proposal demonstrate a tin ear to the echoes of even the recent past, such as the suspicions of the New Labour and Northern Way era of small local authorities regarding the overwhelming ambitions and influence of the larger Core Cities within regional plans (Goodchild and Hickman 2006: 129). Etherington and Jones rightly raise a note of caution about the implications for 'ordinary' cities and places outside the orbit of the starring cities in Powerhouse drives (2016: 3).

This seeming willingness to build a 'Northern Powerhouse' from very few parts of the North prompts attention to questions of poverty. Today the North sees starkly higher rates of poverty and lower overall health expectancy relative to the rest of England, yet has faced disproportionately high per capita public spending cuts over the course of recent administrations (Maxwell 2014). As we have argued, concerns over social welfare have undergirded the imaginations and interventions that have shaped and reshaped the North over many decades. Osborne's prescriptions for a Northern Powerhouse are perhaps no exception, yet concerns with poverty and equity have largely been eschewed in favour of a general focus on wealth creation, arguably at the expense of other policy goals. In a broad survey of recent arguments for devolution, the New Economics Foundation (2015) found that more than four in ten 'focus on achieving economic growth as the main justification for devolving power', while only a fraction address questions of poverty and power. The Powerhouse agenda, lest we forget, arises from the same political grouping that founded the Policy Exchange think-tank and whose recommendations for the economically and socially excluded populations of Northern English cities implied an exodus for those who are able to the honeyed hi-tech hubs of London, Oxford and Cambridge and a retrenchment of financial support for less lucky places in the North (Leunig and Swaffield 2008). Far more than a rhetorical pivot, the extent to which the Government's current devolution and urban growth agendas will prove equitable, inclusive and meaningful to communities beyond the preferred spaces of the Core Cities remains in question (New Economics Foundation 2015). The backroom, invitation only processes through which devolution plans, proposals and deals have been formulated have all but ignored civil society's leadership role in this area— including the very voluntary and community organisations working the ever-growing front lives of poverty alleviation and community development across the North (Bubb 2012; Whillans-Welldrake 2015).

When it comes to poverty, advocates of the Powerhouse, including those in the North itself, seem impervious to the lessons of the recent past, as in the failed aspirations and logics of the Northern Way, which were backed by many of the current political leaders in the North. The Northern Way's argument for increased investment in the North to drive economic productivity was not part of 'a national commitment to reduce regional inequalities' per se, as might have been the case in the interventions of earlier post-war Labour administrations, because merely 'reducing the gap in regional growth rates does nothing to reduce disparities in economic conditions in absolute terms' (Goodchild and Hickman 2006: 130). This is an observation which Northern political leaders should reflect on when considering not only what the Powerhouse might do for their cities, but also who it should really serve. Paring down the

Powerhouse rhetoric to its core suggests that the current devolution discourse is not at all about making people less poor, or addressing issues of entrenched social and economic inequality, but rather about making *certain* places (London as well as Northern cities) more wealthy and productive in a narrowly financial sense.

The continued centrality of all four themes within contemporary discussions of the North has been made even clearer by the reactions to Brexit. The choice voters made to ignore the spatial developments funded by the European Union in favour of a political solution with very unclear outcomes is part of the long tradition of tension, as outlined above, between these two forms of intervention. London is once again the shining emblem, the North once again both a problematic space and a poor one (Williams 2016). As Zoe Williams notes, 'This story about the deprived North, however, will have lasting and profoundly misleading consequences for the political landscape, if we don't think more deeply about it'. This has been true now for more than 150 years.

NOTES

1. The necessity of this historical perspective has only been heightened by the results of the Brexit referendum and the subsequent change in government. While the impact of the latter we will leave to our other colleagues in this volume to explain, the clear role of the North, and Northern poverty and anger (Williams 2016), in the result of the vote, are clear evidence that a more profound consideration of North/South relations is overdue.
2. See the recent proposal by Michael Heseltine to create a mayoral development corporation responsible for the redevelopment of Redcar (Davies 2016).
3. Although archival documents show that there were debates at Cabinet level at that time as to whether national policy towards Liverpool may have better followed a process of 'managed decline', to use the words of the then Chancellor, Geoffrey Howe (Travis 2011).

REFERENCES

Alsop, W. 2005. *Will Alsop's supercity*. Manchester: Urbis.

Belchem, J. 2000. *Merseypride: Essays in Liverpool exceptionalism*. Liverpool: Liverpool University Press.

Bubb, S. 2012. ACEVO urges Chancellor to work with third sector on devolution, public services, employment and extremism in pre-budget letter.

ACEVO, 8th July 2015. Available from: https://www.acevo.org.uk/news/acevo-urges-chancellor-work-third-sector-devolution-public-services-employ-ment-and-extremism. Accessed 20 Sept 2016.

Burnet, A. 2002. North to Elizabetha. *Prospect*, 20th December. Available from: http://www.prospectmagazine.co.uk/magazine/northtoelizabetha. Accessed 12 Nov 2016.

Caunce, S. 2003. Northern English industrial towns: Rivals or partners? *Urban History* 30 (3): 338–358.

Centre for Cities. 2014. *A manifesto for a more prosperous urban Britain*. London: Centre for Cities.

Centre for London. 2014. *The brightest star: A manifesto for London*. London: Centre for London.

Chadwick, E. 1965 [1842]. *Report on the sanitary condition of the labouring population of Great Britain*. Edinburgh: Edinburgh University Press.

Cities and Local Government Devolution Bill [HL]. 2015–2016.

Clifford, C. 1997. The rise and fall of the Department of Economic Affairs 1964–1969: British government and indicative planning. *Contemporary British History* 11 (2): 94–116.

Cockin, K. (ed.). 2012. *The literary north*. Palgrave: Houndmills.

Core Cities. 2013. *Keys to the city: Unlocking urban growth through devolution*. Manchester: Core Cities.

Daily Mash. 2015. Northern Powerhouse relocated to London. *The Daily Mash*. www.thedailymash.co.uk/.../northern-powerhouse-relocated-to-london.

Davies, R. 2016. Lord Heseltine outlines plans to regenerate Redcar steelworks site. *The Guardian*, 19th February. Available from: https://www.theguardian.com/business/2016/feb/19/heseltine-regenerate-redcar-steelworks-site-jobs. Accessed 12 Nov 2016.

Department for Business, Innovation & Skills. 2012. *Closing the RDAs (Regional Development Agencies): Lessons from the RDA transition and closure programme*. London: Department for Business, Innovation & Skills.

Department for Communities and Local Government. 2010. *National evaluation of the local enterprise growth initiative programme: Final report*. London: Department for Communities and Local Government.

Department of Economic Affairs. 1965. *The north west: A regional study*. London: HMSO.

Department of Economic Affairs. 1966a. *A review of Yorkshire and Humberside*. London: HMSO.

Department of Economic Affairs. 1966b. *Challenge of the changing north*. London: HMSO.

Dickens, C. 2001 [1854]. *Hard times: An authoritative text, contexts, criticism*. New York: Norton.

Disraeli, B. 1998 [1845]. *Sybil, or the two nations*. Oxford: Oxford University Press.

Engels, F. 2009 [1892]. *The condition of the working class in England*. Oxford: Oxford University Press.

Etherington, D., and M. Jones. 2016. The city-region chimera: The political economy of metagovernance failure in Britain. *Cambridge Journal of Regions, Economy and Society* 9 (2): 371–389.

Faulkner, W. 1975 [1951]. *Requiem for a Nun*. New York: Vintage.

Frost, D, and P. North. 2013. *Militant Liverpool: A city on the edge*. Liverpool: Liverpool University Press.

Gaskell, E. 1998 [1855]. *North and south*. Oxford: Oxford University Press.

Giovannini, A. 2016. Towards a 'new English regionalism' in the North? The case of Yorkshire first. *The Political Quarterly* 87 (4): 590–600.

Goodchild, B., and P. Hickman. 2006. Towards a regional strategy for the north of England? An assessment of 'The Northern Way'. *Regional Studies* 40 (1): 121–133.

González, S. 2006. *The Northern Way: A celebration or a victim of the new city-regional government policy?* Economic and Social Research Council.

Greenwood, W. 1969 [1933]. *Love on the Dole*. London: Penguin.

Hatherley, O. 2010. *A guide to the new ruins of Great Britain*. London: Verso.

Hebbert, M. 2000. Transpennine: Imaginative geographies of an interregional corridor. *Transactions of British Geographers* 25 (3): 379–392.

Heseltine, M. 2012. *No stone left unturned in pursuit of growth*. Independent report.

Hill, J. 1986. *Sex, class and realism: British cinema, 1956–1963*. London: BFI.

Hunt, T. 2004. *Building Jerusalem: The rise and fall of the Victorian city*. London: Phoenix.

IPPR-North. 2014a. *Transformational infrastructure for the North: Why we need a Great North Plan*. Manchester: IPPR-North.

IPPR-North. 2014b. *Decentralisation decade: A plan for economic prosperity, public service transformation and democratic renewal in England*. Manchester: IPPR-North.

IPPR-North. 2015. *Transport for the north: A blueprint for devolving and integrating transport powers in England*. Manchester: IPPR-North.

Jones, M., and G. MacLeod. 2004. Regional spaces, spaces of regionalism: Territory, insurgent politics and the English question. *Transactions of British Geographers* 29 (4): 433–452.

Kay-Shuttleworth, J. 1970 [1832]. *The moral and physical condition of the working classes employed in the cotton manufacture in Manchester*. London: Cass.

Kidd, A. 2006. *Manchester: A history*, 4th ed. Lancaster: Carnegie.

Leunig, T., and J. Swaffield. 2008. *Cities unlimited: Making urban regeneration work*. London: Policy Exchange.

Malpass, P. 2005. *Housing and the welfare state*. Basingstoke: Palgrave.

Martin, D. 2010. Mobilities-Based Urban Planning in the North of England. *Mobilities* 5 (1): 61–81.

Martin, R. 2015. Rebalancing the spatial economy: The challenge for regional theory. *Territory, Politics, Governance* 3 (3): 235–272.

Martin, R., A. Pike, P. Tyler, and B. Gardiner. 2016. Spatially rebalancing the UK economy: Towards a new policy model? *Regional Studies* 50 (2): 342–357.

Maxwell, J. 2014. Of course there is a north-south divide—and of course it matters. *New Statesman*, 7th May. Available from: http://www.newstatesman.com/politics/2014/05/course-there-north-south-divide-and-course-it-matters. Accessed 12 Nov 2016.

Milne, S. 1994. *The enemy within: The secret war against the miners*. London: Verso.

New Economics Foundation. 2015. *Democracy: The missing link in the devolution debate*. London: New Economics Foundation.

Northern Economic Futures Commission. 2012. *Northern prosperity is national prosperity: A strategy for revitalising the UK's economy*. Manchester: IPPR-North.

ODPM. 2004. *Making it happen: The Northern Way*. London: Office of the Deputy Prime Minister.

One North. 2014. *One north: A proposition for an interconnected north*. Manchester: Manchester City Council.

Orwell, G. 1937. *The road to Wigan Pier*. London: Gollancz.

Osborne, G. 2014. We need a Northern Powerhouse. [Speech]. Manchester, June 23. Available from: https://www.gov.uk/government/speeches/chancellor-we-need-a-northern-powerhouse. Accessed 12 Nov 2016.

Osborne, G. 2015. *Building a northern powerhouse*. [Speech]. Manchester, May 14. Available from: https://www.gov.uk/government/speeches/chancellor-on-building-a-northern-powerhouse. Accessed 12 Nov 2016.

Parkinson, M. 2004. *Competitive European cities: Where do the Core Cities stand?* London: ODPM.

Payling, D. 2014. 'Socialist Republic of South Yorkshire': Grassroots activism and left-wing solidarity in 1980s Sheffield. *Twentieth Century British History* 25 (4): 602–627.

Peck, J., and A. Tickell. 2007. Conceptualizing neoliberalism, thinking Thatcherism. In *Contesting neoliberalism: Urban frontiers*, ed. H. Leitner, J. Peck, and E. Sheppard, 26–50. New York: Guildford Press.

Pilmott, B. 1981. The north-east: Back to the 1930s? *The Political Quarterly* 52 (1): 51–63.

Porter, T. 2010. *Will Alsop: The noise*. London: Routledge.

Raco, M. 2007. *Building sustainable communities: Spatial policy and labour mobility in post-war Britain*. Bristol: Policy Press.

Raco, M., and R. Imrie (eds.). 2003. *Urban renaissance? New Labour, community and urban policy*. Bristol: Policy Press.

Ravetz, A. 1974. *Model estate: Planned housing at Quarry Hill, Leeds*. London: Croom Helm.

Rawnsley, S. 2000. Constructing 'the north': Space and a sense of place. In *Northern identities*, ed. Neville Kirk, 3–22. Hants: Ashgate.

Robson, B. 2002. Mancunian ways: The politics of regeneration. In *City of revolution: Restructuring Manchester*, ed. J. Peck and K. Kevin Ward, 34–49. Manchester: Manchester University Press.

Robson, B., J. Peck, and A. Holden. 2000. *Regional agencies and area-based regeneration*. Bristol: Policy Press.

Russell, D. 2004. *Looking north: Northern England and the national imagination*. Manchester: Manchester University Press.

Savage, M., et al. 2015. *Social class in the 21st century*. London: Pelican.

Simmons, J.R. 2005. Industrial and 'condition of England' novels. In *A companion to the Victorian novel*, ed. P. Brantlinger and W. Thesing, 336–352. Oxford: Blackwell.

Sykes, O., et al. 2013. A city profile of Liverpool. *Cities* 35: 299–318.

Taylor, P. 1993. The Meaning of the North: England's 'foreign country' within? *Political Geography* 12 (2): 136–155.

Travis, A. 2011. Thatcher government toyed with evacuating Liverpool after 1981 riots. *The Guardian*, 30 December. Available from: https://www.theguardian.com/uk/2011/dec/30/thatcher-government-liverpool-riots-1981. Accessed 12 Nov 2016.

Wallace, A. 2010. *Remaking community: New Labour and the governance of poor neighbourhoods*. Aldershot: Ashgate.

Ward, K., and A. Jonas. 2004. Competitive city-regions as a politics of space: A critical reinterpretation of the new regionalism. *Environment and Planning A* 36 (12): 2119–2139.

Watt, N. 2008. Tories' favourite thinktank brands northern cities failures. *The Guardian*, 13th August. Available from: https://www.theguardian.com/politics/2008/aug/13/conservatives.regeneration. Accessed 12 Nov 2016.

Whillans-Welldrake, A.G. 2015. Don't lose sight of devolution's role to empower. *New Start*, 28th May 2015. Available from: https://newstartmag.co.uk/articles/dont-lose-sight-of-devolutions-role-to-empower/. Accessed 12 Nov 2016.

Wilks-Heeg, S. 2003. From world city to pariah city? Liverpool and the global economy, 1850–2000. In *Reinventing the city? Liverpool in comparative perspective*, ed. R. Munck, 36–52. Liverpool: Liverpool University Press.

Williams, R. 2004. *The anxious city: English urbanism in the late twentieth century*. London: Routledge.

Williams, Z. 2016. Think the north and the poor caused Brexit? Think again. *The Guardian*, 7 August. Available from: https://www.theguardian.com/commentisfree/2016/aug/07/north-poor-brexit-myths. Accessed 12 Nov 2016.

Willett, J., and A. Giovannini. 2014. The uneven path of UK devolution: Top-down vs. bottom-up regionalism in England—Cornwall and the north-east compared. *Political Studies* 62 (2): 343–360.

Wyke, T. 1996. *A hall for all seasons: A history of the Free Trade Hall.* Manchester: Charles Hallé Foundation.

AUTHORS' BIOGRAPHY

Daryl Martin is Lecturer in Sociology at the University of York. His research is located at the intersection of architecture, embodiment and health, and he has published articles in academic journals such as *International Journal of Urban and Regional Research, Antipode, City* and *Mobilities.*

Alex Schafran is Lecturer in Urban Geography at the University of Leeds. His research focuses on the contemporary restructuring and retrofitting of urban regions. He has published articles in academic journals such as *International Journal of Urban and Regional Research, City and Environment and Planning A,* and is currently leading the multi-year research and organising project *Developing Impact-Driven Megaregional Research: Northern England after the Northern Way.*

Zac Taylor is doctoral researcher at the University of Leeds. His research focuses contemporary debates about urban innovation and resilience, looking at the interplay between finance, climate change adaptation and systems of urban reproduction in Florida cities. He is also Research Assistant on the project *Developing Impact-Driven Megaregional Research: Northern England after the Northern Way* (led by Alex Schafran).

PART III

Inequality and Austerity in the Northern Powerhouse Agenda

Regionalisation and Civil Society in a Time of Austerity: The Cases of Manchester and Sheffield

David Beel, Martin Jones and Ian Rees Jones

Abstract Within the UK and further afield, the spatial delineation of the 'city-region' has seen a renaissance as the de facto spatial political unit of governance driven by economic development. This spatial realignment has been central to the construction of Northern Powerhouse and has rested alongside other agendas such as devolution, localism and austerity. The chapter presents an original case study empirical research from two city-regions (Manchester and Sheffield), looking at the ways in which the city-region is being constructed differently and the different ways in which 'civil society' is negotiating its way through this changing governance landscape. The chapter considers the ways in which city-regions are

D. Beel · M. Jones (✉)
Staffordshire University, Stoke-on-Trent, Staffordshire, UK
e-mail: martin.jones@staffs.ac.uk

D. Beel
e-mail: david.beel@staffs.ac.uk

I.R. Jones
Cardiff University, Cardiff, UK
e-mail: JonesIR4@cardiff.ac.uk

© The Author(s) 2018
C. Berry and A. Giovannini (eds.), *Developing England's North,*
Building a Sustainable Political Economy: SPERI Research & Policy,
https://doi.org/10.1007/978-3-319-62560-7_10

241

being built and the ways in which this process is being limited or undermined through austerity.

Keywords Agglomeration · Austerity · City-region · Civil society
Devolution · Governance

Introduction

Since 2010, the UK Government has sought to reshape the ways in which economic development takes place and although this shift in governmental delivery began under New Labour, there has been a continuing emphasis on developing the city-regional scale to unlock economic growth. This was much vaunted by the Coalition Government elected in 2010 (Deas 2013), as underlined by the replacement of the Regional Development Agencies (RDAs) with Local Enterprise Partnerships (LEPs), and latterly by the morphing of LEPs into Combined Authorities (CAs). These policies were subsequently taken forward by the following Conservative administrations (Conservative Party 2015) through a variety of locality-specific devolution deals (for a full account, see Giovannini in this volume). In this context, the rhetoric of the Northern Powerhouse as a flagship policy for delivering economic growth for the North of England (Lee 2016) has sat alongside a severe austerity programme that has seen Local Authority (LA) budgets cut significantly. This, therefore, raises difficult questions with regards to the ability of CAs and LAs to address the current and future needs of their populations (Etherington and Jones 2016b). Finally, although in the context of Brexit and with the changes at the head of the Conservative government the future of the Northern Powerhouse remains uncertain, the political territorialisation and regionalisation (Harrison 2014) of the city-region has problematised the position of civil society actors working in their respective city-regions.

Concurrent to this and historically within geography as well as more broadly the social sciences, there have been a series of parallel debates simmering away for the past decade (see Jonas and Ward 2007). These have revolved around a series of discussions that consider the ways in which city-regional 'spatial-fixes' either foster economic development through agglomeration (Harding 2007) or continue to exacerbate uneven development and spatial disparities (Etherington and Jones 2009). This chapter seeks to connect these themes with the *realpolitik* concerns of delivering devolution at the city-regional scale. To achieve this, we follow the development of city-regionalism through these different discourses and in the context of the current devolution deals, and we seek to address the following question: within a language of localism, devolution and austerity, how have civil society actors in Greater Manchester and Sheffield City-Regions (GMCR and SCR) sought to deal with city-regional development approaches and the new governance structures that have been created? GMCR and SCR are two key city-regions in the North, and were the first areas within the Northern Powerhouse to sign devolution deals with the government (although the SCR deal has recently come to halt; see Giovannini in this volume). Thus, focussing on their cases is central to understand what kind of Northern Powerhouse growth is being built, and whose interests are being represented, if this to be more than an empty policy husk (Lee 2016). In turn, the chapter maps out the missing elements from the Northern Powerhouse recipe book for economic growth and social cohesion. By looking at the cases of GMCR and SCR, if the Northern Powerhouse is a coordinating frame for city-regions in the North of England in terms of their interactions, we are interested in understanding how these bodies are being shaped by devolution, and what role civil society plays within this.

Accordingly, the chapter offers an empirical contribution[1] that sheds light upon the ongoing processes of LA restructuring in GMCR and SCR towards combined authority (city-region) approaches. Therefore, it will highlight how 'policies are not, after all, merely being transferred over space; their form and their effects are transformed by these journeys' (Peck and Theodore 2015: 29). This will be achieved by engaging with the views of civil society actors 'on the ground', focussing on how they have responded to a shifting governance framework at the local state/city-regional scale. The chapter will, therefore, address the positioning of civil society within these processes by first, giving greater context to the development of city-regions as a process of regionalisation—i.e. the way in which 'new regions', namely GMCR and SCR, are created territorially through changes in governance structures. In doing this, this chapter will also consider how austerity has impacted upon these processes. Second, the chapter will also assess how, in this context, civil society is being repositioned due to the economic rationale of city-regions, the changes in governance scale and the creation of new 'citizenship regimes' (Jenson and Saint-Martin 2010; also Rutherford 2006). By focussing upon the repositioning of civil society actors, the chapter will highlight how city-regionalism and the Northern Powerhouse, more broadly, raise serious questions about developing notions of an 'inclusive growth' approach (RSA 2016a, b). The findings suggest that the main issue emerging from these complex processes concerns whether failure to deliver inclusive growth at the city-regional scale will reflect a failure to deliver equitable growth within the Northern Powerhouse.

BUILDING THE CITY-REGIONS OF THE NORTHERN POWERHOUSE

The current government has sought to reshape the map of governance in England through a series of reforms implemented from 2014 onwards (see Giovannini, and Gray, Pugalis and Dickinson in this volume). One part of the solution to this has been the creation of the Northern Powerhouse. The Northern Powerhouse can be seen as a policy framing device, in which a series of ongoing projects have been placed (Lee 2016). In many respects, the Powerhouse represents what Jessop (2015: 38) defines as a 'spatial imaginary'—a discursive phenomenon that distinguish, by carving out distinctiveness, specific places and spaces 'from the inherently unstructured complexity of a spatialised world'. This is well represented rhetorically in Fig. 10.1, whereby economic success and growth is emphasised by the role Northern Powerhouse cities have in providing employment in their metropolitan centres.

The Northern Powerhouse agenda has framed the more substantial restructuring of (some) local authorities into combined authority city-regions. This has been based upon a 'city first' approach whereby; to date city-region devolution has focussed around the existing metropolitan footprints of the core UK cities (Jones et al. 2015; Harrison and Heley 2014). The momentum for this is based on a number of issues which the UK government has attempted to deal with. First, it was very much a post-crisis reaction in order to stimulate economic growth, with the city-region vaunted as the de facto scale for growth (Overman 2012). This reflected both a dominant policy discourse in urban development (see Storper 2013 for such an example) and a perceived failure of RDAs (Pugalis and Townsend 2012). Second, it has sought to address the long-standing issue of rebalancing the UK economy, whereby an overheating South is contrasted by an underperforming North

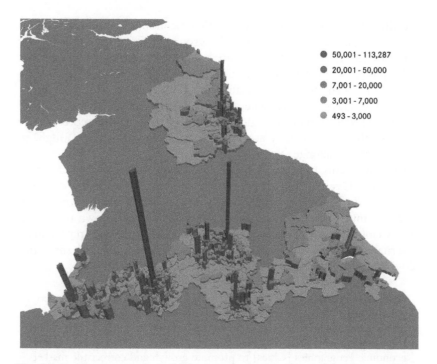

Fig. 10.1 The geography of jobs across the Northern Powerhouse. *Source* Centre for the Cities (2015), based on NOMIS 2015, Census 2011 occupation, MSOA level

(Clarke et al. 2016; Martin et al. 2016; Gardiner et al. 2013). Third, England is often considered as one of the most centralised in Western Europe—in the light of this, with the failure of regional devolution (beyond Wales, Scotland and London) under New Labour (Goodwin et al. 2005), devolution to a suitable scale within England has been sought by the current government (Pike et al. 2012). Fourth, via the current deal-making approach, the government has attempted to embed austerity into the reformulation of combined authorities through a process of block grant reduction and rationalisation.

The city-regional scale has become the dominant discourse in urban development policy (see Storper 2013). This is due to a number of reasons and analytical frames such as the rise of 'New Regionalism'

(Keating 2003) and the influence of 'New Economic Geography' (NEG) in placing specific emphasis upon the growing of regions for economic purposes (MacLeod 2001). Within both these accounts of economic and regional geography, there is an implicit understanding that the city-region is both the 'natural' and 'functional' scales for economic development. It is suggested that where nation-states have failed to deal with macroeconomic shifts in the global economy, city-regions represent the most suitable scale, as they are 'small enough' but also 'big enough' to deal with this challenge (Scott 2001).

Central to this has been a belief in agglomeration theory (Overman et al. 2007; Overman 2012; cf. Haughton et al. 2014) as the driver to economic development, whereby city-regions open themselves up to attract as much investment as they can, so that trickles down in turn to their vicinities and populations. The city-region, therefore, represents a governance strategy that seeks to harness agglomeration and share this geographically. According to an important account of this logic:

> The policy implications of theories of agglomeration is that enabling people and firms to benefit from proximity to centres of activity, bring beneficial economic outcomes ... This implies empowering and incentivising local government, firms and people across economic centres and natural economic geographies [Cities] to promote growth and correct the market and government failures which are acting as barriers to economic development. (BIS 2010: 25)

The BIS quote illustrates the rationale underpinning the current government's approach, and it sees local government and business as having to address the past failures of both the market and the state. Key to this, from the government's perspective, is to create an agglomerative economy in each of the city-regions; quite simply, everyone can win. As Fig. 10.1 suggests, this links up, or agglomerates, to form the Northern Powerhouse, which is presented as the 'spatial imaginary' that could allow the North to match London in economic terms (HM Government and Transport for the North 2015).

Within this context, the Northern Powerhouse agenda—and the devolution deals that are associated with it—have a strong economic focus, which is also emphasised by the goal of addressing the North–South divide, but also by the development of soft-institutional organisation (Haughton et al. 2013) such as Local Enterprise Partnerships

The Greater Manchester City Region
- £1.2 Billion via 'earn back' model
- Investment framework
- Growth hub
- Skills and the local economy
- Low Carbon Demonstrator
- Inward Investment Beacon
- Health and social care
- Coming Mayor (2017)

The Sheffield City Region
- £900 million over 30 years
- Six of Nine LAs are constituent members
- Investment framework
- Skills and the local economy
- Low Carbon Demonstrator
- Coming Mayor (2017) for constituent members only

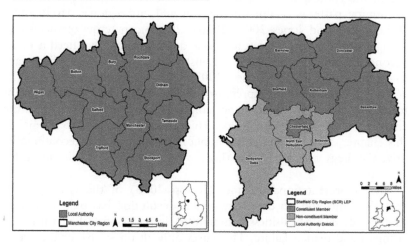

Fig. 10.2   Outline of GMCR and SCR devolution deals and LA membership

(LEPs). Crucially, this leads to a rescaling of the 'representational regime' of the city-region (Jessop 2015; Macleod and Goodwin 1999; Cox 1997), in a spatially specific and strategic way. This, in turn, is linked to the creation of 'new citizenship regimes' for the governance of city-regions. The concept of new citizenship regimes captures that:

> Who qualifies and is recognized as a model citizen is under challenge. The legitimacy of group action and the desire for social justice are losing ground to the notion that citizens and interests can compete equally in the political marketplace of ideas. (Jenson and Phillips 1996: 112)

In the context of GMCR and SCR (see Fig. 10.2 for broad outline), the new business-orientated representational regime, by design, places civil society at the margins of the process. This means that what could broadly be termed as the 'social reproduction of the city' is given secondary status to its economic drivers (Jonas and Ward 2007). This, in turn, positions civil society actors as no longer directly and centrally relevant within the context of chasing agglomerative growth.

Many scholars have been critical to this approach for a number of reasons (see Beel et al. forthcoming for a more in-depth account of this), but there are three important areas of critique to consider here, within the context of a Northern Powerhouse. First, there seem to be continuing patterns of uneven regional and city-regional development (Etherington and Jones 2009, 2016a, 2016b), in terms of the failure for agglomerative approaches to trickle down to those that need it most. Second, this pitches city-regions against each other in a competitive race to capture investment (Harrison 2007), questioning the potential of the Northern Powerhouse as represented in Fig. 10.1. Third, it is important to understand who such strategies empower and disempower within the city-region (see Rutherford 2006). This last point is central to the aim of this chapter, as it highlights the implications that such an economically driven strategy could have for those who sit outside of this rubric for growth.

The 'representational regime' (Jessop 2015) of the city-region is central to this and, to date, city-region devolution has only sought to strategically engage business communities in terms of dealing with government and market failure. This raises difficult questions for the actors that operate within what could be broadly termed 'civil society', who are often working with those sectors of the society that benefit least from agglomerative strategies. This reflects a failure to properly integrate a social or inclusive dimension into devolution, due to their stubborn and narrow focus on economic development. Despite many devolution deals have been proposed by CAs and agreed by the government, the social and inclusive dimension of the reform is only now starting to be discussed as a concern, in the continuing process of implementing devolution. An example of this can be seen in the RSA's Inclusive Growth Commission, which is seeking to identify practical ways to make local economies across the UK more economically inclusive and prosperous (RSA 2016a).

The aim of the next sections is to build on these arguments and frame the role of civil society in process of devolution in GMCR and SCR, and address the position of civil society more directly within this rescaling of governance.

PLACING CIVIL SOCIETY IN THE CITY-REGION

This section assesses the role and place of civil society within GMCR and SCR in the context of the unfolding devolution and the Northern Powerhouse agendas. To achieve this, it draws on the findings of thirty semi-structured interviews with civil society actors in GMCR and SCR that were undertaken by the authors in 2015–2016. In the context of this research, civil society is used as a catchall term for a number of different types of organisation, which are separate from both the state and business. These include organisations such as charities, those termed third sector, voluntary groups, community groups (of both place and identity), social enterprises and housing associations. They all have very different relationships with the local state and business in terms of how they operate. Some have contractual relationships, whereby they deliver specific services. Others act to give specific representation to minority groups, and different groups work on very different spatial scales—ranging from across the city-region to very localised, neighbourhood development. What ties them together as a set of groups is their individual organisational remit to produce or engender some form of social benefit for their perceived communities. The interviews were not discussing the development of the Northern Powerhouse specifically, but more broadly the development of the city-region building agenda. However, as has been previously stated, the development of city-regions is central to the development of the Northern Powerhouse as a 'spatial imaginary' and GMCR and SCR are two key cases in point in this respect. Hence the following responses should be viewed in the context of what such approaches to city-regions mean for discourses surrounding the Northern Powerhouse.

In framing current developments in devolution from a UK state perspective and from within both SCR and GMCR, it is important to consider the ways in which civil society actors are dealing with this changing governance structure. For example, Jones et al. (2015) highlight how in Liverpool and Bristol, the changing governance landscape and the reduction in funding opportunities through austerity have made things more difficult for groups that sit within civil society. This has been reflected also in GMCR and SCR, as austerity has had a hard impact on civil society actors—especially in the most deprived areas of each city-region (Beatty and Fothergill 2016), where such groups are more active and needed. However, civil society members have also highlighted a number of opportunities to mitigate this (despite being problematic) within the context of devolution and in the face of stringent austerity measures. Below we analyse how civil society actors have struggled with devolution, but also have attempted to find new positions and strategies on which to see their social agendas addressed against the economic framework.

Struggling With the Economic Rationale

For many civil society groups, there have been a number of problems that devolution and the rhetoric of the Northern Powerhouse have failed to address. These issues initially focused upon the economic emphasis of city-regions, which places civil society on the outside but also misses the need to help those who are most disadvantaged within city-regions. According to a source:

> I think of Greater Manchester as having a ring donut economy, it's a lot like a North American city. So you have thriving city centre, which it didn't have twenty-five years ago. The suburbs actually doing OK and then the middle bit. If they do not do something about that is really meaningful in that ring donut, the powers that will be devolved will never achieve their economic goals of achieving a fiscal balance for this conurbation. (Salford Social Enterprise representative 2016)

The extract above highlights how from the outset there is a perception that the growth model proposed for GMCR fails to address the broader problems faced by the city-region. This is caused by the ongoing geohistory of inequality in the area, but it also shows how this is compounded by pursuit of an agglomerative growth strategy. Similar views emerged also in SCR:

> Trickledown doesn't work for the most vulnerable and disadvantaged and you have to have strategies around social regeneration (for want of a better word) alongside economic regeneration. Those two things should come together and I don't think they do because the LEP is very purely focused on the economic policy... Feels like I'm in a rowing boat and my colleagues are in a rowing boat and we're trying to turn round this big tanker. (Sheffield Community Development Group representative 2015)

For both respondents, one a social enterprise, primarily focussed upon projects in Salford, and the other a community development organisation in a deprived area of Sheffield, the urban growth machine strategy (Logan and Molotch 1987; Jonas and Wilson 1999) is deeply problematic. As they pick out how the 'trickledown' approach that implies a strategy of developing high level GVA uplift by bringing people to jobs within the city-region (Etherington and Jones 2016a) does little for the disadvantaged citizens they are attempting to support. This means that because they question the rhetoric of this growth model, they are left on the periphery of its strategic delivery. This is also reflected in the above quote, which highlights how such groups, operating at a local level, have little ability or remit in the context of devolution to act at the city-region level and there is an ongoing lack of accountability that marginalises local civil society through institutions such as the LEPs. As underlined by an interviewee in SCR:

> What opportunity will there be to genuinely involve civil society in the process? Because I think the LEP has been and I know it is an economic driver, fine and it's about inward investment, economic growth and the private sector is at the heart of that but there is very little in terms of any wider involvement. And maybe that's ok but when it comes to the combined authority, there needs to be more direct lines of accountability into localities and into local areas. (Sheffield Community Development Group representative 2015)

This suggests that the construction of a new 'representational regime' for the city-region based upon economic interests purposefully excludes civil society actors from the outset. This, in turn, allows for an uncontested agglomerative growth model to be developed. The following section addresses this by assessing how civil society is being positioned and marginalised differently at different scales.

DEALING WITH SCALE

The difficulty to have a voice within processes of devolution, due to the failure for civil society groups to be integrated into the representational regime of the city-region, has left some squeezed between the 'scale jump' of the city-region (Cox 1997) and austerity that are occurring at the same time. According to an interviewee:

At one point they talk about localism but if you look at regionalisation, it's huge, it's huge and actually the local voluntary community sector can't even hope to engage with, let alone deliver against that agenda. Therefore civil society is finding itself squeezed behind/between a rhetoric that emphasises its importance but a reality which mitigates against its ability to capture the resources to deliver against that agenda. (Bolsover Voluntary Organisation representative 2016)

This quote highlights the difficulties for civil society organisations to deal with austerity and devolution at the same time. It also shows the way in which civil society groups are co-opted and recast into a neoliberal growth model. In short, civil society groups are both needed for the continuing function of the city-region, but at the same time they are marginalised within rescaling processes too. There is also an appreciation of how LAs are struggling to deal with this rescaling process within the context of austerity:

To be honest, they are holding what they can, both in Tameside and Oldham, they are holding everything that they can. We are predominantly funded through the local authorities, Tameside get us a fair bit from their CCG [Clinical Commissioning Group] but actually, we don't, as an organisation the make-up is a much greater split for local authorities. So they are doing all they can to protect us. I think the voluntary organisations with smaller grants are dwindling, the smaller amounts of funding for the sector are dwindling, which is in itself a risk and that's something that we fight hard against. But strategically they do view us as important in terms of achieving their public service reform and in fact it has been said by the cabinet portfolio holders around in Oldham and others, that we are their answer to that, that's how they see the change in the relationships between citizens and the wider population and the public services. (Oldham Voluntary Organisation representative 2016)

The end of this quote touches on the important shifts within the positionality of civil society, as it acknowledges how the local state is a deeply contradictory 'agent and obstacle' (Duncan and Goodwin 1989). On the one hand, civil society is drawn into the local state as a necessity of funding. On the other, it is also somewhat powerless in the context of restructuring and cuts, as civil society groups are further distanced from having a strategic voice. Here, the paradox of austerity in the context of scale suggests that at local level, civil society actors are needed more than ever, stepping into the austerity void (DeVerteuil 2016; Dear and Wolch 1987) and increasingly being relied on to deliver public services. However, at a city-region level, the same actors are being afforded a marginal voice. This is especially true within GMRC, due to the fact that the devolution deal for this area includes also health and social care. But similar issues have been notes also in SCR:

> I think it's probably changed enormously actually. I think – well there's a number of pros and cons, I think with the current government policy and the austerity measures everything that's going on in terms of shrinking the states, promoting using third sector organisations and growing civil society has brought some opportunities for the third sector. There's definitely, for example, funding streams that the third sector can access that statutory organisations can't access...but having said that, they are highly competitive. (Sheffield Youth Development Organisation representative 2015)

As illustrated above, within the context of austerity, opportunities have arisen for civil society groups, even in the face of the highly competitive nature of funding. However, the jumping of scale to the city-region and the realignment of governance alongside austerity has also created destabilising experiences. The following sections looks at how civil society organisation have responded to these.

Responding and Repositioning Within City-Regions

In this section, the responses of civil society groups to ongoing and overlapping processes of devolution, city-regionalism and austerity will be assessed focusing primarily on GMCR, as this is the only area where, to date, a devolution deal has developed to a sufficient extent.

Indeed, within GMCR the problematic background highlighted in the previous sections has generated a coordinated response from civil society groups via the Greater Manchester Voluntary, Community and Social Enterprise Devolution Reference Group (VCSE 2016). The group was formed in response to devolution due to the failure of Greater Manchester Combined Authority (GMCA) to engage such organisations in any meaningful way in the ongoing debate on the future of the city-region. VCSE represents an attempt by the various civil society actors operating in the area to find a voice and influence the direction of devolution (and potentially, in turn, of the Northern Powerhouse) by means of their collective knowledge and access to different parts of GMCA. According to an interviewee:

> The reference group was set up when we realised that all this was going on around us and nobody was going to come banging down our door...So from that a little coalition of the willing emerged, completely undemocratically but again I think that's part of it. Stop waiting for permission, stop feeling like you have to get every detail right. Because actually things are moving so fast, we have to trust each to advocate for what our sector wants to collectively achieve. (Manchester Voluntary Organisation representative 2016)

This quote sheds light on a very important point. Although the VCSE includes 'self-selected' groups and therefore does not give full democratic representation for civil society at large, its creation reflects a considerable attempt to 'jump scales' (Cox 1997) by organisations that for the most part do not exist on a city-regional scale. In this way, it could be argued that the VCSE epitomises a joint effort on the part of local civil society actors to exert agency at city-regional level, and influence the process of devolution in Greater Manchester. However, the same extract also highlights how, to date, GMCA has failed to address the needs of civil society groups within the context of devolution, and the desire of these actors to be included in the process. This shows the shortcomings of the representational regime emerging in GMCR. One interviewee develops this further:

> The pace of change of devolution has been about the public sector thinking about the public sector and their internal mechanism ways of working override that belief that we're important partners. I think we as a group, I'm going to use your term, 'civil society' but voluntary sector and social enterprises. By having that collective group that is able to in some part have representative round tables, to have the ability to talk to some of the key individuals, as a collective to be able to do that, that is important. (Oldham Voluntary Organisation representative 2016)

While the voice of business leaders plays a prominent role in the devolution debate in GMCR, as the LEP work in conjunction with the GMCA, civil society groups have had to find alternative ways to reposition themselves within the CA. The VCSE is an attempt at generating a 'critical mass' able to influence the process of devolution—but their impact is still marginal compared with that of the LEP. In this sense, the case of

GMCR shows how the UK government, with its emphasis upon economic development in the context of 'devo deals', has sought to shape devolution from the top-down creating a distorted narrative of 'inclusive growth' which affects, in turn, also the Northern Powerhouse agenda. By its very structure, this approach has defined who is and who is not involved in the debate that will shape the future of devolution deals to CAs and city-regions—empowering certain groups (in particular business leaders), whilst marginalising and disempowering others (such as civil society groups). Although each city-region will implement devolution deals differently, the 'rules of the game' have been shaped in a univocal direction in terms of creating a new 'citizenship regime' under devolution (Jenson and Phillips 1996; Rutherford 2006). This raises serious questions about representation and recognition of civil society groups in the pursuit of economic growth, and this is something that all the interviewees have emphasised. By recognising this 'representation gap', civil society organisations have attempted to find new ways to place their agendas on inequality and the social reproduction of the city-region back into the processes of 'city-region building' and devolution. However, as these new attempts at repositioning civil society are still unfolding, their potential impact and success will only become clear as (and when) devolution to city-regions CAs will be delivered in full, in the coming years.

Conclusions

This chapter has addressed the changes being created by the unfolding process of devolving power to two of the Northern Powerhouse's key city-regions—GMCR and SCR. Within this, it has attempted to understand how civil society is being (re)positioned. The findings have emphasised how if the Northern Powerhouse is to be successful and be more than just a 'spatial imaginary' (Jessop 2015) in which a 'rag bag' set of policies falls (Lee 2016), there is a need to deal more seriously with issues surrounding inequality, representation and uneven development within (and across) its city-regions.

As emphasised in other chapters in this volume, the Northern Powerhouse is often presented as a project that will bring prosperity to the North of England. However, evidence suggests that its model of agglomerative economic growth, fostered on trickledown economics, will only continue to exacerbate uneven development and undermine the project of spatial rebalancing, especially if this keeps perpetuating uneven dynamics of empowerment and disempowerment. By analysing the findings of interviews with civil society actors in GMCR and SCR, this chapter has highlighted how in the context of city-region building, the current approach to city-regional economic development and devolution is falling short of its promises. We have suggested that this is due, in part, to a clear divide between those who have been enabled to have a voice and 'lead' within the devolution city-region agenda, and those who have been marginalised in this process. Further to this, findings in GMCR and SCR suggest that the new citizenship regimes implemented within city-regions place civil society outside of decision-making processes that underpin devolution deals, whilst simultaneously—and somewhat paradoxically—expecting civil society to deal with the fallout from continuing uneven development, socio-spatial inequalities and austerity. Importantly, in areas such as GMCR, where devolution deals are unfolding at a fast pace, civil society groups are trying to reverse these processes of representational marginalisation, as emphasised by the recent creation of the VCSE. However, it remains to be seen whether these attempts at repositioning civil society will be successful.

The Northern Powerhouse faces an uncertain future since the vote to leave the European Union, and also due to the recent switch towards an industrial strategy for the UK and the largely repacking of existing committed expenditure with little new to create regional distinctiveness (compare Berry 2016; HM Treasury 2016). The pendulum of UK economic development may have at least partially turned away from the spatial imaginaries of the Northern Powerhouse and the city-region to focus on the national level again, but the spatial dimensions and subnational dynamics of this remain unclear. Moreover, as we have argued here, there remains a need to rebalance relationships between the economy, state and civil society, so that a more representative and 'just' form of devolution can be delivered. We would suggest that this requires a much stronger attempt to integrate 'the social' alongside the 'economic' within both devolution and the Northern Powerhouse if a more inclusive growth strategy is to be achieved.

NOTE

1. All empirical material is based upon 30 semi-structured interviews with key civil society stakeholders in both GMCR and SCR that were conducted between 2015 and 2016, supported by funding from the ESRC, Grant ES/L0090991/1 WISERD Civil Society.

REFERENCES

Beatty, C., and S. Fothergill. 2016. *The uneven impact of welfare reform*. Sheffield: Sheffield Hallam University.

Berry, C. 2016. Industrial policy change in the post-crisis British economy: Policy innovation in an incomplete institutional and ideational environment. *The British Journal of Politics and International Relations* 18 (4): 829–847.

BIS. 2010. Understanding local growth. BIS Economics Paper Number 7. London: Department for Business, Innovation and Skills.

Centre for the Cities. 2015. Northern Powerhouse factsheet, 2 June. Available form: http://www.centreforcities.org/publication/northern-powerhouse-factsheet/.

Clarke, G., R. Martin, and P. Tyler. 2016. Divergent cities? Unequal urban growth and development. *Cambridge Journal of Regions, Economy and Society* 9 (2): 259–268.

Conservative Party. 2015. Conservative Election Manifesto 2015. The Conservative Party. Available from: https://www.bond.org.uk/data/files/Blog/ConservativeManifesto2015.pdf. Accessed 15 December 2016.

Cox, K. 1997. Spaces of dependence, spaces of engagement and the politics of scale, ore looking for local politics. *Policitcal Geography* 17 (I): 1–22.

Dear, M.J., and J.R. Wolch. 1987. *Landscapes of despair: From deinstitutionalization to homelessness*. Cambridge: Polity Press.

Deas, I. 2013. Towards post-political consensus in Urban Policy? Localism and the emerging agenda for regeneration under the Cameron Government. *Planning Practice and Research* 28 (1): 65–82.

DeVerteuil, G. 2016. *Resilience in the post-welfare inner city: Voluntary sector geographies in London, Los Angeles and Sydney*. Bristol: Polity Press.

Duncan, S., and M. Goodwin. 1989. *The local state and uneven development*. London: Polity Press.

Etherington, D., and M. Jones. 2009. City-regions: New geographies of uneven development and inequality. *Regional Studies* 43 (2): 247–265.

Etherington, D., and M. Jones. 2016a. *Devolution and disadvantage in the Sheffield city region: An assessment of employment, skills, and welfare policies*. Sheffield: University of Sheffield.

Etherington, D., and M. Jones. 2016b. The city-region chimera: The political economy of metagovernance failure in Britain. *Cambridge Journal of Regions, Economy and Society* 9 (2): 371–389.

Gardiner, B., et al. 2013. Spatially unbalanced growth in the British economy. *Journal of Economic Geography* 13 (6): 889–928.

Goodwin, M., M. Jones, and R. Jones. 2005. Devolution, constitutional change and economic development: Explaining and understanding the new institutional geographies of the British state. *Regional Studies* 39 (4): 421–436.

Harding, A. 2007. Taking city regions seriously? Response to debate on 'city-regions: New geographies of governance, democracy and social reproduction'. *International Journal of Urban and Regional Research* 31 (2): 443–458.

Harrison, J. 2007. From competitive regions to competitive city-regions: A new orthodoxy, but some old mistakes. *Journal of Economic Geography* 7 (3): 311–332.

Harrison, J. 2014. Rethinking city-regionalism as the production of new non-state spatial strategies: The case of peel holdings Atlantic gateway strategy. *Urban Studies* 51 (11): 2315–2335.

Harrison, J., and J. Heley. 2014. Governing beyond the metropolis: Placing the rural in city-region development. *Urban Studies* 52 (6): 1113–1133.

Haughton, G., I. Deas, and S. Hincks. 2014. Making an impact: When agglomeration boosterism meets antiplanning rhetoric. *Environment and Planning A* 46 (2): 265–270.

Haughton, G., P. Allmendinger, and S. Oosterlynck. 2013. Spaces of neoliberal experimentation: Soft spaces, postpolitics, and neoliberal governmentality. *Environment and Planning A* 45 (1): 217–234.

HM Government & North, T. for the. 2015. *The Northern Powerhouse: One agenda, one economy, one north.* Available at: https://www.gov.uk/government/uploads/system/uploads/attachment_data/file/427339/the-northern-powerhouse-tagged.pdf. Accessed 15 Dec 2016.

HM Treasury. 2016. *Northern Powerhouse strategy.* Available at: https://www.gov.uk/government/publications/northern-powerhouse-strategy. Accessed 15 Dec 2016.

Jenson, J., and S.D. Phillips. 1996. Regime shift: New citizenship practices in Canada. *International Journal of Canadian Studies* 14: 111–136.

Jenson, J., and D. Saint-martin. 2010. New routes to social cohesion? *Citizenship and the Social Investment State* 28 (1): 77–99.

Jessop, B. 2015. *The state: Past, present, future.* Cambridge: Polity Press.

Jonas, A.E.G., and K. Ward. 2007. Introduction to a debate on city-regions: New geographies of governance, democracy and social reproduction. *International Journal of Urban and Regional Research* 31 (1): 169–178.

Jonas, A.E.G., and D. Wilson. 1999. *The urban growth machine: Critical perspectives, two decades later.* London: SUNY Press.

Jones, G., R. Meegan, P. Kennet, and J. Croft. 2015. The uneven impact of austerity on the voluntary and community sector: A tale of two cities. *Urban Studies* 53 (10): 2064–2080.

Keating, M. 2003. *The new regionalism in western Europe territorial restructuring and political change.* Cheltenham: Edward Elgar.

Lee, N. 2016. Powerhouse of Cards? Understanding the "Northern Powerhouse." *Regional Studies.* Online First see http://dx.doi.org/10.1080/00343404.2016.1196289.

Logan, J.R., and H.L. Molotch. 1987. *Urban fortunes: The political economy of place*. Berkeley: University of California Press.

MacLeod, G. 2001. New regionalism reconsidered: Globalization and the remaking of political economic space. *International Journal of Urban and Regional Research* 25 (4): 804–829.

Macleod, G., and M. Goodwin. 1999. Reconstructing an urban and regional political economy: On the state, politics, scale, and explanation. *Political Geography* 18: 697–730.

Martin, R., P. Sunley, P. Tyler, and B. Gardiner. 2016. Divergent cities in post-industrial Britain. *Cambridge Journal of Regions, Economy and Society* 9: 269–299.

Overman, H. 2012. Investing in the UK's most successful cities is the surest recipe for national growth. In *LSE Politics and Policy Blog*, 12 January 2016. Available from: http://blogs.lse.ac.uk/politicsandpolicy/. Accessed 15 Dec 2016.

Overman, H., P. Rice, and A.J. Venables. 2007. *Economic linkages across space*. London: Centre for Economic Performance, London School of Economics and Political Science.

Peck, J., and N. Theodore. 2015. *Fast policy: Experimental statecraft at the thresholds of neoliberalism*. Minnneapolis: University of Minnesota.

Pike, A., J. Rodriguez-Pose, J. Tomaney, G. Torrisi, and V. Tselios. 2012. In search of the "economic dividend" of devolution: Spatial disparities, spatial economic policy, and decentralisation in the UK. *Environment and Planning C: Government and Policy* 30 (1): 10–28.

Pugalis, L., and A.R. Townsend. 2012. Rebalancing England: Sub-national development (once again) at the crossroads. *Urban Research & Practice* 5 (1): 157–174.

RSA. 2016a. *Inclusive growth commission emerging findings foreword* (September). Available at https://www.thersa.org/discover/publications-and-articles/reports/emerging-findings-of-the-inclusive-growth-commission. Accessed 15 Dec 2016.

RSA. 2016b. *Inclusive growth for people and places* (September). Available at https://www.thersa.org/discover/publications-and-articles/reports/inclusive-growth-for-people-and-places-challenges-and-opportunities. Accessed 15 Dec 2016.

Rutherford, T.D. 2006. Local representations in crisis: Governance, citizenship regimes, and UK TECs and Ontario local boards. *Environment and Planning D: Society and Space* 24 (3): 409–426.

Scott, A.J. 2001. Globalization and the rise of city-regions. *European Planning Studies* 9 (7): 813–826.

Storper, M. 2013. *Keys to the City: How economics, institutions, social interaction, and politics shape development*. Princeton: Princeton Univerity Press.

VCSE. 2016. *Greater manchester voluntary, community and social enetprise (VCSE) devolution reference group.* Available at https://www.gmcvo.org.uk/system/files/gm_vcse_devolution_reference_group_-_information_sheet.pdf. Accesssed 15 Dec 2016.

Authors' Biography

David Beel is Senior Researcher at Staffordshire University, having previously worked as a Research Associate in the Department of Geography at the University of Sheffield, and as a Research Fellow at the University of Aberdeen. He works with Professor Martin Jones on the ESRC-funded project 'Spaces of New Localism - Stakeholder Engagement and Economic Development in Wales and England'. He has published on local economic governance and related issues in *The Scottish Geographical Journal* and *Journal of Rural Studies*.

Martin Jones is Deputy Vice Chancellor at Staffordshire University, and formerly Professor of Urban and Regional Political Economy at the University of Sheffield. He is one of the world's leading scholars of regional economic development, governance and state theory, and has published in journals such as *Environment and Planning A, Regional Studies, Urban Studies, Antipode* and *Territory, Politics, Governance*. He published *Rescaling the State: Devolution and the Geographies of Economic Governance* in 2012 (with Mark Goodwin and Rhys Jones) and *The Nature of the State: Excavating the Political Ecologies of the Modern State* in 2007 (with Mark Whitehead and Rhys Jones).

Ian Rees Jones is Professor of Sociological Research and WISERD director at Cardiff University. Previously, he was Professor of Sociology and Head of School at Bangor University. He is Fellow of the Learned Society of Wales and Fellow of the UK Academy of Social Sciences. Currently, he is undertaking a series of research projects that addresses processes of social change and their impact on individuals, institutions, communities and civil society.

CHAPTER 11

Civic Financialisation: Financing the Northern Powerhouse

Kevin Muldoon-Smith and Paul Greenhalgh

Abstract This chapter examines how the Northern Powerhouse agenda will be financed, in part, through the Government's Business Rate Scheme (BRRS). It begins with a brief summary of local government finance in England, describing the transference from a centralised model to one based on the parallel rubrics of localism and local economic growth. The central findings are structured around three interrelated themes: liability and growth potential, demand divergence, and the nature of local commercial property markets. It concludes that the BRRS has begun to roll out the conditions that will provoke parts of the Northern Powerhouse to enter an era of civic financialisation and entrepreneurial activity. However, asymmetries between commercial property markets, economic conditions and welfare need could result in a defined set of winners and losers—those that can take part in autonomous civic financialisation and those that remain reliant on a system of redistribution and equalisation.

K. Muldoon-Smith (✉) · P. Greenhalgh
Department of Architecture and Built Environment, Northumbria University,
Newcastle upon Tyne, UK
e-mail: kevin.muldoon-smith@northumbria.ac.uk

P. Greenhalgh
e-mail: paul.greenhalgh@northumbria.ac.uk

© The Author(s) 2018
C. Berry and A. Giovannini (eds.), *Developing England's North*,
Building a Sustainable Political Economy: SPERI Research & Policy,
https://doi.org/10.1007/978-3-319-62560-7_11

261

Keywords Business rate retention · Civic financialisation · Northern Powerhouse · Property markets · Urban finance

INTRODUCTION

Since its launch, the Northern Powerhouse has quickly been adopted as a narrative of change for the North of England. The device evokes memories of industrial power, recalling the confidence of economic stability—it also frames the contemporary concern with rebalancing England and combating years of uneven development that led to a discernible North–South divide (Martin et al. 2015). Underneath the rhetorical surface of this largely positive discourse, it is difficult to discern (neither) what is meant by 'Northern'—whether it is a hollow political gambit or substantial plan of action—nor how this Powerhouse agenda will be delivered in practice. However, what is certain is that the Northern Powerhouse has gained traction in the national and international consciousness (even though some Northern locations do not quite know what it means for them). The agenda has typically been received favourably alongside the equally blurred notions of devolution and localism—with the implicit meaning that any economic resurgence in the North is its own business (Berry 2016).

This chapter focuses on one part of this agenda: the recent decentralisation of financial powers in England (examined through the lens of the Business Rate Retention Scheme) and its implications for the funding of local public services, economic development and regeneration in the Northern Powerhouse. The BRRS is frequently heralded as one of the central pillars of the Northern Powerhouse—namely its administration and payment. However, it is rarely taken beyond the implicit assumption that the proceeds of commercial property tax (the basis for the BRRS) will fund the future welfare, economic development and infrastructure requirements of local areas in the North. For all the rhetoric of devolution and new powers found in the Northern Powerhouse agenda, there has been little scrutiny afforded to how it will be funded.

This leaves a gap in knowledge that must be filled in order to understand how these new forms of public finance administration will interact with, and help underpin, the Northern Powerhouse. That is the aim of this chapter. The research underpinning this work is informed by observations garnered through the ongoing CLG Select Committee Consultation into business rate retention (to which the authors participated) and is supported by a comprehensive interpretation of central government policy documents, guidance notes and local government policy directives. The central argument in this chapter is that the BRRS has begun to roll out the conditions that will provoke parts of the Northern Powerhouse to enter an era of civic financialisation and entrepreneurial activity. However, asymmetries between commercial property markets, economic conditions and welfare needs could result in a defined set of winners and losers (Muldoon-Smith and Greenhalgh 2015; Hunter 2016)—those that can take part in autonomous civic financialisation and those that remain reliant on a system of redistribution and equalisation.

The article addresses some of these issues in relation to the Northern Powerhouse by reflecting on one central research question:

How will the Government's BRRS fund the Northern Powerhouse?

The research question is deliberately tentative, although the BRRS has been under way since 2013, enough time has not lapsed to fully analyse the relationship between property tax and the Northern Powerhouse agenda—one of our central concerns is the speed in which these new polices have been adopted without monitoring and evaluation. Instead, some preliminary observations are made in relation to the likely impact of the BRRS around three central themes:

i. Growth potential (examined in relation to risk and liability);
ii. Demand divergence (examining potential asymmetries between welfare requirements and the local property tax base); and,
iii. The nature of local commercial property markets (examining the relative characteristics of commercial property in local areas).

First of all, we set out the recent move towards fiscal decentralisation and its creation of potential civic financialisation in the Northern Powerhouse.

DEVOLVING GOVERNMENT FINANCE TO THE NORTHERN POWERHOUSE

After a debate stretching at least 35 years (Shakespeare et al. 2011), government in England has begun to address the nagging issue of how society funds the future of local public services. In 2013, the Coalition Government introduced the BRRS. This new model of urban finance gave local government the potential to retain 50 per cent of commercial property tax (worth an estimated £13bn) and up to 50 per cent of any of growth in property tax revenue during that time frame, synonymous with construction of new employment (commercial and industrial) floor space. This new way of working coincided with an overall income reduction of almost 40 per cent for local government under austerity.

Since the Coalition Government came into power in 2010, there has been a growing decentralisation of funding and responsibility to local actors who are increasingly expected to pay for their own welfare requirements. Initial forays into devolution coalesced around giving local governments more powers over economic development, regeneration and public services. The more recent engagement with local business rates has transferred this emphasis towards fiscal decentralisation. The intention is to afford local government control over revenue streams in order to underwrite devolution. Indeed,

> The purpose of fiscal devolution is to provide communities with the financial independence, stability and incentives to push for local growth and pioneer new models of public service delivery. (Rt. Hon Greg Clark. page 5 DCLG 2016)

Post-1990, all commercial property tax collected by local government was aggregated in a single national pot before being redistributed amongst local governments in England (Local Government Association 2013). A further surprise announcement in October 2015 (and confirmed in the 2016 budget) by the then Conservative Chancellor of the Exchequer, George Osborne, disclosed that local government would be able to retain 100 per cent of local commercial property tax (worth an additional £13bn) and any additional commercial property tax growth from 2020. However, within the fanfare, it was also announced that 'new responsibilities' would be devolved to match the additional local tax revenues in order for changes to remain 'fiscally neutral'. More recently, it has been announced that the Greater London Authority (GLA) will be able to take advantage of full business rate retention earlier from 2017 alongside the Northern Powerhouse stalwarts Greater Manchester and Liverpool City-Region Pilots.

The intention behind these 'big bang' models of urban finance is to break down a perceived dependency on central government for financial underwriting and grant assistance (Shakespeare et al. 2011: 3). This is in order to provide financial incentives for local governments in the Northern Powerhouse to play their own role in economic growth and to move toward a self-financing model for public services based on locally generated income streams. After 2020, local business rates, a tax levied on commercial property, will be one of the primary methods of funding local government in the Northern Powerhouse as the revenue support grant (RSG) is reduced and eventually phased out in favour of a local government finance model entirely funded by local resources. This means that the performance and construction of local commercial (office, retail and leisure property) and industrial property markets, characterised by unique textures and rhythms (Beauregard 2005), will become a central concern not only for local authority financial planning and investment but the wider business sector and the local electorate as each location in the Northern Powerhouse competes for new business rates (Muldoon-Smith and Greenhalgh 2015, 2016).

In a literal exposition of Harvey Molotch's (1976) urban growth machine thesis, local authority areas in the Northern Powerhouse are being commoditised into socially and economically valued land and property. In certain locations, where property value can be securitised efficiently, it is possible to leverage growth and new value in order to take part in entrepreneurial civic financialisation. That is, to take part in and exploit exotic financial instruments based on debt, such as tax increment financing and accelerated development (Strickland 2013; O'Brien and Pike 2015). Recently, Pike and Pollard (2010: 29) have defined financialisation as 'the growing influence of capital markets, intermediaries and processes in economic and political life'.

Yet, commercial real estate markets have been financialised for decades, transfused by international capital, debt and investment (Jowsey 2011). Similarly, it has long been known that government policy sets cities against one another (Jessop 1998; Harvey 1989). However, what is new are the recent methods of urban finance, such as the BRRS, which has brought the civic realm, understood as town and city administration and duties (Oxford English Dictionary 2016) into closer proximity to already financialised property markets—hence civic financialisation. The central logic is that

> Coalitions of actors and organisations (i.e. growth machines), all sharing an interest in local growth and its effects on land values, compete with growth machines elsewhere for scarce mobile capital investment, while simultaneously attempting to gain the tacit support of local publics for such urban growth. (Rodgers 2009: 4)

Internationally, the transition to local financial control can be associated with decentralised government provision and subsidiarity (Rodriguez-Pose and Gill 2003), 'roll back' and 'roll out' neoliberalism (Peck and Tickell 2002; Peck 2010) and urban financialisation and infrastructure provision (Pike and Pollard 2010; Christopherson et al. 2013). In the Northern Powerhouse, it can be viewed as a result of government austerity since 2010 (MacKinnon 2015) and the argument for enhanced territorial powers associated with growth-based market reforms (Goodwin et al. 2012; Cox 2009; Brenner 2003).

Unfortunately, these new government mechanisms of urban finance are poorly understood and have been hastily adopted as a new means of governing logic without any meaningful critical oversight. Drawing on the later work of Foucault (2002) into governmentality, this is concerning, primarily because these new models of urban finance introduce new knowledge-power dynamics. Potentially, not all locations in the Northern Powerhouse will have the institutional expertise to manage local property and exploit financialised products while there can be pressure on local authorities to conform to a new set of norms—for example, the utilisation of exotic debt instruments (technologies of the market) to prove their willingness to diversify into new forms of debt in the future. The final regulations and components of BRRS reform where only disclosed at the end of 2012 ahead of the formal introduction of the new model in April 2013 (a matter of months). The ability to control local finance budgets and go for 'growth' is frequently portrayed as a compelling opportunity for the Northern Powerhouse. Yet, the institutions and mechanisms that connect these new finance models to society, place and local government in the Northern Powerhouse remain obscure and have received very little investigation (Wissoker et al. 2014).

Those who study models of urban finance and the process of financialisation, for example, through Tax Increment Finance (Weber 2002, 2010, 2015), local business tax retention (Muldoon-Smith and Greenhalgh 2015), rental housing (Fields and Ufer 2014) subprime mortgages and disaster relief funding (Gotham 2009, 2014) and the international mortgage securitisation market (Aalbers 2012), consistently suggest that these financial models are beset by risks and do not account for spatial variegation and local agency.

FISCAL DECENTRALISATION IN ENGLAND

Until recently the UK had one of the most centralised government finance models in the world. Figure 11.1, based on research conducted by the Organisation for Economic Co-operation and Development (OECD 2010), illustrates this situation. Although it must be noted that the USA, Spain and Germany have federal systems of government, compared to the UK, the OECD calculated that local authorities in the USA, Spain, France, Germany and Japan all have greater control over local budgets than do their counterparts in the UK.

According to the Department of Communities and Local Government (DCLG 2011), traditional methods of financial redistribution (most notably the Formula Grant methodology introduced by Margaret Thatcher's Government in 1989) denied local authorities control over locally raised income. Formula Grant is the blanket term given to the main sources of general Government funding for English local authorities. Formula Grant, as it was conceived, comprised three main

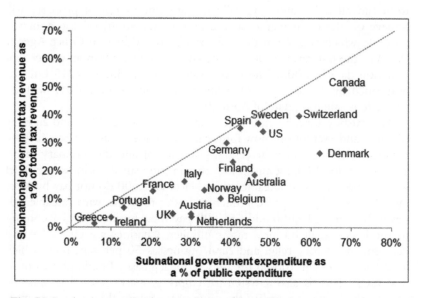

Fig. 11.1 An international comparison of local fiscal autonomy. *Source* 3rd report, 2015 (Session 4): New powers for Scotland: An interim report on the Smith commission and the UK government's proposals

elements, an allocation of funding from the National Non-Domestic Rates pool (a figure sometimes referred to as the Distributable Amount), the Principle Police Formal Grant (for qualifying authorities) and a top-up grant, the RSG.

These methods deprived local authorities of the ability to raise income and capped their spending powers which in turn reduced the financial certainty that is needed to plan investment over the long term.

In response to this perceived lack of local control and autonomy, the consultation document for the BRRS (DCLG 2011) echoed the work of Molotch (1976) into urban growth machines by arguing,

> Developers will find local authorities have greater incentives to grant planning permissions for appropriately-sited and well-planned non-residential development in order to go for growth. (DCLG 2011, p. 12)

The modern system of business rates in England, the NNDR, replaced the local rate in 1990 (a poundage known as the Uniform Business Rate is set nationally and is updated each year). It is a property tax derived from the rateable value (typically the amount of rent a property will achieve on the open market at the time of valuation) of non-domestic property which is assessed every 5 years by the Valuation Office Agency (VOA)—the last revaluation took place in 2010 based on an antecedent valuation date in 2008. The next revaluation was due in 2015 but was postponed by 2 years by the Coalition Government until 2017 with an antecedent valuation date of April 2015.

The existing business rate system has evolved since 1990, and an array of reliefs and exemptions now form part of the mechanism. These include mandatory measures set by central government and discretionary reliefs awarded by local billing authorities that include small business rate relief where properties with rateable values below £12,000 do not pay business rates followed by a tapered reduction until properties with rateable values in between £15,000 and £51,000 pay their business rates according to the lower small business rate multiplier. Charities are entitled to 80 per cent mandatory relief and rural businesses 50 per cent relief which local authorities can top-up on a discretionary basis. In addition to business rates, there is also a system of empty property rates that must be paid by the landlord equal to the value of the national business rate multiplier—all commercial landlords get an initial 3-month exemption period (6 months for industrial properties) while listed properties are exempt.

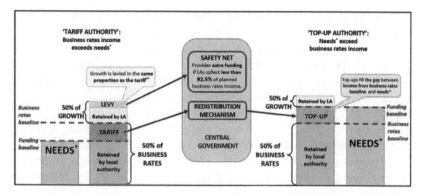

Fig. 11.2 How business rate retention works. *Source* CLG select committee enquiry into business rate retention

Government estimates that the total national business rate income in 2016/2017 will be £24 billion collected from almost 1.8 million non-domestic properties—this is anticipated to increase to 31 billion in 2020/2021 the first years of 100 per cent retention. Figure 11.2 describes the processes at the heart of the current BRRS model in England which is based on 50 per cent retention of existing business rates and 50 per cent of any business rate assessments.

The first stage in the development of the business rate retention model in 2013/2014 was to set a baseline for each local authority. Then, in order to achieve a 'fair' starting point, central government calculated a tariff or top-up amount for each local authority. Those authorities with business rates in excess of their baseline level of funding are asked to pay a tariff to central government; those authorities with business rates yield below their baseline would receive a top-up grant from central government (top-ups and tariffs are adjusted in proceeding years against RPI). This results in a distinction between tariff and top-up authorities that recognises that some local authorities will receive more business rate income than they did under the previous Formula Grant system while others will receive considerably less.

In future years, local authorities would keep a significant proportion of any growth in business rates above the initial baseline. If business rates decreased or did not grow as much in future years, they would see revenue fall. If some local authorities experience disproportionate growth, such as those with high business rate tax bases, a levy is imposed to recoup a share of this growth in order to redistribute it to those authorities that see significant reductions in business rate income. The model is adjusted to take into account movements in the business rate yield resulting from periodic national valuation assessments. Then, every 10 years, the model is evaluated and reset (the next reset is scheduled to take place in 2020) to ensure that local authority resources meet the needs of service pressures sufficiently and that the gap between growing and disadvantaged areas is not too great. The final stage gives local authorities the opportunity to pool their resources with neighbouring authorities. The following section examines the initial roll-out of the BRRS mechanism since 2013 in order to examine its implications for the Northern Powerhouse once 100 per cent retention starts to operate from 2020.

LIABILITY AND GROWTH POTENTIAL: LEARNING FROM 50 PER CENT RETENTION

Although relatively recent, the initial operation of the 50 per cent BRRS, first introduced in 2013, offers some important insights in relation to the future operation of fiscal decentralisation and potential civic financialisation in the Northern Powerhouse. The foremost concern of local authorities in England is the impact of ratepayers appealing their business rate bills and rateable valuation (see Greenhalgh et al. 2016 for a detailed discussion of this issue). In the event of an appeal, a local authority must hold in reserve a sum of money in case of success. This has two consequences: first, large sums of money are often unavailable for significant periods (decades in some cases); and second, in the event of successful appeals, large sums of money could be paid out to ratepayers. These sums often eclipse the value of any new business rate growth constructed through new development or repurposed floor space. Local authorities expressed frustration about the appeals system at the recent CLG enquiry because the appeals system exists largely outside of the control of local councils yet they are forced to carry its financial burden—it is administered by the national VOA—part of HM Treasury.

For example, the Assistant Head of Financial Resources at Sunderland City Council summed up this situation,

In Sunderland we have roughly 1,429 appeals still outstanding. The value of these appeals, if successful, is over £11.3 million. That just gives you an idea of the context and the scale of things that are beyond the local authority's control. (CLG Public Enquiry, 2016)

Greater Manchester Combined Authority supported this argument and predicted its consequences for 100 per cent retention,

It is already clear that the fluctuations in revenue caused by the appeals process are so large that they are likely to swamp growth incentives. Unless this is addressed, there is a significant risk that the Government's reforms will fail to meet their productivity and growth objectives. (CLG Public Enquiry, 2016)

The difficulty of setting an accurate budget in order to fund activity within the Northern Powerhouse is evidenced by the losses incurred by the City of Leeds due to appeals between April and July 2015:

In the period from April through to June this year (2015) we lost £9m to back dated appeals, and in the month of July we lost a further £9m. We have lost £18m so far this financial year and the provision we set was £17m for the whole year, so already by the end of July we have used all our provision. To make things worse, when we look at appeals still outstanding we have to make a provision of £26 million for next year – this is an enormous problem. (Finance Officer, Leeds City Council, 2015)

Unless this situation is improved, the cost of appeals will undermine the system before it has had an opportunity to gain traction. In other words, even those councils with buoyant property markets (with potential to grow) will not be able to engage in financialisation because they must hold a financial reserve at least equal to the cost of any appeals.

At the other end of the spectrum, other contributors to the CLG committee, for example, Stockton-on-Tees Borough Council, argued that the Safety Net provision—designed to protect those local authorities who see their business rates decrease—does not provide enough immunity to shortfall nor recognise graduated reductions in revenue. Stockton argues that the Safety Net is set too low. Under the current system, business rates in Stockton would need to reduce by £5 million before the Safety Net was activated. It is estimated that roughly 130 local authorities, many of them in the Northern Powerhouse, may need a Safety Net contribution under 100 per cent business rate retention. It is worth noting that when 100 per cent retention was announced by George Osborne in 2015, he declared that the levy on disproportionate growth would be abolished by 2020. The intention was to allow local authorities to fully benefit from growth. However, since 2013, the growth levy has funded the Safety Net mechanism. There is no suggestion that the Safety Net will cease to function after 2020, yet it must be noted that this commitment is no longer funded.

TERRITORIAL DIVERGENCE

The amount of additional local tax revenue resulting from 100 per cent retention is uncertain; different figures have been quoted, and the extension of Small Business Rates Relief and the up-rating of the multiplier by the Consumer Price Index will affect the amount available. Whatever new responsibilities are devolved to local authorities (the intention is for 100 per cent retention to be fiscally neutral) must therefore be carefully chosen to ensure that they remain proportionate to the additional revenue generated and are suited to local authorities' devolution ambitions.

This is to safeguard against the potentially harmful union of increasingly complex local welfare and development demands and declining incomes streams. However, it is not only economically disadvantaged locations that face uncertain futures. More affluent locations with rapidly ageing populations with fewer economically active participants still have complex welfare demands. In such locations, there is concern that Government expects business rate retention to fund welfare demand despite demographic growth and change likely surpassing potential growth in business rates.

The North East of England illustrates this situation. Sunderland is a top-up authority reliant on the current equalisation measures in the 50 per cent retention model. It is fearful of 100 per cent retention because of the uncertainty associated with equalisation—without additional funding, local authorities are not able to fund their basic council services. This shows the need for continued equalisation after 2020. Sunderland can raise £90 million in business rates per year—equating to £325 per head of population. Newcastle can produce £153 million business rates per year—this equates to £531 per head, the third highest in the country. Gateshead, which has a comparatively smaller population than Sunderland, can initiate £95 million business rates per year—equating to £476 per head. The composition and performance of local commercial real estate markets are variegated and do not match respective local demand upon services. So, not only are there regional imbalances between North and South, there are also local variations with, the Northern Powerhouse. The risk under BRRS is that we manage to rebalance the North in relation to South but create greater uneven development within the Northern Powerhouse.

Consequently, we believe there are some key areas where the model could be improved (considered in the following section) in order to give more locations in the Northern Powerhouse the opportunities to exploit civic financialisation. It is important to not underestimate the significance of these financial reforms, which, while incentivising councils to promote local growth and economic development, could lead to significant divergences in authorities' spending power. Without the RSG, it is likely to prove very difficult to allocate resources to authorities in direct response to need in all circumstances.

THE TEXTURES OF LOCAL PROPERTY MARKETS

The performance of local commercial real estate markets, measured through *ad volorem* tax, underpins the BRRS. However, not all types of commercial property can be utilised in the BRRS and this has significant implications for the productive operation (and property tax accumulation) of all locations in the Northern Powerhouse. If more parts of the commercial built environment were brought into productive use, more locations in the Northern Powerhouse would have the ability to engage in civic financialisation.

Traditionally, there are three ways of generating growth (additional tax receipts) in urban finance:

1. Maximise the value of existing commercial premises, i.e. attract new businesses into vacant commercial premises creating new business rates and jobs. This is a proficient way of supporting small and medium size businesses who do not necessarily want to be in the highest value premises during their initial business development—instead favouring flexibility in order to accommodate changing conditions of business expansion and contraction.

2. Increase the value of existing commercial premises through regeneration, new infrastructure, etc. This is a proficient method for locations that do not have space to construct new floor space or simply don't want to redevelop their existing stock because it is an integral part of the built environment and local economy. It also supports urban sustainability by promoting investment in existing stock and locations.

3. Expand the local business rate portfolio through the addition of net-new floor space. In other words, a local authority can create new floor space through new construction or repurposing existing premises.

Under business rate retention, local authorities in the Northern Powerhouse are only really able to benefit from the latter scenario—the addition of new floor space. This is because local authorities do not benefit from attracting new businesses into vacant premises because they already receive empty property rates from landlords (further exacerbated by the recent extensions of reliefs for small business which has removed even more businesses from retention) while any increase in property value (captured through the national revaluation exercise) is stripped out of the BRRS because of the perverse impact of national revaluation which is skewed by high-value locations such as Westminster and the core cities. For example, it is not possible to gain any economic benefit, reflected in property value uplift, from local regeneration activities or infrastructure improvements. The implication of this situation is that non-productive behaviour is rewarded in vacant premises in the Northern Powerhouse while the growth potential in the existing built environment is entirely ignored.

Relying almost entirely on net-new floor space construction benefits those areas in the Northern Powerhouse with the economic potential and space to do so but also runs the risk of undermining the strategic balance of employment land and premises within and between locations in the Northern Powerhouse. The creation of too much supply in buoyant areas (for instance the core cities of Manchester, Leeds and Liverpool) could potentially depress long-term rents and encourage displacement of businesses from older locations to new. This form of growth is reliant on speculative investment and build out rates and the expectation that new property will be let. This effectively mortgages the Northern Powerhouse upon the uncertain trajectory of property performance which is historically cyclical and increasingly influenced by globalisation.

The empty property rate issue could be rectified quite easily if the empty property rate (currently equal to the maximum business rate multiplier) was reduced in order to create an incentive to fill vacant properties with new businesses. The second issue is more complex, i.e. how to leverage the value (and potential growth) held in the existing built environment. Significant research needs to take place into how potential growth can be harnessed from existing properties without disadvantaging those authorities who achieve growth below the national average—considering that the current national average is artificially high because of the gravitational pull of high-value locations such as Westminster. Any solution will likely require a structural redesign of the existing Business Rate system and should not be entered into without caution. However, not doing so ignores a huge section of the built environment in the Northern Powerhouse due to the inefficient nature of the national method of property taxation.

Under this form of business rate retention, economic growth in the Northern Powerhouse is not being stimulated, rather, the emphasis is on new construction—but these are two separate things. This does not provide the right level of incentive and reward to local councils in the Northern Powerhouse locations—particularly those working closely with local businesses and together as Combined Authorities—that pursue policies that drive additional growth in their area. Yes, there is an incentive in place for the construction industry (and associated commercial real estate investors) to build large high-value floor plates (above the relief thresholds) but the intended link between business rate retention and economic growth (a central policy objective alongside localism) is tenuous. This is because business development is not supported (due to empty property rates) and because local investment in existing local resources is not rewarded.

The BRRS rests upon the performance and operation of local commercial real estate markets. This has consequences for the even distribution of welfare provision in England. We have already observed the limiting nature of the BRRS as it interacts with local commercial real estate markets. However, the nature of local commercial real estate markets (and associated economies) can also place restrictions on the operation of BRRS revealing some of the inconsistencies in its design and at the same time revealing its less than straightforward relationship with economic growth.

For instance, any town or city economy that is characterised by industrial or manufacturing businesses will be at a disadvantage because the associated business premises, although space hungry, are not very valuable in terms of rent which means that business rate receipts in such areas will always be smaller than those economies associated with office or retail uses which traditionally have greater financial worth—this indicates that the composition of local real estate markets influences the financing of the Northern Powerhouse a great deal. However, it also indicates the lack of synergy between the BRRS and economic growth. Some of the highest growth areas in recent years have been in the manufacturing and industrial sectors (traditionally the bedrock of economic activity in the Northern Powerhouse)—furthered recently by a weakened pound and talk of an export-led economic recovery—yet, this is not rewarded in the BRRS.

Industrial- and manufacturing-dependent Sunderland illustrates this situation. A typical 11,000 square metre supermarket would produce circa £1.2 million business rates. However, comparably sized manufacturing premises, upon which Sunderland relies, only generate £200,000 business rates. It is not only the composition of overall local business rate portfolios that influences the BRRS in the Northern Powerhouse but also locational reliance on discreet businesses or niche industries. Although towns and cities in Wales do not fall under the BRRS (as a devolved administration Wales has the autonomy to set its own business rate rules), some recent structural changes offer an insight into the potential workings of the BRRS. In Port Talbot, the rateable value of the recently closed Tata steelworks is worth half of the County's rateable value—a similar issue has recently hit Redcar in Cleveland when the SSI plant closed.

In the past, local authorities have been protected from the consequences of structural economic change by mechanisms of national redistribution controlled by central government. The situation in Port Talbot and Redcar offers a glimpse of how this will change under BRRS post-2020. The BRRS, and by extension civic financialisation, is inextricably linked into and at the mercy of globalised economic conditions and volatility. In this case, Tata Steel, a Thai company, has closed a major source of employment and business rates in Port Talbot (similarly in Redcar) because, in part, the Chinese government flooded the international steel market with artificially cheap produce. The city of Detroit in North America also provides an example of municipal bankruptcy after the proceeds of the traditional car industry dried up. The steel works in both locations are unlikely to be utilised again due to their specialised nature leading to dereliction and eventual demolition.

During the CLG enquiry the Industrial Communities Alliance (which represents sixty local authorities in industrial areas many of which are located in the Northern Powerhouse) reinforced this point by arguing that:

> It doesn't require a degree in economics to recognise that the full retention of business rates, without any redistribution via central government, runs major risks for areas where the business rate base is weak. Most of England's older industrial areas, where there have been substantial job losses over many years, fall into this category. (CLG Enquiry, 2016)

The variable composition of the property-based business rate tax base marks a significant difference from a traditional tax base which is typically characterised by lots of taxpayers paying similar levels of income tax. Property tax is very different; a small amount of businesses often accounts for a disproportionate amount of tax. Perhaps the most significant problem with the current scheme is that it is not sufficiently robust to cope with shocks.

The District Councils Network (part of the Local Government Association representing 201 district councils) noted this point in the CLG consultation describing an amplified Pareto effect (an economic theory according to which 80 per cent of the output from any given economic scenario is generated by 20 per cent of the input) where less than 1 per cent of businesses often dominate property tax contributions. This exposure to volatility exposes local authorities in the Northern Powerhouse to a potential torrent of interconnected risks and liability. If dominant businesses cease trading, business rate and corporation tax decline while the welfare bill increases—exacerbating the divergence outlined in the previous section.

CONCLUDING REMARKS

Until 2013, local government finance in the Northern Powerhouse was controlled almost entirely by central government and the Formula Grant method of funding which ensured a degree of equal distribution of financial resources. Consequently, the relatively sudden adoption of the BRRS in 2013 can be considered game changing in its provision for local self-governance. Indeed, it has created the conditions whereby respective local governments in the Northern Powerhouse now have a potential mechanism to attract global capital in order to construct growth-orientated commercial real estate assets. In a short period of time, some local governments in the Northern Powerhouse, most prominently buoyant segments of Greater Manchester, have started to fulfil the entrepreneurial modes of government anticipated by Jessop (1998), Harvey (1989), and Weber (2010).

However, we feel that most local authorities in the Northern Powerhouse are not yet at the stage where they can contemplate repackaging growth accrued on top of their business rate portfolios into new financial instruments (they have not had enough time or they have been undermined by rate appeal liability). Consequently, they are somewhat behind the financialised urban redevelopment policy described by Rachel Weber (2010) in North America and suggested by Molotch in the 1970s. So, perhaps it is more accurate to argue that we are potentially on the cusp of true civic financialisation. It is also inappropriate to suggest that all of Greater Manchester is at the vanguard of civic financialisation and this would ignore the high levels of deprivation in less privileged areas of Oldham, Rochdale and Bolton and sections of wealth in parts of the North East—where Newcastle has the third highest business rate to constituent ratio in England.

It is tempting to relate this moment in time to neoliberal ideology, new urban economics and theories of agglomeration—the rhetoric of the Northern Powerhouse certainly fits some of this context. However, the authors take the view that the uneven nature of the BRRS in the Northern Powerhouse is also a consequence of the pragmatic evolution of property tax in England over many decades combined with an element of speculation and experimentation. This perspective discounts the possibility that the Coalition and Conservative Governments intentionally designed the BRRS to operate in this way. Irrespective, whether a flawed technocratic response to devolution, accident of history or intentional neoliberal state project, the consequences are the same. The BRRS effectively helps select a small minority of winners (typically those that are already winning) in the Northern Powerhouse to benefit from fiscal decentralisation (e.g. Greater Manchester and Liverpool will get full business rates retention early, from April 2017) while conceding that a majority of less affluent locations will lose out under the BRRS.

Supporting this contention and in tentative response to the underlying research question in this chapter—*How will the Government's BRRS fund the Northern Powerhouse?*—our findings suggest that all locations in the Northern Powerhouse do not have an equal ability to exploit the BRRS. A special minority of locations in the Northern Powerhouse will perform efficiently under the BRRS, those areas with resilient rental levels combined with the ability and space to build new commercial floor space (see Muldoon-Smith and Greenhalgh 2015). Key cities, such as Manchester (but also) Leeds, Sheffield, Liverpool and Newcastle, have the potential to flourish under this agenda. However, other locations have less certain futures under fiscal decentralisation, for instance, post-industrial areas suffering from economic restructuring (e.g. Stockton and Redcar), industrial and manufacturing locations associated with space hungry but low value stock (e.g. Sunderland and Middlesbrough), seaside towns with high levels of vacancy (e.g. Blackpool and Scarborough) and non-urban areas which simply do not have commercial real estate markets (any location in the countryside)—all of which can have high demand for public services but little potential to pay for them. Reflecting this argument, a recent report by Paul Hunter (2016) on behalf of the Smith Institute, warns that Business Rate Devolution could reduce the resources of suburban councils. In other locations, this is because it is difficult to generate any return from existing commercial real estate assets (e.g. Durham and York) due to the nature of the empty property tax regime in England and the operation of the national commercial property valuation exercise. Moreover, it should not be forgotten that some locations simply do not have a significant business rate base (e.g. South Tyneside, Darlington, Bury and Oldham).

Consequently, in the lead up to 2020, all focus should be on the redistribution measures built into the BRRS, such as the Tariff and top-up mechanism and the potential Safety Net which is designed to protect those locations with less buoyant business rate portfolios and those locations that see significant drops in business rate income. The Treasury stated that these mechanisms would remain after 2020 and will likely be enhanced to ensure that an element of redistribution remains. However, the form and efficacy of these mechanisms remain unclear. Indeed, the levy on disproportionate growth, which has funded the Safety Net since 2013, has been removed in order to allow the strongest local authorities to benefit from the full proceeds of growth. Furthermore, although combined authorities have made considerable progress in setting out plans to address maldistribution at the local level—there are also existing pooling arrangements where local authorities share resources—these efforts are like shutting the stable door after the horse has bolted. Indeed, it is difficult to see the point in redistributing wealth to less viable locations considering that most of the local businesses have left for the new business premises constructed in the urban core—leading to an erosion of the urban hinterland. Rather, systematic change is needed if the BRRS is going to be fit for purpose in the North's future. For example, steps should be taken to remove the burden of rate appeals, the perverse reward for vacant property implied in Empty Property Rates should be withdrawn and it should be made possible to capture new value from the existing urban built environment.

This line of enquiry is pivotal in relation to the future funding of public services in the Northern Powerhouse, especially as central government intends to devolve more functions and greater responsibilities to local government to make sure that full business rate localisation is fiscally neutral. We believe that any change should only proceed once the results of 50 per cent localisation are fully understood. It is currently difficult to estimate its influence on local authority finances or the local economy as too little time has passed. Therefore, there is clearly an open question in relation to what evidence DCLG has used to formulate the 100 per cent policy or whether the department is frantically reformulating policy after Osborne's surprise announcement in 2015. However, it is possible to reflect on the first four years of business rate retention and recognise some of the hazards and hurdles in the initial model.

One of the principle contradictions in the system is between growth, relative need and redistribution. The BRRS is asked to do two things, to provide the necessary incentives to grow local economies and also to be the basis for redistribution. This is possible under 50 per cent retention, as a proportion of business rates are still held by central government. However, it is unclear how this will function under 100 per cent business rate retention. It must be considered that Government is asking the BRRS to do too much in the Northern Powerhouse post-2020—i.e. to equalise enough to be fair whilst also giving local authorities enough incentive to grow their business rate base.

It is conceivable that local authorities in the Northern Powerhouse will come under increasing pressure to compose planning policies and simplify planning processes to stimulate new commercial development. Furthermore, individual local authorities in the Northern Powerhouse may consider using taxpayer's money, through economic incentives, improvements to local infrastructure and beneficial land deals, to retain existing businesses and attract new ones in the form of entrepreneurial competition with their neighbours. Therefore, we suggest that there is the need for a coherent approach to growth in the Northern Powerhouse. Authorities should be encouraged to collaborate and plan across functional economic geographies to prevent competition between areas through application of the new flexibility to reduce business rates. A regional provision for pooling appeal liability at the regional level should also be considered. Furthermore, local authorities should not be penalised for historic appeals relating to the 2005 and 2010 list.

In addition, we advocate a BRRS that evolves in synergy with the periodic national property valuation process. Confusion surrounds the most recent statutory revaluation exercise that came into effect in April 2017. Largely heralded as a benefit for Northern cities, the general view is that lower business rate bills will strengthen existing balance sheets and attract new businesses. However, this judgement discounts the broad reduction in the overall value of Northern business rate portfolios, which will result in lower commercial property tax returns for local authorities. This situation highlights the complexity involved in capturing economic growth through the BRRS. A revaluation exercise that should favour economic growth in the Northern region will leave it out of pocket.

Clearly, further investigation is needed into methods of fiscal decentralisation and its potential output—civic financialisation. While we have delivered an initial critique of fiscal decentralisation in the Northern Powerhouse, through the lens of business rate retention, we have left the outline construct of civic financialisation largely alone as a potential macroconsequence of contemporary fiscal decentralisation. To this end, further research is needed into civic financialisation in order to test its suitability in the Northern Powerhouse—is it a potential game changer, allowing Northern locations to stand on their own two feet, or has central government dealt the North a busted flush that leads to potential financial risk?

References

Aalbers, M.B. 2012. *Subprime cities: The political economy of mortgage markets. Studies in urban and social change.* Oxford, UK: Wiley-Blackwell.

Beauregard, R.A. 2005. The textures of property markets: Downtown housing and office conversions in New York city. *Urban Studies* 42 (13): 2431–2445.

Berry, C. 2016. Balancing Britain: The 'Northern Powerhouse' and the search for alternatives. *Red Pepper.*

Brenner, N. 2003. Metropolitan institutional reform and the rescaling of state space in contemporary Western Europe. *European Urban and Regional Studies* 10 (4): 297–324.

Christopherson, S., R. Martin, and J. Pollard. 2013. Financialisation: Roots and repercussions. *Cambridge Journal of Regions, Economy and Society* 6 (3): 351–357.

Cox, K.R. 2009. Rescaling the state in question. *Cambridge Journal of Regions, Economies and Societies* 2 (1): 107–121.

DCLG. 2011. Local government resource review: Proposals for business rates retention consultation document. https://www.gov.uk/government/consultations/business-rates-retention.

DCLG. 2016. Self sufficient local government: 100 business rate retention. https://www.gov.uk/government/consultations/self-sufficient-local-government-100-business-rates-retention.

Devolution (Further Powers) Committee. 2015. *New powers for Scotland: An interim report on the Smith commission and the UK governments proposals*. Edinburgh: APS Scottish Parliament Publications.

Fields, D., and S. Uffer. 2014. The financialisation of rental housing: A comparative analysis of New York City and Berlin. *Urban Studies*. doi:10.1177/0042098014543704.

Foucault, M. 2002. *Power: The essential works of Michel Foucault 1954–1984*. London, UK: Penguin.

Goodwin, M.A., M. Jones, and R. Jones. 2012. *Rescaling the state: Devolution and the geographies of economic governance*. Manchester, UK: Manchester University Press.

Gotham, K.F. 2009. Creating liquidity out of spatial fixity: The secondary circuit of capital and the subprime mortgage crisis. *International Journal of Urban and Regional Research* 33 (2): 355–371.

Gotham, K.F. 2014. Re-anchoring capital in disaster-devastated spaces: Financialisation and the Gulf Opportunity (GO) Zone Programme. *Urban Studies*. doi:10.1177/0042098014548117.

Greenhalgh, G., K. Muldoon-Smith, and S. Angus. 2016. Commercial property tax in the UK: Business rates and rating appeals. *Journal of Property Investment & Finance* 34 (6): 602–619.

Harvey, D. 1989. From managerialism to entrepreneurialism: The transformation in urban governance in late capitalism. *Geografiska Annaler B* 71 (3): 3–17.

Hunter, P. 2016. *Towards a suburban renaissance: An agenda for our city suburbs*. London: The Smith Institute.

Jessop, B. 1998. The narrative of enterprise and the enterprise of narrative: Place marketing and the entrepreneurial city. In *The entrepreneurial city:*

Geographies of politics, regime and representation, ed. T. Hall and P. Hubbard, 77–99. Chichester, UK: Wiley.

Jowsey, E. 2011. *Real estate economics.* London, UK: Palgrave Macmillan.

Local Government Association. 2013. *Rewiring public services: Business rate retention.* London: LGA.

MacKinnon, D. 2015. Devolution, state restructuring and policy convergence in the UK. *The Geographical Journal* 181 (1): 47–56.

Martin, R., A. Pike, P. Tyler, and B. Gardiner. 2015. Spatially rebalancing the UK economy: The need for a new policy model. *Regional Studies Association* 50 (2): 342–357.

Molotch, H. 1976. The city as a growth machine. *American Journal of Sociology* 82 (2): 309–332.

Muldoon-Smith, K., and P. Greenhalgh. 2015. Passing the buck without the bucks: Some reflections on fiscal decentralisation and the business rate retention scheme in England. *Local Economy* 30 (6): 609–626.

Muldoon-Smith, K., and P. Greenhalgh. 2016. Surveying business rate decentralisation. *RICS Property Journal*, March–April 2016, 20–21.

O'Brien, P., and A. Pike. 2015. The governance of local infrastructure funding and finance. *Infrastructure Complexity* 2 (3). doi:10.1186/s40551-015-0007-6.

OECD. 2010. *Fiscal policy across levels of government in times of crisis.* OECD Network on Fiscal Relations across Levels of Government.

Oxford Dictionaries. 2016. The Oxford English Dictionary 2016. Oxford University Press, Oxford.

Peck, J., and A. Tickell. 2002. A neoliberalizing space. *Antipode* 34 (3): 380–404.

Peck, J. 2010. *Constructions of neoliberal reason.* Oxford, UK: University Press.

Pike, A., and J. Pollard. 2010. Economic geographies of financialization. *Economic Geography* 86 (1): 29–51.

Rodgers, S. 2009. Urban geography: Urban growth machine. In *International encyclopaedia of human geography*, ed. R. Kitchin and N. Thrift. Oxford, UK: Elsevier.

Rodríguez-Pose, A., and N. Gill. 2003. The global trend towards devolution and its implications. *Environment and Planning C: Government and Policy* 21 (3): 333–351.

Shakespeare, T., T. Simpson, and A. Thompson. 2011. *The rate escape: Freeing local government to drive economic growth.* London: Localis.

Strickland, T. 2013. The financialisation of urban development: Tax increment financing in Newcastle upon-Tyne. *Local Economy* 28 (4): 384–398.

Weber, R. 2002. Extracting value from the city: Neo-liberalism and urban redevelopment. *Antipode* 34 (3): 519–540.

Weber, R. 2010. Selling city futures: The financialisation of urban redevelopment policy. *Economic Geography* 86 (3): 251–274.

Weber, R. 2015. *From boom to bubble: How finance built the New Chicago.* Chicago, USA: Chicago University Press.

Wissoker, P., D. Fields, R. Weber, and E. Wyly. 2014. Rethinking real estate finance in the wake of a boom: A celebration of the twentieth anniversary of the publication of the double issue on property and finance. *Environment and Planning A* 46 (1): 2787–2794.

AUTHORS' BIOGRAPHY

Kevin Muldoon-Smith is Lecturer in Real Estate Economics and Property Development and co-founder of R3intelligence Consultancy in the Department of Architecture and Built Environment at Northumbria University. His expertise is at the interface of real estate development, finance and public policy. He has published articles in leading academic journals, such as *Local Economy* and professional circles.

Paul Greenhalgh MRICS is Associate Professor of Real Estate Economics, Faculty Director of Research Ethics and Founder of the URB@NE Research Group and R3intelligence Consultancy in the Department of Architecture and Built Environment at Northumbria University. He has published widely in the field of Urban Policy evaluation and the spatial analysis of commercial real estate markets, and local economic development and finance, in leading academic journals such as *Urban Studies, Local Economy,* the *Journal of Urban Regeneration* and *Renewal.*

CHAPTER 12

The Recomposition of the Tax System: Exacerbating Uneven Development Through the Northern Powerhouse Agenda

Daniel Bailey

Abstract The tax and investment reforms justified through the Northern Powerhouse discourse have set in place the foundations of a new tax settlement in England. Yet, this chapter argues that these reforms will concentrate capital available for reinvestment in those local economies which are already affluent and growing, and in all likelihood further disadvantage Northern regions. The recomposition of the tax system inaugurates a 'race to the bottom' between politics who will be encouraged to offer increasingly 'business friendly' tax environments. This is being discursively rationalised as part of a strategy to address the UK's uneven development, but instead is likely to exacerbate regional inequalities by impeding the flow of much-needed capital for investment to the North.

Keywords Business rates · Local government · Northern Powerhouse Regional inequality · Tax · Uneven development

D. Bailey (✉)
Sheffield Political Economy Research Institute, University of Sheffield, Sheffield, UK
e-mail: daniel.bailey@sheffield.ac.uk

© The Author(s) 2018
C. Berry and A. Giovannini (eds.), *Developing England's North*, Building a Sustainable Political Economy: SPERI Research & Policy, https://doi.org/10.1007/978-3-319-62560-7_12

285

When George Osborne was relieved of his position as Chancellor of the Exchequer in July 2016 he left behind a noteworthy legacy of institutional reforms, but none more so than the ones which were justified through the Northern Powerhouse agenda. The Northern Powerhouse agenda—which he did so much to reify—encompassed a variety of policy initiatives purporting to boost infrastructure investment, devolve power to 'city-regions' (and more specifically to the Local Economic Partnerships (LEPs) and freshly inaugurated Metro-Mayors within them) and modify local government financing. Whether the Northern Powerhouse discourse will be perpetuated by Theresa May's government or whether the North of England will benefit from 'High Speed 2' (HS2) and the proposed 'High Speed 3' (HS3) is yet to be seen, but the city deal agreements and the reforms to the financial settlements of local governments will far outlive Osborne's tenure in Downing Street. This chapter will focus specifically on the significant restructuring of local government financing which Osborne oversaw, and its relationship to the claim that the Northern Powerhouse agenda would usher in a new wave of prosperity for the unevenly developed Northern regions of England.

This first area of local government financing to be analysed concerns the inauguration of a new architecture of business rate taxation. Local councils will increasingly be 'empowered' to retain the proceeds of the business rates generated locally and to set the level of business rates applicable in their area. Second, the proceeds of infrastructure investments sanctioned by a city-region's metro-mayor—what was termed 'earn back' in the devo-Manc agreement—will further localise tax income in certain cities in England. Osborne reasoned that these changes will both 'incentivise' councils to pursue economic growth and reward the ones who are successful (Osborne 2015).

This chapter will demonstrate that the recalibration of the tax system will blunt the mechanisms of geographical distribution and institute a framework of taxation which will concentrate resources in those areas which are already growing. The winners of these reforms will be those cities currently running a 'budget surplus' with central government; in other words, those cities contributing more to central government than they get back. The losers of these reforms will be those regions which receive more from the state than they contribute who will incrementally be deprived of capital available for local services or investment; many of which are located in the North of England who these reforms purport to 'empower'. The reforms to tax increment financing—designed to inculcate an understanding of fiscal responsibility in local governance—also caps the investment capacity of poorer areas in line with projections of future business rates. Moreover, the abolition of universal business rates encourages local polities to compete with each other on the creation of 'business friendly' environments; a reform which threatens to inaugurate a 'race to the bottom' which favours affluent areas with a greater capacity to compete. Beneath the hubris of the Northern Powerhouse discourse, therefore, these reforms to local government financing will ensure the concentration of resources in affluent areas, whose growth will be 'rewarded'. The poorer areas will suffer a further squeeze on their fiscal capacity as a result of these reforms, compounding the effects of austerity. All of this will mean that governmental resources will increasingly be channelled into the continued success of the UK's 'growth engines' rather than directed toward the investment projects which would help 'rebalance' the UK economy or tackle its uneven development.

This chapter will begin by offering an exposition of the reforms made to the pre-existing tax and investment settlement and their distributional consequences in the UK. It will then outline the competitive framework on business rates being established by the central government which threatens to trigger a deleterious 'race to the bottom'. Thereafter it will analyse the politics of such changes and assess whether these reforms could help generate a wave of growth in the poorer areas of the country which could form part of a strategy to address uneven development.

THE RECOMPOSITION OF THE TAX SYSTEM

The political discourse surrounding the English devolution agreements have, thus far, centred upon its ability to aid economic growth and help address uneven development through boosting 'local competitiveness' (Lyall et al. 2015). Yet this advocacy appears to be very difficult to reconcile with the substantive policy content justified through the 'Northern Powerhouse' concept. In particular, the incremental recomposition of the current tax settlement, in a way which blunts the state's mechanisms of redistributing tax revenue and create the framework for a competitive 'race to the bottom' on business rates, seems to be a starkly regressive reform and one which will have significant implications for the poorer areas of the country.

The pre-existing tax settlement is being remoulded in a multitude of ways but this chapter will be limited to drawing attention to the two most significant reforms, both of which curb existing mechanisms of redistribution through 'localising' tax revenue. Together they promise the opportunity for local policymakers to retain more of 'their' money. First, 'earn back' and its equivalents in other city deals, which have *primae facie* been introduced to 'incentivise and reward growth' by allowing the 'core cities' to keep the rise in tax revenue (up to £900 million) raised through infrastructure investments sanctioned by the new City Mayors (GMCA 2012). The tax revenue accumulated via these growth-creating infrastructure investments will be placed into a 'revolving fund' intended to sustain future investments in the region (GMCA 2012). Such an invention will not produce dramatic or swift changes in the allocation of governmental resources in the short term, but its effects will become steadily more apparent over time as an increasing number of infrastructure investments will be sanctioned through the office of City Mayor.

Second, the Conservative government has introduced a new set of rules regarding the levies imposed upon, and the retention of, business rates. This affects around £26 billion of annual taxation at the present time in the UK (HM Treasury 2015; see also Muldoon-Smith and Greenhalgh in this volume). Between 1990 and 2013, business rates were transferred directly to central government who would then distribute a proportion of the total amount to local areas—based upon a formula which attempted to reflect a notion of fairness and equitability—in the form of grant. The Local Government Finance Act of 2012 and the reforms that followed it, however, permitted local authorities to keep 'up to half' of business rate growth in their area (LGA 2013). Pilot schemes to test the success of 100 per cent business rate retention schemes—again only on the revenue derived from new businesses or the growth of existing business—were announced by George Osborne in March 2015, with 'Manchester and East Cheshire' and 'Cambridgeshire and Peterborough' (that other great engine of the Northern Powerhouse!) chosen to pilot this scheme (Osborne 2015). Only a few weeks later, it was announced that all local authorities would retain 100 per cent of business rates revenue from 2020. This means that Revenue Support Grants (the mechanism of redistributing business rates) will be entirely phased out over the course of two Parliaments, although there will be a safety net for any council which loses 7.5 per cent of their business rates revenue in a year in order to 'ease' the transition.

HM Treasury has rationalised these reforms through the discourse of 'rewarding growth'. George Osborne in particular promoted the idea

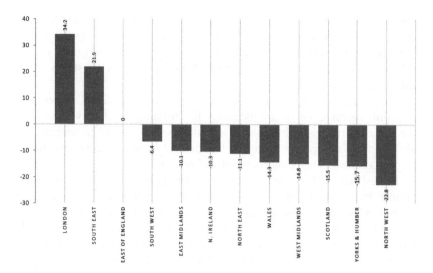

Fig. 12.1 Regional Surpluses and Deficits, 2013/2014. *Source* City of London Corporation (2014)

that 'when local areas take steps to boost business growth in their area, they should see the benefit' (cited in HM Treasury 2015). It is easy to see why this discourse could be seductive to politicians at the local level. The opportunity to 'keep' a larger proportion of 'their' tax revenue is *primae facie* an appealing proposal. Viewing these developments in their entirety through the analytical lens of a macroeconomic perspective, however, reveals that the cities currently contributing less to central government funds than they withdraw need to contemplate resisting the trend towards localising tax income. For the regions who are running 'budget deficits' with central government, the localisation of taxation could produce a tightening of available resources.

Figure 12.1 illustrates the overall tax surpluses and deficits amongst the regions of the UK. It shows that London and the South East contribute significantly more to the Exchequer than they withdraw, whereas the vast majority of the country (and particularly the North West) benefit from existing mechanisms of redistribution through withdrawing more than they contribute. The specific ramifications of the localisation of tax income—via business rates reform and the 'scaling up' of policy pledges such as Earn-Back—on each area in the North will be contingent upon the specific deals agreed by each area, but the regressive effects on the North can be deduced in reference to the graph below. Unsurprisingly, London represents the biggest fiscal winners of this reform whilst the North West and the Yorkshire region are set to be the most significant fiscal losers.

The retention of taxation in local areas is of political importance not only because of its implications for funding local services (which are already struggling because of simultaneous austerity measures), but also because it represents capital which is able to be reinvested in the local economy. This concentration of resources in a discrete selection of English cities threatens to accelerate the uneven development in the country; a troubling realisation given that the UK is already one of the developed world's most unequal countries. This was recognised by the late Jo Cox, then the Labour MP for Batley & Spen and a member of the Communities and Local Government Select Committee (Cox 2015). She estimated that the consequences of this for her local area would be dire. In her own council of Kirklees, she projected a funding gap of 'more than £30 million annually' as a result of these changes, and noted that simultaneously 'Westminster Council's budget will increase 10-fold'. For her, these structural reforms could be seen as a form of austerity for the North of England which compounded the more direct cuts to local government expenditure imposed by the cuts of the coalition government.

The state's mechanisms of redistributing capital from the affluent areas of England to the poorer ones, in order to mitigate geographical inequalities, have been diminished through this recomposition of the tax and investment settlement. It constitutes a reshaping of the distributional arrangement of governmental resources, and one which primarily benefits the most prosperous local areas. The implication of these reforms, despite the language of 'empowering' the Northern Powerhouse, is that governmental capital will increasingly be apportioned to the capital city. The poorest areas that are in desperate need of investment would be penalised by such reforms; undermining the hubris surrounding the Northern Powerhouse agenda as a route to rebalancing the economy and addressing uneven development. This demonstrates the implicitly regressive nature and potential dangers of the 'rewarding growth' discourse. That these reforms of the state's distributional arrangements are being justified by the Northern Powerhouse discourse is strikingly disingenuous.

The business rate revaluation made under Theresa May's Conservative government in February 2017 will compound the fiscal effects for local authorities in poorer areas once the business rate retention scheme is rolled out. Whilst the revaluation delighted private businesses in the North of England and the Midlands when it was introduced, many of whom have been excluded from the tax altogether, the local authorities of those areas will see their tax revenues deplete further. The revaluation also means that rates will be scaled upwards for London businesses, in line with updated assessments on the escalating value of London property, available to the Greater London Authority to reinvest in the local economy or provide tax relief without fear of compromising its fiscal capacity. The reform was widely seen to be 'good news' for the Northern economy (The Financial Times 2017)—itself an expression of the tacit understanding of how economic growth is driven by lowering taxes on private businesses and the diminishing presence of local government—at a time when both public and private investments are low. The erosion of financing available to local authorities, however, stands in stark contrast to the rhetoric of empowerment.

To make matters even worse for the city-regions of the 'Northern Powerhouse', to ensure that cities will remain 'fiscally sustainable'—as if maintaining the state's mechanisms of geographical redistribution were itself inherently unsustainable—changes to investment rules (as part of the 'new development deals' in Newcastle, Sheffield City-Region and Nottingham) mean that Tax Increment Financing will now be contingent on the projection of future business rates in the local area. This reform to the investment settlement also institutionalises an unequal set of parameters in which local authorities can operate. This effectively allows richer areas to indulge in a greater degree of Keynesian stimuli (should they wish) through leveraging future tax earnings, but reduces the policy space for poorer areas. For the poorer areas badly in need of investment, such countercyclical spending would be disallowed in the name of 'fiscal sustainability'. The consequences of this bifurcation of available capital for investment for any attempts by Northern regions to 'catch up' to the South are clear. Both the tax and investment settlement, then, are being reformed in ways which accelerate uneven development.

There are far more layers to the tax system—most of which still constitute mechanisms of redistribution—not analysed here (with income tax perhaps being the most obvious example). Unquestionably, many forms of geographical and social redistribution through the tax system remain in place after the reforms which have been analysed. However, as Simon Lee argues in Chap. 2 of this volume, this takes place within the context of a British state which tends to privilege London's competitive advantage in matters of economic policy. This can be seen in the decision to bail out a selection of financial institutions in 2008 and the following rounds of quantitative easing which served to rebuild balance sheets and reinflate asset prices at the expense of the taxpayer. Moreover, many regressive modes of governmental distribution remain in place (and depoliticised) also. An obvious example of this is the disproportionate funding apportioned to London transport relative to other English cities. IPPR calculated that government spending per head in London was £2604, compared to £314 per head in the North East (IPPR 2015: 5). The reliance of London upon an active state and a range of state subsidies can be thought of as the 'metropolitanisation of gains' which acts alongside the 'nationalisation of the City's losses', according to Adam Leaver (2013). The recomposition of the tax and investment system, therefore, does seem set to establish an even more regressive political economy of the UK which will further privilege the interests of London at the expense of redressing uneven development.

The Only Game in Town: A Race to the Bottom

To compound matters, another component of business rate reform—the abolition of universal business rates across all councils—threatens to prompt a 'race to the bottom' between competing city-regions. The new set of rules for local councils inaugurated by George Osborne authorised councils to lower local business rates as they see fit, but authorised them to raise rates only temporarily and with the proviso that the rises are supported by local business interests (see HM Treasury 2015). This abolition of universal business rates, therefore, establishes a new framework for business rates which encourages tax competition between city-regions, furthering the structural conditions under which mobile capital is able to play polities off against each other.

Constructing this new framework can be viewed as a type of statecraft designed to encourage devolved politics to competitively offer more attractive business environments than neighbouring areas. This could potentially inaugurate a 'race to the bottom' on business rates, and help engender the low tax, business-friendly environments which neoliberal theory posits helps generate economic growth. Lord Heseltine spoke enthusiastically about the prospect of fostering this competition between neighbouring communities in a speech in December 2015. He claimed that devolution enforces 'a community of self-interest, in order to propose plans and ideas that are more exciting than the neighbouring economies with which they are competing', citing the Government's decision to allow councils to determine their own business rates as an example of how local governments would vie to conceive 'a winning strategy' (cited in The Telegraph 2015). John Cridland, of the Confederation of British Industry, concurred that this reform to business rates was 'putting flesh on the bones of the chancellor's commitment to devolution' (cited in The Financial Times 2015). Therefore, the awarding of new tax powers to local areas, within a rules-based framework which enforces stringent conditions upon tax hikes (including acquiring the support of business interests through the LEP), sets the economic conditions for business-friendly competition between city-regions, with the intent of facilitating sites of 'urban entrepreneurialism' (Harvey 1989: 4).

However, it is likely that the reforms to local taxation will lower the overall tax take for local councils (Meadway 2015), and (more pertinently for the uneven development of the UK) there is the likelihood that the losers of this reform will be the poorer areas who are less able or less willing to engage in tax competition. As Berry and White (2014) revealed, poorer councils suffered disproportionately from the form of fiscal consolidation pursued by the coalition government. Austerity politics has left poorer areas far less able to lower taxation, relative to the more affluent areas whose cuts have been less severe, even if they wanted to. This, though, leaves poorer councils at the mercy of mobile capital, which is at liberty to seek out ever lower tax and regulation zones. The reforms thus put in place a framework which facilitates a transforming topology of taxation and regulation across the UK economy in future years, with deleterious consequences for the poorest regions in the North for whom Osborne was purporting to help 'empower' (HM Treasury 2015).

The capacity of less affluent councils to compete on business rates is threatened further by the economic shock of 'Brexit'. The European Uniongrants dedicated to funding regional development throughout the North are set to be withdrawn when the UK formally leaves the EU; resulting in what Berry (2016) described as 'austerity squared'. Even if existing EU regional development grants until 2020 are honoured by Whitehall, as proponents of leaving the EU pledged in the referendum campaign, the long-term fiscal forecasts of less affluent councils will likely deter them from lowering taxes any further.

Whether such a framework will help generate tax competition is not yet known. It is worth noting that the coalition government's Localism Act of 2011 allowed councils in England to create discretionary discount schemes for business rates, but by 2013 only 18 out of 326 councils in the UK had done so. By 2016, a further 56 councils had signed up, meaning that 74 out of 326 councils had participated in the five years after they were enabled to do so, offering discounts amounting to £14 million (The Financial Times 2015). However, the much-trumpeted devolution agreements of recent years could trigger a more intense form of inter-territorial competition. As Neil McInroy of the Centre for Local Economic Strategies predicts, there could be punitive economic consequences for regions which neglect to seek some form of devolution package as the affluent areas around them negotiate deals to retain their taxation. McInroy anticipates that 'in areas with no devolved powers, and maybe even those outlying boroughs (but still within the city-region), there is likely to be an ebb in economic investment, worker flight, and business relocation' (McInroy 2014). It may be that with some diverging capacities and political inclinations between the councils of the UK, we may see the more affluent and Conservative councils show a greater inclination to lower rates and create 'business-friendly' environments. Any resistance from poorer councils to engage in the type of competition being encouraged by central government (either because of inability to compete given fiscal circumstances or because of a predisposition towards progressive policies) therefore could help ensure that the UK economy becomes an 'uneven playing field'.

The areas in the North of England hit hardest by all this may be forced to turn to a 'release valve' suggested by George Osborne. He proposed giving local authorities more freedom to benefit from the sale of assets. This would essentially entail a privatisation of local government assets in poorer regions which conforms to what Pike et al. (2016) refer to as the establishment of subnational 'austerity states'. Such a strategy may be effective as a short-term strategy for councils faced with a liquidity crisis, but the sale of profitable assets can hardly be seen as a form of 'empowerment'.

In sum, the rechannelling of governmental resources is set to have regressive consequences for the less affluent areas of England, in spite of the rhetoric the reforms were couched in. This reconfiguration of the tax system is set to exacerbate uneven development by blunting the mechanisms of redistribution and motivating private capital to locate in the most competitive locations who can offer low business rates as well.

THE POLITICS OF LOCALISING TAX INCOME

Interestingly, the effects of these reforms on the poorer areas of the UK have been recognised in some form by certain groups, which have framed the stymieing of the state's redistributive mechanisms in terms of 'breaking' the 'cycle of dependency' in which some cities are 'trapped'. Respublica is one think-tank which has argued that cities currently running 'budget deficits' with central government—in that they contribute less to state finances than they withdraw—will ultimately benefit from these reforms as it will force them to finally renounce the 'umbilical cord' of the state. This discourse is clearly inspired by the 'culture of dependency' or 'cycle of dependency' imagery often deployed by Iain Duncan Smith's Centre for Social Justice (2007, 2013, 2014) in reference to families who claim welfare benefits, albeit applied to a much larger scale. The policy prescriptions drawn from such an analysis, similarly, centre upon 'liberation' and instigating 'culture change' via the 'incentivisation' wrought through withdrawing state support. A Respublica report on devo-Manc stated that:

> high levels of public funding and low tax yields, are constraining the potential for Greater Manchester to be self-sustaining. Despite significant cuts to some public services over the past few years, total public spending in Greater Manchester has remained largely the same in real terms since 2008, being £22.5 billion in 2012/13. This compares with an estimated total tax take of around £17.7 billion. Greater Manchester is currently a 'cost centre' for the UK, unable to reduce dependency or close the gap - of nearly £5 billion over a single year - between the taxes it generates and the cost of public services. (Blond and Morrin 2014: 5)

Statements such as this demonstrate the perception of some that devolution is potentially a vehicle for lessening the burden of 'cost centres' from the shoulders of London. The report goes on to say that:

> to support genuine local decision making, we do believe measures will be needed to retain and manage tax resources generated locally – for example the local management and retention of income tax. As an operative

principle which we term 'proportionate parity' we would argue that some of the freedoms enjoyed by the devolved nations should be enjoyed by city-regions... In regard to Greater Manchester, we believe that once full placed based devolution of public services has taken place, fiscal devolution should follow. (Blond and Morrin 2014: 6)

In London, the calls for a reconfigured taxation and investment framework long predate the current Northern Powerhouse agenda. Boris Johnson, the former Mayor of London, repeatedly asserted during his tenure that London ought to reclaim a greater share of its tax revenues in order to redress the pressing issues London residents face and reinvest in the city (The Evening Standard 2012). Johnson denounced London's status as a 'cash cow' for the other regions in the UK; citing research that found that £1 in every £5 earned in the capital is redistributed to elsewhere in the country (The Evening Standard 2012). He was quoted as saying that 'London is the powerhouse of the UK economy and it is time to look at formally recognising that and make sure hard-pressed and hard-working Londoners get the benefit of their contribution'.

This position gained a great deal of momentum as the Northern Powerhouse discourse was emerging. In May 2013, the London Finance Commission produced an influential report, *Raising the Capital* which called for the decentralisation of a range of taxes in a plan designed to provide London with a 'greater control over resources' and 'greater autonomy to invest' in infrastructure (LFC 2013: 7). The London Assembly (2013) meanwhile explicitly claimed that obtaining the power to set tax policy and to retain its resulting income was the underpinning rationale of the 'devolution revolution'. After the initial devolution agreements had been announced, the Core Cities group acclaimed the increased retention of business rates in local areas and sought to capitalise on its preliminary successes by arguing that 'London's government should have greater freedom to access the tax resources necessary to make it possible for the GLA and boroughs to invest in projects that would sustain and increase economic growth' (Core Cities 2013: 28).

In the context of the movement for a 'better deal for London', it would have been politically inexpedient for the new London Mayor, Sadiq Khan—given the remit of the role and the palpable need for investment in London housing in particular—to publicly make the case for geographical redistribution from a macroeconomic perspective. Indeed, Khan has instead become one the most vocal proponents of the agenda and has embraced the role of 'doing what's best for London'. On the campaign trail in 2015, he denounced the tax arrangements which he believed left the capital city at a competitive disadvantage with its 'global rivals' such as New York. He made the case that 'only 7 per cent of the taxes raised from London taxpayers and businesses is spent by London's government—compared with 50 per cent in New York' and criticised central government for 'not trusting Londoners to govern [their] own city' (cited in The Evening Standard 2015). Unsurprisingly, then, he has adopted a firmer stance on the devolution agenda than his Labour colleagues, and taken his cue from the departing Boris Johnson, by explicitly arguing in favour of increasing London's 'autonomy' and 'self-determination'. His position echoes, and has been supported by, the range of organisations and think-tanks which rose to prominence in the last Parliament. After Khan's electoral victory, the *Centre for Cities* was quick to assert that 'to ensure that London can continue to compete with other major global cities, Khan also needs to make the case for the Mayor to have greater control of the city's fiscal affairs—such as the power to retain and reinvest revenues raised in the capital through stamp duty, council tax, and business rates' (Centre for Cities 2015).

George Osborne concurred that cities constitute the 'engines of growth' at a time when an economic recovery was proving difficult to instigate. He too invoked the 'incentivising growth' mantra, not least in the March 2015 budget speech, to make the case that growing cities would be 'deserving' of their tax boon. In this speech he stated that 'where cities grow their economies through local initiatives, let me be clear: we will support and reward them... Our ambition for a truly national recovery is not limited to building a Northern Powerhouse. We back in full the long-term economic plans we have for every region' (Osborne 2015; see also Gray, Pugalis and Dickinson in this volume). Therefore, this reconfigured framework of taxation 'locks in' new arrangements for the distribution of government capital. Specifically, it serves to funnel resources in the city-regions of the UK which are already experiencing economic growth, at the expense of less affluent areas. This means that, despite the rhetoric surrounding the 'Northern Powerhouse', resources will increasingly be dedicated to fuelling the continued success of the country's 'engines of growth' rather than to addressing uneven development or 'rebalancing' the UK economy. This, however, is being concealed by a discourse which frames regressive reforms as a strategy to 'reduce dependency', tackle 'unsustainable'

city financing, encourage 'self-reliance' and 'incentivise' poor performing cities to grow; a language with contestable ideological and empirical
underpinnings.

'Unlocking' Growth in the North

The hope of devolution proponents is that, despite the regressive localisation of tax income, the incentivisation of local councils will instigate
internal reforms which will unleash a wave of growth across the less affluent areas of the country. The changes could 'remedy' the tendency for
some councils (particularly in the North) to focus spending on welfare
services rather than on growth-accelerating capital spending projects.
The priorities enforced by these changes, then, could potentially unleash
a wave of growth—perhaps fuelled by a bounty of Chinese investment—
which will offset or completely redress the loss of income caused by the
regressive reforms outlined above.

The economic reforms made as part of the 'devolution revolution'—comprising the localisation of tax as well as the encouragement
of competition—can be understood as a political expression of a certain understanding of wealth creation. It is an understanding encompassing the belief that entrepreneurialism and enterprise are inspired by
low taxation and deregulation, that establishing the competitive conditions between regions is the best mode of promoting it, and the merits
of developing 'partnerships' between business and governance actors so
that policymaking can be systematically informed by the needs of business. This conforms to the prevailing 'neoliberal' economic philosophy,
but it also draws upon two other influential bodies of ideas. The first is
the emerging theory of 'agglomeration'—the idea that the 'clustering'
of businesses can lead to enhanced economies of scale, labour movement
and networking, resulting in increased productivity and growth—which
has grown in influence partly because of the success of the 'Magnet
Cities' in recent decades (KPMG 2014). The second is the lionisation
of cities as the locomotives of economic growth, which has persuaded
policymakers across the globe that supporting economic growth is most
efficiently achieved through redirecting governmental resources to urban
areas (Champion and Townsend 2013; Florida 2002; Glaeser 2011; Katz
and Bradley 2014; Overman 2012; Rosenthal and Strange 2004). At
a time when economic growth of any kind is difficult to inspire, large

and affluent cities where agglomeration is taking place seems to offer the greatest prospects of a 'return' on government capital.

The notion that devolution will 'naturally' produce a wave of growth across the North has been taken as an article of faith by many in recent years, partly instigated by Lord Heseltine's influential report 'No Stone Unturned' (Heseltine 2012). This is a conflation which the academic literature on the 'economic dividend' of devolution does much to undermine (Baskaran and Feld 2009; Pike and Tomaney 2009; Pike et al. 2010; Rodriguez-Pose and Ezcurra 2010; Rodriguez-Pose and Gill 2005), and there is little to suggest that the UK's macroeconomic failings since 2008 have been linked to political centralisation. Ultimately, devolution will do little to address the pathologies of the volatile UK growth strategy, in which demand is supported by a deregulated and highly leveraged financial sector, an influx of capital from Asia (primarily China), escalating private indebtedness, asset bubbles in the South East (particularly the housing market), and a dependence upon the continuation of low interest rates (Crouch 2009; Hay 2013). Nor have the proponents of devolution put forward a strong vision of the economic sectors likely to spur this wave of growth in less developed areas. Devolution, thus, fails to represent a solution to the UK economy's ills or the underlying causes of uneven development. If a wave of growth is set to be unleashed across the less prosperous parts of the UK, the exact dynamics upon which it will be based—as well as the source of the investment fuelling it, in light of the receding resources of local governmental agencies—remain shrouded in opacity.

The forthcoming withdrawal from the EU will carry further economic ramifications for the Northern Powerhouse. In addition to the forecasted economic shock resulting from the withdrawal from the European Union trading bloc (or merely the spectre of it), the poorer regions in the UK will also no longer be the recipients of the European Regional Development Fund. Although still shrouded in uncertainty, it is highly unlikely that Brexit will incline the Conservative Government to compensate poorer areas for the lost investment, such as the funds for fostering the growth of SMEs—known as the 'joint European resources for micro to medium enterprises', or 'Jeremie'—which has helped create approximately 10,000 jobs since 2010 (The Financial Times 2016). Lord Porter of the Local Government Association meanwhile has voiced concerns that they will lose £5.3 billion of regenerations funds to central government in the midst of economic uncertainty (LGA 2016), and the Joseph Rowntree Foundation recently expressed its fears that The Northern Powerhouse is at risk of 'withering' (The Financial Times 2016).

As such, it is difficult to be optimistic that devolution in England constitutes the missing piece of the puzzle to the problem of uneven development as has been suggested. In contrast, the rechannelling of governmental capital to the existing hubs of growth, such as London, may be a recognition of the difficulties in inspiring growth of any kind in the post-2008 economy. In light of the frailty of the economic recovery staged in the last decade, these distributional reforms appear to signify a political desire to maximise growth wherever it is possible, regardless of how much the fruits of that growth will be concentrated in the hands of those who need it the most (Layard 2005; Wilkinson and Pickett 2009). In the desperation to raise the UK's aggregated GDP figures, available governmental capital for investment in the economy is decreasingly being redirected to poorer areas in line with a commitment to tackling uneven development, and more likely to be apportioned to already-affluent 'growth-centres'. Indeed, the influence of ideas such as agglomeration appears to signify the increasing geographic parochialism of 'economic development' as a concept (see Berry's chapter in this volume for a discussion of the meaning of 'development' in this regard).

Conclusion

During George Osborne's tenure as Chancellor, the Northern Powerhouse rhetoric served to conceal the remoulding of the tax settlement and the state's mechanisms of geographical redistribution. Furthermore, his decision to abolish a uniform business rate across the country threatens to establish the conditions for a competitive 'race to the bottom'. These reforms, which were justified through appealing to notion of a Northern Powerhouse, will leave a legacy of capital being increasingly concentrated in those city-regions which are already experiencing economic growth and, as such, 'locks in' the institutional architecture of a more regressive political economy.

The disparity then between the discourse surrounding the Northern Powerhouse—characterised by concepts such as empowerment, local autonomy and prosperity—and the economic restructuring it entails is striking. Where the repercussions of this for geographical inequality have been acknowledged, it has been framed in terms of 'reducing dependency', 'unsustainable' city financing, 'self-reliance' and 'incentivising' poor performing cities to grow; a language with contestable ideological and empirical underpinnings. The concentration of government resources, and potentially private capital, in existing growth hubs indicates that the Northern Powerhouse agenda does not represent the raft of reforms which will finally address uneven development within England. Instead, far from 'rebalancing' the UK economy, these reforms are likely to accelerate uneven development.

This is a crucial issue because, as was revealed by both Brexit and the electoral victory of Donald Trump in the USA, the socio-economic fragmentation in post-industrial societies created by decades of deindustrialisation outside of the major cities, and accelerated by geographically uneven economic growth and socially uneven austerity measures after the 2008 financial crash, is pronounced. The politically contingent economic decisions which created such social fragmentation has raised the stakes for those tasked with contemporary economic governance. At a broad level, perhaps the primary divide revealed by these events can be seen as being between the prosperous and cosmopolitan communities in major cities where economic recovery has taken hold, and those communities outside of the major cities who have suffered decades of deindustrialisation, economic stagnation, increasing job insecurity and escalating levels of private indebtedness. It is the communities outside of the major cities—who have been 'left behind' by economic development—who are now more likely to profess anti-immigration views and their support for illusory anti-establishment figures offering scarcely-believed promises of political–economic change.

The analysis above on the reworking of the tax settlement in a way which increasingly channels government resources to the urban 'engines of growth' will inadvertently exacerbate this socio-economic divide. The political decision to foster growth in those major cities already enjoying economic growth risks exacerbating the social fragmentation which helped fuel the Brexit vote and the febrile political climate of 2016. Theresa May, after a period of indecision, declared that the whole machinery of government was firmly behind the Northern Powerhouse agenda. Whether this will mean leaving the recomposition of the tax system unmodified is yet to be seen. What can be said with some certainty is that the spectre of Brexit particularly has placed even greater political importance on the issue of investment and growth in the North.

REFERENCES

Baskaran, T., and L.P. Feld. 2009. Fiscal decentralization and economic growth in OECD countries: Is there a relationship? CESifo Working Paper Series No. 2721. Available from: http://ssrn.com/abstract=1441152. Accessed 7 Mar 2017.

Berry, C. 2016. Brexit = austerity squared. *SPERI Comment*, June 28, 2016. Available from: http://speri.dept.shef.ac.uk/2016/06/28/brexit-austerity-squared/. Accessed 7 Mar 2017.

Berry, C., and L. White. 2014. Local authority spending cuts and the 2014 English local elections. *Speri Brief 6*, July 2014. Available from: http://speri.dept.shef.ac.uk/wp-content/uploads/2014/07/Brief6-local-authority-spending-cuts.pdf.

Blond, P., and M. Morrin. 2014. Devo max—Devo Manc: Place-based public services. *Respublica*, September 2014. Available from: http://www.respublica.org.uk/wp-content/uploads/2014/10/csv-Devo-Max-Report.pdf. Accessed 7 Mar 2017.

Centre for Cities. 2015. What are the key economic questions for Sadiq Khan to answer in London Mayoral bid? September 11, 2015. Available from: http://www.centreforcities.org/blog/what-are-the-key-economic-questions-for-sadiq-khan-to-answer-in-london-mayoral-bid/.

Centre for Social Justice. 2007. Breakthrough Britain: Economic dependency and worklessness, July 10, 2007. Available from: http://www.centreforsocialjustice.org.uk/publications/breakthrough-britain-economic-dependency-and-worklessness. Accessed 17 Sep 2015.

Centre for Social Justice. 2013. Up to the job? How reforming Jobcentre Plus will tackle worklessness, July 2013. Available from: http://www.centreforsocialjustice.org.uk/publications/up-to-the-job-how-reforming-jobcentre-plus-will-tackle-worklessness. Accessed 17 Sep 2015.

Centre for Social Justice. 2014. The journey to work: Welfare reform for the next parliament. Available from: http://www.centreforsocialjustice.org.uk/publications/the-journey-to-work-welfare-reform-for-the-next-parliament. Accessed 17 Sep 2015.

Champion, T., and A. Townsend. 2013. Great Britain's second-order city regions in recessions. *Environment and Planning A* 45 (2): 362–382.

City of London Corporation. 2014. London's finances and revenues, November, 2014. Available from: https://www.cityoflondon.gov.uk/business/economic-research-and-information/research-publications/Documents/Research-2014/londons%20finance%20and%20revenues.pdf. Accessed 7 Mar 2017.

Core Cities. 2013. *Unlocking urban economies through devolution*. London: Core Cities.

Cox, J. 2015. George Osborne's perfect storm to batter North. *The Yorkshire Post*, December 7, 2015. Available from: http://www.yorkshirepost.co.uk/news/opinion/jo-cox-george-osborne-s-perfect-storm-to-batter-north-1-7610255#ixzz3tqFJmGYo.

Crouch, C. 2009. Privatised Keynesianism: An unacknowledged policy regime. *British Journal of Politics and International Relations* 11 (3): 382–399.

Florida, R. 2002. *The rise of the creative class: And how it's transforming work, leisure, community and everyday life.* New York: Basic Books.

Glaeser, E.L. 2011. *Triumph of the city.* London: Macmillan.

Greater Manchester Combined Authority [GMCA]. 2012. *Greater Manchester City deal.* Available from: https://www.gov.uk/government/uploads/system/uploads/attachment_data/file/406275/Greater-Manchester-City-Deal-final_0.pdf. Accessed 5 Sep 2015.

Harvey, D. 1989. From managerialism to entrepreneurialism: The transformation in urban governance in late capitalism. *Geografiska Annaler—Series B: Human Geography,* 71 (1): 3–17.

Hay, C. 2013. *The failure of anglo-liberal capitalism.* London: Palgrave.

Heseltine, M. 2012. *No stone unturned: In pursuit of growth.* London: Department for Business, Innovation and Skills.

HM Treasury. 2015. Chancellor unveils 'devolution revolution'. *HM Treasury,* October 5, 2015. Available from: https://www.gov.uk/government/news/chancellor-unveils-devolution-revolution. Accessed 7 Mar 2017.

Institute for Public Policy Research [IPPR]. 2015. Rhetoric to reality: A business agenda for the northern powerhouse. Available from: http://www.ippr.org/files/publications/pdf/rhetoric-to-reality-sep2015.pdf?noredirect=1. Accessed 14 Dec 2015.

Katz, B., and J. Bradley. 2014. *The metropolitan revolution: How cities and metros are fixing our broken politics and fragile economy.* Washington, DC: Brookings Institution.

KPMG. 2014. *Magnet Cities.* Available from: https://home.kpmg.com/uk/en/home/insights/2014/07/magnet-cities.html. Accessed 4 Dec 2015.

Layard, R. 2005. *Happiness.* London: Allen Lane.

Leaver, A. 2013. The metropolitanisation of gains, the nationalisation of losses. *Open Democracy.* September 25, 2013. Available at: https://www.opendemocracy.net/ourkingdom/adam-leaver/metropolitanisation-of-gains-nationalisation-of-losses. Accessed 21 Sep 2016.

Local Government Association [LGA]. 2013. Rewiring public services: Business rate retention, December 2013. Available from: http://www.local.gov.uk/documents/10180/11531/The+story+so+far+-+business+rate+retention.pdf/2175c47c-6916-4b93-add8-c2201db60482. Accessed 17 Oct 2015.

Local Government Association [LGA] (2016). Growing risk to EU funding billions and Brexit uncertainty, councils warn, August 3, 2016. Available from: http://www.local.gov.uk/media-releases/-/journal_content/56/10180/7912122/NEWS. Accessed 3 Aug 2016.

London Assembly. 2013. London and England's largest cities join to call for greater devolution to drive economic growth, September 30, 2013. Available from: http://www.london.gov.uk/media/mayor-press-releases/2013/09/london-and-englands-largest-cities-join-to-call-for-greater. Accessed 12 June 2015.

London Finance Commission. 2013. *Raising the Capital*. https://www.london. gov.uk/what-we-do/business-and-economy/promoting-london/london-finance-commission. Accessed 15 June 2015.

Lyall, S., M. Wood, and D. Bailey. 2015. Democracy: The missing link in the devolution debate. *New Economics Foundation*, December 3, 2015. Available from: http://www.neweconomics.org/publications/entry/democracy-the-missing-link-in-the-devolution-debate. Accessed 3 Dec 2015.

McInroy, N. 2014. Will city devolution tackle national inequality? New Start, November 21, 2014. Available from: http://newstartmag.co.uk/your-blogs/will-city-devolution-tackle-national-inequality/. Accessed 14 May 2015.

Meadway, J. 2015. Will tomorrow be a big day in the north? New economics foundation, May 26, 2015. Available from: http://www.neweconomics. org/blog/entry/will-tomorrow-be-a-big-day-in-the-north. Accessed 28 May 2015.

Osborne, G. 2015. Chancellor George Osborne's budget 2015 speech. Speech delivered on March 18, 2015. Available from: https://www.gov.uk/government/speeches/chancellor-george-osbornes-budget-2015-speech.

Overman, H.G. 2012. Investing in the UK's most successful cities is the surest recipe for national growth. *British Politics and Policy at LSE*, January 26, 2012. Available from: http://eprints.lse.ac.uk/44073/. Accessed 2 Aug 2015.

Pike, A., and J. Tomaney. 2009. The state and uneven development: The governance of economic development in England in the post-devolution UK. *Cambridge Journal of Regions, Economy and Society* 2 (1): 13–34.

Pike, A., A. Rodríguez-Pose, J. Tomaney, G. Torrisi, and V. Tselios. 2010. In search of the 'economic dividend' of devolution: Spatial disparities, spatial economic policy and decentralisation in the UK. SERC Discussion Papers, SERCDP0062. Spatial Economics Research Centre (SERC), London School of Economics and Political Science, London, UK.

Pike, A., M. Coombes, P. O'Brien, and J. Tomaney. 2016. Austerity states, institutional dismantling and the governance of sub-national economic development: The demise of the regional development agencies in England. SERC Discussion Paper 206, August 2016. Available from: http://www.spatialeconomics.ac.uk/textonly/SERC/publications/download/sercdp0206.pdf. Accessed 7 Mar 2017.

Rodríguez-Pose, A., and N. Gill. 2005. On the 'economic dividend' of devolution. *Regional Studies* 39 (4): 405–420.

Rodríguez-Pose, A., and R. Ezcurra. 2010. Is fiscal decentralisation harmful for economic growth? Evidence from the OECD countries. *Journal of Economic Geography* 11 (4): 619–643.

Rosenthal, S.S., and W.C. Strange. 2004. Evidence on the nature and sources of agglomeration economies. In *Handbook of Regional and Urban Economics: Vol 4,* ed. J. Vernon Henderson and J.-F. Thisse, 2119–2171. Amsterdam: Elsevier.

The Evening Standard. 2012. 'Give London back its tax': Boris Johnson demands return on cash that capital makes for Britain, April 4, 2012. Available from: http://www.standard.co.uk/news/mayor/give-london-back-its-tax-boris-johnson-demands-return-on-cash-that-capital-makes-for-britain-7618555.html. Accessed 7 Mar 2017.

The Evening Standard. 2015. Sadiq Khan: We must trust Londoners to run the capital, August 26, 2015. Available from: http://www.standard.co.uk/comment/sadiq-khan-we-must-trust-londoners-to-run-the-capital-9691016.html. Accessed 7 Mar 2017.

The Financial Times. 2015. Q&A: Unpicking Osborne's business rate reforms. Jim Pickard, October 6, 2015. Available from: http://www.ft.com/cms/s/0/e866ac2a-6c31-11e5-aca9-d87542bf8673.html#axzz3nudxeknS. Accessed 7 Mar 2017.

The Financial Times. 2016. Funding concerns for UK's northern business after Brexit vote, 22 July 2016. Available from: http://www.ft.com/cms/s/0/173270b2-4f2a-11e6-8172-e39ecd3b86fc.html#axzz4IzmtmYtP. Accessed 7 Mar 2016.

The Financial Times. 2017. Business rates revaluation boosts northern economy, February 17, 2017. Available from: https://www.ft.com/content/d8c3da74-f518-11e6-8758-6876151821a6. Accessed 7 Mar 2017.

The Telegraph. 2015. Lord Heseltine: 'Devolution of power will start new industrial revolution', December 6, 2015. Available from: http://www.telegraph.co.uk/finance/jobs/12036051/Lord-Heseltine-Devolution-of-power-will-start-new-industrial-revolution.html. Accessed 7 Mar 2017.

Wilkinson, R., and K. Pickett. 2009. *The spirit level: Why more equal societies almost always do better.* London: Penguin Publishing.

AUTHOR BIOGRAPHY

Daniel Bailey is Research Associate at the Sheffield Political Economy Research Institute at the University of Sheffield, and formerly an Associate Lecturer in Politics at the University of York. He recently completed his doctoral research at the University of Sheffield, which has been published in leading academic journals such as *New Political Economy* and *British Politics.*

PART IV

Conclusion

Conclusion

CHAPTER 13

A Better Place

Craig Berry and Arianna Giovannini

Abstract This chapter situates the book's analyses of the Northern Powerhouse, devolution and Northern economic development more generally within an emerging 'politics of place'. It argues furthermore that a *political economy* of place is required to more fully understand the pursuit of economic development in the North by both local and national elites. The chapter distills the key lessons we can infer from the book, including the multiple and long-standing nature of development dilemmas in the North, the problematic framing of the North in national debates, the dysfunctional nature of economic governance in the North (and the messy relationship between devolution and existing institutional structures) and the damaging impact of tax reform on Northern cities and regions. The chapter ends by outlining a set of policy reforms designed to place Northern economic development on a more sustainable, progressive and democratic path, focusing on changes at the centre, and in centre–local relations, as well as at the local level.

C. Berry (✉)
Sheffield Political Economy Research Institute, University of Sheffield,
Sheffield, UK
e-mail: craig.berry@sheffield.ac.uk

A. Giovannini
Department of Politics and Public Policy, De Montfort University,
Leicester, UK
e-mail: arianna.giovannini@dmu.ac.uk

© The Author(s) 2018   309
C. Berry and A. Giovannini (eds.), *Developing England's North*,
Building a Sustainable Political Economy: SPERI Research & Policy,
https://doi.org/10.1007/978-3-319-62560-7_13

Keywords Democracy · Devolution · Economic development
Governance · Northern Powerhouse · Place

The increased interest in 'the North' in the UK in the post-crisis period
among scholars, policymakers and, to some extent, the general public
should not surprise us. The apparent over-reliance of the UK economy
(and Exchequer revenues) on industries concentrated in London and
the South East was regularly noted by policy elites, even before 2008.
After the crisis, this notion became one of the major tropes of elite-level
political discourses on the UK's economic predicament (Berry and Hay
2016). However, the (re)emergence of the North as national-level political issue is reflective also of a more profound shift. Crises destroy complacency about the basic foundations of social organisation, of which
physical space is probably the most fundamental. Place, and associated
concerns around identity and belonging, has therefore become a key
dimension of numerous political and policy dilemmas in the UK (Berry
2016b). The North is not the only dimension upon which this emerging politics of place is evident; the crisis appears to have unleashed or
unearthed a wider set of anxieties about the security of forms of spatial
organisation—our home, our neighbourhood, our city, our country—
which were once taken for granted, or more precisely, we once assumed
were immune to the ebbs and flows of the wider economy.

The recent rise of English national identity, and its politicisation, is
perhaps the most important example of this anxiety for our purposes
(see Kenny 2014, 2015; Wyn Jones et al. 2012). The debate over the
role and place of Scotland within the UK, thrown into sharp relief by
the 2014 independence referendum and more recent arguments about a
potential 'IndyRef 2', has also played an important role in accentuating
the political relevance of place. On the one hand, 'the Scottish question'
has helped to reinforce emerging grievances within England, promoting a reactionary type of nationalism which depicts the English people as
being denied the rights enjoyed by other nations. We can speculate that
this version of English anxiety was reflected, at least in part, by the UK's
vote to leave the European Union. On the other hand, and perhaps
more importantly, the Scottish case has also prompted discussions revolving around a more progressive sense of place, especially in areas, such

as the North of England, with distinctive regional identities (Willet and Giovannini 2014). Indeed, there is evidence of an emerging 'place-based self-discovery' from the bottom-up in the North, reflected in the rise of civil society and political groups which uphold the civic and territorial distinctiveness of the North or its constituent parts (Giovannini 2016). While such groups in the North invariably tend towards the pro-remain position of their equivalents in Scotland, their political claims are clearly buttressed by an apparent desire to, in the words of the pro-Brexit campaign, 'take back control' among many local communities in England, not least the North.

Of course, the political achievements of these groups in the North have, to date, been extremely limited. It appears at present that the right is the main beneficiary of England's place-based political anxieties: the Conservative Party's promotion of the Northern Powerhouse (and the devolution and local growth agendas more generally) since 2010 represents, unquestionably, an attempt to capitalise upon concerns about place in order to refresh its base of supporters in a post-crisis environment in which previous political certainties have been undermined. To date, the traditional, nationally constituted centre-left has not produced a compelling alternative (Berry 2016a). Attempts by various centre-left figures to commandeer the mantra of 'take back control' for their rather conventional liberal or social democratic political aims, albeit with support for devolution now more firmly central within their programmes, have yet to coalesce into a realisable political strategy.

It is vital that scholarly attention is turned to the politics of place. But this alone would be insufficient to understand the pursuit of economic development in the North; we argue that a *political economy* of place is also required. What is happening *in* and *to* the North is part of much broader processes of capitalist restructuring, evident long before 2008, in which places are becoming more different and, at the same time, more connected. New, transnational patterns of inequality are one of the main characteristics of these processes, both transforming and reinforcing pre-existing geographical schisms in countries such as the UK (McCann 2016; Peck and Theodore 2007). In short, anxieties around the place are intimately connected to questions around production and distribution. An understanding of both sets of issues is required if we are to explain not simply why policy elites are interested in the North, but why this interest has taken the form that it has, and the implications that related policy initiatives will have on the long-term development of the North and its constituent parts. This book offers only an initial foray into this intellectual agenda, drawing upon work undertaken by academic experts across a range of relevant disciplines. We are convinced, however, that both the rationale and the raw ingredients for a critically oriented 'local political economy' approach exists, combining economic geography's focus on the spatiality of economic organisation, connections between sites of production and the unevenness of socio-economic life, and political economy's abiding interest in the role of power, institutions and ideas—at the national and international levels—in determining how capitalist economies develop (Cox 1987; Jones 2015; MacKinnon et al. 2015; Martin 2015; Watson 2005).

*

While acknowledging the varied empirical focus and disciplinary background of the authors, we believe eight key lessons can be distilled from the book's analyses. First, the multiple developmental dilemmas facing the North are very long-standing in nature. The 2008 economic crisis may have transformed the rubric through which these dilemmas are confronted, but has probably sharpened their bite as well as providing an opportunity to illuminate their obstinacy. Second, many chapters have stressed that the notion of the North–South divide dominates the debate on economic development in the North, and the governance of development, in ways that are no longer particularly productive. It is apparent that the North continues to be framed mainly in negative terms, insofar as it needs to 'catch up' to the South. However, the presence of spatial economic imbalance in the UK is not merely related to the idea of a 'problematic North'; instead it is underpinned by a systemic London-centric bias, and should be understood as an entrenched, persistent and institutionalised feature of the national political economy. As such, the role of the South—and in particular the concentration of economic, financial and political power in London—in relation to the North needs to be problematised. Even if (parts of) the South could be said to represent an exemplar for the North to learn from, we would be required to acknowledge the role that the North's subservience plays in the South's developmental success.

Third, several accounts in the book have shed light on the limits of urban agglomeration in theory and practice. This epistemological framing currently provides a large part of the rationale for the Northern Powerhouse and related agendas, and has been absorbed into elite practices *in* the North, as well as national policy *for* the North. Agglomeration-based theory overlooks too much of what in practice is 'holding back' the

North, and the apparent enablement of agglomerative dynamics through public policy is likely to widen, rather than bridge, existing gaps not only between the North and the South, but also across the North. Fourth, the importance of appraising the politics of economic development in the North via an understanding of where Northern cities and regions are situated within wider domestic and international production processes, and, importantly, how the North's status within these processes is upheld by the maintenance of a national growth model. Whilst the Northern Powerhouse (and, as discussed below, the devolution deals linked to it) touches upon post-crisis concerns around place and empowerment, beyond the rhetoric Northern regions continue to have limited powers over the structures and practices that govern their economic make-up.

Fifth, one of the themes running throughout the book is the dysfunctional nature of the governance of economic development in the North. The introduction of new (and often overlapping) institutional structures from the top-down, adding complexity to an already overcrowded system of governance, is a core trait of the governance system in this regard. Crucially, these new institutional arrangements graft onto a policy framework that is led by central government and lacks coherence, especially in terms of strategic coordination, long-term planning and funding—hindering the development of place-specific architectures and subnational policy. Sixth, and related to this, the disorderly nature of this framework is epitomised by the uneven governance of devolution deals. While presented as key to unlocking economic development in the North, in practice 'devo-deals' are emerging as mere bespoke partnership agreements between national and local elites, which involve modest powers as well as vast liabilities, are based on artificial (and often problematic) functional geographies, and have little resonance among local communities. As emphasised by several contributions in this volume, devolution *could* benefit and empower those areas, such as Greater Manchester, that already have a degree of institutional maturity and experience of cooperation between local authorities. However, by the same token, other parts of the North where such frameworks are nascent or still missing could end up (and in many respects already are) being marginalised, fostering dynamics of local tribalism, competition and suspicion between localities—within which local interests supersede cross-regional and/or pan-northern ones.

This points us towards the seventh main lesson that can be taken from the book, that is, the lack of democratic accountability evident in the devolution agenda and local governance processes in the North more generally. The top-down approach to state restructuring and institutional (re)arrangement promoted by the central government has facilitated practices of inclusion and exclusion in the negotiation and decision-making processes that underpin 'devo deals'. Generally speaking, only certain actors (typically political leaders and business representatives in the so-called 'core-cities') have been granted a voice, and residents are seldom aware of, let alone involved in, the apparent transformation of the means by which their local economies are ostensibly being shaped. That the Northern Powerhouse and related initiatives have been justified precisely on the basis that they enhance local democracy serves to compound a long-standing 'democratic deficit' within the North. Finally, there are a set of specific lessons—explored most extensively in the chapters by Bailey, and Muldoon-Smith and Greenhalgh—around tax reform and fiscal decentralisation. Moves towards making local authorities more dependent on the taxes they raise locally reinforce the structural disadvantage of the North. There are fewer profitable firms and wealthy individuals in Northern cities and regions from which tax revenue can be raised and, moreover, strong incentives for areas in the North to cut local taxes in the hope of attracting such firms and individuals into their jurisdiction (invariably creating mutually destructively competitive relations between different parts of the North). At the same time, local authorities are increasingly expected to shoulder the burden of financing public services in the context of austerity. More generally, the differential impact of austerity on the North features in several of the book's chapters.

*

Politics is about power and, in simple terms, political economy is concerned with the role of political power in shaping economic life. While recognising that power takes many forms, and that the process for devolving some formal, institutional powers to some Northern city-regions is hugely flawed, our view—generally supported by the analyses of this book—is that the opportunity represented by the devolution agenda as it stands must be seized by the North. The devolution on offer is limited and conditional, and in some ways reinforces the North's subservience within the national development model, but also arises in part from evident weaknesses in the UK's over-centralised political economy. There is a chance therefore that the North can push now for a more progressive, ambitious and genuinely empowering model of devolution, and one which assists efforts to construct a new role for Northern cities and regions in a transformed UK growth model. We should of course be under no illusion that more power to the North would allow it to buck the transnational core/periphery dynamics which shape its political–economic environments. Ultimately, however, more power is better than less power—especially given the disappointing track record of national political authorities in the UK in terms of supporting Northern regions in responding to wider shifts in capitalist organisation.

Although it would be impossible to delineate a comprehensive agenda here, we believe several other, related policy reforms should be pursued in order to enable the North to develop its economy in a more sustainable manner. The devolution agenda must be based on a profound rethinking of centre-local relations; we should focus not only on rearranging local government, but also a radical transformation of governance structures at *all* levels, established in a new constitutional settlement. The centre itself would be reformed in this process, via reconsideration of the function of key macroeconomic policy bodies such as the Treasury and the Bank of England, the relocation of some of the core functions of government departments—and perhaps even Parliament—away from the capital. Reform of the upper chamber, the House of Lords, should include elements of regional representation. Moreover, the institutional reforms that do take place within local government in the North should not be constrained by prescriptive forms of governance imposed by the centre, which are increasingly based exclusively on the spatial imaginary of the city-region. We believe that the most suitable solution for the North would be to allow for the creation of multiple layers of political authority, that is, at metropolitan, regional, and pan-northern levels.

Crucially, subnational governance in the North should be democratised as well as federalised. In a political climate characterised by increasing levels of disillusionment, devolution could and should provide an effective way to improve the relationship between citizens and the political system. To achieve this, local communities must be given a say over decisions concerning how the North should be governed, and should be actively engaged in the debate about their political and economic future (Cox 2017). Too often, local political leaders in the North themselves seek to sideline the inputs of the communities they represent. They should instead seize the opportunity to provide a collective voice for their localities, their regions and the North in general—a platform which would in turn enhance their legitimacy in negotiations with the centre over power and resources.

Economic development in the North will be impossible without a UK-wide industrial strategy that builds upon the economic strengths and potential of Northern cities and regions. Industrial strategy means that government thinks strategically about how to utilise its resources and the inherent strengths of the sovereign state (such as its longer time horizons and unparalleled ability to spread risk) to improve the productive capacity of the economy. The UK has remarkably few robust organs of industrial strategy at either national or local levels—and those that have existed at the subnational level have been effectively neutered or abolished in recent years, despite the rhetorical focus on 'rebalancing' among policy elites. At the same time, it is clear that the UK state has pursued an industrial strategy by other means in recent decades, to the benefit of the finance sector and the City of London. That this strategy has proven unsustainable in developmental terms (from a national perspective) underlines the need for an industrial strategy that is place-based rather than place-blind, recognising the particular assets of different areas rather than assuming each can or should seek to replicate the local developmental model of London. Northern cities and regions must be mobilised in service of a new, nationwide industrial strategy and, at the same time, empowered to determine the specific mix of industrial policy measures appropriate to their local economies.

The inherent bias of financial institutions to London-based economic activity—an inevitable consequence of a London-centric growth model—means that reforms to the regulation of the banking sector and capital markets must be central to any industrial policy agenda. This would better enable much-needed infrastructure investment in the North, which is presently disincentivised within finance sector business models, but more generally provide greater opportunities for long-term capital investment by private companies. At a seemingly more mundane level, local authorities must be able to devote greater resources to understanding the local economies over which they preside. The provision of detailed information on the composition and performance of local economies in England is inadequate and, coupled with a lack of economic and industrial policy expertise among local officials, serves to undermine the North's ability to demonstrate its particular needs, and indeed its value to the national economy. Furthermore, it is vital that the interests of the North are central to the Brexit process. At the very least, European funds invested into the North must be replaced, and enhanced, by the UK government in due course. More fundamentally, given the significance to European production networks to productive activity in the North, Northern cities and regions must be treated by the central government as a partner when negotiating a new trading relationship with the continuing EU.

The question of fiscal decentralisation hangs over any attempt to devolve meaningful economic powers to the local level. It is clear that the reform of local taxes associated with the Northern Powerhouse and devolution agendas poses a serious challenge to economic development in the North. New freedoms to raise local business and property taxes is connected to efforts to paper over the cracks in public services created by austerity, and new freedoms to lower local taxes constitutes an attempt by central government to instil a 'race to the bottom' among local authorities in order to attract exogenous investment in high-employment (but low-wage) sectors. The developmental model implied by this scenario is not one that is likely to benefit the North. It is not appropriate for any locality, particularly structurally disadvantaged areas in the North, to become more dependent on the revenue it is able to raise only within its own boundaries to fund local government. Instead, comprehensive tax reform should be subject to a new centre-local settlement, enabling more opportunities, not fewer, for the redistribution of tax revenues between areas—as well as providing for a more nimble tax system that can prevent overheating in certain local economies where necessary, and better ensures the success of prosperous areas is not threatened by a lack of economic resilience elsewhere in the domestic economy that they are inherently dependent upon (Engelen et al. 2016). This does not mean that local authorities should not have some tax powers; they should, for instance, have the ability to adjust national tax policies locally in order combat rent-seeking behaviour connected to land and property holdings, as and when such behaviour stands in the way of local economic development.

There is also an array of more limited and straightforward reforms that could make a significant difference to local economic development in the North (see McInroy et al. 2016). For example, national purchasing frameworks and restrictive procurement practices prevent local economies from utilising the potential of 'anchor institutions' within their economy. Anchors are organisations which have a sizeable local presence, usually through a combination of being large-scale employers, one of the largest purchasers of goods and services in the locality, controlling large areas of land, and/or having relatively fixed assets. Arguably, the North's economy is stronger than it appears, given the location of anchors within 'foundational' economic sectors such as health and education, yet it is not sufficiently able to build upon this strength in the construction of a development model more tailored to the characteristics of constituent cities and regions. Local authorities should be empowered to use their own purchasing power—and direct that of locally rooted employers— to, for instance, encourage suppliers to create quality career progression opportunities for their workforces, provide support to the voluntary and community sector, and indeed invest in local supply chain development. The notion of anchor institutions is usually applied to public sector or pseudo-public sector organisations, but its logic could be extended to the private sector, whereby large private firms were supported to operate in the local economy on the basis of a social license which would ensure their profit-making activities are aligned with local developmental needs (Bowman et al. 2014).

Above all, and encompassing all the points raised thus far, the dominant narrative that portrays the North as inherently problematic should be reversed. In many respects, such top-down, London-centric framing of the North has been internalised by national and local elites, and is reflected in the current devolution and Northern Powerhouse agenda. Yet while the North has distinctive characteristics, it is not uniquely disadvantaged, and the path towards de-development is not set in stone. A national conversation that focuses on the 'divide' between the North and South—while rightly illuminating endemic inequalities—leads to the political–economic interactions between different parts of the UK being overlooked and under-theorised. Similarly, a seemingly progressive agenda focused on helping the North to 'catch up' to more developed local economies is a narrative which paints the North as failing, rather than constrained. We need to turn the current motifs of 'empowerment' and 'localism' from rhetoric into reality. To achieve this, local leaders need to be bolder, and to coalesce, overcoming local tribalism, and focusing on building cohesive political agenda across the Northern regions. They should also mobilise and find strength in the local and regional identities that characterise the North—so as to build an inclusive political project based on shared civic and community values that speak both for and to the people, and aims at actively involving them in the construction of a more progressive and sustainable developmental path.

References

Berry, C. 2016a. *Austerity politics and UK economic policy.* Basingstoke: Palgrave.

Berry, C. 2016b. The resurrected right and disoriented left: Growth model failure and the nascent politics of a transformative narrative. SPERI Paper No. 27. Available from: http://speri.dept.shef.ac.uk/wp-content/uploads/2016/02/SPERI-Paper-27-The-Resurrected-Right-and-Disoriented-Left.pdf. Accessed 1 March 2017.

Berry, C., and C. Hay. 2016. The great British 'rebalancing' act: The construction and implementation of an economic imperative for exceptional times. *British Journal of Politics and International Relations* 18 (1): 3–25.

Bowman, A., I. Ertürk, J. Froud, S. Johal, J. Law, A. Leaver, M. Moran, and K. Williams. 2014. *The end of the experiment. From competition to the foundational economy.* Manchester: Manchester University Press.

Cox, R.W. 1987. *Production, power and world order: Social forces in the making of history.* New York: Columbia University Press.

Cox (ed.). 2017. *Taking back control in the North. A council of the North and other ideas.* Manchester: IPPR North. Available from: http://www.ippr.org/publications/taking-back-control-in-the-north. Accessed 21 Apr 2017.

Engelen, E., J. Froud, S. Johal, A. Salento, K. Williams. 2016. How cities work: A policy agenda for the grounded city. CRESC Working Paper No. 141. Available from: http://www.cresc.ac.uk/medialibrary/workingpapers/wp141.pdf. Accessed 1 March 2017.

Giovannini, A. 2016. Towards a 'New English Regionalism' in the North? The case of Yorkshire First. *The Political Quarterly* 87 (4): 590–600.

Jones, C. 2015. On capital, space and the world system: a response to Ron Martin. *Territory, Politics, Governance* 3 (3): 273–293.

Kenny, M. 2014. *The politics of English nationhood.* Oxford: Oxford University Press.

Kenny, M. 2015. The origins and drivers of English nationhood. *British Politics* 10 (3): 356–361.

MacKinnon, D., A. Cumbers, A. Pike, K. Birch, and R. McMaster. 2015. Evolution in economic geography: Institutions, political economy, and adaptation. *Economic Geography* 85 (2): 129–150.

Martin, R. 2015. Rebalancing the spatial economy: The challenge for regional theory. *Territory, Politics, Governance* 3 (3): 236–272.

McCann, P. 2016. *The UK regional-national economic problem: Geography, globalisation and governance.* London: Routledge.

McInroy, N., C. Berry, T. Hunt, A.G. Whillans-Welldrake, and M. Todd. 2016. *The real deal: Pushing the parameters of devolution deals.* SPERI/CLES. Available from: http://speri.dept.shef.ac.uk/wp-content/uploads/2016/07/The-Real-Deal-SPERI-CLES.pdf. Accessed 1 March 2017.

Peck, J., and N. Theodore. 2007. Variegated capitalism. *Human Geography* 31 (6): 731–772.

Watson, M. 2005. *Foundations of international political economy*. Basingstoke: Palgrave.

Willett, J., and A. Giovannini. 2014. The uneven path of UK devolution: Top-down vs. bottom-up regionalism in England—Cornwall and the North-East compared. *Political Studies* 62 (2): 343–360.

Wyn Jones, R., G. Lodge, A. Henderson, and D. Wincott. 2012. *The dog that finally barked: England as an emerging political community*. London: IPPR. Available from: http://www.ippr.org/files/images/media/files/publication/2012/02/dog-that-finally-barked_englishness_Jan2012_8542.pdf?noredirect=1. Accessed 1 March 2017.

AUTHORS' BIOGRAPHY

Craig Berry is Deputy Director of the Sheffield Political Economy Research Institute at the University of Sheffield. His previous roles include Policy Advisor at HM Treasury, Pensions Policy Officer at the Trades Union Congress, and Head of Policy and Senior Researcher at the International Longevity Centre-UK, and he has taught at the University of Warwick and University of Manchester. He published *Globalisation and Ideology in Britain* in 2011 and *Austerity Politics and UK Economic Policy* in 2015.

Arianna Giovannini is Senior Lecturer in Local Politics at the Department of Politics and Public Policy, De Montfort University (DMU), where she is also a member of the Local Governance Research Unit (LGRU) and the Centre for Urban Research on Austerity (CURA). Before joining DMU she was a researcher at the Sheffield Political Economy Research Institute (SPERI), University of Sheffield, where she is now an Honorary Research Fellow, and a research assistant for the White Rose Consortium for the North of England project at POLIS, University of Leeds. Her research focuses on devolution, territorial and political identity, regionalism and democracy—with a particular emphasis on the 'English Question' and the North of England. She has published widely on these themes in leading academic journals such as *Political Studies, Policy & Politics* and *The Political Quarterly*.

INDEX

© The Editor(s) (if applicable) and The Author(s) 2018

C. Berry and A. Giovannini (eds.), *Developing England's North*, Building a Sustainable Political Economy: SPERI Research & Policy, https://doi.org/10.1007/978-3-319-62560-7